E N G L A N D

1485–1603

Allan Keen
Derrick Murphy
Michael Tillbrook
Patrick Walsh-Atkins

Collins Educational

Published by Collins Educational
An imprint of HarperCollins *Publishers* Ltd
77–85 Fulham Palace Road
Hammersmith
London W6 8JB

© HarperCollins *Publishers* Ltd 1999
First published 1999

ISBN 0 00 327124 2

Allan Keen, Derrick Murphy, Michael Tillbrook and
Patrick Walsh-Atkins assert the moral right to be
identified as the authors of this work.

British Library Cataloguing in Publication Data
A catalogue record for this book is available from the
British Library.

ACKNOWLEDGEMENTS
Every effort has been made to contact the holders of
copyright material, but if any have been inadvertently
overlooked the publishers will be pleased to make the
necessary arrangements at the first opportunity.

The publishers would like to thank the following for
permission to reproduce photographs (T = Top, B =
Bottom, L = Left, R = Right).

Bridgeman Art Library: Sir Thomas More by Holbein the
Younger, Philip Mould, Historical Portraits Ltd, London,
165B; Lord Cromwell by Holbein the Younger,
Collection of the Earl of Pembroke, Wilton House,
Wiltshire, 167L; Queen Mary I of England by Anthonis
Mor, Isabella Stewart Gardner Museum, Boston,
Massachusetts, USA, 198; Queen Elizabeth I in
Coronation Robes, by English School, National Portrait
Gallery, London, 238L; Christie's Images, 168;
Committee for Aerial Photography, University of
Cambridge, 120; Mary Evans Picture Library, 35, 49T,
194; The Fitzwilliam Museum, Cambridge, 129T; The
Fotomas Index, 20, 49B, 72, 83, 117, 125, 129B, 130,
132–3, 135, 147, 154, 159, 165, 167R, 169, 175, 181–3,
202, 207–9, 217–18, 220, 238R, 249, 251, 257, 281, 285,
287, 295, 299, 301, 309, 313; A F Kersting, 148T, 312T;
National Museums & Galleries of Wales, 213; National
Portrait Gallery, London, 29, 81, 166; The Royal
Collection © Her Majesty the Queen, 78, 158;
Shakespeare Birthplace Trust, Shakespeare Centre
Library, 311; C & S Thompson, 148C; Wigan Heritage
Service, 312B.

Cover photograph: Nonsuch Palace © Fitzwilliam
Museum, University of Cambridge

Text extracts from the following titles are reprinted by
permission of Addison Wesley Longman Ltd: *The Age of
Plunder* by W. G. Hoskins (1976); *Elizabeth I* by
Christopher Haigh (1988); *England and Europe
1485–1603* by Susan Doran (1986); *The Age of Elizabeth:
England under the Later Tudors 1547–1603* by
D. M. Palliser (1983); *The Emergence of a Nation State* by
A. G. R. Smith (1984). Cambridge University Press for
permission to reproduce the extract from *Cardinal
Wolsey: Church, state and art* by S. J. Gunn and
P. J. Lindley (1991). The extracts from *Tudor England* by
John Guy (1988) and from *The Later Tudors 1547–1603*
by Penry Williams (1995) by permission of Oxford
University Press. The extract from *The King's Cardinal:
The rise and fall of Thomas Wolsey* by Peter Gwyn by
permission of Barrie and Jenkins (1990). Yale University
Press for extracts from *Henry VIII* by J. J. Scarisbrick
(1983) and the extract from *Henry VII* by S. B. Chrimes
(1972). Extract from *Power in Tudor England* by
D. Loades (1996) by permission of Macmillan Press Ltd.

Edited by Steve Attmore
Design by Derek Lee
Cover design by Derek Lee
Map artwork by Tony Richardson
Picture research by Caroline Thompson
Production by Anna Pauletti
Printed and bound by Scotprint Ltd, Musselburgh

Contents

Study and examination skills 4

1 England 1485–1603: a synoptic assessment 11

2 The reign of Henry VII 28

3 The age of Wolsey 71

4 Social and economic change, 1485–1547 110

5 Religious change in Henrician England – the beginnings of the Reformation? 126

6 Government, politics and foreign affairs 1529–1547 163

7 'A Mid-Tudor crisis'?: the reign of Edward VI, 1547–1553 181

8 'A Mid-Tudor crisis'?: the reign of Mary I, 1553–1558 197

9 English government under Elizabeth I, 1558–1603 213

10 Religion in Elizabethan England 233

11 Elizabethan foreign policy 262

12 Social and economic history in the reign of Elizabeth I 292

Further Reading 314

Index 317

Study and examination skills

- Differences between GCSE and Sixth Form History
- Extended writing: the structured question and the essay
- How to handle sources in Sixth Form History
- Historical interpretation
- Progression in Sixth Form History
- Examination techniques

This chapter of the book is designed to aid Sixth Form students in their preparation for public examinations in History.

Differences between GCSE and Sixth Form History

- **The amount of factual knowledge required for answers to Sixth Form History** questions is more detailed than at GCSE. Factual knowledge in the Sixth Form is used as supporting evidence to help answer historical questions. Knowing the facts is important but not as important as knowing that factual knowledge supports historical analysis.

- **Extended writing is more important in Sixth Form History.** Students will be expected to answer either structured questions or essays.

Structured questions require students to answer more than one question on a given topic. For example:

1. In what ways did Henry VIII bring religious change to England?

2. To what extent was England a Protestant country by 1547?

Each part of the structured question demands a different approach.

Essay questions require students to produce one answer to a given question. For example:

To what extent did Elizabeth I's foreign policy have consistent aims and objectives?

Similarities with GCSE

- **Source analysis and evaluation**

The skills in handling historical sources which were acquired at GCSE are developed in Sixth Form History. In the Sixth Form sources have to be analysed in their historical context, so a good factual knowledge of the subject is important.

● Historical interpretations

Skills in historical interpretation at GCSE are also developed in Sixth Form History. The ability to put forward different historical interpretations is important. Students will also be expected to explain why different historical interpretations have occurred.

Extended writing: the structured question and the essay

When faced with extended writing in Sixth Form History students can improve their performance by following a simple routine that attempts to ensure they achieve their best performance.

Answering the question

What are the command instructions?

Different questions require different types of response. For instance, 'In what ways' requires students to point out the various ways something took place in History; 'Why' questions expect students to deal with the causes or consequences of a historical question.

Are there key words or phrases that require definition or explanation?

It is important for students to show that they understand the meaning of the question. To do this, certain historical terms or words require explanation. For instance, if a question asked 'how far' a king or politician was an 'innovator', an explanation of the word 'innovator' would be required.

Does the question have specific dates or issues that require coverage?

If a question mentions specific dates, these must be adhered to. For instance, if you are asked to answer a question on Elizabethan Parliaments it may state clear date limits such as 1559 to 1571. Also questions may mention a specific aspect such as 'domestic', 'religious', 'economic' or 'foreign policy'.

Planning your answer

Once you have decided on what the question requires, write a brief plan. For structured questions this may be brief. This is a useful procedure to make sure that you have ordered the information you require for your answer in the most effective way. For instance, in a balanced, analytical answer this may take the form of jotting down the main points for and against a historical issue raised in the question.

Writing the answer

Communication skills

The quality of written English is important in Sixth Form History. The way you present your ideas on paper can affect the quality of your answer. Since 1996 the Government (through SCAA and QCA) have placed emphasis on the quality of written English in the Sixth Form. Therefore, punctuation, spelling and grammar, which were awarded marks at GCSE, require close attention. Use a dictionary if you are unsure of a word's meaning or spelling. Use the glossary of terms you will find in this book to help you.

The introduction

For structured questions you may wish to dispense with an introduction altogether and begin writing reasons to support an answer straight away. However, essay answers should begin with an introduction. These should be both concise and precise. Introductions help 'concentrate the mind' on the question you are about to answer. Remember, do not try to write a conclusion as your opening sentence. Instead, outline briefly the areas you intend to discuss in your answer.

Balancing analysis with factual evidence

It is important to remember that factual knowledge should be used to support analysis. Merely 'telling the story' of a historical event is not enough. A structured question or essay should contain separate paragraphs, each addressing an analytical point that helps to answer the question. If, for example, the question asks for reasons why the war with Spain began in 1585, each paragraph should provide a reason for the outbreak of war.

Seeing connections between reasons

In dealing with 'why'-type questions it is important to remember that the reasons for a historical event might be interconnected. Therefore, it is important to mention the connection between reasons. Also, it might be important to identify a hierarchy of reasons – that is, are some reasons more important than others in explaining a historical event?

Using quotations and statistical data

One aspect of supporting evidence that sustains analysis is the use of quotations. These can either be from a historian or a contemporary. However, unless these quotations are linked with analysis and supporting evidence, they tend to be of little value.

It can also be useful to support analysis with statistical data. In questions that deal with social and economic change, precise statistics which support your argument can be very persuasive.

Source analysis

Source analysis forms an integral part of the study of History. In Sixth Form History source analysis is identified as an important skill in Assessment Objective 3.

In dealing with sources you should be aware that historical sources must be used 'in historical context' in Sixth Form History. Therefore, in this book sources are used with the factual information in each chapter. Also, a specific source analysis question is included.

Assessment Objectives in Sixth Form History

1 knowledge and understanding of history
2 evaluation and analysis skills
3 a) source analysis in historical context
   b) historical interpretation

How to handle sources in Sixth Form History

In dealing with sources a number of basic hints will allow you to deal effectively with source-based questions and to build on your knowledge and skill in using sources at GCSE.

Written sources

Attribution and date

It is important to identify who has written the source and when it was written. This information can be very important. If, for instance, a source was a private letter between Elizabeth I and William Cecil (Lord Burghley) on the issue of the French Marriage Negotiations of 1578 this information could be of considerable importance if you are asked about the usefulness (utility) or reliability of the source as evidence of Elizabeth's foreign policy.

It is important to note that just because a source is a primary source does not mean it is more useful or less reliable than a secondary source. Both primary and secondary sources need to be analysed to decide how useful and reliable they are. This can be determined by studying other issues.

Is the content factual or opinionated?

Once you have identified the author and date of the source it is important to study its content. The content may be factual, stating what has happened or what may happen. On the other hand, it may contain opinions that should be handled with caution. These may contain bias. Even if a source is mainly factual, there might be important and deliberate gaps in factual evidence that can make a source biased and unreliable. Usually, written sources contain elements of both opinion and factual evidence. It is important to judge the balance between these two parts.

Has the source been written for a particular audience?

To determine the reliability of a source it is important to identify to whom it is directed. For instance, a public speech may be made to achieve a particular purpose and may not contain the author's true beliefs or feelings. In contrast, a private diary entry may be much more reliable in this respect.

Corroborative evidence

To test whether or not a source is reliable, the use of other evidence to support or corroborate the information it contains is important. Cross-referencing with other sources is a way of achieving this; so is cross-referencing with historical information contained within a chapter.

Visual sources

Maps

Maps which appear in Sixth Form History are either contemporary or secondary sources. These are used to support factual coverage in the text by providing information in a different medium. Therefore, to assess whether or not information contained in maps is accurate or useful, reference should be made to other information. It is also important with written sources to check the attribution and date. These could be significant.

Statistical data and graphs

It is important when dealing with this type of source to check carefully the nature of the information contained in data or in a graph. It might state the information in old forms of measurement such as pre-decimal currency: pounds, shillings and pence. One pound equalled 20 shillings, or 240 pence. Be careful to check if the information is in *index numbers*. These are a statistical device where a base year is chosen and given the figure 100. All other figures are based on a percentage difference from that base year. For instance, if 1500 is taken as base year for wool exports it is given a figure of 100. If the index number for 1505 is 117 it means that wool exports have risen 17% since 1500.

An important point to remember when dealing with data and graphs over a period of time is to identify trends and patterns in the information. Merely describing the information in written form is not enough.

Tudor currency
1 guinea = 21 shillings
£1 = 20 shillings
1 shilling = 12 pennies
1 penny = 4 farthings

Historical interpretation

An important feature of both GCSE and Sixth Form History is the issue of historical interpretation. In Sixth Form History it is important for students to be able to explain why historians differ, or have differed, in their interpretations of the past.

Availability of evidence

An important reason is the availability of evidence on which to base historical judgements. As new evidence comes to light, historians today may have more information on which to base their judgements than historians in the past. For instance, sources for Tudor history include the Calendar of State Papers – correspondence between individuals and reports by foreign ambassadors to England. Occasionally new evidence comes to light which may influence judgements about Tudor England.

Also archaeological evidence is important in Tudor History. The archaeological study of the *Mary Rose*, which sank off Portsmouth in 1545, has produced considerable evidence of naval warfare and weapons in the later years of Henry VIII's reign.

'A philosophy of history?'

Many historians have a specific view of history that will affect the way they make their historical judgements. For instance, Marxist historians – who take the view from the writings of Karl Marx, the founder of modern socialism – believe that society has been made up of competing economic and social classes. They also place considerable importance on economic reasons in human decision making.

The role of the individual

Some historians have seen past history as being moulded by the acts of specific individuals who have changed history. Henry VII, Cardinal Wolsey and Elizabeth I are seen as individuals whose personality and beliefs changed the course of 16th-century history. Other historians have tended to 'downplay' the role of individuals; instead, they highlight the importance of more general social, economic and political change. Rather than seeing individuals as having changed the course of history, these historians tend to see them as representing the views of a broader group of individuals.

Placing different emphasis on the same historical evidence

Even if historians do not possess different philosophies of history or place different emphasis on the role of the individual, it is still possible for them to disagree because they place different emphasis on aspects of the same factual evidence. As a result, Sixth Form History should be seen as a subject that encourages debate about the past based on historical evidence.

Progression in Sixth Form History

The ability to achieve high standards in Sixth Form History involves the acquisition of a number of skills:

- Good written communication skills

- Acquiring a sound factual knowledge

- Evaluating factual evidence and making historical conclusions based on that evidence

- Source analysis

- Understanding the nature of historical interpretation

- Understanding the causes and consequences of historical events

- Understanding the themes in history which will involve a study of a specific topic over a long period of time

- Understanding the ideas of change and continuity associated with themes.

Students should be aware that the acquisition of these skills will take place gradually over the time spent in the Sixth Form. At the beginning of the course the main emphasis may be on the acquisition of factual knowledge, particularly when the body of knowledge studied at GCSE was different.

When dealing with causation students will have to build on their skills from GCSE. They will not only be expected to identify reasons for a historical event but also to provide a hierarchy of causes. They should identify the main causes and less important causes. They may also identify that causes may be interconnected and linked. Progression in Sixth Form History will come with answering the questions at the end of each subsection in this book and practising the skills outlined through the use of the factual knowledge contained in the book.

Examination techniques

The ultimate challenge for any Sixth Form historian is the ability to produce quality work under examination conditions. Examinations will take the form of either modular examinations taken in January and June or an 'end of course' set of examinations.

Here is some advice on how to improve your performance in an examination.

● **Read the whole examination paper thoroughly**
Make sure that the questions you choose are those for which you can produce a good answer. Don't rush – allow time to decide which questions to choose. It is probably too late to change your mind half way through answering a question.

● **Read the question very carefully**
Once you have made the decision to answer a specific question, read it very carefully. Make sure you understand the precise demands of the question. Think about what is required in your answer. It is much better to think about this before you start writing, rather than trying to steer your essay in a different direction half way through.

● **Make a brief plan**
Sketch out what you intend to include in your answer. Order the points you want to make. Examiners are not impressed with additional information included at the end of the essay, with indicators such as arrows or asterisks.

● **Pace yourself as you write**
Success in examinations has a lot to do with successful time management. If, for instance, you have to answer an essay question in approximately 45 minutes then you should be one-third of the way through after 15 minutes. With 30 minutes gone you should start writing the last third of your answer.

Where a question is divided into sub-questions make sure you look at the mark tariff for each question. If in a 20-mark question a sub-question is worth a maximum of 5 marks then you should spend approximately one-quarter of the time allocated for the whole question on this sub-question.

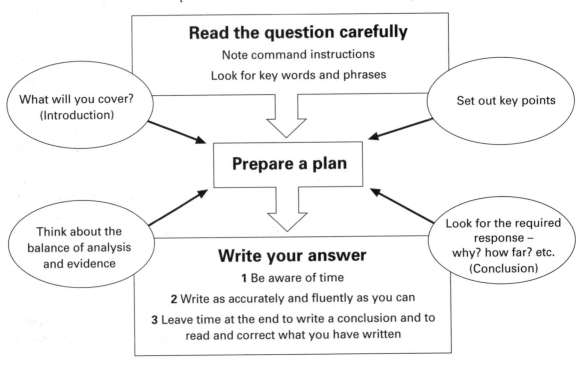

Read the question carefully

Note command instructions

Look for key words and phrases

What will you cover?
(Introduction)

Set out key points

Prepare a plan

Think about the balance of analysis and evidence

Look for the required response –
why? how far? etc.
(Conclusion)

Write your answer

1 Be aware of time

2 Write as accurately and fluently as you can

3 Leave time at the end to write a conclusion and to read and correct what you have written

England 1485–1603: a synoptic assessment

1.1 To what extent did the Tudors face threats to their rule in England between 1485 and 1603?

1.2 In what ways did English government and administration change in the years 1485–1603?

1.3 How far did the economy and society change in the period 1485–1603?

1.4 How important was the issue of religious change?

1.5 To what extent did England dominate the British Isles between 1485 and 1603?

1.6 Why did England's relations with France and Spain alter in the years 1485–1603?

Key Issues

● *To what extent did English government change in the period 1485–1603?*

● *How important were the social, economic and religious changes in the period 1485 to 1603?*

● *In what ways did England's relations with Scotland, Ireland and Europe change in the period 1485–1603?*

Overview

ENGLISH history in the Tudor period saw major development in English government, religion and in the relations between England and other parts of the British Isles. It also brought major changes in English foreign policy. The England which began to emerge from the political chaos of the Wars of the Roses in 1485 was a very different place by the time the King of Scotland, James VI, became England's James I in 1603.

English government and administration went through considerable change. The historian Geoffrey Elton even spoke of a Tudor Revolution in government. Changes in government were mirrored in the changes in the power and authority of the English monarchy.

In the 15th century the English monarchy faced the threat of powerful local aristocrats (**magnates**). Under the first Tudor, Henry VII, the power and influence of the monarchy increased. This was achieved mainly through establishing the financial independence of the King. Under Henry VIII, England was declared an empire. This means an independent, sovereign state. The monarch's power was also increased with the removal of the Pope's authority over the English Church. By the death of Elizabeth I, the monarch was head of both Church and State.

English rule also increased during the Tudor era. Although Calais was lost in the reign of Mary I, English influence over Wales and Ireland increased considerably in the 16th century. Even Scotland, which had been a traditional enemy, had adopted the Protestant religion in the 1560s. It had also formed close links with England, which led to the Union of Crowns in 1603.

England's relations with western Europe also experienced considerable change. The first half of the Tudor period saw France as England's main enemy.

Magnates: Rich people who have gained a lot of money, originally from inheritance and landowning. With this wealth comes power and possibly authority. Since Tudor times, the term 'magnate' has become associated more with money earned from a business or industry.

However, during Elizabeth I's reign, Philip II's Spain became England's foe. From 1585 to 1604 England and Spain were at war.

Although England remained a predominantly agricultural country, society saw major changes. The religion of the vast majority of the population changed during the century from Catholicism to moderate Protestantism. The Tudor government, both local and national, took on more responsibility for the problem of poverty and **vagrancy**. Eventually a government system was established which survived until 1834.

Vagrancy: The act of being a vagrant or vagabond. These were people who did not have a home. They roamed the countryside, usually begging.

Finally, the Tudor period saw the development of education and learning, which led to the development of a golden age of literature during Elizabeth I's reign.

This chapter will allow you to identify the main themes of Tudor History. Although they appear in distinct sub-sections, you should be able to make links and connections between them. At the end of the chapter is an exercise that will enable you to make historical connections.

An introduction to Tudor History

Population and communications
As one would expect, England in the Tudor period (1485–1603) was markedly different from England today. England has a population of 49 million today. During the 16th century the population was between 2 and 4 million. However, like today, most of the population lived in the South-East, with London as the major city. The most effective way to travel or move goods was by coastal shipping or along navigable rivers. Movement by road was slow. Today, to travel by road from Manchester to London would take about three and a half hours. In Tudor times, travel by road, on horseback, over the same distance would take five days.

The political decision makers
The vast majority of the population engaged in subsistence agriculture, living in village communities. Most of the population was illiterate. The 'political nation' – those who made political decisions at local and national level – numbered approximately 20,000. The most important political decision makers below the monarch were the **aristocracy**. They dominated national politics. Many also had considerable regional power.

Aristocracy: A Greek word meaning, literally, 'the government of a state by its best citizens'. In the period covered by this book, the aristocracy consisted of titled families whose wealth passed down the generations by inheritance. About 200 or so families controlled most of the nation's wealth and dominated the political and social leadership (see map on page 21).

One problem for students studying the Tudor period is the use of aristocratic titles. For instance, John Dudley (1502–1553) was known as Viscount Lisle from 1524 to 1527, then the Earl of Warwick until 1551 when he became Duke of Northumberland. Perhaps the most confusing title was that of Duke of Anjou. This was held by Henry of Valois, who became Henry III of France in 1574. The title then passed to his younger brother, Francis Duke of Alençon, who was Duke of Anjou from 1574 to 1584.

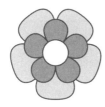

Religion

This was very important in Tudor society. The Church was one of the most important institutions in England for a number of reasons. It had a lot of influence over the population and possessed considerable wealth and land. In politics, bishops and abbots were represented in the House of Lords and many clerics held posts in the Royal government. For much of the Tudor period England and Europe were affected by the religious conflict brought about by the Reformation. In England, from the reign of Henry VIII, the power and influence of the monarchy grew at the expense of the Church. Nevertheless, religion remained one of the most powerful influences on Tudor life.

The limited powers of government

Unlike today, central government was very limited in power and influence at the beginning of the Tudor period. To the vast majority of people 'government' meant local government. Several aristocratic families controlled areas of England, in particular on the borders of Scotland and Wales. During the Tudor period the organisation and influence of central government increased.

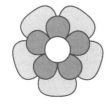

Privy Council: Under the Yorkists and Henry VII there was a Council to advise the monarch. This usually consisted of peers, courtiers, judges and the like. Many did not actually attend meetings; so the main work was done by an inner ring. By the end of Henry VII's reign this 'inner ring' of 20 or so members became the Privy Council. There is evidence that a Privy Council appeared for a few months in 1536–37, and re-emerged in 1540 after the fall of Thomas Cromwell.

Improvements in the operation of government, particularly during the 1530s, made the **Privy Council** the most important central government body. Also the Church declined in power and wealth from the reign of Henry VIII. Local government also improved with the development of the offices of **lord lieutenant** and **justice of the peace**. By 1603 government regulation and influence had increased. The establishment of the Poor Law and the raising and training of the militia (see page 264 for details) are examples of these.

Justice of the peace (JP): Appointed for every shire (district) and served nominally for a year at a time. They first appeared in the late Middle Ages as the Crown tried to cut down on the powers of the sheriffs. Most of them were local gentry who were unpaid. Their chief task was to see that the laws of the country were obeyed in their area. Both their powers and their numbers increased steadily during the Tudor period. The parliaments of Henry VII's reign saw laws passed concerning the role and work of JPs. Even a small shire would have 15 or so JPs, while a major county such as Kent had about 80.

Lord lieutenant: Appointed by the monarch. There was one appointed for each county by the end of Elizabeth I's reign. A lord lieutenant's main task was to organise the militia (for fuller description see Chapter 10).

What were the major changes to affect England during the Tudor period?

1.1 To what extent did the Tudors face threats to their rule in England between 1485 and 1603?

The British Isles in the 16th century, showing Tudor territory and language boundaries

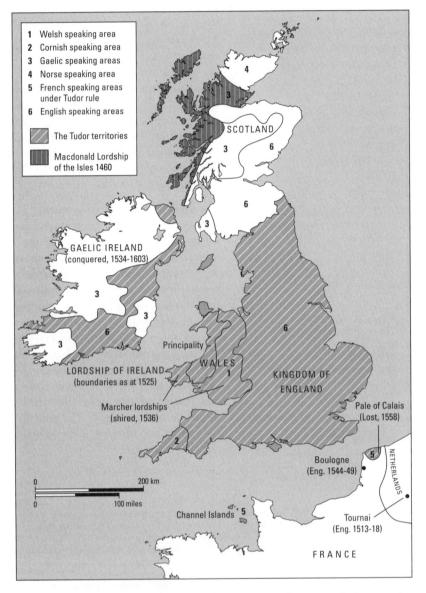

1. Welsh speaking area
2. Cornish speaking area
3. Gaelic speaking areas
4. Norse speaking area
5. French speaking areas under Tudor rule
6. English speaking areas

The Tudor territories

Macdonald Lordship of the Isles 1460

SCOTLAND

GAELIC IRELAND
(conquered, 1534-1603)

Principality

WALES

LORDSHIP OF IRELAND
(boundaries as at 1525)

Marcher lordships
(shired, 1536)

KINGDOM OF
ENGLAND

Pale of Calais
(Lost, 1558)

Boulogne
(Eng. 1544-49)

NETHERLANDS

0 ——— 200 km

0 ——— 100 miles

Channel Islands

Tournai
(Eng. 1513-18)

FRANCE

The Tudor period of English History (1485–1603) is regarded as a relatively stable period when compared to either the 15th century or the 17th century. The period was preceded by considerable political instability, known as the Wars of the Roses. Following the death of Elizabeth I in 1603, England entered a period of political instability, which led to the outbreak of civil wars in the 1640s.

However, the Tudor period was affected by a number of different threats to political stability. One type of threat were attempts to replace a Tudor monarch by a different dynasty. These were mainly associated with the reigns of Henry VII and Elizabeth I. However, in a technical sense, the only monarch to 'rule' in the period 1485 to 1603 who was not a Tudor was Lady Jane Grey, the Nine Days' Queen, in 1553 (see family tree on page 16).

Other threats included regional rebellions which affected the reigns of all the Tudor monarchs. These rebellions were caused by a variety of reasons such as economic hardship, religious and political factors. Finally, Tudor government was affected by factional conflicts between leading members of the Court and Government.

When Henry VII became king in 1485, England was in the grip of a period of political upheaval, known as the Wars of the Roses. In contrast to the 15th century, the 16th century was dominated by one dynasty. During this period England was saved from the problem. However, Henry VII's reign could have come to an abrupt end at the battle of East Stoke, in 1487, if he had not defeated the Yorkist pretender to the throne, Lambert Simnel. In this sense it was this battle, rather than Henry VII's victory at the battle of Bosworth Field, which marks the end to the Wars of the Roses. Later in his reign Henry VII was faced with a threat from another Yorkist pretender, Perkin Warbeck. Warbeck had powerful allies in Ireland and the continent but unlike Simnel he never posed a major military threat to Henry VII. In 1497 a major regional revolt broke out in Cornwall over taxation. For a brief period the Cornish Rebellion posed a major threat to political stability. The rebels were only defeated when they had reached Blackheath, just south of London.

Henry VIII also faced threats to his rule. Rioting and opposition to the Amicable Grant of 1525 was the only time when government policy had to be abandoned in the face of widespread national opposition. The religious and political changes of the 1530s created opposition which led to the Pilgrimage of Grace of 1536. Although initially successful in the north of the country, Henry VIII's government was able to suppress the rebellion ruthlessly in 1536–37.

Henry's immediate successors perhaps faced the most serious threats of all. The reign of Edward VI (1547–53) coincided with a period of considerable political and religious change as well as social and economic problems. The Ket Rebellion and the Western Rebellion, both in 1549, were important factors in the overthrow of Protector Somerset's government. Edward VI's successor was faced by the most serious threat of all in Wyatt's Rebellion of 1554 against the Spanish marriage between Mary Tudor and Philip II. It began in Kent and reached London.

During Elizabeth I's long reign (1558–1603), political opposition was associated with religious and regional issues. The Rebellion of the Northern Earls of 1569–70 was the last major regional rebellion in English History. Also, the period 1571–86 saw the discovery of numerous Catholic plots, associated with replacing Elizabeth by the catholic Mary Stuart.

All of these rebellions and attempts to overthrow Tudor monarchs failed. Their failure was due in part to the fact that they were localised. Anthony Fletcher in the third edition of *Tudor Rebellions* states: 'Tudor Rebellions ... were essentially the responses of local communities to local grievances.' Anthony Fletcher also notes that 'only one clear theme of national significance ran through the rebellions. This was the opposition of a conservative and pious society to the English Reformation.'

This factor was important in the Pilgrimage of Grace, in 1536, and in the Rebellion of the Northern Earls in 1569–70. However, their failure also reflects other reasons. There was a strong feeling of support for royal authority in England in the 16th century which made potential rebels reluctant to challenge the monarch directly. Instead rebels challenged the

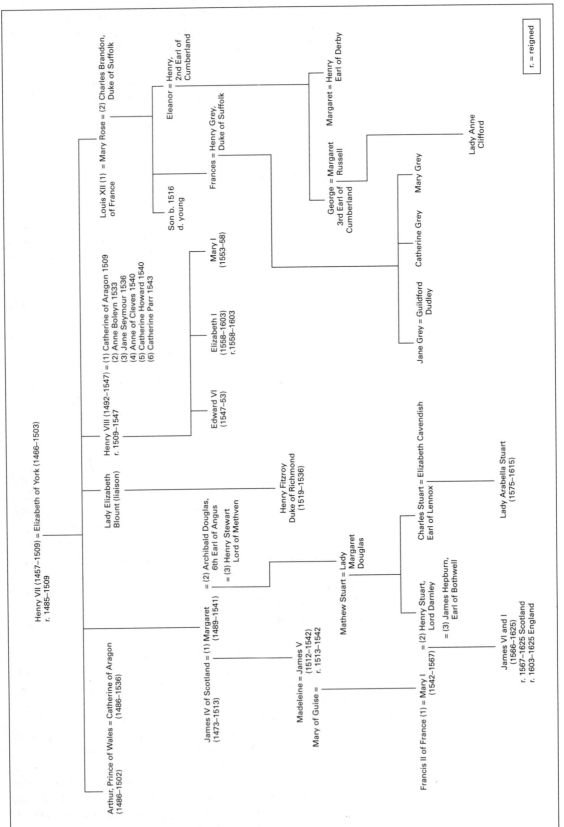

The Tudor dynasty

authority of royal officials. In the Pilgrimage of Grace in 1536 opposition was centred on the King's advisers, in particular Thomas Cromwell. Even the Wyatt Rebellion of 1554 was more against the marriage of Mary I to Philip II of Spain than against the queen herself. Defeat of these rebellions could also be explained by the growing power and stability of Tudor monarchs to deal with political and social threats. Although the 1590s was a decade of war, harvest failure and economic hardship, Elizabeth I's government did not face any serious challenge from the general public. Conflict in the 1590s was centred on political faction at Court and in the Privy Council.

In the Tudor Court, and the major government institution, the Privy Council, the aristocracy and leading government officials formed political groupings to further their own interests. Faction proved to have a significant impact on Tudor government and policy on a number of occasions. In the reign of Henry VIII, factional rivalry helps explain the rise and fall of Anne Boleyn and Thomas Cromwell. During Edward VI's reign, factional conflict led to the rise and fall of the Duke of Somerset. In Elizabeth I's reign, the Earl of Leicester's faction supported the pursuit of a Protestant foreign policy and direct aid for the Dutch against Philip II of Spain. The last years of Elizabeth's reign saw the Council split between rival factions led by Robert Cecil and the Earl of Essex. In 1601 the Earl of Essex failed in an attempt to defeat the Cecil faction, which led to his arrest and subsequent execution for treason.

The issue of faction should not be seen in isolation. The political rivalry at Court and in the Council helps explain both the Pilgrimage of Grace of 1536 and the Rebellion of the Northern Earls in 1569–70.

1. What kind of political threats did Tudor monarchs face?

2. During whose reign do you think political threats to Tudor rule were the most serious?

1.2 In what ways did English government and administration change in the years 1485–1603?

During the Tudor era the operation of government and administration altered considerably. To the vast majority of England government meant local government as administered by a local member of the aristocracy. These local magnates maintained law and order. This was most apparent in the borderlands with Scotland, along the Welsh border and in eastern Ireland. The area of effective control for a Tudor monarch was limited. Even Elizabeth I, who was noted for her tours of her kingdom, never visited the West Country, the North or Wales. The failure to control local magnates (see reference to 'over-mighty subjects' in Chapter 2) was a factor in the political instability of the Wars of the Roses.

Henry VII is credited with reducing the power of the aristocracy and establishing a financially independent monarchy. These developments have been regarded by some historians as creating a 'New Monarchy' in England, similar to those created in France and Spain. However, as Alexander Grant has pointed out in *Henry VII*, the first Tudor monarch did not introduce a new system of government and administration to England but used traditional methods of government and finance in new ways. Rather than see 1485 as the beginning of a new era for English government, Henry VII's reign had more in common with his immediate Yorkist predecessors, in particular Edward IV (1469–70; 1471–83) and Richard III (1483–85). In securing financial independence, Henry VII was fortunate not to have

Star Chamber: Nickname given to members of the Royal Council who dealt with certain legal matters and some aspects of law enforcement.

brothers to reward. His avoidance of war also aided the growth of financial independence. Nevertheless, the rise of the Council Learned (see page 29) and the use of the **Star Chamber** give an indication that Henry VII was willing to develop new aspects of administration.

A traditional form of government employed by Henry VII was the use of regional magnates to rule borderlands. In Ireland the earls of Kildare were used to enforce control in the Pale and in eastern Ireland, just as his Yorkist predecessors had done. In the Marches of Wales and the border with Scotland (see map on page 14) control and jurisdiction was given to families such as Percy and Dacre.

Under his son Henry VIII, historians have talked of a 'Tudor Revolution in Government'. Geoffrey Elton stated that during the 1530s English government was transformed and modernised by Thomas Cromwell. Although considerable change did occur, it is questionable whether they constituted a revolution. In many ways Cromwell improved the system of government and administration which was already in existence. Nevertheless, the 1530s did see major changes. Cromwell centralised the control of finance in the Exchequer at the expense of the Chamber. The Privy Council headed a more centralised administration which served the king's leading ministers. Cromwell also oversaw the incorporation of Wales into English-style county administration and the administrative changes brought on by the religious changes of the 1530s. These are discussed in detail in Chapter 6 on government, politics and foreign affairs 1529–47 (section 6.3).

Also of significance was the recognition in the 1530s that England was an independent sovereign state. The preamble to the Act of Supremacy, 1533 claimed that England was 'an empire' free from outside authority. In addition, Henry VIII's reign saw the Act of Union with Wales in 1536 and the creation of the Kingdom of Ireland in 1540. By 1547 the beginnings of a 'British' state had been established.

Much debate about the nature of Tudor government and the importance of faction has centred on the reigns of Edward VI and Mary I. So much so that, in the past, this period has been referred to as 'A Mid-Tudor Crisis'. However, during the years 1547–58, there was a considerable degree of continuity both with Henry VIII's and Elizabeth I's reigns. The Privy Council continued to develop as the main instrument of government.

Throughout the Tudor period the Privy Council was the most important government institution. The historian Geoffrey Elton regards the Privy Council as one of the important 'points of contact' linking the monarch with the influential figures in England who comprised the political nation. It contained leading aristocrats, churchmen and administrators and it fulfilled the role most closely associated with the Cabinet today. The size of the Council varied through the period. However, its role ranged from offering advice to the monarch and giving instructions to justices of the peace (JPs) and lords lieutenant, to attempts to regulate wages.

Also regarded as one of Geoffrey Elton's 'points of contact' was the Royal Court. This institution did not possess the formal powers and procedures of the Privy Council but still had political influence and was most closely associated with political faction. The Court contained those members of the aristocracy who attended the monarch for social rather than political reasons. Its function did not change radically during the Tudor period. However, in the 1530s and 1590s, Court politics associated with faction became a major issue. The fall of Anne Boleyn and the fall of the Earl of Essex were closely associated with political faction at Court. For a more detailed discussion see Chapter 9 (section 9.2).

The role of parliament in the Tudor period has been a major issue among historians for a considerable period of time. Whig historians (in the 19th century) – who saw English political history as the gradual rise in political power of parliament at the expense of the monarch – regarded the 16th century as an important period of development, laying the foundations for the conflict between monarch and parliament in the 17th century.

There is evidence that the power and authority of parliament did increase. The judge's decision of 1489 decreed that the House of Commons had to agree before a bill could become an Act. Also, during Henry VII's reign, parliament began to develop its own administration outside the **Court of Chancery**.

However, the two significant developments in parliamentary history are associated with religious change. Between 1529 and 1536 the Reformation Parliament passed wide-ranging legislation which established England as an independent state in control of its own Church. In doing so it established clearly the idea of the king working with parliament as the ultimate legal authority in England.

Parliament was also important in the Elizabethan Church Settlement, at the start of the reign of Elizabeth I. The Acts of Supremacy and Uniformity of 1559 were the foundation stones of the Church of England. However, parliament did not exist as a permanent institution. It could be called only on the authority of the monarch. Throughout the Tudor period it fulfilled its traditional role as a source of revenue for the monarch and a method of disposing of potential rivals through the use of Acts of attainder (see page 54).

The belief among historians that 'a Protestant choir' in the House of Commons forced Elizabeth I to produce a more radical church settlement in 1559 is no longer accepted. Nor is the belief that the House of Commons was developing its independence by the 1590s. During Elizabeth's reign the monarch was effective in silencing parliamentary opposition to the religious settlement of 1558–59. The opposition to monopolies (see page 115) in the parliaments of 1597 and 1601 was more an exception rather than the rule in the role of Tudor parliaments.

It must be remembered that the House of Lords played a very important role in Tudor parliaments. The House of Lords contained the aristocracy who dominated political and economic life.

An important change in government and administration in Tudor England was in local government. The Councils of the North and the Welsh Marches still existed by 1603. However, most of England and Wales was administered through county administrations where justices of the peace played a major role. This unpaid office became the backbone of Tudor local government administering justice and the poor law. In addition to the JP, the lord lieutenant became an important local official. Charged with the responsibility of raising troops to fight for the monarch, lords lieutenant were appointed from time to time. After 1585 and the outbreak of war with Spain they were appointed in each county on a permanent basis. The improvement in the English army by 1603 can be attributed to the 'trained bands' established by lords lieutenant.

Court of Chancery: A court which could override decisions of the ordinary law courts in the interests of fair play. This court came into being by the time Henry VII came to the throne.

1. Draw a diagram showing the different parts of government in Tudor England.

2. Which part of government do you think changed most during the Tudor period? Give reasons to support your answer.

In the past historians have referred to the creation of a 'Tudor despotism' (dictatorship) in the 16th century. They have pointed to the Statute of Proclamations of 1539 as an example of this development. It is clear that there was an improvement in the quality of administration and control from London as the century progressed. However, it would be difficult to describe the Tudor regime as a dictatorship when local government played such an important part in the government of the country.

1.3 How far did the economy and society change in the period 1485–1603?

Throughout the Tudor period England was overwhelmingly an agricultural country. The wealth of the country was linked directly to events such as the size and quality of the harvest. Periods of harvest failure led inevitably to a rise in grain prices and, in some cases, starvation. The 1590s saw one of the worst periods of harvest failure and starvation in the whole Tudor period.

Map of the British Isles produced in about 1534

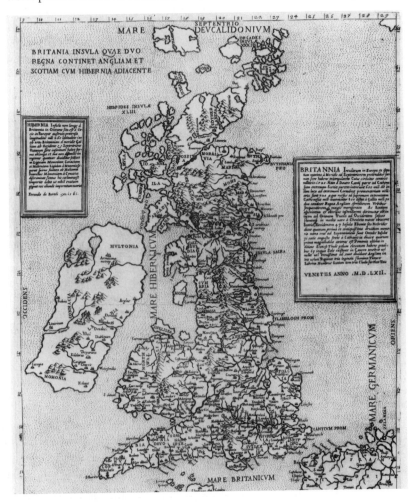

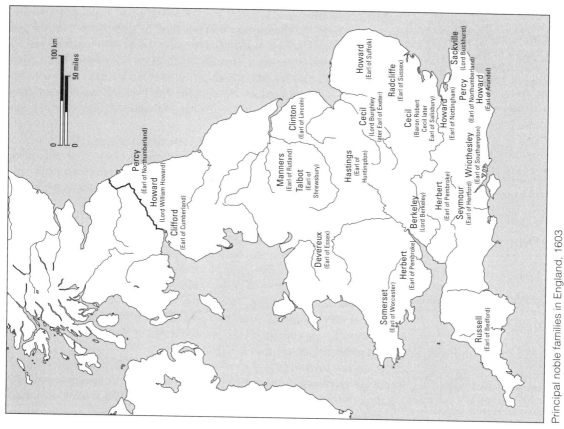

Principal noble families in England, 1603

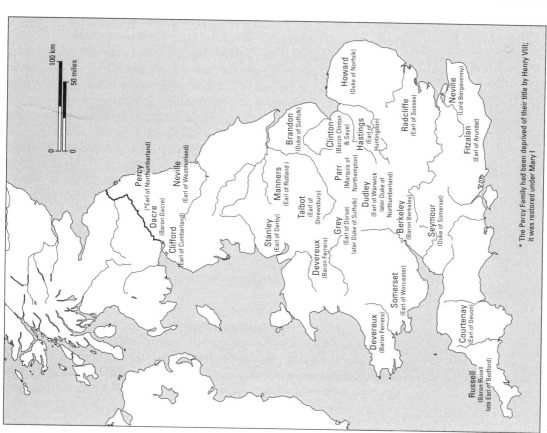

Principal noble families in England, 1547

* The Percy Family had been deprived of their title by Henry VIII;
it was restored under Mary I

In what ways did the principal noble families change between 1547 and 1603?

Staple: A place where a company or organisation, such as the Merchant Adventurers, had the exclusive right to buy and sell goods.

Chartered companies: Donations from the monarch to certain companies granting them rights and privileges.

Most Englishmen and women lived in villages and engaged in subsistence agriculture, producing just enough food to feed themselves. In the early part of the period some enterprising landowners attempted to improve agriculture through creating enclosures (see page 111). This process created considerable debate about its effects on rural unemployment and rural depopulation throughout the century. As late as 1598 Parliament passed an Act on husbandry and tillage (see page 301) in a bid to prevent rural depopulation.

England possessed a wide variety of agricultural regions. The historian Joan Thirsk, in *The Agrarian History of England 1500–1640,* identifies farming practices associated with different types of landscape and soil from marshland associated with cattle raising, through vales, downlands, forest, heathlands and moorland.

Sheep farming was an important activity which provided the raw material for England's main exports, wool and woollen cloth. The export of woollen goods remained the backbone of English trade throughout the Tudor period. Under the control of the **Staple** and the Merchant Adventurers (see page 46) this trade was centred mainly on the Netherlands city of Antwerp. During the Dutch Revolt and the war with Spain after 1585, this trade was disrupted. Although alternative outlets for English wool were sought at Emden and Hamburg, Antwerp remained the chief port for these exports.

As the century progressed, new outlets for English trade were developed. These are usually associated with **chartered companies** given responsibility for trade. The Muscovy and Levant companies handled trade with Russia and the eastern Mediterranean respectively. However, these new outlets of trade remained small in comparison to the wool trade. In this respect, the Tudor period can be seen as laying the foundations for the future. This is illustrated with the creation of the East India Company in 1600.

The dominant class in England was the aristocracy. They numbered about 200 families. They were the largest landowners and were the most influential group in politics. They were represented at Court and in the Privy Council. They also had considerable local power. Some, like the Percy family of Northumberland, played a major role in the government of the Scottish borders. Others, like the Stanleys in Lancashire and the Howard family, controlled regions of north-western and central England respectively (see maps on page 21).

Some historians have suggested that the aristocracy declined in importance during the 16th century. This was due to the rise in importance of a new class of landowner, the gentry (see page 111). There were several thousand gentry families. Events such as the Dissolution of the Monasteries helped members of the gentry to acquire land. However, although the gentry grew in numbers and social and economic status there is only limited evidence to suggest any change in the position of the aristocracy by 1603.

An important feature of 16th-century economic history is the price revolution. Today this is known as a period of price rises, or 'inflation'. The Tudor period faced two major periods of inflation: the 1540s to the 1550s and the 1590s. A wide variety of explanations have been put forward for the rise in prices. One view is that a rise in population without a significant increase in food supplies caused prices to rise. However, the link between these two factors is most apparent at times of harvest failure, which leads to a major drop in the supply of food. The first major period

Renaissance: Period of European history covering the 15th century to 17th century. It was associated with the re-discovery of Ancient Greek and Roman literature and the study of man. Also associated with the spread of literacy to the lay (non-clerical) population.

1. Produce a time chart using the three sub-headings: *Economy, Social affairs, Learning and literature.*

Write down the major changes which took place during the Tudor period.

2. *Which aspect of the economy and society of England changed most during the Tudor period? Give reasons to support your answer.*

of inflation (1540s–1550s) is associated with the rise in the cost of warfare and the debasement of the coinage (see page 115 for definition). One of the successes of the first years of Elizabeth I's reign was a revaluing of the coinage and an end to inflation. In the 1590s the rise in prices was associated more with harvest failure than anything else. But price rises were not limited to England. Across Europe prices rose in the second half of the 16th century. This has been explained, in part, by the arrival in Europe of large quantities of silver from the Spanish mines in Peru (south America).

One of the major problems facing Tudor government at both local and national level was poverty and vagrancy. During the 16th century a large number of measures were taken to help the poor and to deter vagrancy. The Dissolution of the Monasteries removed one possible source of aid for the poor, especially in the North of England. However, during Elizabeth I's reign legislation was passed by Parliament which provided the basis of a national scheme of aid for the poor and a deterrent to vagrancy (for a more detailed coverage, see Chapter 12).

In education and literature the 16th century is seen as a period of significant development. The **Renaissance** led to the 'New Learning' (see page 74). By the reign of Henry VII, scholars across Europe were studying the ancient world of Greece and Rome as well as subjects such as medicine and science. In England this development helped the growth of grammar schools and university learning at Oxford and Cambridge. Perhaps the most significant impact of these changes came later in the century, during the reign of Elizabeth I. The literary works of William Shakespeare (1564–1616), the poetry of Edmund Spenser (1552–1599) and the plays of Ben Jonson (?1572–1637) make the Elizabethan period a 'golden age' of English literature.

1.4 How important was the issue of religious change?

In 1485 England comprised two provinces of the western Christian or Catholic Church, Canterbury and York. By 1603 a separate and distinct Church of England had been created. The Pope's authority over England had been abolished. The monarch had become Supreme Governor of the Church of England. Why did these changes take place?

There has been considerable debate about the popularity and strength of the Catholic Church in England before 1530. Protestant writers have emphasised issues such as corruption and lack of enthusiasm among the general public for the Church at that time. However, research by historians such as J. J. Scarisbrick and Eamon Duffy has shown that the Church was popular in England on the eve of Henry VIII's break with Rome. In fact, the traditional Catholic religion remained the religion of the majority of the population well into Elizabeth I's reign. Protestantism was centred in London and south-east England until the reign of Queen Elizabeth I. One of Elizabeth's achievements was the establishment of the moderate Protestant Church of England by the time of her death.

Although Protestant ideas had reached England by the 1530s, Henry VIII's break with Rome was based mainly on dynastic reasons. Henry VIII's failure to get an annulment of his marriage to Catherine of Aragon led directly to the end of the Pope's authority in England through laws passed by the Reformation Parliament from 1529 to 1536. Henry VIII also acquired considerable wealth by confiscating Church property through the Dissolution of the Monasteries. Some changes did occur in religious belief and practice by 1547, such as the provision of an English Bible in each church. However, by Henry VIII's death in 1547 religious belief in England was very similar to that followed before 1530. The English Church could be regarded as a form of National Catholicism.

The reign of Edward VI is associated with more radical changes in religious belief and practice. The Books of Common Prayer of 1549 and 1552 moved the Church closer to the Protestant churches of Germany and Switzerland. However, the short length of Edward's reign allowed his sister, Mary I, to re-introduce the Catholic religion relatively quickly after 1553.

A major turning point in the development of religious change came with the reign of Elizabeth I. The Church Settlement of 1559 established the Church of England in terms of its organisation and religious belief. The Church was a distinct version of moderate Protestantism which was disliked by both Catholics and more extreme Protestant, known as Puritans. In spite of this opposition, Elizabeth I's reign saw the permanent establishment of the Church of England without any fundamental change after 1559.

> *1. What do you regard as the most important religious changes which took place in the Tudor period?*
>
> *2. When do you think England became a Protestant country? Give reasons to support your answer.*

1.5 To what extent did England dominate the British Isles between 1485 and 1603?

In 1485 the British Isles was divided into a number of political units. The most important state was the Kingdom of England. The independent state of Scotland existed to the north. To the west of England lay Wales which was technically part of the English Kingdom but had its own administration which was under the control of the local aristocracy (see map opposite). Although English monarchs were Lords of Ireland, English control was limited. A small area around Dublin, known as The Pale, was under direct English control. Much of eastern Ireland was under the control of Anglo-Irish aristocrats such as the earls of Kildare who administered the area for the English monarch. Most of western and southern Ireland was outside any form of English control. This area was inhabited by Gaelic-speaking Irish clans (see map on page 14). In Europe England controlled the Pale of Calais, the last remnant of the English Empire in France which had been lost in the years before 1453 during the 100 Years' War.

By 1603 things had changed. Calais had been lost during Mary I's reign. English county administration had been extended to include all of Wales. The accession of James VI and I had brought a 'union of Crowns' between England and Scotland. In Ireland the defeat of the Tyrone Rebellion at the battle of Kinsale in 1601 had brought Gaelic Irish resistance to English rule to an end. These developments laid the foundations for the eventual political unification of the British Isles in the 18th century.

Important developments in this process took place during the reign of Henry VIII. The Act of Union with Wales and the proclamation of Henry as King of Ireland in 1540 reinforced the claim that England was an 'empire', or independent state made in the Act of Supremacy, 1533.

During the reign of Mary I, attempts were made to increase English influence in Ireland. The policy of 'surrender and regrant' was used to

The British Isles

encourage Gaelic chiefs to abandon their Gaelic noble titles and replace them with English titles, such as earl. Mary I also established the English colonies or plantations of King's and Queen's counties where Englishmen replaced the Gaelic Irish (see map on page 66).

The most important phase in the establishment of English control over Ireland came during the reign of Elizabeth I. English colonisation through plantations was extended to include the south of Ireland and east Ulster. These developments sparked off rebellions by the Gaelic Irish. The most serious began in the north Irish province of Ulster in 1596, led by the Earl of Tyrone. It took the English government six years and considerable financial expense to defeat the rebellion. However, by Elizabeth I's death in 1603 England had broken the resistance of the Gaelic Irish chiefs.

England's relations with Scotland went through several changes in the period. Scotland had been a traditional enemy throughout the Middle Ages. The Scots usually allied themselves with England's other traditional enemy, France, to form the 'Auld Alliance'. When Henry VIII went to war with France in 1512 the Scots used the opportunity to invade north England. In 1513, at the battle of Flodden, the Scots suffered a serious defeat and the death of their king, which ended the Scottish threat for a generation. Towards the end of his reign, in the 1540s, Henry VIII again became involved with war against Scotland, at the same time as the renewal of war with France.

During the short reign of Edward VI, the Duke of Somerset adopted an expensive and ultimately unsuccessful policy towards Scotland. He established English garrisons (soldiers in towns) across central and southern Scotland in an attempt to maintain English control. Unfortunately for Somerset, he had to abandon these garrisons. His Scottish policy was, in part, responsible for his fall in 1549.

Relations with Scotland deteriorated during Mary I's reign. With England's entry into war with France in 1557, Scotland provided a base for French troops. The 'Auld Alliance' was made more effective through the marriage of Mary Stuart to a French prince, who became king in 1559.

It was the reign of Elizabeth I which finally saw the end of the Scottish threat to England. In the years 1559 to 1560 English military action brought to an end the French presence north of the border with the Treaty of Edinburgh. Through much of Elizabeth I's reign support was given to Protestant Scottish noblemen who were sympathetic to England, such as the Earl of Morton. However, the main issue in Anglo–Scottish relations was the exile of Mary Stuart in England from 1568 to 1587. As a Catholic and an heir to the English throne, Mary created problems for Elizabeth I in domestic politics as well as for England's relations with Scotland and Europe. Mary became the centre for Catholic plots to remove Elizabeth I. The execution of Mary Stuart, for treason, and the English support for her Protestant son, James VI, ensured good relations between the two countries. These relations reached their peak when James VI succeeded Elizabeth as monarch in 1603.

1. Produce a time chart with the sub-heading of Scotland and Ireland. Write down the major changes which took place in England's relations with these two areas during the Tudor period.

2. How far did England dominate the British Isles by 1603?

1.6 Why did England's relations with France and Spain alter in the yea. 1485–1603?

1. Why did France rather than Spain become England's main enemy during the Tudor period?

2. Study the changes which took place in politics, government, the economy, society, religion and England's relations with other states. In which of the following periods did (a) most change occur; (b) least change occur? Give reasons to support your answer.

1485–1529

1529–1547

1547–1558

1558–1603

Throughout the period 1485 to 1603 England was regarded as a second-class power in western Europe, compared with France and Spain. Traditionally, England's main enemy had been France. In the period before 1453 England and France had engaged in the 100 Years' War. Although at one stage England had controlled large areas of France, such as Normandy and Gascony, after 1453 English rule was limited to Calais and the Channel Islands (see map on page 14). This did not mean English monarchs gave up the hope of recapturing England's lost possessions.

During the reign of Henry VII, the main aim was to establish the Tudor dynasty. As a result, England followed a peaceful foreign policy. The marriage of Henry VII's sons to Catherine of Aragon and the marriage linking the houses of Tudor and Stuart (see family tree on page 16) were aimed at achieving this end. Henry VIII returned to a policy of warfare to recover England's French lands. In wars with France in 1512–14 and again in the 1540s attempts were made to win territory. However, English victories were limited to the temporary capture of Tournai and Boulogne.

The loss of England's last possession on the continent occurred in the reigns of Mary and Elizabeth. The French War of 1557–59 saw the capture of Calais by the French army. However, it was not until the Treaty of Troyes in 1564 that Elizabeth I gave up the hope of the return of Calais to English rule.

In many ways the 1560s mark a turning point in England's relations with western Europe. Before that date France was seen as England's main enemy. From 1562 to 1598 France was affected by the Wars of Religion. Instead the new threat to England was Spain under Philip II. In the space of a decade, from 1554 to 1564, Spain went from being England's ally to a possible threat. This was in part due to the religious conflict between Catholic and Protestant in late 16th-century Europe. Throughout his reign Philip II hoped to win England back to Catholicism. However, trade and economic considerations were also important. Philip II controlled the Netherlands, the main export market for the woollen trade.

Anglo–Spanish relations began to deteriorate rapidly between 1568 and 1572 because of the revolt of the Netherlands against Spanish rule. By 1585 fear of a Spanish victory in the Netherlands and a possible Franco–Spanish Catholic alliance against England had driven a reluctant Elizabeth I into war. From 1585 to 1604 England and Spain fought a war in the Netherlands, France, Ireland and across the north Atlantic.

The reign of Henry VII

2.1 How did Henry VII establish himself as king 1485–1486?

2.2 What were the dangers posed by conspiracies and rebellions to Henry VII (1485–1506)?

2.3 Why was foreign policy so important in establishing the Tudor dynasty?

2.4 How successful was Henry VII in dealing with the English nobility?

2.5 What were the main features of Henry VII's government of England?

2.6 Historical interpretation: To what extent did Henry VII create a 'new monarchy'?

Key Issues

● *How successful was Henry VII in dealing with threats to his rule?*

● *What problems did Henry VII face in foreign policy?*

● *Did Henry VII create a 'new monarchy'?*

Framework of Events

1485	August: Henry Tudor defeats Richard III at Bosworth Field and becomes Henry VII
	November: Henry's first Parliament
1486	January: Henry marries Elizabeth of York
1486–87	The Simnel conspiracy
1487	June: Battle of East Stoke – defeat of Simnel
	November: Henry's second Parliament. Acts of attainder are passed against those who had supported Simnel
1489	January: Henry's third Parliament – votes taxes for intervention in Brittany
	February: Treaty of Redon with Brittany
	March: Treaty of Medina del Campo with Spain
	October: Final French defeat of the Breton army
1491	October: Henry's fourth Parliament votes taxes for a war against France
	November: beginning of the Warbeck conspiracy in Ireland
1492	October: Henry invades northern France
	November: Treaty of Etaples. Henry receives a French pension
1493	Embargo on Anglo–Flemish trade is imposed by Henry
1494	September: Sir Edward Poynings sent to Ireland
	November: Irish Parliament passes Poynings Law
1495	February: Sir William Stanley is executed for treason
	October: Henry's fifth Parliament. The De Facto Act is passed
1496	Kildare is reappointed as Lord Deputy in Ireland
1497	January: Henry's sixth Parliament votes taxes for the war against Scotland
	June: Cornish rebels are defeated at Blackheath
	September: capture of Perkin Warbeck
1498	Renewal of Treaty of Etaples
1499	Execution of Warwick and Warbeck
1501	Marriage of Prince Arthur and Catherine of Aragon
1502	February: Anglo–Scottish Treaty
	April: death of Prince Arthur

1503	February: death of Elizabeth of York
	August: marriage of James IV to Princess Margaret
1504	Henry VII's last Parliament
1506	January–April: Philip and Joanna of Castile in England
	Malus Intercursus: trading agreement between Philip and Henry much to the disadvantage of Flemish merchants
1509	April: death of Henry VII.

Overview

Henry VII (1457–1509) – painting by Michiel Sittow, 1505

Usurper: A person who seizes power by using unjust or unlawful force.

Trade embargo: When ships are forbidden to leave port to trade with other countries.

Council: The king's ministers and advisers who met together regularly to run government as well as to give him advice. The membership of the Council varied but its regular members were leading ministers such as the Lord Chancellor (see page 72), the Lord Privy Seal and the Lord Treasurer, as well as other leading noblemen.

Council Learned: A small body of Royal Councillors set up in 1495. Its job was to deal with all problems concerning the Crown lands and the king's feudal rights. In the last years of Henry VII's reign the Council Learned became very unpopular.

O N 22 August 1485 Henry Tudor defeated Richard III at the battle of Bosworth Field and became King Henry VII of England. At the time Henry may have appeared to be just one more **usurper** rather than the founder of what was to be the Tudor dynasty.

Much of Henry's reign was to be concerned with securing his position on the English throne. He was to face frequent problems with conspiracies and pretenders who often received foreign support. Henry's insecurity was seen in the famous **trade embargo** which he imposed on Flanders between 1493 and 1496 because of their support for the pretender Perkin Warbeck. After the execution of Warbeck in 1499, Henry's position was still insecure due to the deaths of two of his sons, Edmund and Arthur in 1500 and 1502 respectively, and the future of the Tudors depended on the survival of the remaining son, Prince Henry. As late as 1506 there were still mutterings about the succession to the throne once Henry VII was dead.

Henry VII's foreign policy, apart from avoiding expensive wars, was much concerned with obtaining his fellow rulers' recognition of his dynasty. The Treaty of Medina del Campo with Spain in 1489 was for Henry welcome recognition of his dynasty by one of Europe's leading powers, especially with its proposed marriage between Arthur, Henry's heir, and Catherine of Aragon. Other treaties, such as Etaples with France in 1492 and Ayton with Scotland (1497) helped to secure international recognition for Henry. Also, the king was interested in promoting trade, provided that it did not interfere with security, as the commercial clauses of the Treaty of Medina del Campo indicated.

Within England Henry was determined to ensure good government by control of the nobility, encouraging law and order in the localities and increasing the wealth of the Crown. In spite of his inexperience, Henry soon developed as a hard-working king who learnt from his mistakes. He also appointed able men to advise and serve him on his **Council**; many of whom had served his Yorkist predecessors too. Henry soon established a firm control over the nobility by using **acts of attainder** against the actively disloyal and a system of **bonds and recognisances** imposed on those whose loyalty he doubted (see panel on page 54 for definitions).

During the last years of his reign through the **Council Learned** the majority of the nobility and many of the gentry found themselves under financial threat from the king, which was much resented. However, in the absence of much in the way of machinery of government and much of an army, Henry made effective use of the nobility and gentry to control the outlying regions and localities of England.

Local gentry: The leading landowning families in each area of the country were called 'the gentry'. This was a reference to their status as gentlemen who were entitled to bear arms because they were looked on as being of 'gentle birth'.

Sir Reginald Bray (?–1503)
One of Henry VII's chief councillors. Firstly, he was in the service of Henry's mother, Margaret Beaufort. When he was Chancellor of the Duchy of Lancaster his responsibilities covered all of the king's estates.

Henry made increasing use of **local gentry** acting as justices of the peace (see page 13) to enforce his will in the localities and his parliaments passed Acts which increased the scope of their powers over many aspects of law and order and everyday life.

Henry VII was quick to appreciate that a rich king was also a strong king. He worked hard to increase the royal revenue through efficient management of the royal estates and of customs revenues and trade. The king was ably assisted in this by his councillors, such as Sir Reginald Bray. In the last years of his reign, Henry was also assisted by the work of the Council Learned enforcing the king's feudal rights, although its activities were much resented. At the time of his death, Henry's revenues were in surplus but he did not leave his son a large treasury – as an earlier generation of historians believed. He called seven parliaments during his reign. Six of them were summoned between 1485 and 1497, often at times of insecurity and danger. Parliament sat for less than 18 months out of the 24 years of Henry VII's reign. Its continuous presence was unnecessary to government. Its role was to grant Henry taxes and to pass laws to help him to govern England more effectively, which it did. Also Parliament was a way of consulting those among the king's subjects who mattered, and at times this was what the king did. The age of parliamentary democracy and 'one person, one vote' lay in the future.

The major debate among historians about Henry VII's reign has been how far did he create a 'new monarchy'? Many historians have seen considerable continuity between Henry VII's government of England and that of his Yorkist predecessors, Edward IV and Richard III. There is no doubt that between 1471 and 1509 much was done to restore the power of the Crown and that Henry followed many of the methods established by his predecessors in governing England. It would have been unusual if the king had not, as many of his leading councillors – such as Archbishop John Morton (see page 35) and Bishop Richard Fox – had served as councillors to the Yorkist kings too. However, Henry himself brought a new vigour to the government of England and made its machinery, both locally and nationally, work much more efficiently. In spite of constant security worries Henry succeeded in establishing his dynasty; as a result, his successor was able to sit securely on his throne. As one of Henry's biographers, Francis Bacon, wrote of him in 1622: 'what he minded he compassed'.

2.1 How did Henry VII establish himself as king 1485–1486?

On 22 August 1485 at the battle of Bosworth Field, the naked body of King Richard III was slung across the back of a horse and hurried away for burial at nearby Leicester Abbey. England had a new king, Henry VII. The battle of Bosworth was seen as a turning point in English history. From Tudor times onwards the battle is viewed by many historians, such as J. R. Green, as marking the beginning of modern times and the end of the Middle Ages. However, it is unlikely that the 28-year-old victor of Bosworth, or his supporters, would have realised that they had begun a new age. In many ways the victory would have seemed to people at the time to be just another chapter in the round of intermittent wars, which had been going since the later 1450s, now known as the Wars of the Roses.

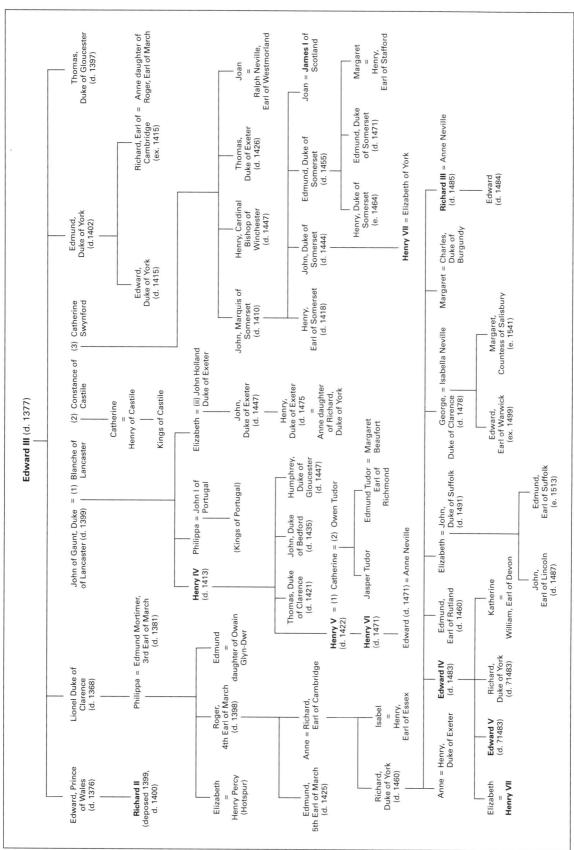

The houses of York and Lancaster, and Henry Tudor

Henry VII, an unlikely king?

Henry was born in January 1457 at Pembroke Castle in south-west Wales. He was the only child of the marriage of Edmund Tudor, Earl of Richmond, to Margaret Beaufort (only 14 when married). Edmund Tudor had been killed three months before the battle of Bosworth Field and Henry was to see little of his mother after 1462 when Lord Herbert became his guardian. Originally Welsh gentry, Henry's family had risen rapidly in 15th-century England. The new king's grandfather, Owen Tudor, had charmed Henry V's widow, Catherine, into marrying him and the resulting children, Edmund and Jasper, were thus half-brothers to the then king of England, Henry VI. The royal connection was advantageous to the Tudors until 1461, but with the victory of the Yorkists the family fortunes became dangerous. In 1470–71 Henry VI was briefly restored to the throne but the Lancastrian defeats at Barnet and Tewkesbury led to the deaths of both Henry VI and his only son, Edward, Prince of Wales. This left Henry Tudor as the new head of the House of Lancaster (see family tree) due to his claim to the throne from his mother Margaret Beaufort. The Beauforts were descended from King Edward III through the marriage of his third son, John of Gaunt, to Catherine Swynford (see family tree). However, Catherine's and John of Gaunt's children were illegitimate as they had been born before their parents' marriage. Although the family was later legitimised by Act of Parliament, they remained excluded from succeeding to the throne. In view of Henry's claim to be the heir to the House of Lancaster, his uncle Jasper thought it best to flee with him to the relative safety of Brittany which was outside Edward IV's grasp.

The next 14 years of Henry's life were spent in exile in Brittany or France. Henry is the only English king who has had to spend his formative years between childhood and adulthood waiting outside the chambers of the great, hoping for an audience or favours. This experience may have helped him to develop patience and the ability to mask his feelings in what were frustrating times with Edward IV firmly established on the English throne. However, with Edward's death in 1483 and the usurpation of his brother, the Duke of Gloucester, who became Richard III, Henry's prospects improved. By 1484 with the defeat of the Duke of Buckingham's rebellion which Henry and his followers had supported, Richard III put pressure on the Duke of Brittany to hand over Henry. Wisely, Henry fled to France where he was joined by disaffected Yorkists angered by Richard's usurpation and the disappearance of Edward IV's young sons (often referred to as the 'Princes in the Tower').

Why did Henry Tudor succeed in taking the English throne in 1485?

Henry's chances of toppling Richard III remained slim. That is, until the French king, Charles VIII, decided to back the Lancastrian pretender. He offered money, a fleet and a small army of **mercenaries** to Henry hoping that if he succeeded he would have a new and grateful ally on the English throne. With this support, Henry and his small band of loyal followers landed in south-west Wales, near Milford Haven, on 7 August 1485. From there, gathering support as he went, Henry marched into England by way of Shrewsbury, Stafford and Lichfield. Richard III did not act immediately

Mercenaries: Professional soldiers who sold their services to the highest bidder. They were therefore not motivated by any sense of loyalty to the cause they were fighting for.

against the threat of Henry and his supporters, as he thought they would be defeated long before they reached the Midlands.

However, once the king realised his mistake he moved his forces to Leicester. The two armies met just outside Market Bosworth on 22 August. Richard's army apparently outnumbered Henry's two to one but accounts of the battle vary greatly. Richard III may have lost the day because of his unwise decision in the middle of the battle to try and win it by killing Henry in hand-to-hand combat. At the crucial moment when Richard had fought his way to within a few metres of Henry his horse was killed under him. Henry's step-uncle, Sir William Stanley, who had been hovering on the edge of the battle with his men waiting to see which way it would go, decided to intervene against Richard.

This intervention was decisive. The Yorkist army, seeing Richard alone and surrounded by his enemies, fled leaving the king to die fighting bravely.

How did Henry secure the throne in his early months as king?

Papal dispensation: The granting by a Pope (Head of the Roman Catholic Church) of a licence to a person to do what is usually forbidden by the laws of the Church.

Tudor propaganda: Putting out the message that the Tudor monarchs wanted their subjects to accept. For example, saying that by his victory at Bosworth and his marriage to Elizabeth of York Henry VII had put an end to the 'Wars of the Roses': he had united the Houses of York and Lancaster, the white rose and the red.

Now that he was king, in effect by rights of conquest, Henry set about securing his new kingdom. His first act was to date the official beginning of his reign from the day before the battle of Bosworth Field. This condemned Richard III and all who had fought for him as traitors. Their estates became the property of the new king. Also, Henry VII arranged his coronation for 30 October, just before the Parliament which he had summoned to meet on 7 November. This was done to make it clear that Henry VII, in becoming king, owed nothing to parliamentary support.

This parliament granted Henry the income from the customs revenue that all new kings received – for life. Parliament passed acts of attainder confirming the king's earlier seizure of his enemies' lands. This was followed in January 1486 by Henry's marriage to Elizabeth of York, Edward IV's daughter. The marriage had had to wait for the arrival of the necessary **papal dispensation**, as the young couple were distant cousins. However, this delay made it clear to all that Henry did not in any way owe his throne to his wife. Nevertheless, the marriage strengthened Henry's position as afterwards he was able to claim that he had united the rival houses of York and Lancaster, and restored national unity. In future, **Tudor propaganda** was to make much of this marriage and its good effects – such as the ending of the so-called 'Wars of the Roses'.

What threats did Henry VII face in the early years of his reign?

John de la Pole, Earl of Lincoln (1464–1487)
Son of John de la Pole, 2nd Duke of Suffolk, and Elizabeth, the sister of Edward IV and Richard III. After the death of his own son Edward in 1484, Richard III recognised the Earl of Lincoln as his heir. However, after Bosworth Field Lincoln recognised Henry VII as king and was made a member of the Royal Council. Early in 1487 he fled from England to join his aunt Margaret of Burgundy in the Netherlands. He may have been involved in the conspiracy led by Lambert Simnel. Certainly, de la Pole accompanied Simnel to Ireland and later fought on the pretender's side at the battle of East Stoke, where he was killed during the fighting.

Besides meeting Parliament and getting married, Henry VII was not idle in other areas in the early months of his reign. There were still a number of important Yorkists alive who had a strong claim to the throne. The most important of these was the Earl of Warwick, the ten-year-old son of another of Edward IV's brothers, the Duke of Clarence, who was sent to the Tower of London. Another claimant, John de la Pole, who had been named as heir to the throne by his uncle Richard III, was invited to join the Council after he had declared his loyalty to Henry.

Others who had supported Richard at Bosworth were treated carefully by the new king. The Earl of Northumberland, who sat on the sidelines during the battle of Bosworth Field, was soon sent back to rule the North of England. The Duke of Norfolk and his son the Earl of Surrey, who had

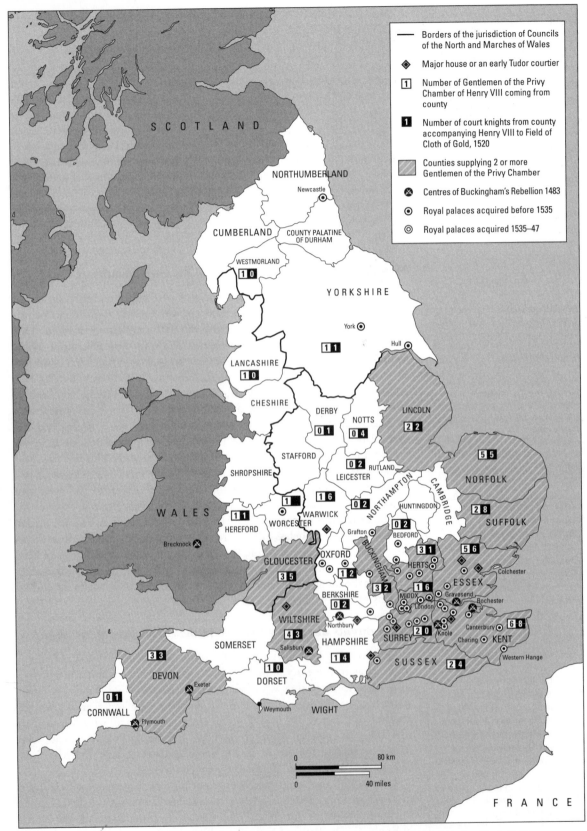

Map showing early Tudor political structure: rule was based in the South East

Thomas Howard, 13th Earl of Surrey (1443–1524)
Son of John Howard, first Duke of Norfolk, who was killed fighting for Richard III at the battle of Bosworth. Surrey was imprisoned in the Tower by Henry VII for his part in the battle, and his estates were confiscated. In 1489 he was released and some of the Norfolk estates were returned to him. He was sent north to suppress the Northern Rising. Remained Henry's lieutenant in the North until he was recalled to London to become Lord Treasurer in 1503. Surrey was sent back north to command the forces which defeated the Scots at the battle of Flodden in 1513. In 1514 the title of Duke of Norfolk was restored to him. In his later years he was a consistent enemy of Cardinal Wolsey.

John Morton (1420–1500)
A Lancastrian until the 1460s, Morton allied himself with the Yorkists after the battle of Tewkesbury (1471). In 1473 he became a Royal Councillor and in later years was made Bishop of Ely. He resisted Richard III's usurpation and was an important figure in Buckingham's unsuccessful rebellion. He fled to join Henry Tudor in exile. After Henry became king, Morton was made Lord Chancellor and in 1486 he became Archbishop of Canterbury. He was Henry's leading councillor until his death in 1500. In 1493 Morton was made a cardinal by the Pope. He was known for his taxation of the nobility by means of benevolences (free gifts to the king, usually unwillingly given).

Sanctuary: Under the law (canon law) of the medieval church, a fugitive from justice was immune from arrest in a holy place such as a church, abbey or cathedral. By Tudor times there were exceptions to this rule.

1. No one expected Henry Tudor to become king of England in August 1485. Explain why he succeeded.

2. How did Henry VII make himself secure as king during the first year of his reign?

both fought for Richard at Bosworth, were imprisoned by Henry. Other Yorkist lords, especially in the North of England, had to give promises for their good behaviour but provided they remained loyal there was no barrier to gaining the new king's favour.

Besides Yorkists, Henry enjoyed the support of hose who had shared his exile before 1485. The king's uncle, Jasper Tudor, soon to be made Duke of Bedford, became a vital figure in the Royal Council, along with John de Vere (Earl of Oxford). John Morton, who became Chancellor and Archbishhop of Canterbury from 1486, was another key figure, along with Richard Fox (Lord Privy Seal) and the king's step-father, Thomas Stanley (Lord Stanley, later Earl of Derby).

In spite of his friendly approach, Henry VII soon found himself facing trouble from those Yorkists who refused to accept him. In March 1486 Henry travelled to the North on a royal progress to boost support for the Crown in Yorkshire, which had been the centre of Richard's power. At York the King and Queen were received with great celebrations but not before they threat of a plot and uprising. This plot was the work of Thomas, Lord Lovell (Richard III's chamberlain) and the Stafford brothers who had broken **sanctuary**. The threat was avoided by promises of a royal pardon to the ordinary rebels. Lovell fled abroad while the Staffords, who had failed to raise the West Country against Henry, were dragged from their new sanctuary and imprisoned in the Tower of London.

The judges assured Henry that sanctuary did not apply to the crime of treason and Humphrey Stafford was executed, although later his brother was pardoned and released by the king. In September 1486, Elizabeth gave birth to a son, who was called Arthur, which seemed to make Henry's rule safe. The name Arthur was chosen because of ancient stories and Henry's wish to identify the Tudors as descended from Cadwaladr, the last truly great king of Britain before the Saxon invasion succeeded. These ideas came from Geoffrey of Monmouth's book *History of the Kings of Britain*, which was written in the 1130s and 1140s and linked Britain to the glories of King Arthur. It allowed Henry VII to make good use of what then passed for real history. It gave the Tudors a firm link to Britain's glorious past: good propaganda for the new dynasty.

2.2 What were the dangers posed by conspiracies and rebellions to Henry VII (1485–1506)?

The first Tudor monarch was an usurper who spent much of his reign securing his position. This is a key fact to remember about him. Henry VII was the first member of the Tudor dynasty, which was to rule England. It is easy to forget that for much of his reign Henry VII was politically insecure. Within two years of becoming king, Henry faced a major conspiracy organised around the ten-year-old Lambert Simnel. For much of the 1490s his attention was taken up with the threat of the impostor Perkin Warbeck. Even as late as 1506 Henry was receiving reports of leading officials at Calais discussing who would succeed him as king.

How serious a threat to Henry VII was Lambert Simnel?

Just as Henry VII was establishing his government and winning the support of the political nation, which was then the nobility and the men of prosperity, news came of what was the first serious conspiracy of the reign. An Oxford priest, Richard Symonds, realised that in the unsettled nature of England in 1485–86 many people were prepared to believe even the wildest of rumours. He passed off a pupil of his, the ten-year-old Lambert Simnel, as at first Richard, Duke of York, the youngest of the two 'Princes in the Tower'. However, when rumours began to spread about the possible death of the Earl of Warwick, Symonds changed his mind and decided that Simnel could now be passed off as the earl. Symonds managed to get the boy to Ireland, which was then the centre of Yorkist plotting against the new king. This was because Ireland's nobility had favoured the Yorkist cause since the popular Lord Lieutenancy of Richard, Duke of York in the 1450s. The **Lord Deputy** there, the Earl of Kildare, and other members of the Irish nobility happily supported Simnel. The 'pretender' was also supported by Margaret of Burgundy, the sister of Edward IV and Richard III, who as an enemy of Henry VII was determined to do all in her power to overthrow him. The duchess lent money and an army of 2,000 mercenaries, led by Martin Schwarz, which landed in Ireland in May 1487.

In spite of Henry's generosity to him, the Earl of Lincoln suddenly fled to Margaret's court and with Lord Lovell, who had resurfaced to plot against the Tudors, accompanied the mercenary army on its voyage to Ireland. This growth in support for Simnel led to him being crowned in Dublin as 'Edward VI'. Now Henry was faced by the first major challenge. In spite of having the real Earl of Warwick paraded through London to expose Simnel's imposture, support for the conspiracy did not weaken.

Henry VII was extremely worried by the threatened invasion and he offered pardons to the rebels, which they refused. The king had no means of knowing how much support the rebel army might attract once it landed in north-western England. However, when the rebel force arrived in England in June 1487 it attracted much less support than Henry had feared. The north of England remained generally unenthusiastic for the Earl of Lincoln and his army. This may have been because of the presence of numbers of ill-disciplined Irish troops, which deterred many people from joining the rebels. Henry had prepared for an invasion and on 16 June the two armies met just outside Newark, at East Stoke. The battle was hard fought but after a few hours the rebels were defeated. Lincoln,

Lord Deputy: The title given to the person who rules Ireland on behalf of the king. For much of Henry VII's reign it was the Earl of Kildare.

Margaret of Burgundy (1446–1503)
Sister of Edward IV and Richard III, Margaret was the third wife of Charles the Bold, Duke of Burgundy (who was killed in 1477). After 1485 Margaret was a bitter enemy of Henry VII. She supported both Lambert Simnel and Perkin Warbeck in their impostures.

Schwarz and the Irish leaders were killed in the fighting. Lambert Simnel and Richard Symonds were captured. Symonds, as a cleric, was imprisoned for life rather than executed. Simnel, who had been used by ruthless and ambitious men, was put to work in the royal kitchens. This last action was a good example of how Henry realised that an act of calculated mercy could only help his reputation in his subjects' eyes.

The Simnel conspiracy was a threat to Henry VII as well as indicating how unsettled England remained. That an impostor such as Simnel was considered a dangerous threat to Henry is clear evidence of how insecure the king's hold on the English throne remained two years after the battle of Bosworth. Simnel owed his success to powerful backers, such as Margaret of Burgundy, anxious to avenge her brother, the late Richard III. Also Maximilian, ruling Burgundy on behalf of his young son Philip, had been rebuffed by Henry when he sent heralds to congratulate him on his accession in 1485. This led Maximilian to back Margaret in supporting the Simnel conspiracy. There may have been other powerful figures behind Simnel, such as Henry's own mother-in-law, Elizabeth Woodville. In February 1487 she had been deprived of her lands on the authority of an assembly of peers and was later confined to a nunnery.

'The last battle of the Wars of the Roses', as the historian R. L. Storey called the battle of East Stoke in his biography of Henry VII, did not give the king much satisfaction. During the battle the two wings of Henry's army had held back and had not committed themselves until it was clear that the king would win. Also Henry had wanted Lincoln taken alive so that he could discover who had supported the earl, but this order was not obeyed. Perhaps the earl was killed so that there was no danger of his secret backers being discovered by Henry VII. Certainly, Henry's insecurity was shown in the Parliament which he called in November–December 1487. Those nobles and gentry who had fought against Henry at East Stoke were attainted and had their lands confiscated by the Crown. Also Henry was quick to repair relations with Maximilian: a new treaty in January 1488 restored friendly relations and close trading ties between England and Burgundy.

Why were Warbeck's adventures such a threat to Henry VII?

The next conspiracy against Henry VII was to last for nearly ten years (1491–99). It caused the king considerable anxiety before it was finally defeated.

In 1491 a young man of 17, the servant of a Breton merchant (from Brittany), was showing off his master's fine products around the streets of Cork in Ireland. He impressed the townspeople with his appearance and bearing. They told him that he must be the Earl of Warwick. When he denied this, the young man was 'changed' into Richard, Duke of York, the younger son of Edward IV who had supposedly been murdered in the Tower of London. Thus began the adventures of Perkin Warbeck. In reality, it is unlikely that Warbeck's career as an impostor began quite so casually as he was later to suggest.

Originally, Warbeck came from Tournai in Flanders. It is likely that he had been 'discovered' already by Margaret of Burgundy and her agents. Seeing that he resembled her late brother, Edward IV, when young, Margaret of Burgundy decided to send the young Warbeck to Ireland – always a centre for Yorkist plots. These were difficult times for Henry VII, with the developing situation in Brittany and his poor relations with both Scotland and France. Warbeck's backers may have decided that this was the best moment to try to overthrow the king. It was unlikely that any of those who supported Warbeck's imposture were fooled into believing that he really was Richard, Duke of York, because most of them would have been aware of the real duke's death even before Richard III was defeated at Bosworth. However, the 'pretender' was to be of great nuisance value to those foreign rulers who wanted to bring diplomatic pressure to bear on Henry VII during the 1490s.

Warbeck received some support in Ireland but it was not enough to give him a safe base, especially when Henry sent a small army there. By 1492 Warbeck had found his first protector in King Charles VIII of France who by then was at war with England. The Treaty of Etaples put an end to this phase of the impostor's career and he and his small band of followers moved on to Flanders where he was welcomed by his 'aunt', Margaret of Burgundy. This worried Henry so much that in 1493 he placed a ban on trade with Flanders, even though it threatened England's vital cloth trade. At this point Warbeck found an even more powerful backer when his cause was taken up by Maximilian who had recently succeeded his father as **Holy Roman Emperor**. Maximilian had been annoyed by Henry VII's supposed treachery in making the Treaty of Etaples without his agreement and now saw a chance of getting his own back on the English king. The Emperor recognised Warbeck as Richard IV, King of England, in 1494 and promised him help in recovering his crown. However, Maximilian lacked the money to fit out a proper invasion force for Warbeck. Charles VIII's decision to invade Italy in the same year took further pressure off Henry VII. As the French king wished to gain glory there and to dominate the Iberian peninsula, he needed peace on his northern borders and with England in particular.

However, Warbeck's supporters had not been idle. In England their influence reached into the royal court itself. In December 1494, Sir Robert Clifford, who had earlier fled to Flanders to join Richard IV, made his peace with Henry VII and returned home with detailed information. For this he was pardoned and rewarded. This led to the fall and execution of Sir William Stanley, Henry's Lord Chamberlain and a key player in the victory at Bosworth. It was clear that the price of Henry's survival on the English throne was unending vigilance. In early 1495 it had paid off handsomely. With the discovery of the English branch of the Warbeck conspiracy by Henry's agents the pretender's plans for invading England with much hope of success collapsed, but nevertheless it was attempted.

In July 1495 Warbeck, sailing from the Netherlands, appeared off Deal in Kent, where he landed the bulk of his small force. This was a failure, with the local authorities easily dealing with the pretender's men. Warbeck, who had sensibly remained on board ship, then sailed off for Ireland. However, times had changed since 1491 and after an unsuccessful 11 days' siege of Waterford, Warbeck decided to sail for Scotland.

The Scottish King, James IV, was pro-French in his sympathies and more than happy to welcome the pretender. It is uncertain how far, if at all, James was taken in by Warbeck but he gave him a generous pension and married him to his cousin, Katherine Gordon. These actions offended Henry VII and put the English king's proposed marriage alliance with Spain in doubt.

Holy Roman Emperor: In theory, the most important and powerful ruler in western Europe; in practice, by the end of the Middle Ages the emperor was the sovereign of an empire which included what is now Germany and Switzerland. The Habsburg family, who had been emperors since the later 13th century, only exercised real authority over their own hereditary lands, while the remainder of the empire was ruled by virtually independent princes. Apart from a glamorous title, the Holy Roman Emperors were in reality less powerful than the rulers of France, Spain and even England.

In January 1496 James IV launched a massive border raid into England but it achieved nothing for Warbeck received no support there. Later that same year, when Henry VII began to seek to marry his daughter, Margaret, to James IV he decided that such an alliance would be to Scotland's advantage. Realising that he could not count on any further support from James IV, Warbeck decided to leave Scotland in July 1497 and try his luck once again in Ireland. The Scottish King, who had no further use for the pretender, was delighted to see him go.

Once he landed in Ireland Warbeck found that the situation had changed. The Earl of Kildare, once again Lord Deputy, decided to remain loyal to Henry VII and so Warbeck departed on one last desperate adventure. The south-west of England had been disturbed by the Cornish Rebellion in 1497 and the pretender hoped to exploit the situation. After landing in the west, Warbeck was joined by several thousand discontented peasants, but no one of any importance in the region supported him. Henry had been warned of Warbeck's arrival and an army had been sent westwards to intercept him. Warbeck's poorly-led and ill-equipped army was halted at Exeter where its attempt to besiege the city was met with vigorous resistance. As soon as Warbeck heard that the King's army was advancing towards him, he decided to abandon the siege. He left his army to fend for itself and fled with a few companions to the safety of sanctuary at Beaulieu Abbey near Southampton. Once there, Warbeck was soon persuaded into giving himself up and making a full confession.

In return, Henry treated Warbeck well, considering the trouble he had caused him, and allowed him to remain with his wife at court. In 1498 Warbeck decided to escape, but was soon recaptured. This time Henry was not so merciful. The pretender was publicly humiliated before being imprisoned in the Tower. Once there, it was not long before Warbeck was in contact with the Earl of Warwick and plotting with him to escape. The plan was hairbrained and whether Henry VII or his agents were behind it will probably never be known. In 1499 Warbeck was accused of trying to escape and this time he was hanged.

The Earl of Warwick appears to have been a rather helpless figure, but as long as he was allowed to live he would be there for others to make the centre of their plots against the king, and Henry did not want this situation to continue. So a few days later, after a brief trial, the Earl of Warwick was found guilty of treason and executed.

Conclusion

Perkin Warbeck was an exceptional threat to Henry VII, especially between 1491 and 1497. He was handsome, intelligent and able to carry off an imposture that caused Henry a great deal of trouble. Warbeck had been taken up by the Irish nobles who wished to weaken further the already diminished influence of the English Crown in Ireland. Kildare's support for Warbeck led to Henry making a determined attempt to increase the power of the Crown in Ireland (see section 2.5). The outcome was the ensuring of Irish loyalty to Henry VII for the future – as Warbeck found when he tried to promote his own cause there in 1495 and 1497, and was rebuffed. Burgundian support for Warbeck was a considerable threat to Henry, especially between 1493 and 1495, as his decision to place a ban on Anglo–Flemish trade indicated.

The fact that Sir William Stanley, Henry VII's Lord Chamberlain, could plot against the king in Warbeck's interests was clear proof that Henry was still insecure. However, it is a credit to the competence and loyalty of Henry's agents in rooting out what was dangerous conspiracy, as well as to the king's own increasing success in undermining his enemies' plans. Warbeck's plotting in Scotland between 1495 and 1497 nearly led to a major Anglo–Scottish war and was a direct cause of the 1497 Cornish Rebellion which he later tried unsuccessfully to exploit.

Warbeck's own landing in the West Country ended in failure. His own inadequacies as a leader and general were fully exposed and the gentry and nobility of the region remained loyal to Henry. In spite of the trouble he had caused, Henry VII was at first lenient with Warbeck. It was only after his attempted flight and supposed plotting with Warwick that Henry had the pretender executed.

There had also been pressure on Henry from Ferdinand and Isabella of Spain to execute both Warwick and Warbeck so that the projected marriage between Arthur and Catherine of Aragon could go ahead. An alliance with one of the most powerful royal houses in Europe was very welcome to Henry VII as it gave him both further security on his throne and valuable foreign recognition. Warbeck had been used by others – Maximilian, Margaret of Burgundy and James IV of Scotland – to weaken and embarrass Henry VII and at times, particularly in 1495, their plots nearly succeeded. In 1499 Henry VII was still far from being totally secure on his throne.

How serious were the conspiracies against Henry VII after 1499?

With Warwick's execution in 1499 it might have seemed that at last Henry VII was safe. Unfortunately, this was not the case. The chief Yorkist claimant to the throne was now Edmund de la Pole (Earl of Suffolk and brother of the Earl of Lincoln who had died fighting against Henry VII at East Stoke in 1487). The Earl of Suffolk, who had appeared to be reconciled to Henry's rule, suddenly fled abroad in July 1499. Henry persuaded him to return and the king and he were reconciled. Then two years later, while part of the escort bringing Catherine of Aragon to England, the Earl of Suffolk and his brother Richard fled to the court of Maximilian who was quite prepared to encourage yet another Yorkist plot against Henry VII.

Henry was also soon to find himself head of a dynasty that seemed very unsafe. In 1500 his third son, Edmund, died; followed in April 1502 by the eldest son and heir, Arthur. This left Henry VII with the ten-year-old Prince Henry as his only male heir. The king's disappointments were made worse by the death of his wife, Elizabeth of York, in 1503. Henry began to look abroad for a new wife, while at home he struck out ruthlessly at possible enemies. Those members of Suffolk's family who remained in England were imprisoned, while the Parliament of 1504 passed more attainders than any other parliament of the reign: a sure sign that the king felt highly insecure.

Nevertheless, in spite of his ruthless actions, it appeared that speculation about Henry VII and his dynasty continued as an informer's report to the Council from this time made clear. It appeared that important officials at Calais discussed what might happen after Henry VII died and none of them apparently considered that Prince Henry would be the next king.

However, Henry VII's luck changed. In 1506 a storm forced the Archduke Philip of Burgundy and his wife, Joanna of Castile – who were on their way to Spain to claim her kingdom – to take shelter in

Weymouth. Henry made much of his unexpected guests and agreed to surrender the Duke of Suffolk to him provided that the duke's life was spared. In return, Henry agreed to support Philip in his attempts to become king of Castile and persuaded him to agree to the 'Malus Intercursus' ('Evil Settlement'), a trading treaty which was very unfavourable in its terms to the archduke's Flemish subjects. However, Henry kept his word in regard to Suffolk who was imprisoned in the Tower where he remained until Henry VIII had him executed in 1513.

Did rebellions rather than conspiracies pose the greater threat to Henry VII's rule?

The two rebellions against Henry VII – the Yorkshire rebellion of 1489 and the Cornish rebellion in 1497 – were both about what was seen as heavy and unjust taxation by the king, although other factors played their part.

In 1489 Henry was intending to assist Brittany against the French and Parliament had granted him a subsidy to allow him to raise troops to do so. This tax was resented, not least because people were facing more realistic charges on their income. People in Yorkshire particularly resented the tax; the king's representative, the Earl of Northumberland, was murdered while trying to collect it. Although the earl was unpopular because he supported the tax, other factors may also have played a part. The leader of the rebels, Sir John Egremont, was an illegitimate member of the Percy family and a sympathiser with the Yorkist cause. Henry sent a large army north to deal with the revolt. But by the time it had reached York, the rebels had largely melted away, probably frightened by the king's reaction. The Earl of Surrey easily defeated what remained of the rebels and a royal pardon was granted but no more tax was collected. Henry VII appointed the Earl of Surrey as his new lieutenant in the North. This made good sense as Surrey had no estates or interests there and was able to spend many years reconciling the region to Tudor rule.

The second rebellion, in Cornwall, was sparked off when Parliament agreed to vote Henry VII a subsidy and other taxes to deal with the possible invasion of England by James IV of Scotland and Perkin Warbeck. The Cornishmen refused to pay taxes for the defence of the north of the country and against an invasion which in their view was no threat to them. There may have been other causes of the rebellion: some historians have suggested that Henry's representatives in the region were too grasping and that their maladministration and corruption had inflamed local resentment against the government.

The rebels were led by Thomas Flamanck, a lawyer, and Michael Joseph, a blacksmith. A march was launched across England to take the rebels' complaints to the king. The march was peaceful and once out of Cornwall attracted little active support in Devon. In Somerset the rebels gained the support of Lord Audley, who was in financial difficulties and out of favour with the government. The march continued across the south of England and many people either joined or sympathised with the rebels. It was remarkable that the rebel force was allowed to reach Blackheath, just south of London, and that it moved far outside its home region (unlike other Tudor rebellions). Its success suggests that the government's taxes were widely resented and that its handling of local gentry was at times insensitive to their local concerns.

1. 'An adventurer who was no real threat to Henry VII between 1491 and 1499.'

How far do you agree with this view of Perkin Warbeck?

2. The Simnel conspiracy, Perkin Warbeck and the Cornish Rebellion of 1497 all presented dangers to Henry VII. Which one of these three dangers came closest to overthrowing Henry VII? Explain your answer.

Henry VII was surprised by the revolt and troops had to be sent quickly south under the command of Lord Daubeney, while the king raised further forces. Henry was determined to defeat the rebels. On 17 June the King's forces smashed the rebel army, already weakened by desertions, and entered London in triumph. Many rebels were killed in the battle and its leaders were captured and executed. After this, Henry fined all those involved in the rebellion throughout southern England and the West Country. This financial severity worked as there was no more trouble in the west until the later 1540s. Henry learnt a lesson from the rebellion – no expensive wars. Instead of fighting James IV, Henry began negotiations with him for peace.

2.3 Why was foreign policy so important in establishing the Tudor dynasty?

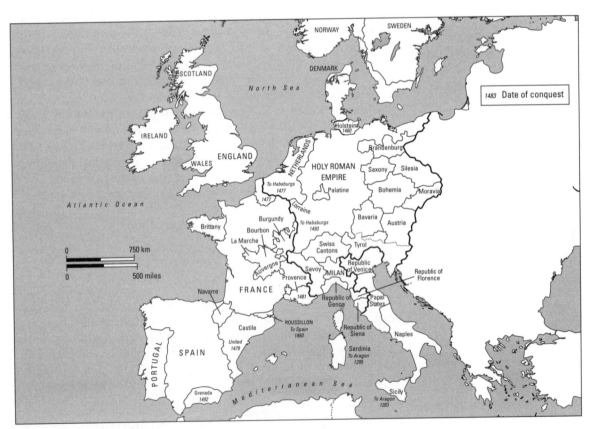

Europe, late 15th century

A brief survey of western Europe, 1485

When Henry VII became king the European political scene was changing (see map on page 42). During the reigns of Charles VII (1422–61) and Louis XI (1461–83) France had emerged as a much stronger power than England. This period had seen the end of the Hundred Years War (1137–1453) with the final expulsion of the kings of England from what remained of their French lands, except for the small enclave of Calais on the Channel coast. The French kings had tamed their **over-mighty nobility**. Apart from Brittany, they had re-absorbed areas such as the **semi-independent Duchy of Burgundy** into their kingdom. By the 1480s the kings of France enjoyed revenue from taxation which was much larger than that of English kings. With these resources the French kings built up a powerful army. Henry VII owed his throne in part to French support and he had to work out relations very carefully with his powerful neighbour.

Besides France, a new power had been created with the marriage of Isabella of Castile to Ferdinand of Aragon in 1479 – Spain. The Spanish monarchs were able to create a powerful joint-kingdom in which the nobility were controlled and revenue generated which could pay for large armies. This emergence of Spain meant that England was reduced to the second rank of powers in Europe and France had a powerful new rival on the international stage. This new rivalry was increased by both Spanish and French ambitions in Italy, where both powers had interests. It was there that the conflict between them became centred. So the concerns of European diplomacy shifted southwards, leaving England very much on the edge of important international events.

The other important figure with whom Henry VII had to reckon at times was Maximilian, heir to the Holy Roman Emperor Frederick III (whom he succeeded in 1493).

The other country that Henry had to consider was Scotland. Anglo–Scottish relations had not been good through the Middle Ages. They had not been improved by Edward IV's war with the Scots in 1480–83 when the towns of Berwick and Dunbar were captured (see page 44). In September 1484 Richard III had arranged a three-year truce with the Scots, but they ignored it. After Henry's victory at Bosworth in 1485 the Scots took advantage of the new king's problems to recapture Dunbar.

Over-mighty nobility: For much of the Middle Ages France had been mainly ruled by independent nobles, such as the dukes of Burgundy. This had kept the French kings weak.

Semi-independent Duchy of Burgundy: The dukes of Burgundy (a younger branch of the French royal family) inherited extensive lands outside the territory ruled by the duke in 1384, as a result of a fortunate marriage (see map) – the Low Countries (now known as the Netherlands). During the early 1400s their lands continued to grow and the dukes of Burgundy became as powerful as the French Crown. There was bitter rivalry between Louis XI and Charles the Bold (1467–77). When Charles was killed, Louis repossessed the French lands of the duchy. The remainder passed into the Habsburg family as Charles' heiress had married the Archduke Maximilian (later Holy Roman Emperor). Maximilian's family, the Habsburgs, had acquired lands by a series of good marriage alliances stretching over two centuries. In 1485 Maximilian was ruling the non-French Burgundian lands centred in Flanders, on behalf of his son Philip (who was married to Mary, heiress to Charles the Bold – another successful Habsburg marriage). During much of his reign Henry had to endure Maximilian and his varying support for Yorkist pretenders – which was an added complication after 1485.

Why was foreign policy so important to Henry VII?

In 1485 Henry VII was a successful usurper who owned some of his success to foreign support. The early years of the reign (especially 1485–87) were very insecure and during his time as king Henry had to deal with pretenders, conspiracies and rebellions (see previous section). Foreign policy was a key area of Henry's concerns. Its importance to him was due to the following factors:

● *Security* – Henry, himself, was an usurper and it was vital that the support of other powers for any conspiracies and pretenders threatening the English throne was kept to a minimum.

● *Recognition* – as the head of a new dynasty it was important that Henry VII obtained the acceptance of other powers. This made him more secure on his throne and gave him prestige both at home and abroad. The Spanish marriage and later the Scottish marriage were vital to this process of obtaining international respectability.

Anglo–Scottish border region

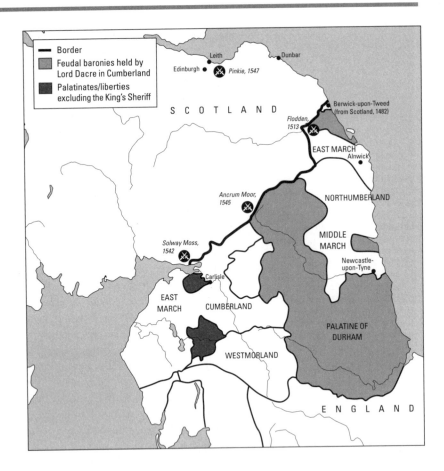

- *Prosperity* – Henry was well aware that a rich king was more respected both at home and abroad than a poor one. When circumstances allowed, Henry was anxious to ensure that relations with other countries filled his pockets and improved the trading position of England's merchants. An excellent example of this was the 1492 Treaty of Etaples which saw Henry VII obtain an annual pension from France which was to be paid to him for the remainder of his reign.

What issues affected England's relations with France and Brittany in 1485–1492?

The French monarchy had spent much of the 15th century increasing its control over France. By 1485 only one important area – Britanny – remained outside its control. Anne of Beaujeu, the French regent who ruled France on behalf of her younger brother, Charles VIII, was determined to make Brittany a part of the French kingdom. This was a problem for Henry VII, as it had been with French help that he seized England in 1485 and he wanted to remain on good terms with them. However, if Brittany came fully under French control its ports would be very convenient places from which to launch another invasion of England.

In 1487, faced by the French takeover threat, Duke Francis II, offered his daughter Anne in marriage to Maximilian. This annoyed a section of the Breton nobility who called on the French to intervene. Anne of Beaujeu sent troops in to the duchy, but the Breton army, helped by foreign volunteers, managed to put up a strong resistance. Henry was able to sit on the sidelines hoping that a settlement between the Bretons and the French would be worked out.

In July 1488 the situation changed when the Breton army was defeated and Francis had to accept the Treaty of Sable. This treaty made certain that Anne of Brittany could not be married without French consent. Shortly afterwards, Duke Francis died and Anne became Duchess of Brittany. The French claimed custody of Anne but the Breton nobility, fearing a French takeover, opposed them and war was renewed.

This time Henry could not remain neutral. The king consulted the leading men of England to make sure that he had their support in deciding to help Brittany. In February 1489 Parliament voted money to raise an army and Henry obtained Maximilian's and Spanish support, but in practice neither provided soldiers or money for the war. In the Treaty of Redon (February 1489) the Bretons agreed to cover the costs of English military help. A force of 3,000 men was sent to Britanny, while Henry gave further military help to Maximilian against the Flemish rebels who had been stirred up by France. However, Maximilian did not help Henry in Brittany, but instead made peace with the French so that he could pursue his ambitions in Hungary. Spain also began to negotiate peace with France and in October 1489 the Breton army was defeated. To obtain peace with France Anne had to agree to dismiss the English troops who had been helping her. Henry's plans to keep Brittany independent were in ruins.

However, Henry did not give up. Instead he sent more troops to help the Bretons. He also persuaded Maximilian to give Brittany further support and in December 1490 the archduke married Anne – not in person but **by proxy**. The French launched further attacks and by May the next year Anne was appealing to Henry VII for further help.

Henry summoned Parliament in October 1491. Parliament granted the king more money to continue the war. However, it took time to collect the taxes and for Anne time was running out. In December 1491, Anne had no choice but to accept defeat, give up Maximilian and marry the French king, Charles VIII.

In spite of the defeat of his plan, Henry VII did not give up. For him to have accepted defeat in Brittany would have meant international humiliation. Also, the French were probably involved in the promotion of the new pretender, Perkin Warbeck (see section 2.2) which Henry could not ignore. However, in spite of all this, Henry decided on action against France. In October 1492, having raised an army of 12,000 men, Henry landed at Calais and besieged Boulogne. The campaign was launched very late in the fighting season and its real aim was to persuade the French king to negotiate. Through his informants in France, Henry was well aware that Charles VIII burned with the ambition of invading Italy and would rather settle with England than waste time, men and money fighting. Also, after the Breton defeat, Henry wanted to win back prestige at home and ensure that the English nobility remained loyal to him.

Henry's campaign achieved its aims. In November 1492 the Treaty of Etaples was signed between the English and the French kings. The French agreed not to help Yorkist pretenders (Warbeck in particular) and to pay Henry a pension of £5,000 a year. In return, Henry agreed to withdraw his troops from Brittany. All in all, Henry turned the defeat in Brittany to his advantage and restored good relations with France. In

By proxy: When a substitute stands in for the intended bride or groom at a ceremony. When someone marries someone else 'by proxy' the proposed marriage is binding.

terms of the expedition, Henry made a profit: besides the renewed pension (first granted to Edward IV in 1475), much of the parliamentary grant was unused and so went into the King's treasury instead.

Why were relations with Spain and Burgundy so important between 1485 and 1509?

Burgundy, which by the later 15th century was made up of what was beginning to be called the Franche Comte (see map on page 85), was England's major trading partner. Good relations between the two powers was essential. By the later Middle Ages woollen cloth was England's major export. The chief market for this was to be found in the Netherlands (the Low Countries) where both English wool and woollen cloth were much in demand for finishing off into good quality textiles in the workshops of the Flemish merchants.

However, despite the importance of these commercial links, Margaret of Burgundy was the promoter of constant plots against Henry VII after 1485 (see section 2.2). Also, Maximilian, who ruled the Burgundian lands for his son Philip during the 1480s and early 1490s, was untrustworthy. He was quite prepared to plot against Henry if it appeared to be in his best interests to do so, This meant that Henry's relations with Burgundy were at times delicate, as well as being vital to his security.

In 1493 Philip took over direct rule of Burgundy when Maximilian succeeded his father as Holy Roman Emperor in what was to be an interesting year in Anglo–Burgundian relations. Henry protested to Philip about Margaret of Burgundy's support for Perkin Warbeck. However, Philip chose to ignore the English. Henry retaliated by banishing all Burgundian merchants from England and put an embargo (see page 29) on trade with the Low Countries too. This action was as harmful to English trade as it was to Burgundy's but it was clear that Henry put the safety of his throne and dynasty before matters of trade. However, Henry did make some attempt to delimit the damage by instructing the **Merchant Adventurers** to move their centre of trading activity from Antwerp to Calais. The embargo lasted until 1496 by which time both Henry and Philip had had enough. The departure of Warbeck from Burgundy in 1495 made it easier for the two sides to reach a settlement. In an agreement made a year later – the Magnus Intercursus ('Great Settlement') – Henry and Philip removed all the barriers to trade between England and Burgundy. Thereafter trade improved but diplomatic relations between Philip and his father Maximilian and Henry remained difficult at times as the former continued to give support to Yorkist pretenders.

Where relations with the new power of Spain were concerned, Henry was determined to strengthen his links both in terms of trade and dynastic interests. The Treaty of Medina Del Campo (1489) was partly concerned with the Breton war, and Ferdinand was probably trying to obtain English support against France at the least cost to himself. However, from Henry VII's viewpoint, the treaty had other advantages:

- Ferdinand and Isabella agreed not to support pretenders against the English throne, which strengthened Henry's position.

- There were some advantages for English trade with Spain.

- An agreement was made that Henry's eldest son, Arthur, would be married to Ferdinand's and Isabella's younger daughter Catherine.

Merchant Adventurers: A group of merchants who traded individually but were regulated (i.e. acted under an agreed set of regulations). They shipped their cloths together in fleets of ships, and displayed them at shows in Antwerp (before moving to Calais) on specific days. The Adventurers did not live up to their name: they pursued a safety-first policy of easy profits and they did not try to find new markets. However, they did control English cloth exports and operated a form of 'closed shop', stopping other wool merchants from trading.

This proposed marriage was very important for Henry as it marked his acceptance as King of England by Europe's rising power after what had been four insecure years on the throne. The marriage provided both recognition and valuable security for the new Tudor dynasty. The final agreement to the marriage, however, did not take place until 1496 due to both Henry and Ferdinand being expert at bargaining to get the best advantage for their own country from the arrangement. In the end it was agreed that Catherine would come to England in 1500 to marry Arthur.

Dowry: A bride's marriage portion. It could be paid to the groom or his family in money or jewels, or it might consist of land. Catherine of Aragon's dowry was in money and jewels. Her father, Ferdinand of Aragon, was very slow in paying it and the full amount was never received.

Ferdinand also agreed to pay Catherine's **dowry** to Henry in instalments (although he never finished paying!). In 1501 Catherine finally arrived in England and married Arthur amid great celebrations. However, five months later Arthur was dead (April 1502). Henry VII, who hated waste, proposed that Catherine should marry his only surviving son, Henry (later to be Henry VIII). After further haggling, Ferdinand agreed. In June 1503 Catherine was betrothed to Henry, now Prince of Wales, after a papal dispensation (see page 33) had been obtained from Pope Julius II. The marriage still had to wait for nearly six years due to important changes in the international scene following the death of Isabella of Castile in 1504.

The effects of Isabella's death were far reaching. The new kingdom of Spain was in danger of falling apart, as Ferdinand was now only the ruler of his own kingdom of Aragon as Isabella had left her kingdom to her oldest daughter Joanna. Joanna was married to Philip of Burgunda and he now claimed Castile on her behalf. During 1505 Philip began to plan an expedition to Spain to assert Joanna's rights. He expected Henry VII to pay for it. Why? Simply because Philip had given his protection to the Yorkist pretender Suffolk and Henry felt it was worthwhile to pay to keep his dynasty safe.

At the same time Henry did not want to fall out with Ferdinand, although an alliance with him was now less valuable than it had been. In order to keep his options open, Henry now claimed that he was uncertain that the proposed marriage between Prince Henry and Catherine was valid. His father made Prince Henry claim that as he had been under age at the time of the marriage agreement in 1502, it was worthless. Ferdinand, feeling isolated, looked around for a new ally and by the Treaty of Blois (October 1505) he patched up his differences with Louis XII, and married the French king's niece in 1506.

In January 1506, Philip and Joanna were forced by storms to land at Weymouth while on their way to Castile. For Henry this was too good an opportunity to miss. He lavishly entertained his reluctant guests for three months. The secret Treaty of Windsor (1506) between Henry VII and Philip saw the English king recognise his guests as king and queen of Castile, while he promised them further help in gaining control in Castile. In return, Philip agreed to arrange Henry's marriage to Margaret of Savoy (Philip's sister who was then ruling the Low Countries for him) and to hand over the pretender Suffolk to the king provided he was not executed. Also, Philip agreed to a trade treaty with England – the so-called 'Malus Intercursus' ('Evil Settlement') because it was so favourable to English merchants.

It seemed that Henry's diplomacy had achieved a great success in 1506, but the actual results of the Treaty of Windsor were rather limited. The only solid gain was the surrender of Suffolk whom the king imprisoned in the Tower. The Malus Intercursus never came into effect as it was never agreed to by the Burgundians. Margaret of Savoy refused to marry Henry in spite of pressure to do so.

In Spain, Philip died suddenly in September 1506. Ferdinand declared that Joanna was mad and took the regency of Castile on behalf of her son, the six-year-old Charles, who also became duke of Burgundy. Once again, Spain's unity was assured as the young Charles was the heir to his grandfather Ferdinand's kingdom of Aragon too.

Henry's plans had been seriously upset, but that did not stop him from making further diplomatic moves. Soon he was once again assuring Ferdinand that the marriage plans for Prince Henry and Catherine were safely in place. Also, Henry offered to marry the 'mad' Joanna, but that was rejected by Ferdinand. The Spanish King, happy with the new French alliance, refused to pay Henry VII the remaining portion of Catherine's dowry as he no longer needed English support.

Henry now tried to make alliances with both Burgundy and France in a bid to isolate Ferdinand. In 1507 Henry agreed to give up the Malus Intercursus. The regent of Burgundy, Margaret of Savoy, agreed that her nephew Charles would eventually marry Henry's younger daughter Mary. At the same time, Henry was proposing a marriage between one of Louis XII's many nieces and Prince Henry instead of the Spanish marriage. In the end, nothing came of these proposals and as the centre of international events was in Italy Henry found himself left on the diplomatic sidelines during the last years of his reign.

How did Anglo–Scottish relations develop during Henry VII's reign?

Anglo–Scottish relations had long been difficult (see page 40). In his early years as king, Henry VII did not want trouble with the Scots. The Scottish King, James III, wanted to make a settlement with England and in 1486 a three-year truce was agreed.

When James was defeated and killed by his enemies in 1488, Anglo–Scottish relations suffered a setback. The men ruling Scotland on behalf of the young James IV were no friends of England and wanted to renew the 'auld alliance' with France. Henry's attempts to overthrow the hostile Scottish government were successful in 1492, but the coming of age of James IV was a fresh setback for Henry. The new Scottish king wanted war with England and the arrival of the pretender Perkin Warbeck in Scotland in 1495 gave his plans a boost. However, Warbeck proved to be of limited value to James IV and by the autumn of 1497 he was making peace with England. In the truce of Ayton, James IV agreed not to attack England, but neither did he abandon the French alliance.

However, Ayton was a great achievement for Henry as there had been no worthwhile agreement between England and Scotland since 1328. This truce became a full treaty of peace only after Warbeck's execution. It was finally confirmed in 1502. Henry's efforts were completed by the marriage of his eldest daughter, Margaret, to James IV one year later. For the rest of his reign, Henry enjoyed peace with Scotland but the continued Scottish friendship with France remained. It was to be a source of trouble to Henry VIII when he decided to go to war with France in 1511. However, the Scottish marriage was a notable achievement for Henry and was another sign that the Tudors were acceptable to other kings in spite of their rather recent arrival on the Scottish throne.

John Cabot (1425–1500)
Born in Genoa, Giovanni
Caboto (John Cabot) later
became a Venetian citizen.
About 1490 he settled in
Bristol, England. Backed by
Henry VII and the merchants of
Bristol, John set sail in 1497
across the Atlantic to discover
a western route to the riches of
China and the Indies. Instead
he discovered the mainland of
North America and its rich
fisheries.

Sebastian Cabot (1474–1527)
John Cabot's son. In 1498 he
commanded another major
expedition – to discover the
North West Passage. In reality
the expedition was
commanded by his father, but
Sebastian took all the credit.
The elder Cabot did not return
from this voyage. After 1509
Sebastian worked for a number
of patrons, including Charles V,
Ferdinand of Spain and
Henry VIII (between 1517 and
1519).

Hanse: A commercial and shipping
organisation based on several Baltic
cities which specialised in importing
and exporting goods throughout
Europe. Their main base in London
was known as the Steelyard.

How important were trade and overseas exploration to Henry VII?

Trade was important to Henry because his encouragement of it brought in more income for the Crown in the form of customs revenue. Also, the king was well aware after his rather poverty-stricken years as an exile that a full treasury was vital if he was to be able to sit securely on his throne. A rich king was much more secure than a weak king.

Due to Henry's efforts the income from customs revenue rose from about £33,000 in 1485 to more than £40,000 yearly by 1509. How much of this was due to Henry's encouragement is uncertain but there is no doubt that the Crown benefited from it. Many of Henry's important treaties contained trade clauses, such as that concluded with Spain at Medina Del Campo in 1489 and the Treaty of Etaples with France in 1492.

England's chief trading area was in Burgundy. The trade with Flemish merchants in wool and, later, cloth had grown in importance during medieval times and was encouraged by English rulers. However, in spite of its importance, Henry had no hesitation in placing an embargo on it between 1493 and 1496 due to Margaret of Burgundy's support for Warbeck. When it came to the security of his crown, trade in Henry's eyes came a poor second. However, when occasion allowed Henry pushed for greater trading advantages for English merchants. The 'Malus Intercursus' of 1506 was a good example of this: Henry took advantage of Archduke Philip's wish for his support to obtain excessive privileges for English merchants in Burgundy. These were much resented there and by 1507 common sense had reasserted itself in matters of Anglo–Burgundian trade.

Besides Burgundy, Henry made trading agreements with other powers too (see map on page 50). In 1489 Henry renewed an earlier treaty of friendship with Portugal which encouraged Anglo–Portuguese trade. Venice was a major player in Mediterranean trade and English merchants who were increasingly making inroads there found their activities limited by the Venetians. However, Henry was able to improve the position for his merchants by making a treaty in 1490 with Florence, one of Venice's trading rivals, which allowed English wool to be marketed at the Florentine-controlled port of Pisa.

In 1492 Henry put a heavy import duty on wine brought to England in Venetian ships. This aggressive policy did little initially to improve Anglo–Venetian relations. However, after 1504 Venice was caught up in the Italian wars and had little time to plan effective retaliation against England. For the remainder of Henry VII's reign English Mediterranean trade continued to increase.

In northern Europe, Henry faced the power of the Hanseatic League. This was a powerful group of northern German ports and cities, which had by the 1400s established a stranglehold on much of northern European trade, especially in the Baltic. They had long had dealings with English kings. In 1471 the League had provided Edward IV with the ships which allowed him to regain his throne. Unsurprisingly, Edward then granted them considerable trading privileges in England, such as lower rates of taxation and import duties than English merchants in their bases (for example, the London Steelyard). During his reign, Henry VII's attitude towards the **Hanse** varied depending on the security of his dynasty from foreign threats and pretenders. At times he tried to limit their influence by restricting or redefining their privileges, but without much success. He also tried to get his merchants direct

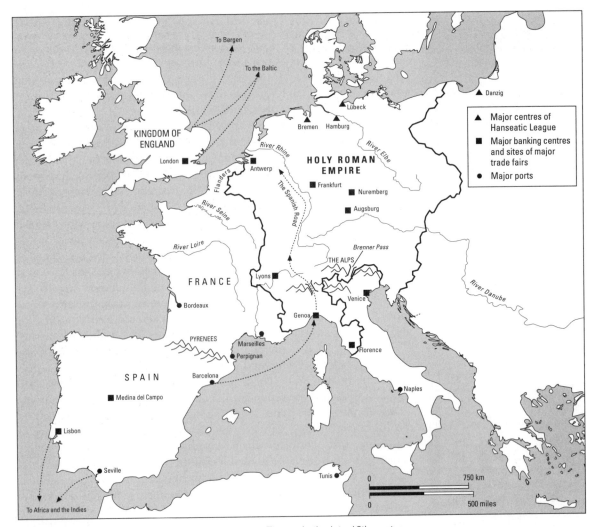

Trade in western Europe in the late 16th century

1. Explain the main problems facing Henry VII in his handling of foreign policy at the beginning of his reign.

2. What actions did Henry VII take to protect England's trade interests between 1485 and 1509?

3. 'Above all, security dominated Henry VII's conduct of foreign policy during his reign.' How valid is this judgement?

access to northern European trade, as another way of limiting Hanse power. For example, in 1489–90, a treaty with Denmark gave English merchants trading opportunities in Denmark and Norway.

Overseas exploration

Henry VII also had an interest in overseas exploration. Due in part to his resentment of Venice's control of much of the rich trade in silks and spices from the East, Henry was prepared to support explorers who believed that a new route to the East could be found by sailing westwards. He patronised John Cabot in his westward voyages, especially that of 1497 which led to the discovery of Newfoundland and its rich fisheries.

Henry also supported John's son, Sebastian. He encouraged Sebastian's voyage of 1509, which explored Hudson's Bay and the North American coast. By the time Cabot returned, Henry VII was dead and his son had no interest in such activities. It was not until the reigns of Mary I and Elizabeth I that there was active English royal support once again for such voyages of discovery.

? Source-based questions: *The Spanish marriage 1497–1502*

SOURCE A

Although we before entertained singular love and regard to your highness above all other queens in the world, as well as for the common blood between us, and also for the eminent dignity and virtue by which your Majesty so shines and excels that your most celebrated name is noised abroad and diffused everywhere; yet more has this our love increased and accumulated by the accession of the most noble affinity which has recently been celebrated between the Lord Arthur, Prince of Wales, our eldest son and the most illustrious princess, the Lady Catherine, the infanta, your daughter … Therefore we request your serenity to certify us of your estate and of that of the aforesaid most illustrious Lady Catherine our common daughter. And if there be anything in our power which would be grateful or pleasant to your Majesty, use us and ours as freely as you would your own.

From a letter of Queen Elizabeth (Henry VII's wife) to Queen Isabella of Castile following the betrothal of Prince Arthur to Catherine of Aragon, December 1497.

SOURCE B

On the 12th of November the Princess made her entry into the capital accompanied by such a multitude of prelates, high dignitaries, nobles and knights, and with the acclamation of such masses of people as never before have been seen in England. On the 14th of November the Princess was conducted with great splendour to our Cathedral of St Paul … and the Prince and Princess of Wales were solemnly wedded. Although the friendship between the houses of England and Spain has been most sincere and intimate before this time, it will henceforth be much more intimate and indissoluble. Great rejoicings have taken place. The whole people have taken part in them. Banish all sadness from your minds. Though you cannot now see the gentle face of your beloved daughter, you may be sure that she has found a second father who will ever watch over her happiness, and never permit her to want anything that can be obtained for her.

From a letter of King Henry VII to Ferdinand and Isabella describing the arrival and marriage of Catherine of Aragon to Prince Arthur, November 1501.

SOURCE C

The King of France [Louis XII] is on his way to Milan with an armed force, and has sent a force against us with the intention, it is said, of endeavouring to take from us our possessions there. He has also sent to the frontier of Perpignan many armed men, foot and horse. All the time this was going on we were at ease here, for we did not believe that he would break the agreement which he had made and sworn.

But now you must see how much importance it is that there should be no delay in making the agreement for the contract of marriage with the Prince of Wales who now is [Henry, later Henry VIII]. It is the more necessary, as it is said that the King of France is endeavouring to hinder it, and is intending to obtain the said alliance for his daughter or the sister of the Duke of Angoulême [heir to the French throne]. Therefore without saying anything about this, since it is already known for a certainty that the said Princess of Wales, our daughter, remains as she was here, endeavour to have the said contract agreed to immediately without consulting us; for any delay that might take place would be dangerous. See also that the articles to be made and signed and sworn at once and if nothing more advantageous can be procured, let it be settled as was proposed.

From a letter of Queen Isabella to Ferdinand, Duke of Estrada, the Spanish ambassador in England, July 1502.

---

1. Study Source A.

How, by her use of language and style, does Queen Elizabeth convey the importance of the Spanish marriage to her husband and herself?

2. Study Sources B and C.

How useful would the sources be to a historian studying Anglo–Spanish relations during the reign of Henry VII?

3. Using all the sources above and the information in this chapter, explain how far dynastic marriage was a vital aspect of diplomatic relations during the reign of Henry VII.

2.4 How successful was Henry VII in dealing with the English nobility?

One of the first concerns of a medieval king was how well he got on with the leading men in his kingdom, especially the nobility. Medieval kings who failed to maintain good working relationships with their leading subjects were always failures, such as King John and his son, Henry III. They could end up losing both crown and life, as in the cases of Edward II and Richard II. How Henry VII handled the nobility was one of the key concerns of his reign and any failure there would have been fatal. However, Henry VII's relations with the nobility were controversial, particularly during the later years of his reign. His death was followed by a backlash against some of his leading councillors and their activities.

A survey of the English nobility in 1485

The numbers of nobles in England in 1485 were not great. About 60 noble families were in existence at the beginning of Henry's reign. These low numbers were not due to the effects of the Wars of the Roses, although deaths on the battlefield and convictions for treason had played their part. Much of the problem of low numbers was caused by the tendency of noble families to die out due to lack of male heirs. This was a time when, by modern standards, survival was hazardous. There were many deaths at birth or in infancy, as well as limited medical knowledge in the face of diseases which were nearly always fatal.

Henry VII was fortunate that the upheavals during the reigns of his Yorkist predecessors had seen the deaths of many powerful nobles, which had left their lands in the hands of the Crown. The death of Richard III and the imprisonment of the Earl of Warwick meant that all of the great Warwick inheritance fell into Henry VII's hands. The Warwick inheritance consisted of extensive estates across the whole of England, but especially concentrated in the Midlands. It had been built up over three generations by a number of fortunate marriages. When the Earl of Warwick was killed at the battle of Barnet in 1471 his estates were divided between Edward IV's brothers, the Duke of Clarence and the Duke of Gloucester (later Richard III), who had each married the Earl's two surviving daughters. The Duke of Buckingham's execution by Richard III put his vast estates under royal control as his heir, Edward Stafford, was only a boy of seven in 1485. The death of John Howard (Duke of Norfolk) fighting for Richard III at Bosworth resulted in his son, the Earl of Surrey, being put into the Tower as Henry's prisoner. The family estates also fell into the new king's hands.

Henry VII was fortunate, unlike Edward IV, in having few living male relatives. His uncle, Jasper Tudor (Earl of Pembroke) was created Duke of Bedford by his grateful nephew but he had no children to succeed him. Among other leading nobles in 1485 the Earl of Northumberland, a Percy, was soon sent back to rule the North of England for Henry. When he was murdered in 1489, his ten-year-old son was automatically Henry's ward and the Percy's estates were in Henry's control for the next ten years. The Earl of Shrewsbury, another powerful noble, was happy to use his influence on Henry's behalf. The Earl of Oxford, one of the king's closest friends and followers, was powerful in East Anglia and promoted firm government in that area.

What was Henry's attitude towards the nobility?

Some historians, such as J. R. Green and A. F. Pollard, have suggested that Henry saw the nobility as a danger. So he set out to control them ruthlessly. However, more recent research has suggested that the nobility were vital to the Crown's effective control of England, especially in the outlying areas of the kingdom – such as the North or the Welsh Marches. As an example, Henry's stepfather, Lord Stanley, was allowed to exercise considerable local control in Lancashire and Cheshire on Henry's behalf. The same was true for other nobles elsewhere in the country.

Standing army: An army which is regularly recruited and employed. The English Crown was too poor to employ large numbers of full-time soldiers.

Nobles were vital to Henry in controlling their localities. In the absence of a **standing army** or an effective police force, the king rarely interfered with the nobles' local authority. When he felt more secure, however, Henry VII did on occasion replace the regional influence of a noble with his own men. In 1489 after the Earl of Northumberland's murder, Henry made his own son – the three-year-old Prince Arthur – ruler of the North, but in practice the Earl of Surrey exercised power. Surrey had no lands or influence in the North of England and could be relied on to support royal power in what was a region where loyalty to Henry was dubious.

Unlike his predecessors, Henry VII did not try to win the loyalty of the nobility. The only way to obtain royal reward under Henry VII was by loyal service over many years; for example, men such as Jasper Tudor and the Earl of Oxford were rewarded for their loyalty during Henry's dangerous years in exile. Otherwise, reward depended on loyal and able service; the best-known example being Thomas Howard (Earl of Surrey) who after many years' service regained all the family estates and his father's title of Duke of Norfolk (see page 168).

Henry was sparing in his creation of new nobility. He created only one earl during his reign – his stepfather, Lord Stanley (who took the title Earl of Derby). Only five new barons were created during the reign, including Lord Daubeney, one of Henry's leading commanders. The result of such economy was that Henry was able to avoid giving away much of the Crown lands to his new peerage creations, unlike Edward IV before him. Another consequence of this policy was that the number of peerage families was reduced as noble families continued to die out. However, Henry found another way to reward his subjects for loyal service other than creating new peerages: to give the award of the **Order of the Garter** for loyal service. This knighthood gave prestige to its holders but it did not involve the Crown in much expenditure or in it having to give away Crown lands.

Order of the Garter: An order of knighthood introduced by Edward III (1327–77). By the 1400s it had become England's highest order of chivalry.

How did Henry control the nobility?

Henry VII kept close control of his nobility. More perhaps than either Edward IV or his own son, Henry VIII, was to do. This was understandable in a man who only became king by force and throughout his reign faced both conspiracies and rebellions (see section 2.2). This control took a number of forms. It was concerned with **attainder, bonds** and **recognisances** and the restrictions on **livery** and **maintenance** (see panel overleaf).

The greater the noble the more likely they were to be under financial pressure from Henry. For example, the Marquis of Dorset (Edward IV's stepson and half-brother to Henry VII's wife, Elizabeth of York) was suspected by the king of having Yorkist sympathies. It was believed that

Sir Richard Empson (1450–1510)
Trained as a lawyer and sat in a number of parliaments as an MP. He became important as a member of the Council Learned in the later years of Henry VII's reign. Empson became hated for his activities as a royal debt collector, along with Edmund Dudley. He was arrested soon after Henry VII's death and in the next year was executed on false treason charges.

Edmund Dudley (?1462–1510)
Also trained as a lawyer and in 1494 was Speaker of the House of Commons. He was a member of the Royal Council and the Council Learned. Dudley was responsible, with Richard Empson, for overseeing Henry VII's system of bonds and recognisances. On Henry's death in 1509 he was a victim of the resentment of the upper classes. He was falsely accused of treason and executed in 1510, but not before he had written *The Tree of Commonwealth* – in which the fallen minister offered the new king advice on how to reform England, but it is unlikely that Henry VIII ever read it.

Acts of attainder
An Act of Parliament passed to declare someone guilty of a particular crime against the Crown, usually treason, without putting them on trial. This allowed the Crown to seize the person's title and all their possessions. It was a favour given by both Henry VII and Henry VIII for disposing of their political enemies.

Bonds
A bond was a written document binding one person to another to perform some action or to pay a sum of money if they broke the bond. Henry VII made many of the leading men of the country sign these.

Recognisances
This was when one acknowledged formally a debt or some other obligation. It could be enforced by means of penalties, usually of a financial nature such as a heavy fine.

Livery
This was the badge from a gentleman's or nobleman's coat of arms, which servants wore. It was a sign that they were 'in service'.

Maintenance
This was bringing unlawful pressure to bear on others in court cases (influencing juries etc.).

Dorset had had some connection with the Simnel conspiracy and with further plots against Henry. The earl and his friends had to sign bonds totalling £10,000 as a pledge of their continued good behaviour. It has been estimated that out of 62 peerage families in existence during Henry VII's reign, the great majority were at his mercy, through acts of attainder or bonds and recognisances for at least some of the time. The majority of these controls were imposed in the later years of Henry's reign, after the death of Arthur in 1502, when the king felt much less secure on his throne.

Henry VII's financial policy towards the nobility has been much commented on by historians, not because his methods were new, but because he used them more widely than his predecessors. In the later years of his reign Henry used the Council Learned (see page 29 and section 2.5) to supervise the system of bonds and recognisances, and to collect the money owing. This body was headed by Sir Richard Empson and his colleague, Edmund Dudley. The Council Learned was hated by landowners for its energy and efficiency in doing its job. Perhaps the non-noble background of the two councillors did little to endear them to the nobility. This was to result in Empson's and Dudley's downfall and execution during the period of the so-called 'noble backlash' during the early months of Henry VIII's reign. In spite of his harshness, it is unlikely that Henry VII was anti-noble. He depended on the support of nobles, both locally and nationally, and it was an important feature of the king's wish to control his subjects firmly.

The same can be said of Henry VII's policy of livery and maintenance (see above). Neither practice was new and they had been in use for generations; kings before Henry VII had also tried to control both practices. Livery was an excellent way to raise or retain men. It could be used by a noble to control his locality, or to provide men for the king's army in times of rebellion or war. However, the disturbed period of the Wars of the Roses had shown that powerful lords could manipulate the law in the interests of their own followers. Maintenance had come to mean, not a great man protecting the lawful interests of his men, but actively abusing the law to promote his own interests at any price.

From the beginning of his reign Henry made it clear that he wished to control retaining and the Parliaments of 1487 and 1504 both passed laws against it. The Act of 1487 was intended to prevent unlawful retaining but a strict interpretation of lawful retaining was set out too. Henry also tightened further the interpretation of lawful retaining in his 1504 Act. In future, there was to be a system of licensing by the Crown and a lord's retinue of followers had to be listed for Henry VII's approval.

Henry VII enjoyed some success with his policy to limit retaining. The numbers of men retained by the nobility fell but this may have been because they were careful to keep no written records or indentures (contracts), unlike the period before Henry became king. Certainly, if nobles broke the law on retaining and were found out, they were treated harshly. The best-known example was Lord Burgavenny who in 1506 was fined the massive sum of £70,550. However, Henry set the fine aside in favour of a recognisance and eventually accepted a payment of £5,000 which was to be paid off in ten yearly instalments. The point of the **Burgavenny Case** was to deter others from keeping over-large retinues and to punish a noble whose loyalty Henry had suspected.

There was also the probably fictional case of the Earl of Oxford, one of Henry's closest followers, who was heavily fined for illegal retaining in 1504. The point of the Oxford Case was to make it clear to all men of importance in England that Henry was determined to enforce the law and there should be no exceptions to this, even among the King's closest friends. As he intended, Henry controlled retaining, but he did not wish to stop it. Retaining continued under his successors as an important aspect of raising armed forces to fight wars and to deal with rebellions and uprisings.

Earlier kings had used recognisances as a way of controlling their nobles, but it was Henry VII who erected a whole new system for the first time. In this sense, Henry VII can be regarded as an innovator. The historian Alexander Grant wrote in his pamphlet 'Henry VII', in 1985:

> Recognisances … were the basis of a technique for exerting control over the nobility, through a system of suspended sentences requiring good behaviour, which could, in the most serious cases, threaten complete ruin for a magnate if he displeased the king. In this respect Henry VII can … be contrasted with his other predecessors.

Conclusion

Henry succeeded in controlling the nobility by creating few new peerages, thereby limiting their numbers. He also enforced laws against livery and maintenance firmly without fear or favour. In the last years of his reign, when due to Arthur's death he felt insecure, Henry began to use the system of bonds and recognisances harshly. This resulted in a backlash from the nobility after his death.

Burgavenny Case: George Neville (?1469–1535), Lord Burgavenny, was believed to be one of the wealthiest men in England. His richest estates were in Kent. He was unwilling or unable to control his retainers who threatened others living in the county. In 1506 Burgavenny was a victim of Henry VII's 1504 Act against retaining. He was fined the sum of £70,550, which was increased after the king made him give recognisances for good behaviour to £100,000. In practice, Burgavenny never paid anything like this sum: he paid some £5,000 in ten instalments to the King. However, his Case acted as a warning to other nobles or gentry who failed to control their retainers.

1. Why was Henry VII more fortunate than Edward IV and Richard III in his dealings with the English nobility?

2. 'Henry VII was too harsh in his treatment of the nobility, especially in the later years of his reign.' Do you agree with this view?

In spite of his harshness, Henry still made good use of the nobility to help him rule at both local and national level and they were an important presence in the Royal Council too. Early Tudor England was a society that believed in good rule from above and in providing this for his subjects Henry VII's nobility played a key role.

2.5 What were the main features of Henry VII's government of England?

In 1485 Henry VII was one of the least experienced men to have sat on the throne of England in regard to his knowledge of government and its workings. Most of his life had been spent in exile, and before that in Wales. His first-hand knowledge of England was strictly limited. For instance, this ignorance was shown in the early years of Henry's reign when direct royal control of much of Crown revenues through **the Chamber** was allowed to lapse. However, Henry VII had more immediate worries than finance, while establishing himself as king (see sections 2.1 and 2.2 above).

From the first the new king was wise in his appointment of Councillors who were to serve him well. Both Court and Council (see page 29) were at the centre of Henry's rule in England between 1485 and 1509. Within a few years Henry had realised that a rich king is a strong king, so he kept a strong eye on the royal finances. From the first, the new king appreciated that law and order was vital to good government. Respect for the throne and its agents, not least in the localities, was to be vital to his success.

The key areas in the government of England in the later 15th century which it is necessary to consider when assessing Henry VII's success are:

● the Royal Court and especially the Council

● law and order, especially the localities

● the handling and administration of finance

● relations with Parliament

● the outlying regions of the kingdom and Ireland.

This section will consider the extent of Henry VII's success in each of these areas.

The Royal Court and Council

The King's Court was an important aspect of Tudor government which has been recognised for its true importance by historians such as David Loades in his study of the Tudor Court and David Starkey in *The Reign of Henry VII: politics and personalities* (1985). The king was the chief executive, as well as the head of state, unlike modern monarchs. It was

The Chamber: This was a method of financial control whereby the king had revenue paid directly into the Chamber, rather than the Exchequer. The Chamber was a part of the Royal Household under the king's control, which allowed him to supervise his income directly.

Royal government during the reign of Henry VII

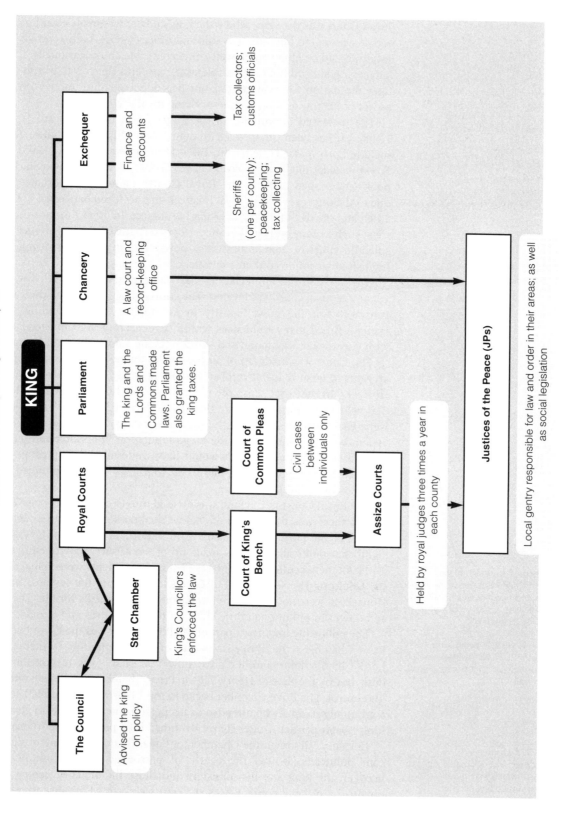

KING

The Council

Advised the king on policy

Royal Courts

Parliament

The king and the Lords and Commons made laws. Parliament also granted the king taxes.

Chancery

A law court and record-keeping office

Exchequer

Finance and accounts

Sheriffs (one per county): peacekeeping; tax collecting

Tax collectors; customs officials

Star Chamber

King's Councillors enforced the law

Court of King's Bench

Court of Common Pleas

Civil cases between individuals only

Assize Courts

Held by royal judges three times a year in each county

Justices of the Peace (JPs)

Local gentry responsible for law and order in their areas; as well as social legislation necessary both for the royal image and its prestige, both at home and abroad, that the king was surrounded by splendour and ceremony. The Royal Court was the place where the king's power was made clear for all to see. It was where honours, rewards and offices (jobs), both centrally and locally, could be obtained by well-connected, able and occasionally 'lucky' subjects. A shrewd king kept a splendid court and Henry VII, in spite of a later reputation for **avarice**, did not begrudge spending money on this aspect of his role as king, as his surviving royal accounts show.

Avarice: The sin of greed. It was supposed to be one of Henry VII's major shortcomings as king, especially his love of money.

The increased importance of the Royal Court under Edward IV and Henry VII has been the message of many recent historical studies. These include *Early Tudor Government, 1485–1558* by Steven Gunn (1995) and *Power in Tudor England* by David Loades (1997), as well as David Starkey's book (mentioned above). The Royal Court's increased importance was due to the improvement in royal finances that occurred between 1471 and 1509, and the decline of the over-mighty subject. In other European countries, such as Burgundy and France, rulers recognised the importance of a splendid court in maintaining their power and it is not surprising that English kings followed their example.

One key point to appreciate is that wherever the king was living was where the royal court was located. The courts of later medieval kings were constantly on the move, mostly in London or its surrounding area. Henry VII had many residences within easy reach of Westminster Palace with Greenwich, Richmond and Windsor being among the most favoured.

The Court was made up of all those who attended the monarch, from servants to great nobles. Numbers attending would vary from day to day. However, in the strict sense the Court's membership was restricted to all that held a paid position or had the right to receive free food. This system went back centuries and was by today's standards extravagant and very expensive, but it was vital to the king's reputation. If a king reformed his court by cutting out waste, it would have undermined his prestige and offended his subjects. A king had to be seen to be both magnificent and generous in his subjects' eyes.

The Royal Court in England was divided into two parts (see page 219). Firstly, there was the household 'below the stairs' which was under the control of the Lord Steward, usually an important nobleman. It was not significant politically and was made up of the service departments, such as the kitchen, **scullery** and **buttery**. These departments were managed by the Counting House of Board of Greencloth. Most of the servants in the Household were not gentlemen but had a safe job, usually for life. The ups and downs of politics had little effect on their daily lives and duties.

Scullery: Department of the Royal Court which was a part of the 'below stairs' organisation, which included the kitchens. It was a vital part of the catering arrangements.

Buttery: Another 'below stairs' department which was responsible for the purchase and storage of food and drink.

The politically important part of the Royal Court was the Chamber and Privy Chamber – the 'above stairs' part of the organisation. In theory, the Lord Chamberlain (another great officer of state) was responsible for both, but by the time of Henry VII the Privy Chamber was largely outside his control. The Privy Chamber began in the 1490s when Henry VII set up a group of servants who attended to his personal needs. It was to give the king greater privacy. Under Henry VII it had little political importance.

In Henry VII's reign the Chamber, or Great Chamber, was more significant politically. It was the centre of **patronage** and communication between the king and his ministers and those hundreds of gentry who obtained a place at court. Places at Court were valued because they gave access to the powerful in the country and provided opportunities to

Patronage: The disposal of jobs and offices – which were the gift of the king or his leading ministers. This was one way in which men and women could be bound to the royal service and remain loyal to the king.

promote family and local interests. As long as the king was in control of government, its focus was the Court, and the Chamber was vital to this process. It was there that the spectacle of monarchy was centred.

How important was the Royal Council?

The Royal Council was vital to Henry VII's rule in England. Fortunately, Henry appointed the right men to help him (see section 2.1) and his councillors were both able and effective. One key point to remember about Henry's Council was that many of its members had served his Yorkist predecessors. For example, Archbishop John Morton had been a leading councillor to Edward IV, but had then fallen foul of Richard III. Soon he became a leading member of the conspiracy which led to Henry Tudor's success at the battle of Bosworth Field and his own return to power. Others who were the most regular attenders at Council were also former Yorkist councillors, so an important element of continuity and experience was maintained to balance Henry's own initial inexperience.

In theory, Henry's Council appears to be a very unwieldy body. During his reign some 227 men were named as councillors. However, many of these were given the status to enhance their position when they were sent on foreign embassies or to represent the king in outlying parts of the kingdom. In practice, Henry's effective council was much smaller. It was mostly made up of important ministers of state, such as the Lord Chancellor and Lord Privy Seal, who met regularly to deal with the business of government on a day-to-day basis. Its most regular attenders were men such as Reginald Bray, Thomas Lovell, Richard Fox (Lord Privy Seal) and Archbishop Morton. No doubt, important matters of policy were discussed in the Council but it was Henry VII who in the end made all of the important decisions.

The Royal Council under Henry VII was not a formal body with laid-down rules. During Henry's reign a number of sub-committees of the Council were set up to deal with specific problems which arose. The first of these was the so-called 'Star Chamber' court set up by the Act of 1487. It was believed that this court was given powers by Parliament to deal with over-mighty subjects, but in practice it met rarely. There is little surviving evidence regarding its meetings but it may at times have been an effective way for Henry to enforce control over the great men of his kingdom. More important was the emergence after 1485 of the Council Learned in the Law.

Duchy of Lancaster: A court which was responsible for administering the royal estates which had been part of the Duchy of Lancaster since the mid-1300s. Many of these were in Cheshire and Lancashire.

Relief: Money paid over to the Crown by members of the nobility or gentry when they inherited their estates on the death of a relative.

Wardship: When a child or young person under the age of majority (14) inherited an estate he or she became a royal ward until they came of age. The Crown (or its appointee) acted as the ward's guardian and ran their estates.

This body was set up to look after the king's interests as the feudal landlord of England. Its membership was small and all members possessed legal knowledge. It was headed by Reginald Bray in his capacity as Chancellor of the **Duchy of Lancaster**. Soon it was extending its role to not only looking after the king's existing feudal rights but to deal with all the Crown lands. Matters such as marriage and **relief** and **wardship** of all the king's tenants-in-chief (landowners) and the collection of money owed to him were soon being dealt with by the Council Learned.

This body actively promoted the extension of the king's prerogative. In the final years of the reign the Council was increasingly unpopular with the landowning and propertied classes. It became responsible for supervising Henry's use of bonds and recognisances. After Bray's death in 1503 it was dominated increasingly by Edmund Dudley and Richard Empson. The Council's exactions were especially resented in the closing years of Henry VII's reign.

Other important offshoots of the Council Learned resulted due to Henry's approach to governing the outlying regions of his kingdom. In the early years of his reign the Earl of Northumberland was left to control the North of England, until his murder in 1489. Thereafter Henry set up a council to rule the North and its nominal head was his eldest son, Prince Arthur. In reality, the head of the Council of the North was the Earl of Surrey who as he had no interests of his own in the region was no threat to royal power. When Surrey became Lord Treasurer in 1501 he was replaced by another council under the charge of the Archbishop of York.

In Wales and the Marches another council was set up under Prince Arthur, based at Ludlow. After Arthur's death in 1502 it was headed by the Bishop of Lincoln, who like the Earl of Surrey had no influence of his own in the region.

So Henry's Council was vital in helping him run his kingdom in terms of day-to-day government. Much of the routine correspondence with local and regional officials was no doubt carried out by them, as was the effective enforcement of the king's feudal rights and helping to maintain law and order in the localities. It is likely that the advice of leading councillors was considered by Henry before he made important decisions, such as going to war, but in the last resort it was the king who made government policy.

How successful was Henry VII in enforcing law and order?

Besides controlling the nobility, another major concern of Henry VII was to make sure that the laws were obeyed by all of his subjects. The provision of good government, which included the right of ordinary subjects to go about their everyday business, was a key requirement of kingship and Henry VII was determined that this should be so.

Henry had a few paid officials in the Customs, the Exchequer and the Duchy of Lancaster, but to enforce the law he was dependent on the support of the nobility and the gentry. Henry was content to allow the nobles their regional influence provided they remained loyal to him. The Stanley family was left to wield influence in Lancashire and Cheshire as long as they upheld the law and did not step outside it themselves. The Earl of Oxford in East Anglia, and other families such as the Courtneys in Devon and the West and the Dacres in the North West, were left with or were given considerable influence in their own areas.

The other much larger group of people on whom Henry VII relied across the country were the justices of the peace (JPs – see page 13). A problem in the past had been that JPs were often under the influence of some over-mighty subject or used their position in their own interests. Henry VII did much to end these evils by his system of bonds and recognisances (see page 54) which he applied to gentry wrongdoers as much as to members of the nobility.

Also, Henry put much emphasis on ensuring that in the counties of England he was seen as the most important landlord locally. To this end Henry passed an Act of Parliament in 1487 which laid down that in future men who held royal land or offices could only be retained by the king. To an extent the Act worked, as Henry VII continued to give JPs more powers. In 1495 further Acts laid down means to prevent juries being corrupted or intimidated by great men. Under these Acts JPs could replace suspect jurors. They also found themselves responsible for enforcing the vagrancy laws, checking weights and measures, as well as many other tasks.

By 1509 JPs were the Crown's most important administrators in the English counties and were vital to the maintenance of law and order. Considering that they were unpaid, it is remarkable that Henry found enough men to fill the local benches with JPs. Local gentry saw the office as one of local influence and prestige and so were willing to serve. Undoubtedly, law and order in the English localities improved under Henry VII's rule but it remained a difficult task. The resources at the disposal of the authorities, both locally and nationally, remained limited by modern standards with no regular police force paid for out of taxation.

How successful was Henry VII's financial policy?

Until recently one fact was known about Henry VII by generations of students: that he died rich. At his death in 1509 he left his son, Henry VIII, a considerable treasury – some £1,800,000 (worth approximately £1 billion today). Modern historical research – particularly the work of Bertram Wolfe – has shown this to be myth. However, there is one element of truth in the story: Henry VII was determined to be a rich king. Once he had obtained the throne, a considerable amount of both Henry's time and energy was given to increasing the royal income. As a former penniless exile, Henry was well aware of the value of a full treasury.

The royal income came from a number of sources. There was income from the royal estates and from the exercise of the king's feudal **prerogative**. Further revenue came from:

Prerogative: These were the powers which the king used to govern his realm. Some of these came from the king's rights as feudal overlord of the kingdom and on occasion this allowed him to act outside the law. But even then the king could not ignore the common law of England.

- customs duties which were granted by Parliament to each king for life

- the French pension granted to Henry by the Treaty of Etaples in 1492 (see page 45)

- profits of justice which came to the Crown from the enforcement of law and order

- 'extraordinary' income: such as taxation granted by Parliament to the king in times of emergency or war. It was an unwise king who asked for extra taxation too often as the result could be widespread dissatisfaction and rebellion, as happened to Henry VII in 1497 with the Cornish rebellion (see page 41).

Henry's Yorkist predecessors had increased revenue by careful management of the royal estates. In Richard III's reign (1483–85) this had amounted to an income of £25,000 per year. This achievement had been gained from an all-time low in the later years of King Henry VI (1422–61) by the introduction of new methods of financial management. The Exchequer, the department responsible for financial administration, had become increasingly slow due to its bureaucratic methods. Edward IV (1461–70, 1471–83) introduced a new, streamlined method of managing the royal estates: using the King's Chamber (part of the Royal Household) to handle his finances. The officials paid income from the royal estates directly into the Chamber, where their accounts were checked and an immediate source of income was provided.

However, when he became king, Henry VII, because of his financial inexperience, did not realise the advantage of the Yorkist Chamber system and the Exchequer was allowed to resume control of royal income. This led to a drop in immediate revenue from the royal estates which by 1486 stood at only £12,000 per year. Within a year, Henry realised his mistake and from then onwards the Chamber once again became the centre of royal financial control. By the last half of Henry's reign, the Chamber was dealing with all sources of royal income. The Exchequer still controlled the income which came in from sheriffs and the customs duties. By the end of the reign, income from Crown lands had risen to £42,000 a year and Henry's income from all sources, including parliamentary grants, was over £100,000 each year.

Henry VII also did much to improve his income from customs duties. Following Edward IV's example, Henry continued to tighten up the collection system by cracking down on dishonest officials. The Book of Rates of Customs Duties was updated by Henry twice during his reign. However, the increase in income from customs duties was not as great as that from the royal estates and feudal dues, but nevertheless it provided nearly 40% of the royal income by the end of the reign.

This success was achieved by Henry VII's own personal involvement. He worked alongside his chief officials checking the accounts himself and signing each page. He also made wise appointments. The successive Treasurers of the Chamber during his reign – Sir Thomas Lovell (1485–92) and Sir John Heron (1492–1512) – both gave the king loyal and efficient service. Henry's most trusted financial adviser, however, was Sir Reginald Bray. He was much concerned with Henry's financial reforms until his death in 1503. Henry VII's healthy finances were helped by his foreign policy in which he was careful to avoid war. He was quick to grasp that fighting wars was expensive and quickly emptied the royal treasury – as his son, Henry VIII, was to demonstrate in the 1540s.

Overall, Henry VII's financial policy was a success. Although the king was not very original as he adopted the financial policies of his predecessors, Henry made his policies work effectively by choosing good servants and checking their work thoroughly. At the time of his death, the Crown's finances were very sound in spite of the myth that he did not leave his son any great treasure to squander on wars against France.

What was the relationship between Henry VII and his Parliaments?

> **The Parliaments of King Henry VII**
>
> | | |
> |---|---|
> | 1 | 7 November 1485 – 4 March 1486 |
> | 2 | 9 November 1487 – 18 December 1487 |
> | 3 | 13 January 1489 – 27 February 1490 |
> | 4 | 17 October 1491 – 5 March 1492 |
> | 5 | 14 October 1495 – 22 December 1495 |
> | 6 | 16 January 1497 – 13 March 1497 |
> | 7 | 25 January 1504 – about 1 April 1504 |
>
> Of the seven parliaments, five were in the first decade of Henry VII's reign; only two after that. This reflects the King's increasingly secure position on the throne. Parliaments were not in continuous session. Most parliaments only lasted a few weeks. Often there were long periods between parliaments.

Parliament had been an established part of government since the 1330s but it did not play a prominent role in the government of later 15th-century England. For much of his reign Henry VII managed very well without summoning Parliament. During his 24 years as King he only called seven parliaments, and of these five occurred during the first ten years of his reign when Henry's position was less secure. All in all, parliamentary sessions for the whole reign lasted about 70 weeks, or on average about three weeks for every year that Henry was king. Evidently, Parliament could not be counted as a regular or essential feature of royal government to the extent it was to become after 1529. Nevertheless, it had a vital place in the early Tudor constitution. Firstly, taxes could only be levied with its consent; secondly, its laws were already looked on as being superior to the laws made by other bodies, such as the royal courts of law.

Parliament's structure was largely fixed by 1485. It consisted of two bodies: the Lords and the Commons. The Lords was the most important of the two chambers and its membership consisted of the Lords Spiritual (the bishops and some abbots of great religious houses) and the Lords Temporal (the nobility). These lords met in the royal palace of Westminster, in London, and often statutes were started there, rather than in the House of Commons. The Commons was made up of the land-owning classes – represented by two knights of the shire for every English county – and the prosperous merchants and tradesmen – two of whom were elected to represent every **borough**. The MPs were elected by a small electorate who had to be property owners or, at the least, local taxpayers. Essentially, Parliament represented a privileged and propertied minority of Henry VII's subjects, but late 15th-century England had no concept of modern democracy or of 'one person, one vote'. Parliament was there to represent interests which were essentially those of the propertied men of the kingdom with a vested interest in strong royal government.

Besides Parliament, Henry VII still used **Great Councils**; five were called between 1487 and 1502. This was another way in which Henry VII could obtain support and advice and be seen to wish to consult his subjects before making policy. A wise monarch preferred to obtain the support of the properties and landowning classes for his or her policies, especially when they went to war.

Parliament could only be summoned by the king. It was usually to promote his own security or policies. For example, Henry VII's parliaments, especially those of 1485–86 and 1487, passed acts of attainder (see page 54) against those who had fought him at Bosworth or had later rebelled against his rule. Parliaments usually granted the king taxes vital to government – as when Henry's first parliament voted him the income from customs revenue for life. This was a well-established procedure in the case of new kings by 1485. When the monarch needed 'extraordinary' taxation, usually for war – as in 1491–92 – it was to Parliament that he turned. Henry tended to be sparing in asking Parliament for extraordinary taxation, but in 1497 it voted him a large grant to counter the threat from Scotland and Perkin Warbeck (see section 2.2). Thereafter, Henry was more cautious, perhaps because he had grasped that usually his subjects were deeply resentful about being taxed, especially if they regarded the king's demands as excessive or unjust. Normally, it was preferred that the king lived off his own money, and not that of his subjects.

In the last parliament of the reign (1504), when Henry VII asked for

Borough: A town which had been granted a royal charter. This gave the town the right to run its own affairs and, once Parliament became regularised in the early 1300s, to choose and send two MPs to represent its interests there.

Great Councils: These were meetings of the great men of the kingdom which the king could call to advise him when important decisions, such as whether or not to go to war, had to be made. Henry VII summoned a number of Great Councils during his reign.

two feudal aids – one for the knighting of his son Arthur (after his death) and the other for the marriage of his daughter Margaret to James IV – the king again ran into opposition. Parliament acknowledged that the law was on Henry's side but declared that raising so large an amount (£90,000) would cause 'trouble and unquietness'. The King was quick to compromise and in the end he settled for a grant of £30,000.

Parliament played an important part in Henry VII's policies of control, especially regarding the nobility and law and order. Apart from acts of attainder, it passed the De Facto Act of 1495 which stated that anyone giving the king faithful service would not be later attainted for treason. This had the effect of strengthening Henry's hold on the throne. Also Parliament passed a number of laws concerning the duties of justices of the peace. For example, in 1495 an Act was passed allowing JPs to hear and decide on all offences short of very serious crimes such as murder. Also, JPs were given statutory powers to supervise and control local officials and to change the membership of juries if a sheriff had failed to act impartially.

Besides strengthening the Crown, Parliament dealt with a variety of other business. Statutes (laws) were passed which regulated the towns and London too, if necessary. For example, in 1497 Parliament blocked the Merchant Adventurers' attempt to restrict their membership by charging anyone trading in cloth the then very high fee of £20. The company was forced to reduce the fee by two-thirds. Acts promoting trade by improving the coinage and setting up a system of standard weights and measures were passed by Henry VII's parliaments. Statutes to control economic change and to promote discipline among the king's subjects were another feature of parliamentary legislation. In 1489 an Act was passed against depopulation and unjust landlords evicting tenants; while in 1495 a statute attempted to lay down standards in terms of wage rates and hours of work.

So Parliament was an irregular, but at times essential, part of Henry VII's government of England. It gave force of law to the king's policies regarding the nobility, taxation, and law and order. It was dependent on Henry summoning it and it was the King who initiated policy, but Parliament acted as a useful way of ascertaining the views of the political nation of that day – the powerful and propertied – regarding royal policy. As Henry felt more secure and became richer, he summoned Parliament less and after 1497 only one more was summoned during the remainder of the reign – that of 1504.

To what extent did Henry VII increase royal control of the outlying parts of his kingdom?

In an age of poor communications, and given the limited power of royal government, it is not surprising that Henry VII often preferred to rely on the nobility to help him control the outlying regions of his kingdom. Edward IV had pursued a policy of using great nobles to control the regions and Henry followed him, although his reign did see some innovations.

To the north, Henry was content to leave the Earl of Northumberland in control, in spite of his ambiguous attitude at Bosworth Field. There was also a royal progress to Yorkshire in 1486 which may have helped to create more of a sense of identity between the new king and the people of the region. After the murder in 1489 of the Earl of Northumberland by rioters, Henry VII chose the Earl of Surrey to rule the North. This was perhaps surprising as the Earl of Surrey had fought against Henry at Bosworth, but the king's choice proved to be wise. Until his promotion to Lord Treasurer in 1503, the earl served the king well. After 1503 Henry VII appointed a council under the Archbishop of York to replace the Earl of Surrey, while the fifth Earl of Northumberland was also given a leading role in the North.

Besides the Earl of Surrey, Henry also relied on Lord Dacre to help control Cumberland and Westmorland (in the north-west). However, that region remained disorderly because of the cross-border fighting between the English and the Scots who were forever raiding one another's settlements and carrying off whatever they could seize. However, as that part of the region presented no real threat to Henry's security, he turned a blind eye.

Another great noble of whom Henry VII was suspicious, the Earl of Westmorland, was generally ignored by the king in terms of controlling the North. Westmorland remained the greatest **lay peer** in the county of Durham, but in 1494 Henry VII made his trusted minister Richard Fox bishop of Durham, no doubt in part to reduce the Earl's influence there.

Lay peer: Those members of the House of Lords who were not churchmen.

Henry was proud of his Welsh ancestry and the symbol of the 'red dragon' featured on his banners at Bosworth. In reality, though, Henry was only partly Welsh and once king he was too preoccupied to give the **principality** more than occasional attention. Until Jasper's death in 1495, Henry relied on his uncle Jasper Tudor (Duke of Bedford) to control Wales. Arthur, Henry's eldest son, was created Prince of Wales in 1489 and thereafter a council headed at first by Jasper Tudor ruled the principality. Its chief task was to see that the law was enforced and many surviving marcher lords found themselves bound by bonds and recognisances to keep the peace and help to maintain order.

Principality: An area or region ruled in theory by a prince. Wales was a princedom whose head was the Prince of Wales (the king's oldest son). In practice, Wales was ruled by the king or his representatives.

The marcher lordships were large blocks of land, which had originally been captured by the English aristocracy at the expense of the native Welsh in the 11th and 12th centuries. By the end of the Middle Ages there were some 45 of them, mostly under the control of the Crown. Each lordship had its own courts, financial structure and officials. Those lordships not under the direct ownership of the Crown were the property of great noble families who were often absentees and were only interested in obtaining as much income from them as they could. In practice, they were often run by corrupt local officials, while criminals moved freely across the different jurisdictions – safe from capture and possible conviction for their crimes. Henry VII tried to impose some order on to this chaos.

The Councils, headed at first by Jasper Tudor and later by the Bishop of Lincoln, tried to keep law and order but with variable success. However, after 1485 Wales posed no real threat to Henry's security as king and, due to his many other problems, it was not until the time of Thomas Cromwell in the later 1530s that the lawlessness of the principality was finally sorted out.

To what extent did Henry VII increase royal control in Ireland?

Ireland had been nominally under the rule of the kings of England as 'Lords of Ireland' since the reign of Henry II (1154–89) but, in practice, their control of the country was slender. Under Henry VII, in spite of some efforts made in the mid-1490s, this remained so. In effect, English rule was limited to the 'Pale' – a coastal strip centred on Dublin. The remainder of the country was under the control of the descendants of the

Gerald Fitzgerald, 8th Earl of Kildare (?1455–1513)

Son of the 7th Earl of Kildare; he inherited the title and estates in 1478. On his accession as King, Henry VII re-appointed Kildare as Lord Deputy in Ireland. However, Kildare's loyalty was suspect, especially after he supported Lambert Simnel in 1487 and did little to prevent Perkin Warbeck beginning his imposture in 1491. In 1494 Kildare was replaced as Lord Deputy by Sir Edward Poynings, then arrested and sent to London. However, by 1496 the Earl of Kildare had decided that it was better to serve Henry VII than to oppose him. He was re-appointed as Lord Deputy and served Henry VII and Henry VIII loyally for the remainder of his life.

Anglo-Norman invaders of the later 12th century. Among these were the three great families – the earls of Desmond, Ormond and Kildare. English kings relied on them to rule Ireland.

After 1485 Henry VII found himself relying on Gerald Fitzgerald, the eighth Earl of Kildare, to rule Ireland. The Earl of Kildare would probably not have been Henry's first choice as he had been Lord Deputy under the Yorkists, but as the King lacked the resources to rule Ireland directly he had to rely on him. The major problem for Henry VII in Ireland was security. It was important that the country did not become a base for Yorkist pretenders. However, Henry's rule did not get off to a good start as the Earl of Kildare ignored the King's summons to visit London to advise him on Irish affairs as he did not trust Henry. When Lambert Simnel arrived in Ireland, it was not long before the Earl of Kildare came out in his favour and allowed him to be crowned as 'Edward VI' (see page 36). Although Simnel was defeated at East Stoke in 1487, Henry had to leave Kildare in office for fear that there would be a rebellion in Ireland. In spite of the king's lenient attitude, Kildare was still unreconciled to Henry's rule. In October 1491, when the pretender Perkin Warbeck landed in Ireland, he took no action against him. This led to Henry removing Kildare and after two rather chaotic years the king appointed Sir Edward Poynings, an experienced soldier, as Lord Deputy.

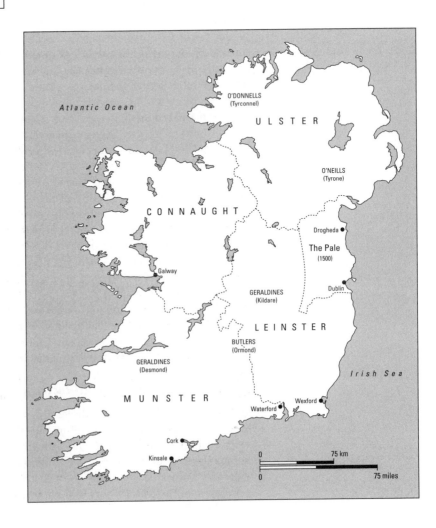

Ireland under the Tudors

Poynings arrived with a small army and his first task was to suppress a rising of the native (gaelic) Irish in Ulster (see map). Before long, convinced of Kildare's disloyalty, Poynings had him arrested and sent to England as a prisoner while his lands were attainted by the Irish Parliament meeting at Drogheda in the Pale. The Drogheda Parliament passed a number of important statutes, including one known as 'Poynings Law' (December 1494). It stated that in future no Irish Parliament could be summoned to pass laws without the approval of the English government. This may have been passed to make it difficult for pretenders to obtain parliamentary approval, as Simnel had succeeded in doing in 1487. However, the cost of ruling Ireland remained excessive and in January 1496 Henry recalled Poynings to England.

Henry VII found Ireland an expensive problem and he had no wish to keep spending money there. So, ever the realist, Henry decided to restore the Earl of Kildare as Lord Deputy. During the Earl of Kildare's time in England, the king and the earl appear to have become friends, and although it is unlikely that Henry fully trusted him, he decided to make use of him once more. The Earl of Kildare's attainder was reversed by the English Parliament and he married Elizabeth St John, a second cousin of the king, before returning to Ireland. It was the clear-eyed recognition of Irish realities, not least that the country was remote from London, that ensured peace in Ireland for the remainder of Henry's reign.

> ? 1. How did the Royal Court and Council work during Henry VII's reign?
>
> 2. 'A rich king is a strong king.' How did Henry VII go about turning this view into reality in his government of England?
>
> 3. What was the most successful aspect of Henry VII's government? Give reasons to support your answer.

2.6 To what extent did Henry VII create a 'new monarchy'?
A CASE STUDY IN HISTORICAL INTERPRETATION

A key concept in the study of the reign of Henry VII is change: how far, if at all, did Henry VII create a 'new monarchy'? Historians have debated this issue for over a century and no doubt it will continue for a long time to come. Compared with the remainder of the Tudor monarchs, we know relatively little of Henry VII's personality but it was an interesting one. Henry was a graduate of the school of hard-won experience, including long, frustrating years in exile which taught him the virtue of patience and developed the capacity to conceal his feelings. The king's portraits reveal an intelligent but essentially reserved man, very different from the overpowering nature of those of his son, Henry VIII. Nevertheless, it was Henry VII, not his son, who established the Tudor dynasty in 24 years of hard work. Henry had the capacity not only to apply himself to the job of governing England but largely learnt from his mistakes in the fields of both domestic and foreign policy. Certainly Henry created and established a new dynasty, but could his monarchy be said to be new?

How the idea of a 'new monarchy' emerged

The idea of a 'new monarchy' owed much to the historian J. R. Green who referred to the events of 1471–1509 in his *Short History of the English People* (published in 1876) as seeing the emergence of a 'new monarchy'. This new monarchy restored the powers of the Crown, weakened by the Wars of the Roses, and set back English freedom by 100 years. This was also the beginning of the '**Tudor despotism**' – an idea supported by early 20th-century historians. Subsequent historians adopted Green's views and expanded on them, shifting the date of the

'**Tudor despotism**': The theory that Tudors restored the power of the Crown at the expense of their subjects' rights and liberties.

Nation state: Usually refers to the situation – increasingly common by the late Middle Ages – when a king ruled over subjects who were mainly of the same race and had a common sense of identity (e.g. England, France, Spain, Portugal).

beginning of the new monarchy to 1485 in the process. This was not surprising given the fact that the date saw the arrival of a new dynasty which successfully established itself on the English throne for well over a century and presided over a period of great change and achievement. This more positive view of the Tudors as being not only achievers but modernisers owes much to the historian Albert Pollard. Writing in the early years of the 20th century, Pollard credited the Tudors with helping to create the centralised **nation state**. Putting the emphasis on the date of 1485 meant that parallels could be made between the Tudors and other modernising monarchies of the time, such as France and Spain. In these countries the power of the Crown was greatly increased too.

Other aspects of the 'new monarchy' were centralisation, an ability to balance the financial books and the use of middle-class men instead of the feudal nobility to run government. In the early 20th century the reputation of the Tudor monarchy stood high as it was seen as having been responsible for the creation of the modern nation state.

'New monarchy' challenged

The last 50 years have seen the concept of the 'new monarchy' slip down from its 'premier league' rating among historians. In *The Earlier Tudors 1485–1558* (published in 1952) J. D. Mackie challenged the idea of a new monarchy:

> In England as elsewhere the new monarchy did not emerge fully developed in the year 1485 or in any other year. This factor was not always recognised.

Another challenge to the idea of 'new monarchy' came from the historian Geoffrey Elton. In *The Tudor Revolution in Government* (1953) he shifted the development of the new monarchy forward to the 1530s. It was the reforming work of Henry VIII's great minister, Thomas Cromwell, that saw the creation of modern government in England; not the contributions of Edward IV or Henry VII which made the vital difference between old and new. Elton also believed that the very idea of a new monarchy was unhelpful and that it 'only confuses and ought to be abolished'.

Since then, other historians have challenged Elton's ideas. S. B. Chrimes wrote an important biography of Henry VII published in 1972. He believed that any idea that the government of the Tudors was a fundamental change to the existing medieval system was wrong:

> His (Henry's) was not an original mind; he was no great innovator. He was rather a highly skilful builder on existing foundations … He could bring an essentially medieval spirit and practice of government to its highest point of effectiveness without in any important way changing its character.

Other historians studying the 15th century have emphasised continuity rather than change as being the chief feature of Henry VII's government of England. In an important study of the idea of a new monarchy, published in 1988, Anthony Goodman wrote that in spite of new interpretations, 'the concept of the new monarchy … still hovers around works on 16th-century England. Its wraith-like presence has proved hard to exorcise.'

Recent views of Henry VII's reign

Latterly, historians have tended to argue as to whether or not Henry VII was continuing the work of his Yorkist predecessors in governing England and their views are varied. Historians of 15th-century England argue that the Wars of the Roses did not see such a breakdown of central government as earlier historians had believed and that the period 1471 to 1534 was one of continuity rather than change. However, others have argued that the idea of continuity between Henry VII and his predecessors has been exaggerated. Alexander Grant, in his pamphlet on Henry VII (1985), believed that although there were similarities between the reign of Edward IV and that of Henry VII the differences were more important. For example, in their administration of Crown lands Henry was more concerned with their revenue-raising potential, while Edward IV was more concerned to use them to reward his family and supporters. In Grant's view it was Henry's personal control over government that made his reign unique rather than any changes in the machinery of government:

> However, the level and extent of Henry's personal control was much greater than that of any of his predecessors; indeed in this respect he is perhaps unique … both through fortunate circumstances and royal policy – Henry came closer to solving the problems of governing England than any of his predecessors had done.

In regard to Henry's use of 'new men', recent historians have stressed continuity. Henry VII's use of the gentry to run his government was not totally new, and in any case the idea of a 'middle class' was then unknown. Also the role of the nobility – both as members of the royal council, while often at the same time exercising important local and regional influence on the king's behalf – has received attention in recent studies. In spite of his use of recognisances as a means of controlling the nobility, the nobles remained vital to successful royal government.

Whatever the changing views on Henry VII and whether or not his rule represented continuity or change, there is no doubt that by the time of his death in 1509 the king had gone a long way to restoring respect for the power of the Crown. As John Guy wrote in *Tudor England* (1988):

> Henry VII's reign was distinguished by sober statesmanship. Bosworth's victor was a stabiliser; he could be ruthless and severe but he was neither bloodthirsty or egoistical … Henry also attempted to centralise English politics. The Tudor court began to exercise magnetic influence, and if much territorial power still lay in the hands of regional magnates, faction was tamed by recognisance and the exaction of royal prerogative rights by the Council Learned. Lastly, Henry's diplomatic and security measures guaranteed his dynastic survival.

Finally, the Italian Polydore Vergil, who knew Henry VII and whose *Anglia Historia* was published some years after the King's death, wrote of Henry:

> He knew well how to maintain his royal majesty and all which appertains to kingship at every time and in every place. He was most fortunate in war, although he was constitutionally inclined to peace than to war. He cherished justice above all things … Consequently he was greatly regretted on that account by all of his subjects, who had been able to conduct their lives peaceably, far removed from the assaults and evil doings of scoundrels.

1. How far can the reign of Henry VII be regarded as a success by the time of his death in 1509?

2. Why do you think historians differ over whether Henry VII created a new monarchy?

Source-based questions: Henry VII and the problems of law and order

SOURCE A

The king, our sovereign lord, remembers how by unlawful maintenances and the giving of liveries, signs and tokens, and retainers by indenture, promises, paths, writing or otherwise; embraceries [corrupting of juries] of his subjects … by taking of money by juries, by great riots and unlawful assemblies; good rule in this realm is almost defeated … The laws of the land have little effect, to the increase of murders, robberies, perjuries and the insecurity of all men and the losses of their lands and goods to the great displeasure of almighty God.

From the Star Chamber Act of 1487.

SOURCE B

A decree made in affirmation of an order taken by the Mayor and commons of Plymouth for the expulsion of Nicholas Lowe and Avice his wife, out of Plymouth for their misdemeanours and evil living in the keeping of brothels, night watching beyond reasonable hours, maintaining and keeping dicers, carders, gamblers and other misgoverned and evilly disposed persons. And Sir John Croker, knight and his sons and servants, by the same decree ordered not to maintain or uphold the said persons in the said case against the Mayor and commons. And for having done so up to the present they are ordered to keep the peace upon pain of a fine of 300 marks [= £200].

A case before the Council in Star Chamber, 6 May 1494.

SOURCE C

The king … reserved from the beginning of his realm the retainer to himself of all his subjects in the county (of Kent), to avoid the divisions, enormities, and inconveniences that otherwise might have ensured among them … It has come to the knowledge of our said Soveriegn Lord (the king) that retainers within his said county, as well as liveries, tokens … promises and badges … do daily increase, against his mind and the laws against them.

His Highness, having tender respect to the governance of his subjects and intending his laws to be observed, charges and expressly commands that none of his subjects, within his said county presume to take upon them to use any retainers, or to be retained by livery or wages … but to

reserve themselves wholly to his person and to be ready to serve him as they will be commanded … when and as often as shall be required.

From a royal proclamation prohibiting retaining in Kent, 1502.

SOURCE D

In government he was shrewd and prudent, so that none dared to get the better of him through deceit or guile … those of his subjects who were indebted to him and who did not pay him due honour or who were generous only with promises he treated with harsh severity.

He knew well how to maintain his royal majesty and all which is owed to kingship at every time and in every place …

He cherished justice above all things; as a result he vigorously punished violence, manslaughter and every other kind of wickedness whatsoever. Consequently, he was greatly regretted on that account by all of his subjects who had been able to conduct their lives peaceably far removed from the assaults and evil doings of scoundrels.

From a description of Henry VII by Polydore Vergil, 1513.

---

1. Explain what is meant in the context of Henry VII's policies on law and order by the following phrases:

a) 'unlawful maintenances' (Source A)

b) 'liveries' (Sources A and C).

2. Study Sources A and B.

How far does Source B reflect the view in Source A that the 'good rule in this realm is almost defeated'?

3. Study Source C.

How useful is this source as evidence of Henry VII's determination to enforce law and order in his kingdom?

4. Using all the sources above and the information in this chapter, explain how successful you think Henry VII was in re-establishing respect for the law and strong government in England between 1485 and 1509.

The age of Wolsey

3.1 How far did Henry VIII break with both his father's policies and style of kingship between 1509 and 1514?

3.2 Why did Thomas Wolsey emerge as the King's chief minister by 1515?

3.3 To what extent did Henry VIII and Wolsey succeed in promoting England as a significant European power, 1515–1529?

3.4 How far was Wolsey's conduct of domestic policy concerned with the reform of the Church and Government?

3.5 Was Wolsey the architect of his own downfall?

3.6 Historical interpretation: Wolsey: an assessment

Key Issues

- Did Henry VIII start a new style of kingship between 1509 and 1529?

- How successful was Wolsey as Henry VIII's chief minister between 1515 and 1529?

- To what extent were Church and State reformed under Wolsey?

Framework of Events

1509	21 April: death of Henry VII and accession of Henry VIII
	11 June: Henry VIII marries Catherine of Aragon
1511	England joins the Holy League (Pope Julius II) against France
1512	Declaration of war on France
	Failure of Dorset expedition to recapture English lands in SW France
1513	Wolsey organises Henry VIII's expedition to France
	22 August: Battle of the Spurs
	September: Scottish invaders defeated at Battle of Flodden. King James IV is killed
1514	Anglo–French treaty signed at St Germaine-en-Laye
	Marriage of Henry VIII's sister Mary to Louis XII of France
	September: Thomas Wolsey becomes Archbishop of York
1515	January: death of Louis XII of France. Francis I becomes King of France
	July: secret marriage of Mary to Charles Brandon, Duke of Suffolk, in Paris
	September: Wolsey is made a cardinal by Pope Leo X
	December: Wolsey is appointed Lord Chancellor
1516	Birth of Princess Mary at Greenwich
1517	Wolsey establishes a commission to investigate enclosures
1518	September: Wolsey is appointed Papal Legate
	5 October: Treaty of London establishes peace between the European powers
1519	Charles, grandson of Emperor Maximilian, becomes Holy Roman Emperor
1520	Field of the Cloth of Gold
1521	May: trial and execution of third Duke of Buckingham
	October: Pope bestows the title 'Fidei Defensor ('Defender of the Faith') on Henry VIII in gratitude for the King's book *In Defence of the Seven Sacraments* which condemned Martin Luther's ideas
1522	July: Treaty of Windsor between England and the Empire
	Duke of Suffolk leads unsuccessful expedition against France

1523	Parliament grants only half the subsidy required by Wolsey for the war. Failed English expedition against France
1524	Wolsey is made Papal Legate for life
1525	Francis I is defeated and captured by Charles V at Pavia. Charles V repudiates Treaty of Windsor and his engagement to Princess Mary. Anglo–French Treaty of the More
1526	England joins the League of Cognac against the Empire
1527	Henry VIII announces his intention to divorce Catherine of Aragon
1528	Divorce campaign continues
1529	July: failure of Legatine Court at Blackfriars to settle the divorce when the case is recalled to Rome. October: fall of Wolsey from power. November: opening of the Reformation Parliament.

Overview

Thomas Wolsey (?1475–1530)

Lord Chancellor: The king's minister responsible for the running and supervision of all the kingdom's law courts. He was senior judge and sat regularly in the Court of Chancery (see page 19). The Lord Chancellor also kept and looked after the Great Seal of England which was used to authorise all important official State business.

THE first half of the reign of Henry VIII has often been regarded as a period lacking achievement. It was dominated by the figure of Thomas Wolsey, who was Henry's chief minister between 1515 and 1529. Wolsey enjoyed a period in power longer than those of most other English statesmen.

In 1509 the accession of the young Henry VIII was welcomed by his subjects, especially the nobility (noble class), who were affected by the policies of Henry VII's later years. Henry VIII was seen as the ideal of the Renaissance prince – well-educated, a sportsman and interested in music and the arts. However, the king wished for war against France and in 1511 he had his way. After early setbacks, an expedition was sent to France in 1513 where success was achieved on the battlefield. At the same time, the Scots were beaten decisively at the battle of Flodden Field, which did much to remove the threat from north of the border for a generation. A successful peace was made with France in 1514 and Henry VIII's younger sister, Mary, was married to the French King, Louis XII. Since Henry VIII was married to Catherine of Aragon, the Tudor dynasty was now related to the royal families of both France and Spain.

The most lasting result of the war with France was the emergence of Thomas Wolsey as chief minister. Wolsey had already shown his abilities both as an administrator and as a diplomat. By 1515 he was a cardinal, Archbishop of York and **Lord Chancellor**. As Henry VIII's chief minister, Wolsey's record was mixed. He combined great abilities with a vast capacity for work and was full of ideas for the reform of both church and government. Wolsey introduced some important legal reforms to Star Chamber and made the law more accessible for poorer people. He also had an interest in social reform and tackled what were seen then as the evils of enclosures, but with limited success. Wolsey had plans to reform the Church. However, they came to little due to pressures of work, while his own lifestyle and vast income from the Church did not suggest an enthusiasm for reform.

Besides domestic policy, Wolsey had to spend much of his time dealing with foreign affairs. Historians are divided on his aims. Was the Cardinal in pursuit of a peace policy? Did he put the interests of the Pope first? Did the interests of

Wolsey's master, Henry VIII, always come first? On balance, Wolsey was probably concerned to promote the importance of England's role in Europe. Perhaps he was unlucky that he was in power during the beginnings of the Habsburg–Valois rivalry (see page 84). Wolsey's attempts to mediate between France and the Empire failed and by 1522 England was an ally of Charles V, the Holy Roman Emperor, in his war against France. Due to lack of resources, the English achieved little in the war, and in 1525 were ignored by Charles V after his decisive defeat of the French at Pavia. This humiliation led to the so-called 'diplomatic revolution', when Henry VIII and Wolsey made peace with France and encouraged the setting up of the anti-Habsburg alliance in the League of Cognac (1526).

By 1526–27 English foreign policy was increasingly dominated by Henry VIII's wish for an annulment of his marriage to Catherine of Aragon. The King feared that the lack of a legitimate male heir would mean chaos if he died suddenly. To him the need for a second marriage was vital for England. Between 1527 and 1529, Wolsey tried to obtain a divorce for his master, but the international situation was against him. The Pope was unable to offend Charles V since his army had sacked Rome in 1527. The Emperor would not agree to his aunt Catherine's marriage being annulled, as that would be an insult to Habsburg honour. By 1529 it was clear that Wolsey had failed. Henry VIII was furious. Partly due to the influence of others, not least Anne Boleyn, the King dismissed Wolsey in October 1529. In 1530 the Cardinal was accused of treason and died on his way south to face trial and probable execution.

Since his death, Wolsey has remained a controversial figure. Was he a great statesman, a man of solid achievements? Or was he merely an able man in love with power, who beyond attempting to serve Henry VIII well, achieved little?

3.1 How far did Henry VIII break with both his father's policies and style of kingship between 1509 and 1514?

The young Henry: an example of all the kingly virtues?

In April 1509 the young Henry VIII, not quite 18 years of age, presented a contrasting image to that of his dead father. Henry VII had died worn down by the never-ending work in governing England and protecting his new dynasty against conspiracies real and imaginary. The last years of his reign had seen the nobility ruthlessly controlled by Henry's system of bonds and recognisances (see page 54), supervised by the Council Learned.

The last years of Henry VII's rule had seen an absence of war and of foreign adventures. The English upper classes were bored with the rule of a strong king, prematurely aged and worn down by the cares of government. The succession of a youthful king, bursting with energy and determined to enjoy himself, was welcomed by the nobility and by the rest of the nation too.

In May 1509, Thomas More wrote to his friend, the great scholar Desiderius Erasmus, about the energetic atmosphere now to be found in England under the new king's rule:

If you could see how all the world here is rejoicing in the possession of so great a prince, how his life is all their desire you could not contain your tears for joy. The heavens laugh, the earth exults, all things are full of milk, of honey and of nectar. Avarice [greed; love of money] is expelled the country … Our king does not wish for gold or gems or precious stones, but virtue, glory and immortality.

So in a few weeks the atmosphere at the English Court had changed totally. But what was the new king really like? Little is known of Henry VIII's personality before he succeeded to the throne in April 1509. This was because the old king had been very worried that nothing should happen to his only surviving male heir. The young Henry was closely supervised by his over-anxious father. We do know that the new king had been born at Greenwich in 1491. Henry received a sound education – his tutor was the poet John Skelton. Henry was taught Latin and French, and later some Spanish and Italian. Apart from languages, Henry had an aptitude for mathematics and to an extent was versed in theology (religious study) too, as his father may originally have intended him for a career in the Church. Henry also received a good musical education although details of this are not well-known.

From his earliest years honours were heaped on the young prince. When he was three he was made Duke of York and Lord Lieutenant of Ireland – but his father kept the revenues. Before 1509 Henry had little in the way of political education. Unlike his brother Arthur, who was sent to the Welsh Marches, Henry had not been in a position to learn how to deal with his future subjects.

Such was the adolescent who found himself king in April 1509. It is not surprising that Henry soon threw off any controls. From the first, he was quick to spend even more time indulging his favourite sport of **tilting**. Besides languages, music and mathematics, Henry VIII had read the **courtly romances** thoroughly and was much influenced by the then fashionable ideas concerning chivalry and the importance of knightly virtues. The idea of the **perfect knight** was fashionable in the Courts of northern Europe, especially Burgundy. The magnificence of that Court was copied elsewhere, not least in England now that the country had its own new king determined to be the perfect knight. Henry was also influenced by the **'New Learning'** of the Renaissance, but was motivated by the traditional concerns of the upper classes to shine in the tiltyard, at the joust and on the battlefield. Not for the new king the boredom of checking the royal accounts: that could be left for others. For much of his long reign, Henry VIII was very unwilling to worry himself with the daily burdens of government and administration. However, when his interest was aroused – as with foreign policy, or later in the matter of the divorce – he was quite capable of sustained hard work. In 1509 such worries lay in the future and Henry enjoyed himself in a round of feasting, hunting, tournaments and other pleasures.

Physically, Henry looked the part as a king. He was six feet two inches [188 cm] tall – when the average height was around five feet six or seven [167–170 cm] for most men. Besides his height, the young king was well-made, strong and knew how to make the best use of his size to impress, especially as he dressed in rich and fashionable clothes. Most of Henry VIII's portraits show how he wished to leave an image of his strength and power. Henry seems to have succeeded in impressing both his subjects and foreign

Tilting: An aspect of the tournament (where knights meet and compete): two horsemen gallop towards one another on either side of the 'tilt', each holding a lance. The point of the exercise is to dismount the other rider.

Courtly romances: These were the novels of the upper classes of early 16th-century Europe. In England Sir Thomas Malory's *Le Morte d'Arthur* was very popular, with stories of King Arthur and the Knights of the Round Table.

Perfect knight: This was ideal for the courtiers of Europe. The perfect knight excelled in feats of arms and upheld the honour of his lady against all comers. Also, he fought for justice and was on the side of those who had been wronged by the wicked and powerful.

'New learning': Reference to the Humanists (see page 133) and their insistence on the study of Latin and the re-discovered Greek language. It also referred to the study of the Bible using its original languages of Hebrew and Greek.

ambassadors. Ten years into his reign (1519) the Venetian ambassador, Sebastian Guistiniani, in what is one of the most famous passages, wrote of the King:

> His Majesty is 29 years old and extremely handsome. Nature could not have done more for him. He is much handsomer than the king of France; very fair and his whole frame admirably proportioned. On hearing that Francis I wore a beard he allowed his own to grow, and as it is reddish, he now has a beard which looks like gold. He is very accomplished, a good musician, composes well, is a most capital horseman, speaks good Latin, French and Spanish. He is very religious … He is very fond of hunting and never takes this diversion without tiring eight or ten horses, which he causes to be stationed beforehand along the way he means to take. When one is tired he mounts another, and before he gets home they are all exhausted. He is extremely fond of tennis, at which it is the prettiest thing to see him play, his fair skin glowing through a shirt of the finest texture.

In which ways was the young Henry VIII such a contrast to his father Henry VII?

What problems did Henry VIII face on becoming king in 1509?

Marriage

The first big problem facing Henry was that of marriage. It was vital that the king should be married as soon as possible so that the process of producing the all-important male heir could begin. Henry had no living close male relatives. His older sister, Margaret, was married to James IV of Scotland, who was an uncertain ally. His younger sister, Mary, was 13 in 1509 and already a pawn in the diplomatic world of royal marriages. The idea of a female monarch if Henry should die did not appeal to the men who controlled and dominated politics in England in the early years of the 16th century.

However, the marriage problem was soon solved. Within a few weeks of becoming king, Henry married the Spanish princess, Catherine of Aragon. Catherine had been married to Henry's older brother, Arthur, in 1501. After Arthur's death the following year, Catherine was kept in England by Henry VII who wanted to maintain the Spanish connection which made his dynasty more acceptable in European royal circles. By 1503 Henry VII had made a new treaty for his remaining son to marry Catherine. However, the law of the Church did not allow a man to marry his brother's widow and permission had to be obtained from the Pope. In 1504 Henry VII received the necessary permission from Pope Julius II for the marriage to go ahead.

Meanwhile, Catherine remained in England, often neglected, as a useful pawn in Henry VII's game of diplomacy with her father, Ferdinand of Spain. In 1509 Catherine's luck changed. The new king, pressured by his Council, married her. Catherine was seven years older than Henry, but perhaps her maturity and strength of character appealed to the young king, as much as her attractiveness. The marriage was to last for nearly 20 years and in 1509 there was no sign of how its failure would help to change English history so decisively. In the shorter term, Catherine from the first used her influence with Henry in the interests of Spain. The historian P. J. Helm wrote of Catherine:

> In her eyes England was a branch of the family business, as it is clear from her letters to her father, Ferdinand of Aragon, in which she wrote: 'These kingdoms of your Highness are in great tranquility.'

Empson and Dudley

The second problem facing Henry VIII was the supposed tyranny of his father's later years and the work of the Council Learned with its use of bonds and recognisances (see page 54) aimed at keeping the nobility and gentry loyal to the king. The new king was soon listening to the many complaints unleashed in the backlash against his father's rule. Soon Richard Empson and Edmund Dudley, Henry VII's most hated 'enforcers', found themselves arrested and in the Tower of London. This backlash was to lead to the abolition of the Council Learned in Henry's first Parliament (January–February 1510). Also the Council set up special commissioners of **Oyer and Terminer** to look into grievances against the late king's government and agents throughout the kingdom. However, the commissioners found that the majority of complaints had been petty and the reaction against Henry VII's government was founded on little hard evidence of oppression. Nonetheless, Henry VIII and his closest advisers were worried by the outburst. In a calculated attempt to enhance the King's popularity, Empson and Dudley were convicted of treason in what were 'show trials'.

Attempts to **attaint** the two men in Parliament failed and after nearly a year in prison, both were beheaded. As the historian John Guy wrote: 'The executions were a calculated ploy to enable the new regime to profit from the stability won by Henry VII without incurring any of its attendant stigma.'

So in the earliest days of his reign Henry VIII exhibited a ruthless streak, as well as a wish to be popular with his subjects – both of which would be seen again during his reign.

To what extent did Henry VIII follow different policies in the years 1509–1511?

Henry VIII had no political experience when he became king. In spite of his early actions, he had to rely on his father's councillors. The most important of these were William Warham (Archbishop of Canterbury and Lord Chancellor), Richard Fox (Lord Privy Seal), John de Vere (Earl of Oxford) and Thomas Howard (Earl of Surrey and Lord Treasurer). The clerics Warham and Fox were particularly important. They preferred the policy of peace of their late master, Henry VII. Peace had the attraction of being cheap, but would Henry VIII follow their advice?

In fact, Henry did not. He yearned to go to war. Also, the king was surrounded by his Gentlemen of the Privy Chamber and other young courtiers, all of whom were bored by the peace of the last years of Henry VII and wanted military glory and adventure.

In spite of Henry VIII's wishes to go to war, especially with France, it took time. In fact, in March 1510 a peace treaty was signed with France. This was the work of those on the Council who were against war, such as Warham and Fox. Their view continued to prevail as late as 1511 when a Great Council discussed the possibilities of war. They argued successfully that it would be expensive and perhaps threaten England's safety. However, soon afterwards Henry VIII's will prevailed and England found itself at war with France. This change was because the Council was divided and the old soldier, the Earl of Surrey, resented the peace policies of the clerical councillors. Also the king listened to the advice of his wife, Catherine of Aragon. She was concerned to promote her father Ferdinand's interests. He wanted a war with France because he wished to

Oyer and Terminer: A commission which was set to hear and decide on whether or not there was a case to answer in specified crimes in a certain region. Its members would normally be named royal judges or members of the nobility and gentry.

Attaint: The loss of rights when a man was convicted by Parliament of treason or some other serious crime. It applied to the man's heirs too and meant the loss of the family estate.

How far do you think the following were the result of Henry VIII's own wishes:

a) his marriage to Catherine of Aragon

b) the execution of Empson and Dudley?

take over the small kingdom of Navarre, then under French influence. Besides these factors, the international situation had changed. In 1508 the League of Cambrai had been formed by Pope Julius II to attack Venice. All of Europe's major powers, except England, had joined it. By 1510 this League had been too successful for Julius' taste. French victories in northern Italy threatened the independence of Italy and of the Papal States (see page 85) in particular. The Pope began to revive his normal policy of playing off the French against the Spanish to keep his own freedom of action. By October 1511 the Pope succeeded in forming the Holy League with Spain and Venice against France. Would England join?

As far as Henry VIII was concerned the answer was 'yes'. The king was an enthusiastic member of the Church. To take up its quarrel with the French, England's traditional enemy, appealed both to his religious and warlike interests. So in November 1511 England joined the League of Cambrai.

Henry's first war, 1511–1514: a success or a waste of resources?

In February 1512 Parliament met and granted Henry VIII the money to fight France. In April Henry declared war. He was guided by the advice of his father-in-law, Ferdinand of Aragon. The English government sent an expedition under the Marquis of Dorset to help the Spanish, which landed near Bayonne. It was hoped that this would be the beginning of the re-conquest of the English Crown's former territories in south-western France. In the event, the English force received little help from Spain. Ferdinand used it to distract the French while he invaded and took over the small kingdom of Navarre. Within a few months ill-discipline, dysentery and drunkenness reduced the Marquis of Dorset's force to a rabble which was recalled to England in disgrace.

At sea, Henry's navy was defeated at Brest (France) in April 1513. The fleet's admiral, a close companion of the king, Sir Edward Howard, was killed in the fighting. So far, the revival of England's military glory looked to be rather premature.

However, setbacks only inspired Henry VIII to further efforts. A new army of about 30,000 men was organised, equipped and sent to Calais, led by the king in person. Henry VIII had decided to become a second Henry V and invade France. The provisioning, equipping and transporting of what was quite a powerful force was the work of the **King's Almoner** – a rapidly rising new political star, Thomas Wolsey.

After landing in France in late June 1513 the English army moved off not towards Paris but towards Flanders. It was on its way to help Henry's ally, the Emperor Maximilian, in capturing the French fortress of Therouanne which was a threat to Maximilian's territories in the Netherlands. A French cavalry force, sent to relieve the fortress, was easily routed in a skirmish by the English. This clash, due to the speed of the French retreat, was dubbed 'the Battle of the Spurs' by the English and claimed as a great victory. Soon after, Therouanne fell to the English who also captured the larger town of Tournai after a brief siege. Henry VIII had achieved his military glory and returned home in triumph. However, the sunshine of the king's achievements was rather dimmed by what had happened in the north of England while he had been campaigning in France.

Since his accession as king in 1509, Henry's relations with his brother-in-law James IV, King of Scotland, had got worse. By 1512 James was in alliance with France. The next year he crossed the border with the largest

---

How far was Henry VIII's decision to go to war with France in 1511 due to his search for glory and adventure?

King's Almoner: The official who was responsible for making those payments which the king wished to spend on charity and deserving causes.

Emperor Maximilian (1459–1519)
Succeeded his father as Holy Roman Emperor in 1493. He married Mary, heiress of Charles the Bold (Duke of Burgundy). Their son Philip married Joanna, heiress to both Aragon and Castile (Spain), so uniting the houses of Castile and Hapsburg. Maximilian was usually short of money and was very unreliable as an ally – as both Henry VII and Henry VIII knew to their cost.

Regent: Person who is given royal authority on behalf of another. It usually applies when the monarch is a minor (under age).

1. *How effectively did England wage war between 1511 and 1514?*

2. *To what extent did the young Henry VIII break with his father's policies and style of kingship between 1511 and 1514?*

raiding party to invade England for generations. Queen Catherine, acting as governor of the realm in Henry's absence, and the King's ministers raised a large army to meet the Scottish threat. Under the able leadership of the Earl of Surrey it defeated the Scots at Flodden in September 1513. This defeat was a disaster for Scotland. James IV and over 10,000 of his subjects, including many of the Scottish nobility, were killed in the battle. However, Henry did little to exploit the victory. He left his sister Margaret to act as **regent** for her infant son, James, hoping that she would look after England's interests there. As far as the war was concerned, Scotland had been neutralised.

The war with France continued in 1514, but it was expensive and increasing pressure was being put on Henry VIII by his ministers to settle for peace. Both the Emperor Maximilian and Henry's father-in-law, Ferdinand of Aragon, made peace with France. It looked as if Henry VIII would have to fight the French alone. Then, in August 1514, a peace treaty was made with France. It was the result of the diplomatic skills of Henry's new minister, Thomas Wolsey. Under the terms of the treaty, Henry kept Tournai and received a much increased annual French pension for agreeing not to try to regain his French inheritance in future. Also, the marriage was arranged between the widowed French King, Louis XII, and Henry's younger sister Mary. It took place in October 1514, much to Mary's personal disgust. However, Henry was well-pleased. He had come out of the war with military glory, a new possession in France and a new chief minister, Thomas Wolsey. Against that the Treasury was bankrupt and Henry had used up any possible treasure left by his father.

The campaign of 1513: detail from a painting at Hampton Court showing Henry VIII's meeting with Maximilian I, the 'Battle of the Spurs' and the siege of Tournai.

3.2 Why did Thomas Wolsey emerge as the king's chief minister by 1515?

By 1514 Wolsey was the rising star at Henry VIII's Court. He had outshone all his other rivals for power. Why did this middle-aged cleric suddenly shoot from junior office in 1509 to become Henry VIII's chief minister and favourite by 1515?

The career of Thomas Wolsey

1472?	Born in Ipswich, the son of a butcher and innkeeper
1487	Takes his BA degree at Magdalen College, Oxford, aged 15 – 'the boy bachelor'
1498	Wolsey is ordained as priest
1499	Appointed bursar of Magdalen College but has to resign
1502–1503	Chaplain to Archbishop Deane of Canterbury
1503–1507	Chaplain to the Deputy (Governor) of Calais (France)
1507–1509	Chaplain to Henry VII. Wolsey is sent on diplomatic missions
1509	Appointed Royal Almoner by Henry VIII
1510	Appointed a royal councillor
1513	Organiser of Henry VII's successful royal expedition to France
1514	As Bishop of Lincoln, negotiates peace with France. Becomes Archbishop of York
1515	Created a cardinal by Pole Leo X. Appointed Lord Chancellor by Henry VIII
1518	Wolsey enjoys the diplomatic success of Treaty of London. Appointed papal legate by Pope Leo X
1520	Wolsey organises meeting between Henry VII and Francis I at Field of the Cloth of Gold
1521	The Treaty of Bruges with Emperor Charles V against France
1522–23	The so-called 'Grand Enterprise' is launched against France with no great success
1523	Wolsey's attempts to raise money for war are opposed in Parliament
1525	Francis I is defeated and captured at Pavia by Emperor Charles V. England's plans to divide France are rejected by Charles. Attempt to raise money by means of the Amicable Grant fails and nearly causes widespread rebellion.
1526–27	So-called 'Diplomatic Revolution': Wolsey negotiates peace with France
1527–29	Wolsey's attempts to obtain annulment of Henry VIII's marriage
1529	Failure of the legantine court held at Blackfriars (London) as divorce case is recalled to Rome. Wolsey falls from power
1530	November: death of Wolsey on his way to London to be tried for treason.

Wolsey's early career to 1509

Thomas Wolsey was born in either 1472 or 1473. He was the son of a butcher and innkeeper of Ipswich in the county of Suffolk. The boy showed great promise. He was sent to Magdalen College, Oxford, where he soon outshone his fellow students. Wolsey graduated with a Batchelor of Arts (BA) degree by the age of 15. He was young even by 16th-century standards. Within a few years he had become both a fellow and bursar (treasurer) of his college, as well as the Master of Magdalen School. Due to his fellowship, Wolsey had to become a priest and it looked as if a promising academic career lay before him. But Wolsey never went on to take the normal next step upwards for an ambitious academic – a doctorate in canon law (the law of the Church). Instead he was to leave Oxford shortly afterwards in some sort of disgrace. According to the stories told about Wolsey's early years, he was sent packing because as bursar he overspent on the building works without first obtaining the proper permission from the other fellows of the college. If true, the story confirms one thing about Wolsey's character – a tendency to use his initiative and to worry about the consequences later.

Chaplaincies: Clerics acting in private chapel of a great person or institution.

The years following Wolsey's departure from Oxford saw him holding a number of **chaplaincies** or tutorships in important households. However, bad luck seemed to follow the future minister's career in finding the patron (page 221) who would be essential if he was to make a career at Court. One employer, Henry Deane, died less than two years after becoming Archbishop of Canterbury in 1503. Another, the Marquis of Dorset, was very much out of favour with Henry VII. It seemed as if Wolsey was going to become just another disappointed middle-aged cleric. The last of Wolsey's domestic appointments was as chaplain to the Deputy (governor) of Calais. The Deputy died in 1507, but not before he had recommended Wolsey to the king, who made him a royal chaplain. At last, Wolsey had arrived at the Royal Court. But would he ever be more than a minor office-holder?

Why did Wolsey rise so rapidly?

The first piece of good luck for Wolsey was the accession of Henry VIII in 1509. The arrival of the new king transformed the Court. The nobility, liberated from Henry VII, flexed their political muscles and the old king's ministers fought to retain their influence. This fluid situation around the new and impressionable king provided opportunities for ambitious men and Wolsey soon found himself drawn into this situation. Late in 1509 Wolsey was made Royal Almoner and a member of the Council. He owed this to the patronage of the Lord Privy Seal, Richard Fox, who recognised in Wolsey a man of ability who could be useful at Court.

As a lower-ranking councillor, Wolsey was one of those who maintained links between the king and his important ministers, who due to the pressure of business could not always be in daily attendance on the king. Wolsey probably kept Fox informed of the actions of the 'war party' in their attempts to encourage Henry VIII's warlike ambitions, as his earliest surviving letter to Fox (September 1511) tells us. At this stage of his career Wolsey was, like his patron Fox, opposed to the war party, but a year later he had totally changed his position on this. Why?

This change of mind was probably because the ambitious Wolsey had grasped the fact that Henry's enthusiasm for war against France and for military glory was deadly serious and not just a passing phase. By the early months of 1512 it was clear that Henry wanted war and the 'war party', especially the Earl of Surrey and his supporters, had won. Wolsey was determined to be on the winning side. If the king wanted war, so be it. As George Cavendish, Wolsey's **gentleman usher** and his first biographer, wrote of the Cardinal: 'he was the most earnest and the readiest among all the Council to advance the king's only will and pleasure without any respect to the case'.

Gentleman usher: An officer in the household of a great person who was of gentry status. His job was to supervise public ceremonies and processions.

However, Wolsey did not succeed by simply assessing which way Henry VIII's mind was working and then agreeing with him. He also possessed the gift of being able to speak well and persuasively, and this impressed the King. Wolsey was outstandingly good at presenting a case in Council or to the King in private. As George Cavendish wrote of him: 'He had a filed tongue and ornate eloquence.'

In addition, it was Wolsey who was given the mammoth task of organising Henry VIII's French expedition of 1513. Faced by the problems of transport, weaponry and supplies, Wolsey overcame them all through his capacity to work exceptionally long hours. He also showed himself to be an excellent diplomat in the negotiations for peace with France in 1514. By the autumn of 1514 Wolsey was established high in the royal favour.

How did Wolsey make certain of his power?

From 1513 onwards Wolsey began to be richly rewarded for his advice and efficiency. Between 1513 and 1515 he received rapid promotion in the Church. In 1513 he became Dean of York and later that year Bishop of Tournai, Henry VIII's recent conquest. In 1514 Wolsey received the bishopric of Lincoln and later that year was made Archbishop of York, the second highest post in the English Church. This position gave him great status and made him a peer of the realm, as well as the possessor of great wealth. The next year saw Wolsey made a cardinal by the Pope, at Henry VIII's urgent request. Wolsey was now a prince of the Church, one of those who could elect a new pope, and he was quick to wear the impressive scarlet robes that marked his new status.

As well as gaining power in the Church, Wolsey now consolidated his position politically. The two lynchpins of much of English government since the early 1500s, Archbishop Warham of Canterbury and Bishop Fox of Winchester made way for Wolsey. In 1515 Warham resigned as Lord Chancellor and withdrew to Canterbury where he was to deny Wolsey his one remaining ambition to succeed him there as archbishop by living on until 1532. In early 1516 Fox resigned the Privy Seal and returned to Winchester to devote his remaining years and energies to his **diocese**. Both men had spent long years in power and were probably happy to leave the field open to Wolsey, especially Fox.

It did not take Wolsey long to overshadow the remaining powerful men in the Council. These were the dukes of Norfolk (formerly the Earl of Surrey), Buckingham and Suffolk (Charles Brandon, created Duke of Suffolk in 1514). Brandon had been a favourite of Henry VIII and his chief jousting companion since 1509. Like Henry himself he was a large, handsome, outgoing and athletic man – just the type that appealed to the king. Also he was a clever courtier, who in spite of occasional falls from Henry's favour, remained close to the king until his death in 1546.

On 1 January 1515, Louis XII, King of France, died suddenly. This meant that Mary Tudor was now free of her hated marriage. Brandon was sent to escort the now ex-queen of France back to England. Mary, determined not to be married off again by her brother in pursuit of one of his diplomatic schemes, married Brandon in secret. Henry VIII was consulted about the couple marrying and was not hostile to the idea, but the secrecy and haste of the actual marriage put the newly-weds in real danger of losing Henry's favour. However, Wolsey offered to mediate with the King and Brandon willingly agreed to this. In the end, the newly-wed couple and the King were reconciled and Brandon found himself hitched to Wolsey's rising star for a while. As for Buckingham and the newly-restored Duke of Norfolk, Wolsey merely sidelined them.

Explain how Wolsey succeeded in establishing himself in the King's favour by the end of 1514.

Diocese: Area under the administrative care of a bishop. Sometimes called a bishopric.

Charles Brandon, Duke of Suffolk (1484–1546)
Son of Henry VII's standard-bearer who fell at the battle of Bosworth Field (1485). Brandon became a favourite of Henry VIII in the early years of his reign as his jousting and tilting companion. In 1514 he was created Duke of Suffolk and in 1515 married Mary, sister of Henry VIII and widow of Louis XII. By the 1520s he was a political opponent of Wolsey on the Council. He was one of those responsible for the cardinal's downfall in 1529. In spite of some periods of disfavour, Brandon remained quite close his brother-in-law, Henry VIII.

By the end of 1515 there were no competing factions on the Council. Wolsey was in charge of government and royal favour centred on him. For the next 14 years until his fall from power in 1529, the cardinal ruled England on behalf of his master, the King. Wolsey's enemies, of whom as the years passed there were increasing numbers, suggested that Wolsey was the real power in the land. Visitors were often so impressed by Wolsey's magnificence that they too began to see him as *alter rex* (literally, 'the other king'). The Venetian ambassador Guistiniani wrote of him in 1519:

> This cardinal is the first person who rules both the king and the entire kingdom. On the ambassador's first arrival in England he used to say to him, 'His Majesty will do so and so'; subsequently, by degrees he began to forget himself, and started to say, 'We shall do so and so'; now he has reached such a height that he says 'I shall do so and so'.

Later the poet John Skelton, formerly a tutor of Henry VIII, was very rude about the cardinal. In 1522–23 in his attack on Wolsey in his poem 'Why come ye not to Courte?' Skelton wrote:

> He ruleth all the roast
> With bragging and with boast.
> Borne upon every side
> With pomp and pride.

Perhaps not great poetry, but its meaning was unmistakable – Wolsey was finally in charge of government, including the king. However, the last was probably very unlikely. Wolsey did know how to influence Henry and to obtain his support for his policies but the Cardinal rarely made the mistake of taking his master for granted. As Wolsey's enemy, the papal tax collector and historian, Polydore Vergil, wrote (probably again around 1522–23) that the Cardinal took care how he influenced the King:

1. Why was Wolsey able to acquire so much power within the English Church?

2. How far was Wolsey's rise to power, and retention of it, due to his own abilities?

> Every time he wished to obtain something from Henry he introduced the matter casually into his conversation. Next he brought out some small present or other, a beautifully made dish, for example, or a jewel or ring or gift of that sort, and while the king was admiring the gift intently, Wolsey would cleverly bring forward the project on which his mind was fixed.

However he achieved and kept power, Wolsey was Henry VIII's chief minister for 14 years. He kept the king's trust, which was no mean achievement in itself.

3.3 To what extent did Henry VIII and Wolsey succeed in promoting England as a major European power, 1515–1529?

From the beginning of his reign Henry VIII had thirsted for glory. He wished to see England become a significant power in the affairs of Europe. Also, he wanted to regain England's lost lands in France. Therefore much of the diplomacy of the early years of his reign had these aims in view. The treaty signed at St Germaine-en-Laye in 1514 with the French was seen as an Anglo–French alliance. It had given Henry VIII the prestige he wanted, as well as ending what had been an expensive war. However, the cold reality of European affairs was that in the west the continent was dominated by

Field of the Cloth of Gold – the setting for the meeting of Francis I and Henry VIII in 1520. What message is this painting trying to convey of Henry VIII as king?

two powers – France and Spain. England did not possess the resources in terms of wealth and population to compete with either of them. English diplomacy could hope to exploit the differences between the two powers in England's interests. By doing so it would appear to be important on the European stage. That was the reality of power.

In 1515 Henry VIII had a chief minister who, like himself, loved pomp, publicity and display, and was happy enough to put considerable effort into that side of the diplomatic game too. If England was to appear to be an important power the image which was created abroad was important. From the start, Wolsey was concerned to impress France and Spain with the power of England and its king, and of course, that of its first minister. Famous diplomatic events such as the Treaty of London (1518) and the meeting between Henry VIII and Francis I at the Field of the Cloth of Gold (see picture) were notable for their magnificence, as this extract from an anonymous account of the Field of the Cloth of Gold meeting shows:

> Henry and the French king, Francis I, met in the valley called the Golden Dale between Guisnes and Arde where the French king had been staying. In this valley Henry pitched his marquee made of cloth of gold near where a banquet had been prepared. His Grace was accompanied by 500 horsemen and 3,000 foot soldiers, and the French king had a similar number of each.

All of this image-building had a serious purpose, namely to promote Henry VIII as an important player on the European stage. Then, as now, image was as important as reality.

What were Wolsey's aims in foreign policy?

Beyond promoting the interests of his master, Henry VIII, what were Wolsey's aims in foreign policy? Historians have often written as if foreign

Papal legate: An official who was appointed by the Pope to head a church mission or to represent him as Head of the Church in a particular country. The legate's orders could only be over-ridden by appealing successfully to the Pope himself.

Habsburg–Valois conflict: Wars which affected western and central Europe for much of the period 1515–59. The conflict was between France, ruled by the House of Valois, and the House of Habsburg which controlled Spain, lands in Italy, the Netherlands and Austria. The head of the House of Habsburg was also the Holy Roman Emperor. Warfare took place mainly in Italy and the Holy Roman Empire. The main period of fighting took place when Francis I was King of France (1515–47) and Charles V was Holy Roman Emperor (1519–56). Wars came to an end with the Treaty of Cateau-Cambresis of 1559.

What different views have historians put forward to explain Wolsey's foreign policy?

policy between 1515 and 1529 was Wolsey's: in fact, often it was not. Henry VIII, although open to persuasion and influence, still had to be convinced and Wolsey spent a great deal of his time doing this, both by letter and in person at his regular Sunday audiences with the king. Unfortunately, many of Wolsey's and Henry's conversations were never recorded, and where letters and treaties exist they have to be treated with great care by historians when they are trying to re-discover what the King and the Cardinal were trying to achieve between 1515 and 1529.

Historians writing over 100 years ago about foreign policy believed that Wolsey was trying to maintain 'the balance of power' between the Emperor Charles V and Francis I, King of France. Other historians, such as Mandell Creighton in his *Cardinal Wolsey* (published in 1888) believed that the Cardinal wanted to dominate Europe in England's interests. The historian Alan Pollard argued in his book on Wolsey (published in 1929), as well as his earlier biography of Henry VIII (1902), that Wolsey conducted England's foreign policy in the interests of the Pope. This tendency to favour Rome was due to Wolsey being a leading churchman, as well as being a **papal legate** in England from 1518. He was bound to favour papal interests, especially in Italy, where the French and the Spanish were in competition from the 1520s. Also according to Pollard, Wolsey hoped to become pope himself and this gave him a further reason for putting Rome's interests first.

These ideas held sway until the later 1960s when the historian J. J. Scarisbrick published his biography of Henry VIII (1968). Scarisbrick demolished earlier interpretations by arguing that Wolsey ignored the papacy as often as he supported it. Wolsey's chief aim was peace and the Treaty of London in 1518 was his greatest achievement, with some 20 European rulers or their agents signing it. Such a policy put England at the centre of Europe. Thus Scarisbrick's view was, to an extent, a re-working of the ideas of earlier historians.

The diplomatic twists of the 1520s, however, have led to historians attributing a range of motives to Henry VIII and Wolsey in their conduct of foreign policy. John Guy in his book *Tudor England* (1988) thinks that Henry VIII's claim to the French crown was an important factor in Wolsey's diplomacy, as was his wish to achieve European prestige for the king. To achieve that end, foreign policy was often opportunistic. Susan Doran, in *England and Europe 1485–1603* (1996), puts forward the view of Wolsey as 'a showman on a grand scale but also a very skilful diplomatist … for a time he placed Henry at the forefront of the international scene'.

The view of another historian, David Potter, in the *Reign of Henry VIII: Politics and Personalities* (1995) is that: 'For a small country of medium power like England, the priority was to survive the exceptionally change-able and unpredictable waters of European diplomacy in the age of the **Habsburg–Valois conflict**.'

Historians' views will continue to change and to develop in the light of new evidence and concerns. That Henry VIII and Thomas Wolsey sought to enhance England's and their own reputations in Europe is a fair view of their aims in foreign policy between 1515 and 1529.

Why did Wolsey's foreign policy face a setback between 1515 and 1517?

In January 1515, the French King, Louis XII, died. He was succeeded by his cousin Francis I. The new king was just 20 years old and was determined to

North Italy in the 16th century

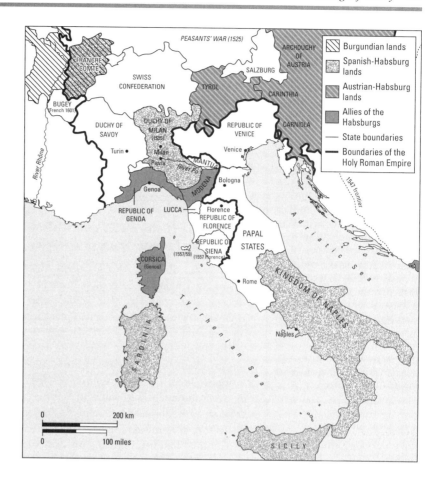

become a significant figure on the European stage. Just like Henry VIII, Francis enjoyed the tournament and the joust. He also patronised the new developments in art and literature while wanting glory. Inevitably, Francis and Henry became competitors and the European situation changed too. Within months of becoming king, Francis intervened in northern Italy to pursue his claims to the Duchy of Milan. The French armies, led by their king in person, defeated the Swiss mercenary army of the Sforza Duke of Milan at Marignano in September 1515. This delivered Milan into the hands of the French King. Soon afterwards at Bologna, Pope Leo X had to come to terms with his French conqueror too. This treaty took the form of a concordat (agreement between Pope and secular ruler), whereby Francis increased his power over the French Church, including the appointment of its bishops. Naturally, Francis' success put Henry and Wolsey and their ambitious plans to make England into a great power into the shade.

Henry VIII and Wolsey hoped that Francis's success would make it possible to build up a coalition against him. The result of this was a treaty with Ferdinand of Spain and an agreement with the Emperor Maximilian whereby England would pay for an army of Swiss mercenaries (for definition see page 32) to be led by him to liberate Milan. As experience ought to have taught Henry VIII to expect, Maximilian took the English money and then let his ally down by defecting to the French.

The year 1516 saw the death of Ferdinand who was succeeded by his grandson Charles, already the ruler of the Netherlands. Charles was not

Francis I (1494–1547)
King of France between 1515
and 1547. He succeeded his
cousin Louis XII. In 1515
Francis I invaded Italy and
captured Milan. He was head
of a brilliant Court and was a
patron of learning and the arts,
as well as increasing royal
control over the nobility and the
French Church. Francis was in
lifelong rivalry with Emperor
Charles V after 1519, so
beginning the Valois–Habsburg
conflict. In 1525 he was
defeated and captured by
Charles V at the battle of Pavia.
However, on his release, it was
not long before conflict was
renewed. Henry VIII saw
Francis as a rival in spite of
their 1520 meeting at the Field
of the Cloth of Gold.

prepared to renew his grandfather's treaty with England and instead signed the Treaty of Noyon with Francis I. This was followed by Maximilian's defection and his making the Peace of Cambrai with Francis I (1517). In addition, English influence in Scotland received a setback when the Duke of Albany, heir to the Scottish throne, was allowed by Francis I to return to Scotland. Once there (1515), Albany managed to replace Margaret Tudor with himself as regent for her infant son, James V. Margaret and her new husband, Archibald Douglas (Earl of Angus) took refuge in England with her brother, Henry VIII. So far, Wolsey and Henry had spent a great deal of money and much diplomatic effort to achieve nothing except English isolation in Europe.

How far did Henry VIII's and Wolsey's diplomacy succeed in restraining Franco–Spanish rivalries, 1518–1521?

At the end of 1517 Wolsey seemed to have achieved little towards advancing England's interests. Francis I of France had emerged as an effective diplomat and war leader who put Henry VIII in the shade. However, 1518 was to see an improvement in England's position on the international stage.

The Pope, Leo X, was very concerned by the threat of the Ottoman Empire advancing into central Europe and wished to see Christendom unite to oppose it. In 1518 Leo sent embassies to the Holy Roman Emperor and the other monarchs and rulers of Europe. The cardinal selected to head the embassy to England was Lorenzo Campeggio. Henry VIII and Wolsey set out to turn this mission to their own advantage. Since 1514 the King and the Cardinal had been putting pressure on the Pope to make Wolsey papal legate in England. Leo X's concern to make peace between Europe's rulers and to launch a crusade against the Turks gave Henry VIII and Wolsey an opportunity to bring further pressure to bear. They refused to admit Campeggio to England until the Pope, not wanting to see the failure of his plans, gave in and made Wolsey co-legate.

Once Campeggio had arrived in London, Wolsey took care to upstage him constantly and to gain credit, while at the same time seizing the diplomatic initiative. Cardinal Wolsey cleverly assumed control of the Pope's plan and made it into an international peace initiative under English chairmanship. The result was to be the universal peace called the Treaty of London (October 1518). The rulers of Europe agreed to keep the peace, and some 20 of them sent embassies to London to sign the treaty. It was a diplomatic triumph for Henry VIII and Wolsey, reversing the humiliations of 1517. Much of the success of the treaty lay in making peace with France. The Anglo–French treaty signed two days after that of London settled the differences between England and France. Tournai, the conquest of 1513, was given back to France and both Henry VIII and Wolsey received French pensions as compensation. The French King also agreed that Henry's infant daughter, Mary, would be married to the Dauphin (title given to the King of France's eldest son). Also, French influence in Scotland would be limited by keeping the Duke of Albany out of that country. So Henry VIII and Wolsey were now set up to become the brokers of European peace, especially between France and Spain. In practice, however, they were to have limited success, in spite of the splendours of 1518–21.

In January 1519 the Holy Roman Emperor, Maximilian, died. This event was bad news for Henry VIII and Wolsey in their role of potential arbiters (peacemakers) of Europe. As the historian R. B. Wernham wrote in his book *Before the Armada* (1966): 'His [Maximilian's] death undid the achievement of 1518 just as that of Louis XII had ruined the work of 1514.'

Maximilian's death meant that there would have to be an election of a new Holy Roman Emperor to succeed him. The two candidates were Archduke Charles of Burgundy – King of Spain, as well as being Maximilian's grandson and the heir to his German lands – and Francis I, King of France. In spite of massive French bribery, the seven German princes who were the electors of the new emperor chose Charles. Wolsey and Henry could not support either side if they wished to be seen as disinterested by both Francis and Charles. However, this did not stop Henry standing as the third candidate, thinking that he had papal support and to stop Francis I becoming emperor. This was not the wisest action, as Leo X had no wish to help Henry after being upstaged by the English the previous year in London. So Charles became the new Holy Roman Emperor. As Charles V, he was now the ruler of his grandfather's German lands, as well as Spain, the Netherlands and Naples. He threatened to encircle France on every side. It seemed that a Habsburg–Valois conflict was only a matter of time and that the Treaty of London would soon be worthless.

In spite of this setback, Henry VIII and Wolsey tried to mediate between France and the Empire and to maintain England's high diplomatic profile. Both Francis and Charles wanted Henry's support and wished to meet with him. It appeared that both the new emperor and the French king were evenly matched, and if war broke out between them it might last for a long time. If one side did win the decisive battle, this would spell danger to the rest of Europe. So Wolsey and his master had every incentive to prevent war and to promote English prestige at little cost to England's own vital interests.

In May 1520, Charles V visited England on his way back from Spain. The meeting was a success and was a clear sign that the Emperor wanted English support. At the same time, negotiations were underway for a meeting between Francis I and Henry VIII. In June the two kings met just outside Calais at the Field of the Cloth of Gold. It was admired at the time for its splendours and again was a good example of Wolsey's ability to arrange and manage great occasions. Not only was it notable for its cloth of gold, but the term 'field' then meant tiltyard. It was a tournament which lasted on and off for 11 days and allowed both Francis I and Henry VIII to show off their sporting prowess. Both kings did best in the jousts, each breaking six spears in a bout, which was the maximum score. However, according to the sources, Francis gave Henry a severe fall in an unplanned wrestling match which did not please the English King. In spite of this, the meeting was judged a success.

In July 1520, Henry and Wolsey again met Charles V at Gravelines. There it was agreed that there would be a three-power conference which would meet at Calais and that neither of them would make a separate treaty with the French. Soon afterwards, however, Charles received news of a serious revolt in Spain which demanded his attention. This meant that for much of the next year Wolsey was able to keep up appearances as the arbiter of Europe.

When the delayed Calais conference did begin, in August 1521, Charles had crushed the Spanish revolt and was now preparing to deal with his

1. What policies did England follow towards France and Spain in the years 1518–1521?

2. How successful was Wolsey in keeping England at the forefront of European diplomacy, 1515–21?

French rival. Therefore little progress was made. Later, in August, Wolsey visited Charles V at Bruges. There, a treaty was made in which it was agreed that Henry was to invade France if Francis I refused to make peace with Charles. Henry agreed to keep the Channel open for Charles, who in return would compensate the English King and Wolsey for any loss of their French pensions in the event of a war with France. There had been rumours for some time past that Charles might agree to eventually marry Princess Mary, Henry VIII's only legitimate child, as by then worries about the succession to the English throne were beginning to surface in Wolsey's calculations. Inevitably, England was drawing closer to Spain. The existence of old friendships and trading ties with the Netherlands counted for much, especially when added to England's traditional enmity for France.

How far were Henry VIII and Wolsey successful in keeping England at the centre of European diplomacy, 1521–1527?

By the autumn of 1521 Henry VIII and Wolsey were committed to Charles V. However, Wolsey had negotiated a delay in England's entering the war against France until 1523. The Cardinal did not wish to appear to be breaking the Treaty of London, so England still appeared to be the arbiter between the Emperor and Francis I. Unlike 1513, if England raised an army to invade France, Wolsey would have to obtain the money through taxation. This was not an appealing prospect for him as taxes were resented. In fact, war was declared on France in May 1522 and an English army was sent to campaign in northern France. However, due to lack of support from Charles V, it achieved little. Henry and Wolsey began to worry that the Emperor would not keep his side of the Treaty of Bruges, and they wondered whether it might be wise to abandon the 'Grand Enterprise' against France.

In 1523 Francis I faced a serious rebellion which gave Wolsey and his master fresh hopes of a successful invasion of France. Charles, Duke of Bourbon, quarrelled with Francis I. After discussions with Charles V and the English, it was agreed that the Duke of Bourbon would raise a revolt in southern France, while the others invaded the country in support. The reward for Henry VIII would be that he would become king of France. Henry and Wolsey sent an army to France in August 1523. It landed at Calais and began to march on Paris. However, the campaign achieved nothing. Bourbon failed to raise a revolt and had to flee into exile, while Charles V had problems raising the necessary money to pay his troops. The English army was successfully opposed by the French, while the severe weather did little to help its advance. As in the previous year, the campaign of 1523 was disappointing. It cost some £400,000, at a time when the war and its financial demands were unpopular in England.

Between the autumn of 1523 and the spring of 1525 Wolsey did nothing, resisting pressure from Charles V to send another expedition to northern France. Also, secret negotiations for peace were opened with France, but these achieved little. The Emperor, through his agents, was aware that his ally was about to desert him if the opportunity offered. Also, a half-hearted contribution of £20,000 from Henry VIII to the cost of Charles' invasion of southern France which failed did little to draw the allies in the 'Grand Enterprise' closer.

By early 1525 the war against the French appeared to be one of stalemate. But suddenly, the situation was dramatically changed by Charles' victory at Pavia, which saw both the conquest of Milan and the capture of Francis I himself. This news was greeted with enthusiasm by Wolsey and his master. Once again, active planning began to send another English army to France. The ambitious English plans envisaged a joint invasion of France by Henry VIII and Charles V. Both monarchs would march on Paris where they would meet. Mary would be given to Charles in marriage and then Henry VIII would march with the Emperor to Rome to see him crowned. Charles would then enjoy the 'whole monarchy of Christendom' and could lead a united Europe against the Turks, so giving practical expression to the plans for union mentioned in the Treaty of London of 1518. However, this dream failed to materialise. Wolsey's attempt to raise money in taxes to pay for the plan failed. The so-called 'Amicable Grant' ran into general resistance from Henry's subjects and had to be abandoned (see section 3.4). There would be no English invasion of France and no repeat of the now distant achievements of Henry V, especially as Charles V refused to agree to Henry's proposals for joint action.

The alliance with Charles had been disappointing. The Emperor had failed to back English invasions of France in 1522 and 1523 and had then denied Henry VIII any gains from his victory in Italy in 1525. Also Charles repudiated the marriage contract with Princess Mary, a sure sign that the English alliance was now of little value to him. It appeared that England was about to be marginalised in European affairs.

Under these circumstances, Wolsey opened separate negotiations for peace with the French. These talks led to five treaties being signed with France, known as the Treaty of the More (August 1525). In effect, a diplomatic revolution had occurred. Henry agreed to give up his claims to France in return for an annual pension. The succeeding months were to see Wolsey helping to construct the League of Cognac (made up of France and the Italian states) to oppose Charles V's possible domination of Europe. English money went into financing the League, but Wolsey did not join as he hoped that he and Henry VIII would be able to act as peacemakers once Charles had been forced to agree terms. However, as in many of their other ambitions since 1518, the English were disappointed. In April 1527, in the Treaty of Westminster, perpetual peace was declared between France and England and the now widowed Francis I, or his second son, would marry Princess Mary. Also, Henry agreed to fight the Emperor if he refused to join the peace and so England would once again be at the centre of European politics. However, by this time English foreign policy was increasingly dominated by Henry VIII's desire for a divorce from Catherine of Aragon, and Wolsey's attempts to obtain it for his master. Foreign policy and Wolsey's political survival now became entangled as never before (see section 3.5).

Between 1514 and 1527 Wolsey had manoeuvred to ensure that England played a prominent role in Europe. This had not been easy, especially after 1519, when England was outclassed in the Habsburg–Valois conflict. Wolsey, driven by a king who above all wished for glory and to regain England's lost lands in France, had often succeeded in keeping his country at the centre of events. England had some value both for Francis I and for Charles V. The latter, who until his victory at Pavia in 1525 which gave him Milan, needed to keep communications open between the Netherlands and Spain by way of the English Channel. The navy which Henry VIII had built up was a factor in Charles' calculations, while his subjects in the Netherlands owed much of their prosperity to the importation of English wool and woollen cloth. Also, England's support would be of use in diverting French resources away from the all-important conflict between the Emperor and the French King to control Italy. These factors, plus traditional ties of friendship, meant that usually Henry VIII's support could be counted on by Charles V. However, the disappointments of the war against France in 1521–25 and the overwhelming victory of Charles V at Pavia had denied Henry VIII his French ambitions, just when it seemed that they might be realised. The result was to drive the English into a French alliance.

In all of these diplomatic shifts, Wolsey played a prominent part and to an extent had enhanced England's international status. The diplomatic events at London in 1518 and at the Field of the Cloth of Gold in 1520 showed that Wolsey had a flair for organising the great occasion which reflected credit on his master, and of course on himself. Then, international relations were to an extent about putting on a good show, and at that the Cardinal was superb, as was his mastery of diplomatic negotiating detail. By 1525 the English had tired of paying for their king's ambitions, as the resistance surrounding the Amicable Grant demonstrated. This showed up the reality of those resources on which Wolsey had to draw in promoting England as an international player between 1514 and 1529: perhaps he made the best of rather restricted and difficult circumstances.

> 1. Explain the problems facing Wolsey in his conduct of foreign policy between 1521 and 1527.
>
> 2. 'It was only Henry VIII's vanity and desire for glory that dominated England's foreign policy between 1521 and 1527.' Do you agree with this view?

3.4 How far was Wolsey's conduct of domestic policy concerned with the reform of the Church and Government?

How did Wolsey keep political control between 1515 and 1527?

On Christmas Eve 1515 Wolsey was sworn in as Lord Chancellor in succession to Archbishop Warham who had resigned. In practice, the Cardinal had been in control of Henry VIII's government since at least 1514, and now he began his tenure of one of the most important offices of state too. From then until his fall in 1529, Wolsey was at the very centre of government. From his residence at York Place, only a short distance from Westminster and the Royal Courts of Justice, Wolsey presided, often daily, in Star Chamber or in the Court of Chancery. This gave Wolsey the opportunity to demonstrate his power as Henry VIII's chief minister, as well as the leading churchman in England (after the granting of his legateship in 1518). Pageantry and display were an important part of royal government in the 16th century and Wolsey was not backward in this respect. His gentleman usher, George Cavendish, described what was the typical day in the Cardinal's routine during his years of power:

> And after mass he would return to his privy chamber again and being told which noblemen and gentlemen were in his outer chambers, he would come out to them dressed all in red in the dress of a cardinal … There was also carried before him first the Great Seal of England, and then his Cardinal's hat … And as soon as he came into his presence chamber, where noblemen and gentry waited to accompany him to Westminster Hall, he went out with two great silver crosses carried before him, with also two great pillars of silver, and his sergeant at arms

with a great mace of silver gilt. Then his gentlemen ushers cried out and said, 'On my lords and masters, make way for my Lord's grace.'

So that was how Wolsey usually began his day during his years of power. For much of this time he was at the centre of government in Westminster where finance, administration and justice were concentrated. Unsurprisingly, his Court attracted the nobility and gentry of England. But Wolsey never forgot the King's Court, more often to be found at Greenwich or Richmond, or within a few miles of London itself. In effect, the Cardinal was often in day-to-day charge of government, but he knew that he had to keep in regular contact with Henry VIII. This was achieved by frequent letters sent to the King through the Royal Secretary, or to those other councillors who might be with him, as well as by Wolsey's own Sunday audience with Henry when he rode to Court. The poet John Skelton daringly suggested that:

> To which court
> To the king's court
> Or to Hampton Court?
> The king's court
> Should have the excellence
> But Hampton Court
> Hath the pre-eminence.

However, Wolsey himself knew, if it was not always apparent to others, that to retain power it was Henry VIII's Court which had to have 'the pre-eminence' and that he neglected the King at his peril. Wolsey could often assume that the King would agree with his policies, especially in domestic affairs. Normally, Henry was uninterested in domestic issues – with the exception of patronage. The King had a low boredom threshold, especially for the routine work of government – unlike his father Henry VII. He was perfectly happy to leave this to Wolsey and his other councillors.

Due to his vast burdens of work, Wolsey could not attend the King on a daily basis. He had to keep careful watch on who surrounded his master on a daily basis. Thus, Wolsey often had to turn his attention to events at Court. Also, he could never totally disregard his fellow Royal Councillors, whether in London or at Court, as he had to depend on them to carry out much of the work of government. When there was a crisis, as in 1525 over the Amicable Grant (see the section on Wolsey as a financial reformer), other members of the Council were quick to grumble that they had not been consulted by Wolsey; just as on occasion Henry VIII himself complained that he was left with inadequate attendance by the Cardinal.

The Royal Court (see Chapter 2) was still, in spite of Wolsey, very much the centre of power. The 'above-stairs' part of the Court – the Chamber and the Privy Chamber – was the politically important part of the organisation. The Privy Council chamber and the rooms beyond it enabled the King to distance himself from the unwanted attentions of courtiers and suitors. It had been treated by Henry VII as such. However, from the beginning of his reign, Henry VIII surrounded himself with young gentlemen, often nearly his own age, especially so after 1515. By being close to the king they were able to exercise considerable influence on him, as well as often control access to his presence. The chief of these gentlemen was the Groom of the Stool (literally in charge of the royal lavatory). The holder of this office became increasingly important politically as Henry VIII's reign progressed.

By 1517 Henry VIII's identification with these young gentlemen was complete. In that year a nickname was given to them: 'the minions' or the 'young favourites'. In 1518 Wolsey was so worried by their influence on Henry that he infiltrated his own man, Richard Pace, both to be a gentleman in attendance on the King and to deal with the royal correspondence. In 1518 Wolsey struck. The minions were expelled from Court for their bad influence on the King and were given jobs away from the centre of power. Hitherto, Wolsey had kept power by encouraging the King in his pleasures, now he hit on another tactic. This was to propose suddenly to reform government. Everything from the Royal Court to government departments and the economy would be affected. The programme caught Henry VIII's interest and he agreed to the expulsion of the minions and their replacement by more serious, middle-aged careerists. However, once he had achieved his objectives, Wolsey dropped the programme of reform.

Soon afterwards, Henry VIII began to re-admit the minions to royal favour. In 1520 they were given the formal title of Gentlemen of the Privy Chamber and, thereafter, Wolsey had to work to diminish their influence with the King in other ways. From 1521 to 1525 they were increasingly used as ambassadors abroad and to take command of military and naval expeditions in the war against France. This too took them away from Court and perhaps helped to maintain Wolsey's influence with the King. However, the peace with France in 1525 meant that Wolsey had to find some other means of continuing to reduce the gentlemen's influence. The turmoil caused by the Amicable Grant in the same year meant that Wolsey also had to find means of countering the influence of his fellow-councillors. They had been complaining that Wolsey had disregarded their advice over levying the Grant, although in practice the dukes of Suffolk and Norfolk and the remainder had gone along with it.

In order to counter his enemies, both on the Council and at Court, Wolsey came up with yet another plan of reform – the Eltham Ordinances of 1526. With these proposals Wolsey dealt with the Privy Chamber by reducing the number of gentlemen from 12 to six. He removed his chief enemies there, such as William Compton, the Groom of the Stool, who was replaced by the politically neutral Henry Norris and others who were no threat to his power. This was done in the name of enonomy, increasingly necessary due to the expense of the recent war and the failure of the Amicable Grant. In regard to his fellow-councillors, Wolsey came up with the idea of the Council Attendant on the King which would be made up of 20 councillors. In practice, Wolsey used the small print of the Eltham Ordinances to see that these councillors carried out their duties elsewhere, leaving the King once more sparsely attended. By means of his still unrivalled influence over Henry, Wolsey had maintained his power, but the onset of the problems surrounding the King's divorce from 1527 were to undermine the Cardinal's influence at Court.

1. Re-read the extract from John Skelton's poem on page 91. Explain what it tells you about the poet's view of the relationship between Henry VIII and Wolsey.

2. How important was Wolsey's use of pageantry and display in helping to remain chief minister between 1515 and 1529?

3. To what extent was the King's Court the real centre of power between 1515 and 1529?

What were Wolsey's relations with the nobility like?

Thomas Wolsey had risen to high office due to his ability to meet the demands which Henry VIII had placed on him, but the King and Court were not the only source of power on which he had to keep a careful eye after 1515. The nobles who were on the Council had re-asserted themselves after the death of Henry VII (see section 3.1) and had been supporters of Henry's war policy. The King was dependent on them as war leaders between 1511 and 1514, and in 1522 when there was once again war with France. Similarly, effective control of the outlying regions of the kingdom depended on the cooperation of the nobility. Effective rule in the borders with Scotland depended on the cooperation of noblemen such as Lord Dacre and the Earl of Northumberland. In the north Midlands and the North-West effective rule depended on the local power of the earls of Derby and Shrewsbury. In the West the power of the nobles, such as the Earl of Devon and the Marquis of Dorset, was important in the effective maintenance of royal power.

It has often been suggested that the relations between Wolsey and the nobility were poor, and that these great men resented the rise of the butcher's boy from Ipswich. While there was some resentment of Wolsey, especially his show of wealth and his accumulation of power, he was in the tradition of powerful clerical ministers, which had been a feature of English government since the time of the Norman Conquest. On a personal level, the evidence would suggest that the Cardinal and most of the nobility could tolerate one another and generally worked well together, especially where the control of the localities were concerned. However, at the highest political level, relations could at times be frosty. There were significant differences between Wolsey and the Howard family, especially the Earl of Surrey who succeeded his father as Duke of Norfolk (the victor of Flodden) in 1524. They were to play an important part in Wolsey's fall from power after 1527 (see section 3.5). Also, relations with the Duke of Suffolk were, on occasion, strained. Like Norfolk, he too played a role in Wolsey's downfall. Certainly, there seems to have been no intention on Wolsey's part to destroy the nobility, just to bend it to his master's will.

The one outstanding exception to this policy was the case of Edward Stafford, third Duke of Buckingham (1478–1521). Buckingham was one of England's greatest noblemen, the owner of vast estates and a remote descendant of King Edward III. It would appear that Buckingham, although not without ability, did not find the role of courtier and servant to the Crown entirely to his liking. He wished Henry VIII to allow him to exercise the hereditary office of **Constable of England**. In spite of the legal judgements in his favour the King insisted that the position remain unfilled. In 1519, after a Star Chamber attack on one of his servants for wearing the duke's livery in the king's presence, Buckingham was reported to be grumbling about the royal councillors. Also, since 1509, the Duke had done nothing to build up support at Court and positively despised the minions around the King. So Buckingham was a reactionary, who did little except talk himself into Henry VIII and Wolsey's disfavour. As the historian David Starkey wrote in his book on the reign of Henry VIII:

> Whatever form of politicking the duke resorted to, he was bad at it. He talked too much and did too little and words and actions alike served only to provide Henry and Wolsey with plausible charges to undo him.

In February 1521 the Duke of Buckingham asked for a licence to visit his Lordships in Wales with a force of armed men. This alarmed Henry VIII, who wrote to Wolsey: 'I would you should make good watch on the Duke of Suffolk, on the Duke of Buckingham, on my lord of Northumberland,

Constable of England: Principal officer in the Royal Court who commanded the royal army in the king's absence or illness.

'The hostility of the Tudor nobility to Wolsey as Henry VIII's chief minister is the invention of historians.' How far do you agree with this statement?

on my lord of Derby, on my lord of Wiltshire, and on others which you think suspect.'

That there was a noble plot against Henry is unlikely, but the King was thoroughly alarmed. Buckingham's royal blood, however remote, worried him. As later in his reign, when he struck against the de la Pole family in 1541, so he moved against Buckingham in 1521. Wolsey's role in the downfall of Buckingham is uncertain but no doubt he was carrying out his master's wishes. In April 1521 the Duke of Buckingham was summoned to Court and arrested. The next month he was tried for high treason and, after a trial of four days, found guilty and executed. No doubt, the trial was 'rigged', but in reality Buckingham was guilty of the basic offence with which he was charged and was largely the author of his own downfall.

The Buckingham case was untypical of Wolsey's relations with the nobility. The Duke's fall probably owed more to Henry VIII's paranoia than to any malice from Wolsey himself.

How important was Wolsey's work as a legal reformer?

Wolsey's preoccupations as Henry VIII's chief minister were foreign policy, and very probably keeping himself in power. Due to his massive energy and capacity for hard work, he has enjoyed a reputation as a legal reformer. The historian Geoffrey Elton, who is in many respects no great admirer of Wolsey, wrote of him in *England under the Tudors* (published in 1955): 'Wolsey gloried in the majesty of a judge, and though he had no legal training that we know of he possessed a remarkable natural ability for the task.'

Most other historians would largely agree with this judgement. As Lord Chancellor, Wolsey had to oversee the whole legal system. He sat in the Court of Chancery as a judge, but according to the historian John Guy his impact there was limited, as there was only a slight increase in the number of cases brought before the court from the days of his predecessors, John Morton and William Warham. This may have been because of Wolsey's other duties, including Star Chamber. Other judges often deputised for him.

If Wolsey's impact on the Court of Chancery was limited, the same was not true of the Star Chamber. In 1516 the Cardinal put forward a plan to improve the legal system, which would ensure that it worked much more efficiently, as well as providing justice which was both fair and cheap. The power house of these reforms was to be an enhanced Star Chamber. It was in future to contain the traditional powers of both the Council and the other statutory tribunals of the reign of Henry VII, to both enforce the law and to see that the delivery of justice was fair. This reformed Star Chamber was a success, if it is to be judged by the caseload which it undertook after 1516. The caseload rose from 12 a year under Henry VII to some 120 a year during Wolsey's time in power.

Under Wolsey's presidency, Star Chamber took on the powerful and did much to curb their abuse of the legal system in their own localities. There were several cases of the court dealing vigorously with the highly-placed, including royal councillors, in pursuit of justice. One case was that of Sir Robert Sheffield, a Royal Councillor and former Speaker of Parliament, who was imprisoned in the Tower of London as an accessory to felony (a serious crime, usually connected with violence), as well as being heavily fined by the Court. In his pursuit of justice, Wolsey encouraged ordinary subjects to bring cases against the mighty – which they were quick to do. Also Wolsey encouraged private individuals to bring their cases to Chancery and the Star Chamber, which greatly increased the workload. This was so much so that the system became overworked. As a result, Wolsey had to establish overflow tribunals, such as that set up at White Hall in London in 1519, which became the forerunner of the **Court of Requests**.

Undoubtedly, Wolsey gave a powerful boost to the modernisation of the legal system, even if he had to leave much of the work to others. In Star Chamber Wolsey's fellow-councillors were kept busy. In this aspect of their activities, they could not complain that the Cardinal had diminished their role. It is unlikely that the nobility and gentry were admirers of Wolsey's legal reforms which probably fed their resentment of him, but he had laid the groundwork for his successors to build upon in modernising English law and its courts. They were able to ensure their effectiveness in maintaining law and order and providing justice for the king's subjects.

How successful was Wolsey as an economic reformer?

As well as his concern for justice for all, Wolsey is remembered for his campaign against the evils of enclosure (see Chapter 4). Once again, it is unlikely that his attempts to deal with this problem made him liked by the nobility and the propertied classes. To people in early Tudor England enclosures meant that they lost their common rights over land, such as that of grazing their animals or gathering fuel. In practice, enclosure meant that common land was taken over by greedy landlords who then built fences and hedges to prevent ordinary people's access to what they saw as their land. Tudor writers on enclosure believed that it caused the decline of villages and the loss of houses and made unemployment inevitable. This process was created by the move in some regions of the country from arable to a pastoral system of farming. That sheep 'ate up men' was obvious because sheep runs needed fewer labourers to maintain them than those needed to plough the fields. Also, it was obvious that the landowners were out to farm the more profitable sheep and in the process 'grind the faces of the poor'. This was made worse by the other evil of engrossing. This was when two or more farms were made into one, often by outside businessmen investing in land – they demolished any unwanted buildings or let them decay. The new property was then enclosed and sold or leased out for a profit. It could mean the loss of homes as well as jobs, and where it occurred it was much resented.

To Tudor commentators, enclosures were a moral problem, an evil of society, and there was no appreciation of the real causes of change in the countryside. Wolsey agreed with these views and insisted that the laws of 1489 and 1514–15 against enclosing and engrossing should be obeyed. In 1517 he launched a national enquiry to discover the extent of enclosure and who had been affected by it. The commissioners reported back and cases were launched against over 260 landlords or corporations such as some Oxford colleges. Some of these cases dragged on for years, but a large number of them ended with clear verdicts against the defendants. Most of the latter were members of the propertied classes and their resentment against Wolsey surfaced in the Parliament of 1523 when he agreed to abandon his enclosure policy for 18 months in return for a large subsidy: the needs of war over-rode social reform. Once again, Wolsey had tackled a perceived evil vigorously, but other pressures led to its gradual abandonment.

Court of Requests: Part of the Royal or Privy Council which dealt mainly with individual requests or petitions for help from ordinary citizens. Under Wolsey and Henry VIII it developed as a court which was separate from the Royal Council.

1. What changes did Wolsey make to the English legal system?

2. Explain how far Wolsey deserves credit for his work as a legal reformer.

1. Why were enclosures seen as a problem in early Tudor England?

2. 'In reality, Wolsey had very little success as an economic reformer.' How far do you agree with this view?

Fifteenths and tenths: The most important tax voted by Parliament from the early 1300s. It was based on property – one-tenth for town and Crown lands, one-fifteenth for the remainder. By the 1500s the sums voted had become fixed and no longer gave much return in tax to the Crown.

Besides enclosures, Wolsey was at times active against what were seen as other social evils. As a leading churchman, the Cardinal was keen on maintaining the idea of the 'just price'. From time to time he attacked the evils of traders whom he accused of charging their customers excessive prices. For example, London butchers, provincial graziers (cattle farmers who fed their animals up ready to sell them at market) and grain dealers all felt the blast of Wolsey's disapproval. But little was done to follow up these condemnations. No doubt, given the increasing demands on him, time was unavailable.

How successful were Wolsey's attempts as a financial reformer and parliamentary manager?

It was in the area of tax reform that Wolsey has been regarded as having made an important contribution to Tudor finance. He has been credited with the invention of the parliamentary subsidy. The problem with raising extra taxation to pay for wars was that by the early 1500s the existing parliamentary taxes of **fifteenths and tenths** had, in effect, become fixed sums. They produced too little money for the Crown. Also, the royal lands produced insufficient revenue, and due to the needs of and the generosity of Henry VIII income from them grew less after 1509. Thomas Wolsey introduced an Act of Resumption in Parliament in 1515 to regain lands for the Crown which had earlier been granted away. This did little to meet Henry's financial demands. Arising out of his experience in organising the French expedition of 1513, Wolsey grasped the need for a new tax which would be flexible in its demands. It was also based on accurate valuations of the taxpayer's wealth. This subsidy was just the tax needed to pay for Henry VIII's constant desire for wars, especially with France, and his extravagance in building, improving and furnishing his growing numbers of palaces.

The subsidy proved to be a success, especially as Wolsey worked out the practicalities of assessment and collection with the able assistance of John Hales, who was a judge in the Court of the Exchequer. It was levied four times in 1513–15 and 1523. All in all, it brought in over £300,000, while separate clerical taxation also produced useful sums. So the Crown was now raising realistic sums by taxing its subjects, but its demands were increasingly resented by the propertied classes who had to pay these parliamentary taxes. Wolsey did not prove adept in managing his first Parliament in 1515, when complaints against the Church dominated and led to its soon being dissolved. This may, in part, explain why there were no more parliaments until 1523. However, the period 1515–21 was one of peace which made calling a parliament unnecessary.

In 1522 war began against France and once again it was necessary to raise large sums in extraordinary taxation. To begin with, Wolsey raised over £250,000 to pay for the war by means of loans from the propertied classes. These were resented – as usual. When parliament was summoned in 1523, the Cardinal demanded £800,000 in extra taxes, on top of the loans of 1522–23. Wolsey tried to overcome resistance, especially from the Commons, by addressing them in person. However, that and his other tactics failed, including keeping Parliament sitting longer than normal, and in the end he had to settle for a rate of two shillings [10p] in the £ on incomes in land or goods of over £20.00 per year. In spite of keeping Parliament sitting between May and July, Wolsey obtained no more from them than they had at first offered. This was no compliment to Wolsey's abilities as a parliamentary manager.

So in trying to meet Henry VIII's demands for money in 1522–23 Wolsey had made himself increasingly unpopular with the political and propertied classes of England. However, the war against France continued and when Henry decided to invade his enemy's country in spring of 1525, again the Treasury was empty. Wolsey knew that he would have to raise money to pay for the war, but he did not want to risk calling a new parliament after the disputes of 1523. Instead he decided to raise a tax based on the valuations of property and goods which had produced the loan of 1523. Wolsey called it an 'amicable grant' and hoped that by appealing to their patriotism people would pay. Both the clergy and the **laity** were asked to contribute, the latter by means of a sliding scale depending on the size of their income.

Laity: The body of people who were *not* clergymen.

This new demand proved to be the final straw for taxpayers. When the commissioners were sent out in March and April 1525 they met with strong resistance, both in London and the provinces. Within weeks Wolsey had to backtrack on his demands and in the end settle for voluntary contributions. However, such a retreat did not occur before discontent had flared into near-rebellion across large parts of England, especially in London and East Anglia where it centred on the wool town of Lavenham. Many of the nobility, although no lovers of Wolsey, were alarmed by the widespread nature of the popular resistance to the taxation and informed Henry VIII of this. The King, whose war policy had been the cause of the discontent, decided to back down in the face of the popular anger. He left Wolsey to arrange a stage-managed display of clemency (apology) at which the defeated Lavenham rebels were pardoned, with the Cardinal himself paying off their prison expenses. This was a humiliation for Wolsey, who had been trying to carry out his master's demands. However, he knew that when affairs went well Henry VIII took the credit and when they did not his ministers and courtiers took the blame.

The Amicable Grant of 1525 was the nearest that England had come to rebellion between the Cornish rising of 1497 and the Pilgrimage of Grace in 1536 (see Chapter 5). Wolsey's very success in devising the subsidy and in raising taxation to pay for Henry VIII's excesses between 1515 and 1523 carried the seeds of its own failure. By 1525 people were tired of taxation to pay for the wars which were expensive and disruptive of economic life. The Amicable Grant caused a display of popular feeling, that in the last resort both Henry and Wolsey were too shrewd to ignore, but it was the Cardinal who took the blame. The King's confidence in him was shaken and his enemies began to 'sharpen their knives'. The near-revolt of 1525 led to the abandonment of the war against France and was a direct cause of the Eltham Ordinances of January 1526 when Wolsey set out deliberately to disarm his enemies, both at Court and in the Council.

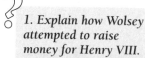

1. Explain how Wolsey attempted to raise money for Henry VIII.

2. How far was Wolsey responsible for the near-rebellion caused by the Amicable Grant of 1525?

To what extent did Wolsey seek to reform the Church?

As in the other areas, Wolsey did on occasions come up with plans to reform the Church. In 1519 when Wolsey announced that he intended to reform the clergy, it was but one aspect of the ambitious plans to overhaul both Church and State which he dangled in front of Henry VIII when he was dealing with his political enemies at Court in that year. In practice, the plans came to little. However, the Cardinal was well aware of the 'New

Learning' and of its impact. He was also aware of the demands for reforming clerical life and the Church which issued from the pens of reformers such as Desiderius Erasmus, William Colet and Thomas More. What is more, Wolsey also knew that often the privileged status of the clergy was resented.

Soon after emerging as Henry VIII's chief minister, Wolsey had to deal with the Parliament of 1515 and its worries over church affairs. A London merchant, Richard Hunne, had been accused of heresy after a quarrel with his parish priest over a mortuary payment. He was then found dead in the local bishop's prison. The City of London was inclined to be anti-clerical, and it took some time for the ill-feeling towards the Church to die down. Also, there was the issue of **benefit of clergy**, which had been cut back by Act of Parliament in 1512 but was due for renewal in 1515. Wolsey managed to avoid this, but only after having knelt before Henry VIII at Baynard's Castle in November 1515 to reassure the King that clerical privileges were no threat to royal power over the Church. Henry VIII in effect got what he wanted – the right to continue to tax the clergy and to control Church patronage. In 1515 Henry had as yet no real interest in asserting total control of the Church – that lay in the future.

Certainly, by 1518, Wolsey was in effect in control of the Church in England by virtue of his power as a papal legate which he had obtained from the Pope that year and which was conferred on him for life in 1524. This office gave him power to reform both the **regular** and the **secular clergy**, but in practice little was done. There were plans to reform the lax discipline of the monks and the friars and to reform the hierarchy of the Church. The last plan would have meant the creation of 13 new bishoprics (area controlled by a bishop) out of monastic foundations. Then the English dioceses would have reflected the population distribution of Tudor England and not that of an earlier age. Also, between 1524 and 1529, Wolsey dissolved some 30 religious houses and used the money raised to build colleges at Oxford and in his home town of Ipswich. The Cardinal had ambitious plans for his foundations and the advancement of learning, but interestingly their proposed endowments were still in his hands at his fall, and so were seized by the Crown. There has been doubt expressed, both at the time and since, as to whether or not Thomas Wolsey was more concerned to build monuments to himself than to promote learning.

In his own person Wolsey was not a good advertisement for clerical discipline and the joys of spirituality. Whatever the Cardinal's own religious sincerity, and there is evidence that he did have genuine religious beliefs, there is no doubt that he knew how to make a good living from the Church. It was not so much that the king's chief minister was a prince of the Church and received a large income from it: that was nothing new. Rather it was the sheer scale of Wolsey's offices which astounded his contemporaries and made him the personification of the vices of **absenteeism** and **pluralism** so condemned by religious reformers and lay critics of the Church. In addition to being Archbishop of York from 1514, Wolsey held other wealthy bishoprics at the same time, such as Durham (1523–29) and Winchester (1529–30). Also, he was Abbot of St Albans, one of the wealthiest abbeys in England, and made other clergy pay him fees for permission to carry out their duties. As legate he poked his nose into everything that could bring him money from **probate** matters to appointments at all levels

Benefit of clergy: This gave any member of the clergy committing a crime the right to be tried only in Church Courts. The punishments given there were less severe than those handed out in the Royal Courts.

Regular and secular clergy: Regular clergy were monks and nuns who followed a Rule (e.g. the Rule of St Benedict). Secular clergy were those who served in the everyday world, such as parish priests and bishops.

Absenteeism: A priest who was absent from his living or benefice, usually under licence to be so from his bishop. His duties would be performed by a deputy.

Pluralism: The practice of holding more than one church office or benefice at the same time.

Probate: Matters to do with wills and property of the dead. At this time, such matters were dealt with in Church Courts.

1. Explain how Wolsey reformed the Church in England.

2. Why was Wolsey able to have such a powerful position within the Church in England?

3. Study the whole of section 3.4 in order to answer the following question:

'In his domestic policy between 1515 and 1529 Wolsey promised much but achieved little.' How far do you agree with this judgement?

of the Church. From all these sources Wolsey derived a vast income, much of it spent on conspicuous consumption and buildings works at Hampton Court, in particular, as well as at York Place in London and his other houses.

In effect, Wolsey was allowed to control the Church by both the Pope and the King. It has been suggested that this weakened the Church in England and so made it easy for Henry VIII and Cromwell to nationalise it in the 1530s. This was not quite true, as the senior clergy, led by the aged Archbishop Warham until his death in 1532, put up a respectable resistance to Henry VIII's claims to be the Head of the Church in the early years of the break from Rome. Certainly, Wolsey himself was very much Henry's creature, as his rather abject submission to the King after his fall from power in 1529 indicated.

3.5 Was Wolsey the architect of his own downfall?

Why did Henry VIII want a divorce?

Sometime between 1521 and 1525 Henry VIII made the decision that he would have to obtain the annulment (end) of his marriage to Catherine of Aragon. Since its beginning in 1509, the marriage had worked as Catherine was the model wife. For many years she produced a succession of children (six in all), but all of them except for Princess Mary (born 1516) were stillborn or only lived for a few days. This fact was distressing both to the King and the Queen, and Henry continued to hope that the longed-for son would eventually appear. However, in this the King was to be disappointed as the biological clock ticked away and Catherine became physically less attractive. More importantly, it became clear by the early 1520s that her childbearing days were over. The Queen was a scholar and patron of the New Learning in her own right. She had used her influence with Henry to advance the interests of her father, Ferdinand of Aragon, and those of her nephew the Emperor Charles V. No doubt, she had some influence on the commitment to the imperial alliance in 1521 and on Charles V, agreeing to marry Mary when she came of age. Wolsey resented Catherine's influence with the King but there was little that he could do about it. Besides, it often suited his diplomatic schemes. Catherine had little time for Wolsey whom she hated, both for his lifestyle and for his influence over the King.

By the early 1500s, Henry VIII was a worried man as the only heir to the throne was the infant Mary. Above all things, the King knew the importance of a male heir. If England was to remain stable after his death there must be no danger of a return to the Wars of the Roses. While the distant example of the country's only female ruler (albeit briefly), the

Empress Matilda in the mid-12th century, was not an encouraging precedent. So Henry and Wolsey made the best of a bad job: Mary would marry Emperor Charles V and the kingdom would gain a protector. However, the imperial victory at Pavia in 1525 and Charles' dismissal of Henry's grand schemes to conquer France, as well as his repudiation of the engagement to Mary, left the King feeling insulted and enraged.

It was these events which led to the so-called 'diplomatic revolution' of 1525–26 and the League of Cognac, Wolsey's anti-imperialist alliance which England would not join (see section 3.3). It was this rebuff by Charles V and worries over the succession which led Henry to elevate his illegitimate son, Henry Fitzroy (born 1519) to the dukedom of Richmond and to the office of Lord High Admiral of England. Henry referred to him as 'my worldly jewel' and intended to settle the throne on him, but this would be no real substitute for a legitimate male heir. All of this left the Queen in a difficult situation as she was seen as the link to a now-discredited alliance and no longer was she personally acceptable to Henry. He drifted away from her in his affections. This situation seemed promising to Wolsey who believed that he could obtain an annulment of Henry's marriage from the Pope and instead marry him off to a French princess.

However, Wolsey was wrong in his calculations. In spite of several mistresses, Henry had essentially stuck by his queen and was, by European standards, hardly a womaniser. But by 1525–26 his affections were drawn to Anne Boleyn (see page 139) and soon the King was becoming infatuated with her. Anne was a daughter of the rising courtier, Sir Thomas Boleyn, who already owed much of his advancement to the fact that his elder daughter Mary had been Henry VIII's mistress for a while. Also, Anne was niece of the Duke of Norfolk, Wolsey's leading enemy on the Council, and he may have been behind the decision to bring her to Henry's attention at Court. If so, the plan was eventually to succeed. Before her final return to England in 1522, Anne had spent a number of years at the Burgundian Court and afterwards the French Court. By the 1520s all that was French was fashionable at the English Court. In her education Anne was French and many found that appealing when she arrived in 1522. Thereafter, information about Anne's progress is vague, but the heir to the Earl of Northumberland, Henry Percy, was warned off making a match with her by Wolsey. From 1525 Henry VIII was to become infatuated with Anne, as his letters to her in French testify. The letters were in themselves labours of love as Henry was at the best of times an unwilling letter-writer. Anne had nerve and intended to go for the highest stakes – she wished to be queen, not mistress – and she stuck to this decision. By 1527 Henry was acknowledged by her as the possessor of her heart, but she made him wait until 1532 before she let him share her bed.

As well as falling in love with Anne Boleyn, Henry had decided by early 1527 that God had cursed his marriage to Catherine, as the death of their many children made clear. Henry had discovered himself that his marriage was invalid by his study of the Bible. In the early weeks of 1527 his wish for a divorce was made clear to Wolsey. The papal dispensation of 1502 was invalid, as a pope could not over-ride scripture. Wolsey saw the weakness in this argument and came up with an ingenious solution (see panel opposite) which Henry in fact chose to ignore. However, in spite of this,

Wolsey saw no great problems given his connections in Rome. Very probably Henry VIII too had no doubts that his minister could obtain an annulment of his marriage.

Wolsey's ingenious solution

Henry VIII claimed that his marriage to Catherine of Aragon was invalid because:

a) in the Bible (Leviticus 20 verse 21) it clearly states that 'if a man shall take his brother's wife, it is an unclean thing'

b) the papal dispensation granted by Pope Julius II to allow the marriage was not valid.

Against this argument, there is a verse in the book of Deuteronomy in the Bible which states that if a brother dies it was the surviving brother's duty to marry his widow.

As early as 1527 Wolsey had seized on the point that Catherine of Aragon had angrily denied that her marriage to Arthur had ever been consummated. If so, then the Deuteronomy text applied. If it had been consummated, then Leviticus applied as there was only the impediment of what canon law (the law of the Church) called 'public dishonesty'. So it ought to be possible to get the Pope to grant an amendment as the original dispensation was based on the belief that the marriage between Arthur and Catherine had been consummated.

However, Henry VIII, already suspicious of Wolsey's motives, did not accept that Catherine was telling the truth. He rejected the idea. Henry's own arrogance and belief in the argument of Leviticus meant that in his mind his case was unarguable. It only remained to make the Pope accept it.

In his campaign for the annulment Wolsey's optimism was to prove ill-founded because of the worsening international situation. In 1526 the League of Cognac had been set up because of fears of the growth of imperial power in Italy after Charles V's victory at Pavia in 1525. Its members were the Papacy, Venice, Florence and France, while it enjoyed English support. In 1527 this League received a fatal setback when the imperial army – which was unpaid, tired and mutinous – ignored its commanders and stormed the city of Rome. Europe was shocked by this event which saw the centre of Christendom sacked and its inhabitants murdered, raped or if they were lucky merely robbed by the imperial troops. Charles V too was shocked by the event but in political terms the Pope was now his prisoner. Also the result of Pavia was confirmed and Italy passed into Spanish control for the next hundred years.

Wolsey now found himself with an impossible task, namely to obtain a divorce from a pope who dared not offend an emperor who felt that his family's honour was under attack by Henry VIII. Between 1527 and 1529 Wolsey did his best but events were against him. In May 1527, Catherine, now aware of Henry's intention to reject her, appealed direct to Rome. This meant that the 'ball' was now in the Pope's court. Over the next two years Wolsey tried his best to obtain the divorce. Firstly, the diplomatic plans, which came to nothing, to free Clement VII from Charles V. Secondly, to get the Pope to set up a commission in England that would give Wolsey the necessary powers to make a judgement on the divorce, which would need no further appeal to Rome. However, Wolsey neglected to keep up good contacts at Rome and ignored Lorenzo Campeggio, the Cardinal-Protector of England, just when he might have been most useful. This meant that Wolsey had to work through diplomats who had little influence or by sending occasional embassies which were unsuccessful.

However, in the summer of 1528 Pope Clement finally agreed to set up a commission. He appointed Wolsey and Campeggio to try the case jointly. In September 1528, the Italian Cardinal finally arrived in England but carefully concealed Clement's private instructions to him to see that the commission was never used when it came to the judgement. The Pope was tired of the bullying of the English envoys, hence the commission. He was not so stupid as to know that in the last event he dared not offend Charles V.

Once in England, Campeggio delayed events as much as he could and tried to get Catherine to enter a nunnery, which would have solved the whole problem. However, on 15 June 1529 the legatine court, with Wolsey and Campeggio presiding, opened at Blackfriars in London. From the first Catherine refused to recognise the court and on 18 July, Pope Clement recalled the case to Rome. The news of this did not reach England until early August, by which time Campeggio had already adjourned the court, following normal church practice. Also, on 5 August, France and the Empire made peace at Cambrai, so that Wolsey's chances of further influencing the Pope were lost. Wolsey's own dismissal would soon follow.

1. Explain why Henry VIII wished to divorce Catherine of Aragon.

2. 'In spite of his best efforts, Wolsey's attempts between 1527 and 1529 to obtain a divorce for the King stood no hope of success.' How far do you agree with this view?

How far was faction responsible for Wolsey's downfall?

Wolsey had always been aware that his survival as Henry VIII's chief minister depended on his keeping the King's favour. For much of his time in power (1515–27) Wolsey managed to outsmart his opponents, not least by the fact that none of them enjoyed the King's trust and affection as much as he. However, with the rise of Anne Boleyn there was a rival for the King's affections which Wolsey could do little to overcome. From the Cardinal's viewpoint, her connections with his enemies on the Council, such as the Duke of Norfolk, did little to help. Also Anne and her family had sympathy with the religious views of the reformers. The ambitions and pretensions of Wolsey, the arch-pluralist, would have had little appeal for them. It appears that at first Anne may have had little personal dislike for the chief minister and may have hoped that he could obtain the divorce. But as events between 1527 and 1529 unfolded, she and her supporters were quick to blame Wolsey for every setback.

By 1527, Anne Boleyn clearly had Henry under her influence and she knew how to exploit this. According to the historians Eric Ives and David Starkey, Anne's rise saw the revival of factional politics. Wolsey had to become the leader of a faction to maintain his power. David Starkey's view is that faction was concentrated in the Council and the Privy Chamber where the gentlemen lined up in support of either Anne Boleyn or the Cardinal, who quickly grasped the new circumstances. As Starkey wrote:

> The cardinal understood the implications immediately and started to pack the Privy Chamber with clients like Sir Richard Pace his former

chamberlain and Thomas Heneage, lately the head of Wolsey's own Privy Chamber. Anne replied by restoring supporters of her own, like her cousin, Sir Francis Bryan and her brother George Boleyn, to their former offices in the department. While even adherents of Catherine of Aragon, like Sir Nicholas Carew, managed with the sudden weakening of the cardinal's control to get their jobs back too. In the course of a few months in 1527–28 the Privy Chamber had been repoliticalised.

This revival of 'faction' can be seen in the appointment of a new Abbess of Wilton in 1528. Wolsey wished to appoint his own candidate but Anne Boleyn had another in mind. In the event, Wolsey went ahead and appointed his own choice. The result was a massive ticking off from Henry for not appointing the person the King wished. Then Wolsey made the situation worse by pretending that he did not know what Henry's views were on the matter. In the end Wolsey managed to smooth the matter over, but it was a sign that times were changing. The Council was now meeting increasingly at Court. When present, Wolsey had to fight his own corner there too. The great concerns of 1529 were the divorce and whether Wolsey stayed as the King's chief minister.

As the divorce campaign started to fail in July–August 1529, councillors began to line up against Wolsey. The nobles' representatives, the dukes of Norfolk and Suffolk, who were no lovers of the minister, united with the followers of Anne Boleyn and those who sympathised with Catherine to bring down the Cardinal. Together they worked on Henry's anger about the failure of the divorce to get Wolsey dismissed. In the last resort, given his unforgiving nature towards those who failed him, the King probably needed little persuasion. Henry VIII had set his heart on the divorce. Wolsey had failed him, so he had to pay the price.

In October 1529 Wolsey was dismissed from the Lord Chancellorship and prosecuted in the King's bench on a charge of **praemunire**. He surrendered himself and his possessions into the King's hands. Wolsey's fate now depended on Henry VIII. The Cardinal was allowed to retire to his house at Esher and was restored to his archbishopric of York. However, Henry kept the remainder of his wealth, including the riches of York Place. At this stage, Henry, in spite of humiliating Wolsey, kept his hopes alive – he might have his future uses.

In April 1530 Wolsey retired to his archdiocese, but he could not stop hoping for a comeback. He started to correspond with French and Imperial agents. No doubt this was known to his enemies. They began to persude Henry VIII that the fallen minister was plotting treason and in early November he was arrested. Wolsey began his slow journey south to face a trial for treason and perhaps execution, but death intervened. He died at Leicester Abbey on 29 November.

Wolsey's career was a remarkable one. Both at the time and since its significance has been much argued over. To people at the time, the Cardinal's career would have seemed a good example of the wheel of fortune. Wolsey had risen high from humble beginnings, but his greed, pride and ambition had led to the wheel humbling him by throwing him back into the dust. As the next section of the chapter will argue, historians have tended to look beyond the vagaries of chance in assessing the significance of Wolsey's years as Henry VIII's chief minister.

Praemunire: This was a law that made any introduction or acknowledgement of papal jurisdiction in England illegal.

1. What actions did Anne Boleyn take between 1527 and 1529 to gain influence over Henry VIII?

2. To what extent was the role of faction rather than his failure to obtain the divorce the key factor in explaining Wolsey's downfall?

Wolsey: an assessment
A CASE STUDY IN HISTORICAL INTERPRETATION

During his time in power, Thomas Wolsey was a controversial figure. His contemporaries were often hostile towards him. This view of him has continued throughout the following centuries.

However, Wolsey has also had his defenders, both at the time and since. The first 20 years of Henry VIII's reign are often regarded as lacking in achievement. Wolsey and his royal master built ambitious diplomatic 'castles' which crumbled under the realities of European diplomacy, while at home, problems such as the reform of the Church were neglected. The accusation was that Wolsey was only concerned with accumulating wealth and offices. He liked displaying his power as Henry VIII's principal minister and the Pope's legate. Debate will continue about Wolsey and his importance in English history. This section will consider this debate, especially whether or not Wolsey was a statesman with significant achievements to his credit.

Contemporaries were often hostile to Thomas Wolsey, especially the poet John Skelton. Until he was bought off by the offer of a good living in the Church, Skelton was vigorous in his denunciations of Wolsey in poems such as 'Collyn Clout' (1522) and 'Why come ye not to Courte?' (1522–23):

> Set up a wretch on high.
> In a throne triumphantly,
> Make him of great estate,
> And he will play check-mate
> With royal majesty
> Count himself as good as he.

Another who was critical of Wolsey was the papal tax collector, Polydore Vergil. In his *Anglica Historia* ('History of the English', written over a number of years and published in 1555), Vergil did little for the reputation of the man who at one stage of his career (1515) had been responsible for his imprisonment in the Tower of London. Vergil wrote:

> To have the abundant good fortune [Wolsey's appointment as Archbishop of York and then Lord Chancellor] must be regarded as most estimable if it showered upon sober, moderate and self-controlled men, who were not puffed up by power, do not become arrogant with wealth, and do not give themselves airs because of their good fortune. None of these qualities appeared in Wolsey. Acquiring so many offices at almost the same time, he became so proud that he began to regard himself as the equal of kings.

As mentioned, Wolsey had his defenders too. The best known was his gentleman usher, George Cavendish. Although writing between 1556 and 1558, Cavendish was well placed to see the public side of Wolsey's work as Henry VIII's chief minister. In the prologue to his account of Wolsey's life, Cavendish wrote:

> I dare be bold to say without displeasure to any person out of affection (for Wolsey) that in my judgement I never saw this realm in better order, quietness and obedience than it was in the time of his authority and rules, nor justice more fairly ministered.

Edward Hall (1498–1547)
He was born in London and for most of his life was closely connected with the city. His education was at Eton and Cambridge University. Hall then trained as a lawyer and later held various legal offices in London. He was elected MP in the 1529–36 Parliament. It is clear from his *The Union of the two noble and illustrious families of York and Lancaster* that Hall was a strong supporter of the Tudor dynasty.

Nicholas Harpsfield (1519–1575)
Harpsfield was a Catholic who became Archbishop of Canterbury in succession to Thomas Cranmer's brother, Edmund. In 1557 he carried out a thorough visitation of the diocese of Canterbury, the records of which survive. He also wrote condemning the Henrician Reformation and the work of Archbishop Cranmer in particular.

So the views of Wolsey's contemporaries and near-contemporaries were mixed, but most were hostile. For a protestant chronicler like Edward Hall, Wolsey was the best-known and most obvious example of the corruption and luxury of the unreformed Roman Catholic Church. For catholic writers such as Nicholas Harpsfield or William Roper (Sir Thomas More's son-in-law), Wolsey was the man who above all others was responsible for Henry VIII's divorce, and thus the disaster of the English Reformation. It seems that Wolsey could not win.

Views of Wolsey over the succeeding centuries remained mixed, but mostly negative. However, Mandell Creighton writing a re-assessment of Wolsey's life and career in *Cardinal Wolsey* (published in 1888 in a series called 'Twelve English Statesmen', which included Henry VII and Elizabeth I), was very complimentary. He saw Thomas Wolsey as the great statesman who was neglected:

> For Wolsey lived in the world as few men have ever done ... for the actual, immediate world of affairs. He limited himself to its problems, but within its limits he also took a wider and juster view of the problems of his time than any English statesman had ever done. For politics in the larger sense, comprising all the relations of the nations at home and abroad, Wolsey had a capacity which amounted to genius, and it is doubtful if this can be said of any other Englishman.

High praise indeed. However, early 20th-century historians were not so complimentary. Alan Pollard in his book on Wolsey (first published in 1929) was critical of the cardinal:

> Had he but known the result of his papal ambitions and the future foreign policy in which they involved him, he might have chosen another path which led to a better end ... He was endowed by nature with unsurpassed ability, an insatiable appetite for work, and a hunger and thirst, sometimes after righteousness but always after wealth and power.

On balance, opinion remained hostile to Wolsey over the next 30 years. In 1965 Geoffrey Elton was even more critical in his introduction to a re-issued edition of Alan Pollard's *Wolsey*:

> It must now look that Pollard's verdict on Wolsey may still err on the generous side ... Responsible for an often mistaken and ultimately disastrous foreign policy, amateurish and uncreative in the government of the realm committed to his care, only moderately successful in ruling its church ... Wolsey had tried to do the impossible, to rule as king when he was not king, to ignore the legal and constitutional traditions of England and substitute for them his own self-confident judgement, to do a highly professional job in a very amateur manner. He had lasted so long because in two things he was not amateur at all: he knew how to promote himself, and for most of the time he knew how to keep Henry satisfied. But there was not really much to be learned from that.

The last 30 years has seen new work on the early years of Henry VIII's reign. This has led to a re-assessment of Wolsey's role. J. J. Scarisbrick, in his 1968 biography of Henry VIII, regarded Wolsey as having been in pursuit of a peace policy. In his view, foreign policy dominated the first 20 years of Henry VIII's reign. Scarisbrick rejected Pollard's thesis that Wolsey 'hitched England to the Holy See [Rome]'. In his view, Wolsey wanted peace because 'war was the quickest way to lose money' and because:

> He [Wolsey] thought in loftier terms. When he praised peace as a good and holy thing – as he often did – and deplored war between Christians as scandalous, it is easy to dismiss his words as the jargon of a cynical diplomat who was merely paying lip-service to convention. But Wolsey was sympathetic to contemporary humanism, as his educational projects, for example, show ... it is at least possible he was touched by the desperate cry of the humanists to contemporary kings and statesmen to cast off amoral diplomacy and put an end to disgraceful war among Christians.

Although not blind to Wolsey's faults, Scarisbrick was also generous about him in his final summing up:

> There had been something lofty and great about him – as a judge, as a patron of education, as a builder, as an international figure. For all his faults he had deserved more generous treatment from his king, and has perhaps deserved more generous treatment from some historians.

Historians have continued to change their opinions of Thomas Wolsey. John Guy wrote about him in *Tudor England* (1988):

> Wolsey had no guiding political principles. He was flexible and opportunist; he thought in European terms and a grand scale; and he was the consummate politican. His policies had the effect of centralising English politics: the firm rule of Henry VII was continued by different means, and political attention was focused on Westminster and the king's court rather than on the territorial feuds of magnates ... But his vision and his originality in Star Chamber were limited by his personality; his management of parliament in 1523 was ham-handed; his success in realising the Henrician fiscal [monetary] potential was seriously reduced by the dêbacle of the Amciable Grant; he over-reached himself in diplomacy. And his lasting achievement – the centralisation of the English Church – was unintentional. Neither evil nor quite a genius, Wolsey was brilliant but flawed.

Another biographer of Wolsey, Peter Gwyn, regards Wolsey as a man of great abilities. However, he does not think that Henry VIII was an easy prey to manipulate. In the end it was the King who was in charge. In *The King's Cardinal* (1990) Gwyn states that Wolsey owed his rise and nearly 15 years at the top to his abilities.

> [He was] a man who combined both enormous ability and unstoppable determination ... If one turns from the literary evidence to the documents that went out under Wolsey's name what immediately impresses is not only their quality and length ... but the range of business they cover ... The multiplicity is endless and the workload staggering, but Wolsey was evidently able both physically and mentally to take it in his stride.

According to Gwyn, when Wolsey was no longer useful to Henry VIII it was the King rather than any others, such as the Duke of Norfolk or Anne Boleyn, who disposed of him.

Other recent historians have largely agreed with Gwyn's views, although S. J. Gunn and P. J. Lindley in *Cardinal Wolsey: Church, state and art* (1991) suggest that other factors explained Wolsey's fall:

> The Cardinal's contemporary reputation must also have suffered from his ready identification with the policies of Henry VII ... In his determination to enforce the king's laws and augment the king's revenues, his confrontations with noblemen, Londoners, reluctant taxpayers and even defenders of clerical privilege – all victims of Henry VII – stirred up widespread enmity ... The completeness of his executive control over the king's affairs opened Wolsey to more general hostility, not only from those who felt themselves excluded from power, but also from all those who conveniently failed to recognise the royal will behind the Cardinal's often painful imposition of the Crown's authority.

In his recent book *Power in Tudor England* (1997) David Loades agrees with the view that Wolsey, although able, owed his position in power to hard work and the retention of the King's support:

> He [Wolsey] dominated the Council, and maintained such a high profile that some observers described him as *ipse rex* – the true king. We now know that that impression was highly deceptive, and that Henry was always in charge of his realm. Nevertheless, it was a contemporary view, and was not simply based upon the cardinal's lavish lifestyle. Wolsey himself never took his ascendancy for granted. Although he did not spend much time at Court, he tracked the king's movements assiduously, and seldom allowed more than a few days to elapse without personal contact. His industry was astonishing, and one of the main foundations of his influence. Henry always listened to other advisers at his pleasure; Charles Brandon, the Duke of Suffolk and his brother-in-law, Sir William Compton, the Chief Gentleman of his Privy Chamber, and in the early days Queen Catherine. Nevertheless the Lord Chancellor shouldered single-handedly virtually the whole executive work of the Council ...
>
> At the same time the cardinal was an isolated figure. Of relatively humble origins, he was resented by well-born councillors and courtiers who were compelled to defer to him, and lacked the support of any affinity or family network. He could find himself in the position of having responsibility without power. Having failed partly through his own mismanagement, to obtain enough money from parliament in 1523 to meet the king's urgent needs, he was virtually constrained to suggest a forced loan or benevolence in 1525. The king accepted his advice with the consent of his whole Council, but when the project failed disastrously, it suddenly became Wolsey's exclusive responsibility. He had no option but to accept the situation, and endeavoured to divert popular anger away from his master by taking it upon himself. However, instead of earning gratitude for such loyal service he found Henry had convinced himself of the truth of his *mea culpa* (my fault) and that his whole position was compromised.

No doubt, in view of the limited and often contradictory evidence, historians will continue to argue about the career and achievements of Thomas Wolsey. However, that he was a man of great personality who made a significant impact on his own contemporaries and since is undeniable. As Geoffrey Elton, not the cardinal's greatest admirer, wrote in 1965:

1. Why have historians differed in their views over Wolsey?

2. How valid is the view that the years 1509–1529 can be regarded as 'the age of Wolsey'?

For 15 years he impressed England and Europe with his grandeur, his hard work, his skill and intelligence, and his very positive action in the affairs of the world … He made a great and deserved name, and his age would have been very different without him. And surely, this is something; surely it is enough.

 ## Source-based question: Contemporary views of Wolsey

SOURCE A

One can surely believe how greatly his arrogance was increased as soon as he was invested with the new dignity (of papal legate) and how much he began to scheme how to satisfy his grandiose plan, seeing that nothing pleased him so much as wordly vanity compared with which he considered true glory of little worth. And so when he saw himself raised to the highest dignity his first consideration was to emphasise his superiority in rank over other people by some outstanding sign … Further he was not satisfied with the one cross which had served him when archbishop of York, but had to have another carried before him … This vanity, more pointless than any known before, aroused both amusement and irritation in everyone, so that all his ostentation was greeted without any applause, without any acclamation. For the people were irritated and took it badly that Wolsey should behave so arrogantly in his good fortune.

From Anglica Historia *by Polydore Vergil, published in 1555.*

SOURCE B

He [Wolsey] kept a noble house and plenty both of meat and drink for all comers, both for rich and poor, and much alms given at his gate. He used much charity and pity among his poor tenants and other, although the fame of this was not a pleasant sound to the ears of his enemies and also to such as bore him no goodwill. Howbeit the common people will report as they find cause. For he was much more friendly among all people than he was accustomed to have been, and most glad when he had an occasion to do them good. He made many agreements and concords between gentleman and gentleman, and between some gentlemen and their wives that had long been parted and in great trouble, and many other

agreements between other persons; making great assemblies for the same purpose and feasting them, not sparing for any costs where he might make a peace and amity, which purchased him much love and friendship in the country.

From The Life and Death of Cardinal Wolsey *by George Cavendish, about Wolsey after his fall from power in 1530.*

SOURCE C

You have heard under the last year how the cardinal of York [Wolsey] was attainted in praemunire, and in spite of that the king had given him the bishoprics of York and Winchester, with great possessions, and had incensed him to live in his diocese of York. Being thus in his diocese, resenting his fall and not remembering the kindness the king showed to him, he wrote to the court of Rome and to several other princes letters reproaching the king and his realm; so much so that various insulting remarks about the king were spoken … and it was said that for the cardinal's sake the king's matrimonial suit would have the worse speed. The cardinal would also speak fair to the people to win their hearts, and always declared that he was unjustly and untruly commanded, which fair speaking made many men believe that he spoke the truth. And to be held in higher repute by the people he determined to be installed or enthroned at York with all possible pomp, and caused a throne to be erected in the Cathedral Church of such a height and design as was never seen before; and he sent to all the lords, abbots, priors, knights, esquires and gentlemen of his diocese to be at his manor of Cawood on the 6th of November, and so to bring him to York with all pomp and solemnity.

The king who knew of his doings and secret communications, all this year pretended to ignore them to see what he would eventually do, until he saw his proud heart so highly exalted that he intended to be so triumphantly installed without informing the king, even as if in disdain of the king. Then the king thought it was not fitting or convenient to let him any longer continue in his malicious and proud purposes and attempts. Therefore he sent letters to Henry, the sixth Earl of Northumberland, willing him with all diligence to arrest the cardinal.

From Chronicles *by Edward Hall.*

1. Using the information contained in this chapter, explain the meaning of the following historical terms:

a) 'papal legate' (Source A)

b) 'praemunire' (Source C).

2. Study Source A.

How, by his use of language and style, does Polydore Vergil show his hostility to Wolsey?

3. Study Sources A and B.

Explain why the two sources differ in their views of Wolsey as a public figure.

4. Study all the sources above and use your own knowledge.

Explain why Wolsey's contemporaries were usually so hostile to him.

Social and economic change, 1485–1547

4.1 Were there any significant changes in the size of the population?

4.2 In what ways did trade and industry change in this period?

4.3 Were there any significant changes in English agriculture in this period?

4.4 Historical interpretation: Was inflation a major issue in the period 1485–1547?

4.5 What major changes took place in the intellectual life and in the educational system of England?

Key Issues

- *How did trade and industry develop between 1485 and 1547?*

- *How far did the agrarian economy change in the years between 1485 and 1547?*

- *Were there any significant changes in society, education and intellectual life in England in this period?*

Framework of Events

1485	Navigation Act – encouraging English shipping
1486	Magnus Intercursus – treaty which encouraged English trade with the Netherlands
1489	Further Navigation Act
1492	Treaty of Etaples – which encouraged English trade with France
1497	Henry VII supports Cabot's voyage of exploration to the Americas
1511	Erasmus is made first Professor of Greek at Cambridge University
1512	New school founded in London, St Paul's, which was not run by the Church
1517	Wolsey's Commission of Enquiry into Enclosures
1535	Major reform of both Oxford and Cambridge Universities by Cromwell
1536	Cromwell's Enclosure Act
1542–43	Major debasement of the coinage

Overview

I N social, economic and cultural matters the period 1485 to 1547 was a time of transition. Trade and industry changed little. Some steps forward were made by Henry VII in the form of an increase in royal interest and support for England's trade, but royal interest declined under his son. England started the period with most of its overseas trade dependent on wool and cloth, and ended the period in the same way. There was little change in either the volume of this trade, or the way in which it was organised. The part it played in England's economy did not change fundamentally either. English agriculture remained basically the same. The vast majority of the population remained **peasants** struggling for survival in a

Peasants: Small-scale farmers who had the right to farm a few tiny strips of land.

Subsistence economy: Where most farmers produced just enough food to live on, with no surplus for profit making.

Enclosure: A process where some landowners put hedges around large fields and created bigger and more productive units of farming.

Gentry: The class, immediately below the aristocracy, which consisted of gentlemen of good breeding.

subsistence economy, and this did not change until the 18th century. There were attempts by the more enterprising landowners to take advantage of the increase in population (which meant rising prices for foodstuffs) to farm more profitably – by a process known as **enclosure**. This happened only on a small scale in some rural areas. With the exception of more impressive looking parish churches in areas where the wool and cloth trade was continuing to boom, and country houses instead of castles which reflected the growing peacefulness of the times, the face of England changed little in this period. Towns were a little, but not significantly, larger and the population of England continued to grow. There was no significant social change in this period either. The aristocracy remained the same size, and there were roughly the same number of members of the House of Lords, although with the departure of the Abbots from the House of Lords after the Dissolution of the Monasteries laymen dominated that Chamber as well as the House of Commons.

However, there were important economic changes. The first was that inflation began to appear in England. There is much debate as to its causes, but it was to have a major effect later in the century. The population grew, particularly towards the end of Henry VIII's reign. Disease was no longer playing its part in keeping the population numbers down. This too was to have an effect both socially and economically. The Dissolution of the Monasteries also caused change, as the impact of putting such a significant amount of the productive land in England on the open market was bound to have an effect. Much of that land was to end up in the hands of the **gentry** (there were several thousand such families in England), as opposed to the aristocracy (which only numbered hundreds). In the 16th century ownership of a lot of land meant social, economic, and ultimately political power, so that may well have played a significant part in the gradual erosion of the power of the aristocracy and the rise of the gentry to being a real power in the land.

Finally, there were important changes in the education of young men. Education had always been seen as the preserve of the medieval Church, but it gradually came into the hands of educated men who were not priests. The Church had seen the purpose of schools to produce a God-fearing and literate clergy and aristocracy, with no need to educate anyone else. The two Universities of Oxford and Cambridge were always seen as the training ground for the Church's senior clergy, but this was to change in this period. Both Universities grew and saw a new role in not only training priests, but also in educating the laity (non-clerical populace). Schools grew significantly in number, no longer seeing themselves as just vehicles for teaching simple literacy and basic theology, but instead seeing themselves as educating the future leaders of society. The study of religion became only one part of the curriculum, as opposed to being the *only* part of the curriculum. Huge new areas of study were opened up – such as the classics and mathematics – and this was bound to have an effect on the life of the nation later on in the century. There was a tremendous cultural development in the second half of the 16th century, of which William Shakespeare was but one part, and this would not have happened without the rapid evolution of education in the first half of the century.

4.1 *Were there any significant changes in the size of the population?*

There seems to have been a slow, but steady, population increase in this period. This had implications in areas such as prices. Evidence is never very accurate in these years, and it was not until Thomas Cromwell started to impose rules and regulations on the keeping of parish records in the late 1530s that figures can be viewed with any certainty. It is estimated that the population in England was approximately:

1430	2.1 million
1522	2.3 million
1545	2.8 million

The death rate at about 30–35 per 1,000 each year, with a high level of infant mortality and many infectious diseases always present, prevented the population rising at a faster rate. The more rapid growth of the population in the reign of Henry VIII should be noted. A relatively high age of marriage among women was also important in keeping the population down, as the older a woman was when she got married the fewer children she was likely to have. The acceleration in the growth of the population in England seems to have come mainly in the period after 1525, when a series of good harvests led to greater prosperity and therefore improved diet. There was also a growing tendency for there to be more and younger marriages. By the end of this period average life expectancy appears to have gone up from 35 to 38 years.

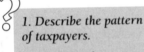

1. *Describe the pattern of taxpayers.*

2. *Compare the information in the map here with the map of England and Wales in the 16th century on page 25. Which counties of England had the highest density of taxpayers per square mile?*

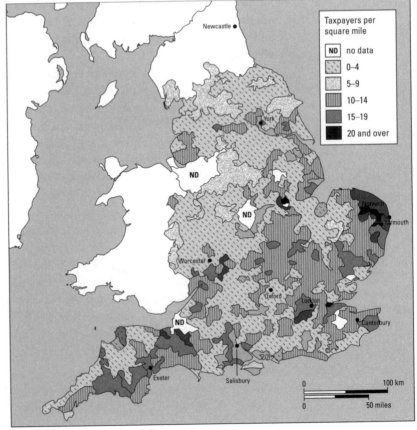

The distribution of taxpayers in England, 1524–25

The death rate was higher in the towns, with their poor sanitation and therefore more disease. However, with the majority of the population living in the countryside this did not have a major impact on the overall figures. It has been calculated that just over 300,000 of the population lived in towns, ranging from London with 60,000 inhabitants through to Norwich with 12,000, Bristol and Newcastle with 10,000, to a group of about 30 towns with between 2,000 and 4,000, such as Worcester and York. A large part of the population were peasants who existed on a subsistence economy, so good harvests meant more people living longer.

Given the unchanging social structure of the population and its relatively slow rate of increase (which could be managed within existing resources), little in the way of change could be expected in this period. Increases in trade and industry on a small scale could be 'manned' by this degree of population growth. The domestic market would see a growth in demand as well, which was bound to have an effect on prices and producers' confidence. However, the population increase was nowhere near as significant as that, for example, seen in the latter part of the 18th century, which had huge social and economic effects. What growth in population there was had little significance at the time, but was to have an impact later in the century.

1. What were the causes and immediate effects of population growth in the first part of the 16th century?

2. Why might the changes in population be more important to those studying the latter part of the 16th century?

Populations of England's main cities circa 1520	
London	60,000
Norwich	12,000
Bristol	10,000
York	8,000
Exeter	8,000
Salisbury	8,000
Coventry	6,000

Populations of some of England's regional centres circa 1520	
Oxford	5,000
Great Yarmouth	4,000
Canterbury	3,000
Ipswich	3,000–4,000
Bury St Edmunds	3,550
Cambridge	2,600

4.2 In what ways did trade and industry change in this period?

England was primarily an agricultural nation in this period; trade and industry only employed a small percentage of the population. Trade and industry were also not a major source of income for the very wealthy or for the Crown. Henry VII took an interest in such matters, in the same way as he took an interest in any matter which might benefit his income and his subjects. His son, however, took none.

Apart from some tin, lead and coal trading, the vast bulk of what could be termed 'industry' was wool and cloth. These dominated exports. Technically these were relatively backward industries, and there are no major advances in the period 1485–1547. The basic processes of making the raw wool into a thread, and weaving that thread into a piece of cloth, were done by hand. This did not change until the 18th century. The export market grew – England exported more manufactured cloth in 1547 than in 1485 – but the amount of raw wool sent abroad declined. What was important here was the fact that the raw wool was heavily taxed, while cloth was not. Well over 80% of all England's exports were cloth, which went out of either London or eastern ports such as Boston (Lincolnshire) or Ipswich (Suffolk) to be dyed and finished (prepared for sale so it could easily be made into clothing) in Antwerp. There was no separate industrial section of society; no factory-type production. The spinning of the raw wool into a thread and the weaving into cloth was done in rural areas by farmworkers. It was almost entirely a cottage-based industry, done in the homes of the peasantry. There were no factories with mass production until the late 18th century. The clothier was the linkman who collected the thread from the spinner, took it to the weavers and then took it on to the export centres. As an industry it provided casual labour for a few, mainly in Yorkshire, East Anglia and the West Country.

Wool and cloth were the most important exports, comprising 90% of total exports. They were vital for the balance of trade. Imports rose throughout the period, especially of wine, and the income from such exports was vital. The fact that customs brought over £40,000 into the Royal Treasury in duties over the years was important to Henry VII. However, this only represented a fraction of the Crown's total income. Henry VIII was less concerned with either trade or income, and his wars in the 1540s were to damage this trade and reduce his income from it.

1. In what ways does the occupational structure differ between the five towns in the table below?

2. To what extent were the towns in the table below centres of trade rather than industry?

Occupational structure of English towns in the early 16th century (classified as percentages)

Trades	Coventry	Northampton	Leicester	Norwich	York
Clothing	14	15	15	8	17
Food and drink	15.5	15	21	13	19.5
Building	4.5	7.5	4	9.5	10
Leather (and allied)	11	23	19	11.5	5
Textiles	33	13.5	8.5	30.5	8.5
Metal	8	3	3	Not known	Not known
Distributive				18	17
Other	14	23	29.5	9.5	23
	100	100	100	100	100

Describe the pattern of English wool exports in the years 1500–1600.

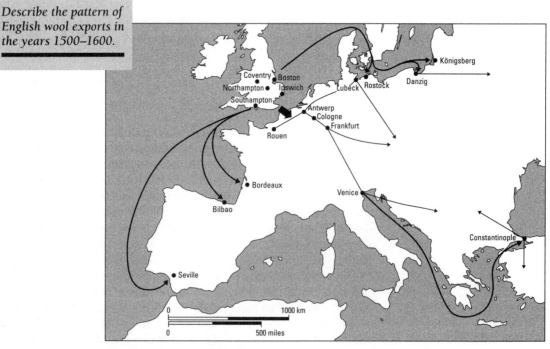

English wool exports, 1500–1600

How much royal support was there for the development of trade and industry?

Henry VII, it is said, 'could not endure to see trade sick'. Unlike his son he took a real interest in England's trade. Foreign treaties not only dealt with vital matters like pretenders and marriages, but also imports and exports. The Magnus Intercursus of 1486 (a treaty with the Netherlands) stabilised the vital cloth trade with Flanders. The Treaty of Medina del Campo with Spain, in 1489, opened new markets there, as well as leading to the marriage of Catherine of Aragon to Henry VII's oldest son, Arthur.

Henry VII also played a major role in the drafting and getting through Parliament of the Navigation Acts of 1485 and 1489. These were designed to encourage English shipbuilding and shipping. The Acts specified that English ships and English crews had to be used to import and export in certain areas. It was not just a defensive measure on Henry's part, to ensure ships in time of war, the King was also aware of the wealth-generating capacity (and thus the taxes raised) of such an industry. The invisible drain of money by having to hire foreign ships to export England's cloth could also be stopped. There was some success here, but by the end of his reign still over 50% of England's exports were carried in foreign ships. There were attempts by the King to break down the virtual monopoly held by the merchants of the Hanse (see page 49 for definition). Henry VII encouraged two main English companies to take part in the wool trade: the Merchants of the Staple, based in Calais, and the Merchant Adventurers who were based in London. He also recognised the Merchant Adventurers as a major importer and exporter in 1486, and again in 1505, in order to encourage their growth and give them an edge over the merchants of the Hanse. They were encouraged to take advantage of the favourable terms Henry always tried to negotiate in treaties such as the Magnus Intercursus. The Merchant Adventurers organised convoys, controlled entry into the trade, tried to set certain standards of cloth and did their best to keep out rivals.

Treaties such as Etaples in 1492, and its renegotiation in 1497, also encouraged trade with France. Further commercial treaties with Florence and Venice showed signs of royal encouragement to move into the Mediterranean. Attempts to develop in the Baltic were less successful as the Hanse was naturally hostile to any attempts to end its shipping **monopoly** in that area.

Henry VII did help to find more outlets for overseas trade, but by the end of the reign had made limited impact. The Netherlands port of Antwerp was convenient and could absorb what England could produce in woollen goods. Dynastic considerations were important as always to Henry VII. He was quite prepared to stop the whole trade in wool and cloth to the Netherlands if they supported 'pretenders' to the English throne. The main example of this came in 1493 when he banned all trade with Antwerp and the Netherlands because they were harbouring the pretender Perkin Warbeck.

There was no significant change under Henry VIII, and virtually no royal interest. The dangers of such a large part of the English 'economy' being dependent on a single product which went to a single market do not seem to have occurred to either the King or their ministers. There was a small boom in the period 1540–47, partly caused by the **debasement of the coinage** and partly by overproduction, but it did not last.

Monopoly: Having total control and therefore no competition. The Hanse had a shipping monopoly at the time, as there were no serious challengers to the Baltic area. The Tudors and Stuarts gave monopolies to businesses partly to fill the royal purse. For instance, by 1601 the Queen had granted monopolies for salt, lead, vinegar and seacoal.

Debasement of the coinage: Reducing the value of currency so it actually bought less. In the 16th century this meant reducing the amount of pure silver in a coin.

1. Describe the pattern of customs revenue for the years 1485–1547.

2. Using information from this chapter, what reasons can you provide which helps explain this pattern?

Annual revenue from customs, 1485–1547

New World: The Americas (North and South) which had been discovered only recently.

1. How important a role did England's wool and cloth trade play in:

a) the economic life of England

b) English foreign policy?

2. How much royal interest was there in England's trade and industry, and what form did it take?

Overall the role of Government was small, and there is no sign of a 'policy' as we know it today. Intervention seems to have been fairly random, with law and order and defence being seen as far more important considerations. Beyond the odd Act of Parliament, such as the Navigation Acts, there was little a monarch or a minister could do, given the power and means at their disposal. Henry VII did support John Cabot and his son Sebastian in 1496 in their attempt to copy the Spanish in tapping the wealth of the **New World**. (The Cabots discovered Newfoundland in 1497.) However, the Cabots seem to have received little support from any other individual or group in England, and there was no sign of any such interest during Henry VIII's reign. England seemed less enthusiastic about the wave of exploration that was clearly benefiting so many of the other Atlantic powers.

4.3 *Were there any significant changes in English agriculture in this period?*

? 1. Describe the activities shown in these contemporary woodcut illustrations which are associated with arable farming.

2. How useful are these contemporary illustrations to a historian writing about agriculture in early 16th-century England?

Capitalism: Economic system based on the theory that possession of capital or money leads to the making of profits through the power of investment.

Real wages: What can be bought with money wages taking into account inflation.

The simple answer to the question 'Were there any significant changes in agriculture in England in the period 1485–1547?' is 'no'. Well over 90% of the population lived off the land. They produced enough to survive on, but little more. In a good year with a good harvest there might be a small surplus for the purchase of luxuries, and an improvement in diet; but in a year with a bad harvest, starvation might be the result. A person leaving the country in 1485 would have seen little change if they did not return until 1547. There are small signs of growing **capitalism** in farming, labour remained cheap and low paid, and there are indications that **real wages** probably declined for many. Living standards probably fell slightly as a result of the fall in real wages. England remained able to feed its population. The rich became slightly richer and the poor became slightly poorer during the period 1485–1547. There were more manor houses to be seen in the countryside and many parish churches were built or rebuilt, which reflected the peaceful nature of the times and the growing wealth of some. The main historian of English farming, W. G. Hoskins, stresses the point that there is virtually no accurate evidence about the industry which employed over 90% of the population – agriculture.

Study the graph below. On balance, did England have good, rather than poor, harvests in the period shown? Give reasons to support your answer.

The pattern of farming varied hugely from area to area – some conformed to the traditional open field pattern, but there were so many local exceptions to this that the rule is not worth having. The only certainties were that there were more sheep than humans (about 4.5 million sheep and 2.8 million humans) and that a bad harvest, such as the one in 1535, could cause real distress for many living in a subsistence economy. The bad harvest of 1535 may have had important implications for the uprising in Lincolnshire and the North in 1536, while the very good harvests of 1537–39 may well explain why the huge upheaval of the Dissolution of the Monasteries passed off so peacefully. There was always a strong connection between disorder and a hungry population.

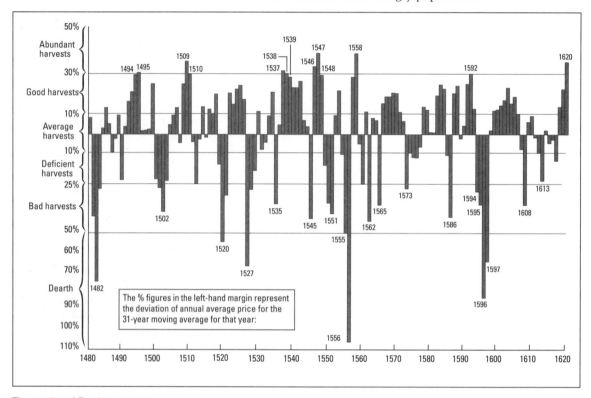

The quality of English harvests, 1480–1620

What was enclosure and what impact did it have?

The one issue which did have an impact on rural England was enclosure. This involved the ending in some areas of the centuries-old practice of the open field system, where each peasant farmer had the right to farm small strips of land in different parts of the village. The peasants also had some rights of grazing on **common land**. It was not an efficient method of farming, as part of the process was that roughly one-third of all the land was left to lie fallow (unused) every third year in order for it to recover. Ideas of rotation and modern fertilisers were unknown, and this had to be done to prevent land exhaustion. In addition, selective breeding of the type practised by the wealthy among their horses was not really possible for sheep and cattle as most were grazed on common land with no supervision. Therefore, poor-quality livestock might breed with better-quality stock and the general standard of the animals would be lowered. An increase in farm prices and the growing profitability of wool led to pressure to make more money out of land.

Common land: Land for grazing in a village that was available for use by all non-landowners. This land was not usually fenced and the cattle had little or no supervision.

Engrossing: The amalgamation of small farming units into a larger one, allowing the houses which went with the 'amalgamated' to decay.

Vagabondage: The state of homeless and unemployed groups who tended to roam in search of casual labour, but could also resort to crime and begging in order to survive.

Tenant farmers: These farmers did not own their own land. Instead they rented it from landowners and were responsible for keeping it productive. The tenant farmer would pay an agreed sum for a lease which gave him the right to farm the land.

The key to profit lay in larger farming units, and two methods were tried in this period. One was **engrossing**, which inevitably led to depopulation. Fewer people were needed to work on larger units. The other method, which caused more concern, was enclosure. The result was that fewer people were employed and some of those who could not prove they had any rights to graze the common land were evicted. Economic factors also caused many people to leave rural areas, resulting in an increase in the numbers of poor people in urban areas.

In some areas it was the lack of labour which actually caused enclosure, as there were too few people to farm the land in the traditional way. There seems to have been some enclosing in the period between 1485 and 1530, but little afterwards. The most intense period for enclosing was between 1500 and 1510. The Crown, monasteries and nobles did some enclosing, but the bulk was done by the gentry. To many it was seen as a 'bad' process, but it did lead to higher productivity.

The process caused national concern, as inevitably there was **vagabondage** and poverty as a result. Quite a few counties were affected. Some communities were shattered – in the same way as the closure of a coalmine does in the 20th century. There were some disturbances in most counties in the first two decades of the 16th century, with enclosure seen as a cause. It should also be noted that the rebels in the Pilgrimage of Grace of 1536 removed hedges and fences which had been put up in some areas.

Thomas Wolsey was the first individual at government level to take the issue seriously. He commissioned a major enquiry in 1517, which provides us with much of the evidence on the topic. The enquiry revealed the harm that enclosure could do to some communities. It also demonstrated that enclosure made money, and that wool brought in more cash than food did to landowners. The main area of genuine concern was in the Midlands, where it highlighted the inefficiency of the old system and the fact that most enclosure was imposed on the peasants from above. Where the **tenant farmers** were freeholders there was little that an enclosing squire could do. However, these were the exception and the majority of the small-scale tenant farmers were not protected by anything more than vague customs dating back centuries. They could not stand up to a literate and wealthy landlord, backed by lawyers in a court of law, and determined to acquire the land for more profitable farming.

There were attempts to ease the problem. Henry VII managed to get legislation through Parliament in 1488 and 1489 which was aimed at preventing depopulation caused by enclosure, but it it was never enforced. Those doing the enclosing were possibly those on whom Henry VII was dependent for supporting his dynasty in the early part of his reign and he was unlikely to do anything to annoy them.

Further anti-enclosure legislation was put through in 1515, but with enforcement left to the landlords it was unlikely that it would achieve much. Wolsey's enquiry of 1517 did not reveal much evidence of mass enclosure, and all that it led to was an increase in the work of both the Star Chamber and the Court of Requests (see Chapter 3) in dealing with enclosure cases. As both organisations were dominated by landlords, as were local juries, they seem to have had little preventative effect. It may have slowed the pace a little, but economic factors were equally important in preventing enclosure.

1. Describe the pattern of enclosure in England during the 16th century.

2. How far does this map support the view that enclosure after 1500 was a minor development?

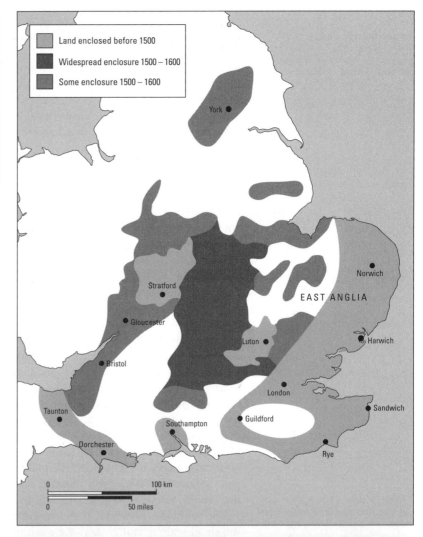

Land enclosed before 1500

Widespread enclosure 1500 – 1600

Some enclosure 1500 – 1600

York

Norwich

EAST ANGLIA

Stratford

Harwich

Gloucester

Luton

Bristol

London

Sandwich

Taunton

Guildford

Southampton

Dorchester

Rye

0   100 km

0   50 miles

Enclosure in England

Enclosure in Wardlow, Derbyshire. The new drystone walls follow the line of older arable strips. Dotted across the landscape are scars left by the pits of lead miners.

Thomas Cromwell was known to have tried to tackle the issue of enclosure, and was instrumental in passing a further Act to stop enclosing in 1536. The fact that particularly sensitive areas such as East Anglia were deliberately left out of this Act (see map opposite) is indicative that the government was reluctant to take on this powerful group of landowners. What had been very worrying about the Pilgrimage of Grace was that some of the gentry got involved, and with no police force or standing army the Crown was totally dependent on local landowners for the maintenance of law and order.

More radical measures, directed against sheep farming itself, were pushed hard by Cromwell. They eventually got through Parliament but only after they had been watered down by both the Commons and the Lords. Given the landed background of most members of both Houses, it was quite an achievement to get any measure through which might have affected their profits.

There is not much in the way of reliable evidence about the size of the problem of enclosure, but overall it was rather a storm in a teacup. It would appear that little more than 3% of all land was enclosed by 1547. It may have got a great deal of 'coverage' at the time as those who were dispossessed protested strongly, and those who stood to make money out of it would do all they could to protect their interests. Governments who were concerned with law and order would inevitably dislike a measure which leads to poverty and destitution. Also, as there was no welfare state, men and their families might be driven to crime and vagabondage.

1. How important an issue was enclosure in the first part of the 16th century?

2. How effective were the actions of government in the early 16th century to deal with the issue of enclosure?

4.4 *Was inflation a major issue in the period 1485–1547?*
A CASE STUDY IN HISTORICAL INTERPRETATION

One major economic issue which started in this period was inflation (a general rise in prices). It was to increase and have a major impact on the economic and then the social and political life of the nation later. There is still much debate as to why it occurred. Given the fact that contemporaries were really unaware of the concept itself as well as the absence of good evidence, the subject lends itself to a great deal of historical speculation.

Prices for grain, livestock and wool 1500–1549
(The figures are in index numbers)

(Prices 1450–1500 = 100)	Grain	Livestock	Wool
Then 1500–1509	112	102	93
1510–1519	115	118	119
1520–1529	154	105	111
1530–1539	161	127	122
1540–1549	187	159	153

(For example, between 1500 and 1509 grain prices were 12% above the 1450–1500 figure, while wool was 7% lower in price than the 1450–1500 figure.)

These are fairly conservative figures. Other historians, such as Peter Ramsey, argue that it was worse, with a 100% increase in basic prices between 1500 and 1510. The figures of most significance to the 90% plus who lived in semi-poverty are the grain prices, as they directly affected the price of their basic foodstuff – bread.

Monopolist: Someone who has the sole right to produce or distribute a product or service.

With all the evidence pointing to a slower rise in wages, a fall in living standards was caused by these price rises. Another factor was the pressure on landlords to produce more food and more wool. What is surprising is that there was so little enclosure.

There are numerous ideas about the causes of inflation. Contemporaries blamed a variety of individuals. The Catholic Church blamed **monopolists** and moneylenders, while Bishop Hugh Latimer in a sermon before the King in the 1540s blamed 'You landlords, you rent-raisers' – who were demanding higher and higher rents. One or two Spaniards at the time were arguing that the big influx of gold and silver from the New World was having an effect, but it is unlikely that it would have affected English prices at the time. This argument was taken up in the 20th century by an American historian, Earl J. Hamilton. The argument was simple: with more money around chasing the same amount of goods, then prices were bound to rise. Current wisdom accepts that it may have had some effect, but not in this period. Some observers at the time argued that inflation resulted from the debasement undertaken by Henry VIII's government, where the main silver coin (testoon = 5p) had its pure silver content reduced from 100 grains to 40 grains. The Royal Mint bought in silver coins at £3, remade the coins, and sold the new product for £7.20. This was a process not dissimilar to a government simply printing more money. This put more money into circulation and that was bound to have an effect on prices if the amount of food available was static.

Peter Ramsey argues in *Tudor Economic Problems* (published in 1968) that population growth was more important to England at this time. We know that population was growing, particularly in towns such as London which it is thought quadrupled in size during the 16th century. This was bound to put pressure on food prices. Ramsey also stresses the possible role of government spending, which was also going to put more money into circulation. Such spending was economically unproductive in that it did not create wealth or jobs. The impact of this has been argued by some historians, such as R. B. Outhwaite, to be marginal. However, perhaps it is more than a coincidence that Tudor inflation began more or less when the warlike Henry VIII came to the throne, and seems to have accelerated during the time of his most expensive wars of the 1540s. Coupled with the debasement of the coinage and the big influx of monastic lands onto the open market, this was bound to have an effect on prices.

At the same time, there is evidence of an increase in borrowing to fund the purchase of ex-monastic land. This expansion of credit would also be inflationary. Peter Ramsey is reluctant to draw any conclusions as to the main causes, placing more emphasis on population growth than anything else. R. B. Outhwaite places more stress on contemporaries blaming it on the debasement rather than greedy landlords. He goes on, in *Inflation in Tudor and Early Stuart England* (1969), to demonstrate how recent economic historians have demolished the Hamilton thesis on the causes of inflation. Instead he stresses the work of two English economists, Brown and Hopkins, who were looking at a much broader period. They argued that population pressures were of greater significance, particularly given the inability of the English economy and agricultural system to increase supply. Outhwaite supports the debasement thesis, but like all others has no strong historical evidence. It seems easier, given the lack of hard evidence, to

Study the table.

a) In which decade were price rises at their lowest level?

b) In which decade were price rises at their highest level?

c) Which year saw the greatest rise in prices?

d) Using the information in this table draw a graph showing the changes in prices in the period 1500–1550.

1. What were the main causes of inflation in the first part of the 16th century?

2. Why and how have historians differed on the causes of inflation in the 16th century?

demolish theories rather than to put forward satisfactory ones to explain the causes of inflation.

Inflation was to have important social, economic and eventually political effects. The growing shortage of royal income is one effect, as it led to a great dependence on Parliament for royal revenue.

Prices for the years 1500–1550

(The figures are in index numbers. The base year is 1508 = 100.)

1500	94	**1510**	103	**1520**	137	**1530**	169	**1540**	158
1501	107	**1511**	97	**1521**	167	**1531**	154	**1541**	165
1502	122	**1512**	101	**1522**	160	**1532**	179	**1542**	172
1503	114	**1513**	120	**1523**	136	**1533**	169	**1543**	171
1504	107	**1514**	118	**1524**	133	**1534**	145	**1544**	178
1505	103	**1515**	107	**1525**	129	**1535**	131	**1545**	191
1506	106	**1516**	110	**1526**	133	**1536**	164	**1546**	248
1507	98	**1517**	111	**1527**	147	**1537**	155	**1547**	231
1508	100	**1518**	116	**1528**	179	**1538**	138	**1548**	193
1509	92	**1519**	129	**1529**	159	**1539**	147	**1549**	214
								1550	262

(For example, between 1500 and 1509 prices fell by 8%; between 1512 and 1513 prices rose by 18%)

4.5 What major changes took place in intellectual life and in the educational system of England?

William Caxton (?1422–1491)
A merchant, a diplomat and a scholar. Caxton learnt printing in Germany in 1471 and set up a press in Belgium where he produced the first book printed in English. After returning to England in 1476, Caxton set up a press in Westminster, London where he printed over 100 books altogether.

The impact of humanist and Renaissance ideas (see page 23) on religious change is dealt with in Chapter 5. However, there were important developments in this period which were to have considerable impact later in the century. One of the main reasons why the men who served Elizabeth I were so able, and why there was such a flourishing intellectual and scientific life in the country, was the huge change in the way in which those leaders had been educated. This started to happen around the time that Henry VIII came to the throne.

William Caxton had set up his printing press in England in 1476, and with the first proper paper mill in England known to be producing by 1496, there was little to stop new ideas spreading. The primary reason behind these educational changes was the return to England of a small group of scholars who had studied in Italy. Also, the arrival in England at their request of one of the best known scholars in Europe, Desiderius Erasmus. The key men who spread what became known as humanist ideas were William Grocyn, Thomas Linacre and John Colet. They advocated a broad education, studying not just the Bible and religious texts. This had been the custom in the few existing schools which were dominated by monks as teachers.

Desiderius Erasmus (?1469–1536)
Born in Rotterdam. As a youth he was a monk. After becoming a priest he went to study in Paris. For a time he was Professor of Divinity (religion) at Cambridge University. Erasmus was a translator and interpreter of the Bible. He was also author of the famous satire on the Church *The Praise of Folly* published in 1511.

Ideas put forward by humanists

Among the educational ideas supported by humanists at the time were:

● The end of the Church's attempted monopoly on learning and thought.

● The study of the huge and influential range of ideas put forward by the great Greek thinkers, Aristotle and Plato.

● Learning should look not only at theology and religion, but also at literature, the arts and science.

● All learning should be opened up to all men and women.

William Grocyn, who had studied at length in Italy – centre of the new Renaissance ideas at the end of the 15th century – started by 1500 to lecture in Oxford on the ideas of Aristotle and Plato. He broadened the curriculum and encouraged debate and re-evaluation of ideas for the first time in decades. Thomas Linacre, another who had studied in Italy, rejecting the idea of a monastic career, returned having absorbed many of the scientific ideas of the great Greek thinkers. He was supported and encouraged by Henry VIII, and became the first President of the Royal College of Physicians early in Henry's reign. John Colet was the third of the 'Greek scholars' who challenged much of the medieval thinking at Oxford University. He played the key role in the creation of St Paul's School in London, which was one of the first schools in the country to be run entirely under lay (i.e. not clergy) control. The reaction against medieval ideas was very strong, and with the support of Henry VIII and Thomas Wolsey it gained influence in the early part of the century.

One of the great 'catches' of these scholars and educationalists was in persuading Erasmus to come and work in England between 1509 and 1514. Erasmus lectured in London, and at both Oxford and Cambridge Universities. He not only added strength to the movement to re-evaluate religious thinking but he was also a strong supporter for a secular (non-religious) education for young men for secular ends. He saw education as a means of forging character for particular ends, for the good of the public for example. Erasmus felt that men are shaped by education and not by birth, and that education ought to challenge and provoke, not just insist on conformity to the religious ideas of the monks who had controlled education in England up to that point.

Although it is easy to dismiss Erasmus and his fellow scholars as being 'out of touch' academics, they did have an impact. Wolsey was strongly influenced by them and his great creation – Cardinal (now Christ Church) College at Oxford University – was made up of some of the outstanding scholars of the day. They studied and taught not only divinity (religion), but also medicine, science and law. As Erasmus suggested, they taught 'pagan' poets as well as Christian writers. This was to prove embarrassing later, as several of the scholars who Wolsey attracted to Oxford were to be seen as **heretics**.

Heretics: Those who departed from the official beliefs of the Roman Catholic Church. Normally such people were burned at the stake.

Cambridge University foundations	Oxford University foundations
Christ's College 1505	Brasenose College 1509
St John's College 1509	Corpus Christi College 1516
Magdalene College 1542	Christ Church College 1546
Trinity College 1546	

Oxford and Cambridge not only expanded in terms of the number of colleges (see insert), but also in number of students. By the early years of the Elizabethan period a growing number of the key ministers of the day had studied there. It became a normal part of the education of a young man of good background. The number of professorships grew throughout the reign of Henry VIII, with new subjects being offered – such as law, science and medicine. What alarmed more orthodox and 'catholic' people was that several of the new professorships of traditional subjects like divinity fell into the hands of men of 'advanced Protestant' ideas. Inevitably, they were having an influence over the young laymen who were studying there, as well as the future leaders of the Church. It is more than a coincidence that the majority of Elizabeth I's bishops and members of the Privy Council who played a key role in the final establishment of Protestantism in England had been students at Oxford and Cambridge between 1525 and 1540 and had been educated in the 'New Learning'.

1. What information does the woodcut contain about life in a Tudor grammar school?

2. How reliable is this illustration as evidence of life in a Tudor grammar school?

A contemporary woodcut of a Tudor grammar school (a school in England for children aged between 11 and 18 who have a high academic ability. The children usually have to pass an exam to gain a place at the school.)

Expansion and change was not confined to the universities of Oxford and Cambridge. During the reign of Henry VIII as least 30 new schools were established in towns across the country. Most of the schools existing today which have 'King's' before the name of a town were set up in this period, ranging from King's, Worcester, to Canterbury and Taunton. These followed the same pattern at St Paul's in London, offering a broad-based education with the focus on studying the classics (Latin and Greek) as well as religion.

Thomas Cromwell, with his hand in everything, played an important part in this educational change. Taking on yet another office and becoming Head of Cambridge University, he ensured that reforms and expansion went through. He used his power as Vice-Regent of the Church to place a close supporter in charge at Oxford to expand and develop that university. His control over the Church also ensured that the Injunctions (orders) to the clergy of 1536 laid down that every holder of a clerical office (such as a bishop) had to fund one scholar at school or university per £100 of his income. Cromwell also ensured that his own son was educated along the lines of the ideal of Erasmus. Perhaps more significant for the future, Henry VIII had his own son educated largely by laymen. He appointed the humanist scholar, John Cheke, as the royal tutor in 1544.

This major change in the purpose of education, as well as in what was actually taught, was to have a huge impact later in the century. It affected all areas of life in England, ranging from the political, through the religious, to the scientific and artistic.

1. In what ways did the humanists have an influence in England?

2. To what extent was humanist influence long term rather than short term?

Source-based questions: The Universities in England during the Reformation

SOURCE A

'I understand that ye are come to us as suitors for your college, and have brought with you a letter of attorney to commune with our council, and to take some good way for the benefit of your house. Surely we propose to have an honourable college there, but not so great and of such magnificence as my lord Cardinal intended to have, for it is not thought meet for the common good of the realm, yet we will have college honourably to maintain the service of God and literature. We wish that you continue as ye have done until Michaelmas next coming, and then wholly to receive your rents and ye shall know at that time our further pleasure, and what way shall be taken for the continuance of that college.'

Henry VIII to the Fellows of Cardinal College, Oxford, August 1530.

SOURCE B

This commission will examine the foundations, statutes and ordinances, and enquire how they are observed and what are the value and nature of all possessions of the colleges and hospitals and … free chapels within the University of Cambridge; and to send certificate of the same with all diligence. The preamble states that this last session of Parliament has given the King full power to order all such colleges at his pleasure and he intends so to order them in the Universities of Oxford and Cambridge, where most of the youth of the realm is nourished in good literature, that students therein may be encouraged.

Part of a letter from Henry VIII to the Vice-chancellor of Cambridge University, January 1545.

SOURCE C

Dr Smythe, their learned advocate, has presented their letters … written in Latin. The letters move her (the Queen) to be a maintainer of the learned state and she thankfully accepts their document. She understands that all kinds of learning flourish among them as at Athens long ago; and she desires them not so to hunger for the knowledge of profane learning as to forget our Christianity, since the Greeks only attained to moral and natural things, but rather to study those doctrines in order to better set forth Christ's sacred doctrine, to the sincere setting forth which she trusts they will always apply their gifts, so that Cambridge may be accounted rather a University of divine philosophy than of natural or moral as Athens was.

Letter from Catherine Parr to the University of Cambridge, 1546.

1. Study Sources B and C.

Using the information contained in this chapter, explain the meaning of the following terms:
a) 'the University of Cambridge' (Source B)
b) 'the knowledge of profane learning' (Source C).

2. What may be inferred from the replies given by the King in Source A and the Queen in Source C about the reasons why the representatives of Cardinal College and Cambridge respectively had written to them?

3. Comment on the reliability of these sources as evidence of royal attitudes to education in the period 1485 to 1547. Use information from this chapter and from the sources printed above.

4. 'Henry's interest in education and learning only went as far as it served his own needs.' Discuss the validity of this statement.

Religious change in Henrician England – the beginnings of the Reformation?

5.1 What was the condition of the Roman Catholic Church in England in 1529?

5.2 What were the reasons behind the religious changes 1529–1536?

5.3 How radical were the religious changes made in the years 1529–1536?

5.4 What was the impact of the Dissolution of the Monasteries in England?

5.5 Who opposed religious change?

5.6 Historical interpretation: The Pilgrimage of Grace, 1536

5.7 To what extent was England a Protestant country by 1547?

Key Issues

- Why did a process of religious change start to take place during the reign of Henry VIII?

- Was the motivation for this change primarily political or religious?

- What form did this change take and how fundamentally was religion in England affected by it?

Framework of Events

1517	Martin Luther publishes his 95 Theses – the beginnings of the Reformation in Germany
1525	William Tyndale publishes translation of the Bible in English
1527	Henry VIII decides his marriage to Catherine of Aragon is unlawful
1528	Cardinal Campeggio arrives from Rome to deal with the Royal Divorce
1529	Hearings on the Royal Marriage open and close in England, then transfer to Rome
	The 'Reformation' Parliament meets – Acts on Probate, Mortuary Fees and Non-Residence passed
1530	Death of Thomas Wolsey
	Start of campaign in universities to get opinions favourable to King's 'side' in divorce
	Thomas Cromwell on the Council
	Clergy charged with praemunire
1531	Convocation accepts that Henry VIII is Head of Church in England 'as far as the law of God allows ... '
1532	The Supplication of the Commons against the Ordinaries
	The Submission of the Clergy
	Lord Chancellor Thomas More resigns
	Thomas Cranmer becomes Archbishop of Canterbury
	Act of Annates
	Anne Boleyn pregnant
1533	Act in Restraint of Appeals
	Henry marries Anne Boleyn; marriage with Catherine of Aragon is declared void
	September: Elizabeth, future Queen of England, is born
1534	Second Act of Annates; Act of Succession; Treason Act; Act of Supremacy; Act of First Fruits and Tenths
	Thomas Cromwell is made Vice-Regent in charge of ecclesiastical matters
1535	Thomas More and Bishop Fisher are executed
	Visitation of the Clergy and the 'Valor Ecclesiasticus' start

1536	Catherine of Aragon dies
	Statute of Uses
	Dissolution of the smaller monasteries
	10 Articles
	Injunctions of 1536
	Pilgrimage of Grace and Lincolnshire Rising
1537	Bishop's Book
1538	Injunctions of 1538
	Bible in English ordered to be placed in every Church
1539	Six Articles
	Dissolution of the larger monasteries
1540	Execution of Cromwell
1543	King's Book published
1547	Regency Council containing many reforming sympathisers appointed by Henry VIII
	Death of Henry VIII.

Overview

Henry VIII (1509–1547) – a miniature painted in 1535

Martin Luther (1483–1546) A Roman Catholic German monk who launched major attack on Roman Catholic Church from 1517 onwards. Luther initially challenged the Pope over the selling of pardons for sins. This grew into a full-scale breach between Lutherans and the Roman Catholic Church. This led to the start of Protestantism.

IT is customary to refer to the changes in religion in England, which started in the second part of the reign of Henry VIII, as the 'Reformation'. This was a process which started in the late 1520s and ended with England becoming a Protestant country by the middle years of the reign of Queen Elizabeth I, probably in the 1570s. The conventional view is that it was a single transition from the traditional Roman Catholic beliefs and practices, which had been a large part of life in England for centuries, to a new set of Protestant beliefs. The old Roman Catholic ways involved obedience to a (usually) Italian Pope in Rome, the traditional Mass and Confession, services in Latin, and monasteries and convents. These dominated much of the social and educational life in England. They were replaced by a new set of beliefs, led by the English monarch in Parliament.

It was also argued that the Church in England in 1529 was a corrupt and inefficient body, disliked by many English people. It was in no state to resist the growing tide of demands for radical reform of the Church and its role in England. Also there was an increased demand for Protestantism of the type spreading in Germany in the 1520s under the leadership of Martin Luther and some German princes.

More recently, historians such as Christopher Haigh have imposed a review of these ideas. They argue that the Roman Catholic Church was not in the state of decline in 1529 that had been made out in the past and that it was a reasonably popular institution in England. It is also now argued that the reasons for the move away from Roman Catholicism in the reign of Henry VIII were mainly political and economic in their motivation. England was by no means a long way down the route to Protestantism when Henry VIII died in 1547. Given a different set of circumstances after his death England could still be a predominantly Roman Catholic country like France.

The first moves in this 'reformation' process started for the simple reason that Henry VIII had decided that not only was his marriage with

**Thomas Cranmer
(1489–1556)**
Priest – Cambridge educated, humanist influenced. Cranmer wrote a book in 1530 defending royal divorce. He became Archbishop of Canterbury in 1533, the year in which he pushed through the Royal Divorce. He supported William Tyndale and the publication of the Bible in English. Author of Protestant Book of Common Prayer in 1549. Executed by Mary for his beliefs in 1556.

Catherine of Aragon illegal, but the reason why he had no male heir was that he was living in sin with her. He also felt that a male heir was needed in order to ensure a peaceful succession and the continuation of orderly rule in England. Henry felt strongly that a female monarch would only lead to trouble. The last time England had had a queen as monarch was Matilda in the 12th century. This had been a time of civil war! Once Henry VIII had got what he wanted by 1534 – had divorced Catherine and married Anne Boleyn – he had no further interest in religious change in England. He wished to die as he had lived, as a 'Roman' Catholic. In the process of gaining his divorce, Henry had abolished the jurisdiction of the Pope in England in some areas. He replaced it with rule by the monarch in Parliament. Matters such as divorce, traditionally seen as part of the Church's work, could now be decided in England by English courts with no reference to Rome. Clergymen now owed their obedience to the English monarch and not to the Pope. However, in most matters of belief and in many of religious practice England remained recognisably Catholic, if not Roman Catholic.

Historians such as A. G. Dickens have argued that two of Henry's key agents in this process – Archbishop of Canterbury, Thomas Cranmer and principal minister in the 1530s, Thomas Cromwell – were both secret 'Protestants' who manipulated events as far as they dared in the direction of Protestantism. Henry VIII, it is argued, knew of their views. This is seen as evidence that Henry intended his legalistic changes of the early 1530s to go much further towards a protestant church. The fact that Henry also ordered the closure of the monasteries and convents of England, seen as strongholds of Papal power and Roman Catholic influence, is yet more evidence of a desire to bring Protestantism to England. The law in 1536 requiring a Bible in English to be placed in every church in the land adds more weight to this case. This was a key feature of Martin Luther's Protestantism, the 'priesthood of all believers'. All individuals could have access to scripture (and not have it interpreted for them, as was Roman Catholic practice). It is very important that what happened in the reign of Henry VIII, as far as religion is concerned, is not seen in isolation. It should also be seen as part of a process which started decades before and was not completed for another 40 years.

5.1 What was the condition of the Roman Catholic Church in England in 1529?

The traditional view put forward by 19th-century historians such as J. A. Froude and J. H. Green (and to a certain extent endorsed by more recent historians such as A. G. Dickens and Claire Cross) was that the Roman Catholic Church in England was in very poor condition by 1529. This unfortunate situation, coupled with the spreading of Protestant ideas coming in from the continent, led to a very strong dislike of the Roman Catholic Church and its clergy. This made it very easy for Henry VIII to topple it and take much of its power and wealth. The opposing views, which had been advocated by Philip Hughes and David Knowles, argue that the Catholic Church was in a healthy condition and that religious changes

Roman Catholic religious practices in early Tudor England

England was part of the western Christian world which accepted the Pope as Supreme Head of the Church. The Pope, in Rome, controlled two provinces of the Catholic Church in England: Canterbury and York.

The Mass: This was the most important religious service. All Catholics were expected to attend Church to hear Mass every Sunday and on Holy Days, such as Christmas Day, Good Friday and certain saints' days. The Mass was said in Latin by a priest. It included readings from the gospel and prayers. The most important part was the Eucharist (when the priest said prayers over bread and wine). Catholics believed in the doctrine of transubstantiation. This stated that the bread and wine became the body and blood of Jesus Christ during the Eucharistic part of the Mass. Lutherans and other Protestants disagreed with this doctrine.

The Sacraments: The Eucharist was one of seven sacraments which Catholics could receive. The others were Baptism, Confirmation, Marriage or Holy Orders (if you became a priest), Penance and Extreme Unction. The latter was given to Catholics who were dying.

Heaven, Hell and Purgatory: Catholics believed they might go to Heaven or Hell when they died. In both cases entry would last for eternity. However, Catholics could only enter Heaven directly if they were free from sin. In the majority of cases most people died in a state of minor sin. They would then go to Purgatory. This was a temporary state of existence where they would have to stay before entering Heaven. The length of time depended on the degree of sin committed. To shorten the possible time spent in Purgatory Catholics could undertake special tasks during their lifetime. These were called 'indulgences' (see page 134). Catholics celebrated Masses for the Dead for the same reason. For this purpose, special chapels were built called **chantries**.

Chantries: Small chapels where the main purpose was to say prayers for the dead to reduce time the dead had to spend in Purgatory.

Pilgrimages: These were journeys taken by people to places of special religious significance. The Pilgrims undertook these journeys to gain Grace which would allow them to enter Heaven. In England two important shrines (the object of pilgrimages) were St Thomas à Becket's tomb in Canterbury and the Shrine of Our Lady of Walsingham in Norfolk. Prayers to Jesus Christ's mother, the Virgin Mary, were a central feature of Roman Catholic practice.

The Church year: Life in England revolved around the religious calendar. Periods of festivity surrounded the two major festivals, Christmas and Easter. There were also periods of fasting, such as the six weeks before Easter (called Lent).

The Clergy: There were two types: secular and regular. Secular clergy included bishops and priests. Regular clergy were monks, friars and nuns. The latter group lived in their own communities and engaged in activities such as helping the poor, education and prayer.

What developments threatened the Roman Catholic Church in England before 1529?

were imposed on the Church by a greedy King chasing after a new mistress and the wealth of the monasteries. This theory has never received much support. The fact that both these two latter historians were Roman Catholic priests as well may have led more uncharitable historians to argue that they were only defending their own organisation. More recent scholarship, particularly the work of Christopher Haigh, J. J. Scarisbrick, and most recently Eamon Duffy, suggests that Hughes and Knowles may well be right.

1. Describe what is taking place in these two contemporary woodcut illustrations. (You may wish to refer to the text on page 131 on Roman Catholic practices.)

2. How reliable are these woodcuts to a historian writing about religion in early 16th-century England?

Lollard: Name given to a set of ideas put forward by an Oxford University clergyman, John Wycliffe, in the late 14th century. He advocated making the Bible in English available to all, the ending of the monasteries and a reduction in the power and wealth of the Church. Many of his ideas were similar to those put forward by Martin Luther, the German clergyman who had led a breakaway movement in Germany against the Pope and the Roman Catholic Church, and which had had huge success in Germany by 1529.

Humanists: A group of scholars who had great enthusiasm for rediscovering the ideas of the great classic Greek and Latin writers, and who wished to apply those ideas to the 16th century. These ideas opposed the excessively religious ideas of the previous age, and stressed the uniqueness of man and his potential.

Sir Thomas More (1478–1535)
Lawyer, scholar, humanist, diplomat and royal servant. Author of *Utopia*, a visionary work about an ideal society, in 1516. Speaker of the Commons in 1523. Lord Chancellor in 1529. Resigned over divorce and its implications in 1532. Executed by Henry VIII in 1535. Thomas More is now a saint of the Roman Catholic Church, along with John Fisher.

John Colet (1466–1519)
A priest and a scholar. Dean of St Paul's Cathedral. Then became Oxford University lecturer. Founder of new school at St Paul's.

John Fisher (1469–1535)
Bishop of Rochester. Humanist priest and educator. Strongly anti-Lutheran and opposed the royal supremacy. Executed for treason as a result in 1535.

Lollard, Humanist and Protestant ideas

The Lollards

Certainly there were threats to the Roman Catholic monopoly on religious belief in England in the 1520s. There is evidence that **Lollard** ideas were still in circulation in some rural areas, although there were in fact few actual Lollards still in England in the 1520s. The movement had been savagely repressed in the early 15th century, and those who still supported these ideas were scattered in rural areas, such as Buckinghamshire, and tended to come from the lower classes. They were not a major force in English religious life, and there is little evidence that they played any significant part in religious change in Henrician England.

The Humanists

More influential perhaps were a group – some of whom were clergy, but others were laymen – known as the **Humanists.** The greatest of all the Humanists was a continental scholar and cleric called Erasmus (see Chapter 4) whose ambition was to reform and to purify the Roman Catholic Church. Erasmus, and his English fellow humanists – such as Lord Chancellor Sir Thomas More and the Dean of St Paul's, John Colet – were out to reform and improve the Church and not to destroy it. They wished to revitalise the Church and cleanse it of all abuses. They wanted to make the Church in England a more effective institution and to return it to what they saw as the ways of the true faith. Colet attacked some of the personal failings of individual clergy, while More, in his great work *Utopia*, portrayed an idealistic and civilised society which he felt was superior to the ideal portrayed by the Roman Catholic Church. Erasmus, in his great satire *In Praise of Folly*, had poked fun at the pretensions and failings of the Church and its members, and had amused both Popes and laymen in the process. They were critics, but not opponents, of Roman Catholicism.

Thomas More and another reforming humanist English Bishop, John Fisher, were later to die for their faith. These men were known as Humanists as they believed in the critical importance of the study of the humanities – such as the ancient Greek, classical authors – as well as the Bible and commentaries on the Bible. They had a real breadth of knowledge. Some of their Catholic critics felt that their ideas were too innovative and showed too much independence from the 'official' line of the Roman Catholic Church, which liked to maintain a monopolistic hold on all religious thinking.

There is no real evidence that this group of men and their ideas weakened the Church in England or laid it open to a Protestant attack. What they may have done is possibly the reverse: by pointing out the failings of the Church in a positive and intelligent way, it may have helped those who wished to reform it and make it more acceptable to the English people.

The Lutherans

Those who wished to alter radically the religion of England were a small group of radical reformers who had ideas similar to those held by Martin Luther in Germany. One part of this group or reformers was led by Robert Barnes, an academic and clergyman based at the White Horse tavern in Cambridge, who advocated Lutheran ideas.

The ideas of Martin Luther

- Criticism of indulgences

- Challenged authority of Pope and Cardinals

- Published Bible in German, not Latin as was usual

- Bible to be basis of belief, not Roman Church's interpretation of it

- Stressed preaching, communion and congregational singing

- Emphasised direct and personal relationship between Christ and the individual believer

- Rejected ideas and ceremonies which he felt did not originate from the Bible

- Disliked Catholic emphasis on worship of Virgin Mary

- Priesthood of all believers – no need for a hierarchical Church in order for ordinary people to be 'saved'.

Kept main practices of old Church, such as baptism, marriage, communion, but in a simpler form.

Bishop Hugh Latimer (1485–1555)
Priest and scholar. Bishop of Worcester. Executed for his Protestant beliefs with Cranmer in 1555.

William Tyndale (?1492–1536)
Oxford-educated scholar, humanist influenced. Tyndale translated the New Testament into English 1524–25. Fled England for fear of heresy charges in 1520s. Executed by agents of Charles V in 1536. It was his Bible that Cromwell and Cranmer placed in all churches.

Indulgences: Originally a relaxation of a punishment by the Church for breaking a religious law in return for a service, such as fighting to defend the Church. It gradually changed into a simple cash purchase of time off from Purgatory in return for money going to a church-approved cause.

This had quite an influence on two men who were to rise to the top of the Church under Henry VIII: Thomas Cranmer, Archbishop of Canterbury and Hugh Latimer, Bishop of Rochester (both of whom were to die for their faith in due course). However, the influence of the Lutherans was mostly confined to academic circles. The main influence men like Cranmer and Latimer were to have was after the break with Rome when they were in a position to advance their Protestant ideas as far as they dared – and Henry VIII would allow. They were not in a position in the 1520s to pose much of a threat to the Roman Catholic Church while it was fully backed by the King.

Luther and his ideas are not felt to have had a major impact on religious change in England during Henry VIII's reign. He was important as an example, and religious radicals in this country saw him simply as one influence among many. Luther was not a significant factor in the English Reformation. led to Protestant faith!

Tyndale and his Bible

The only individual who had a real influence on religious thinking itself was William Tyndale. Although strongly influenced by Lutheran ideas, he was a powerful critic of the Church particularly when it came to what he felt was the low level of education of the clergy, the practice of **indulgences** and the doctrine of purgatory.

Tyndale's greatest impact was to come with his translation of the New Testament of the Bible into English, which was published abroad with great success in 1525. It was soon selling as many copies in England despite strong persecution and censorship. Given that direct access to the Scriptures for all was seen as a fundamental part of Protestant

Title page to the 'Great Bible', first published in 1539. Henry VIII is shown seated beneath a rather small version of God. He is handing Bibles to Cranmer, the Archbishop of Canterbury, and Cromwell as Vice-Regent of the Church. At the bottom of the illustration the Bible is heard, not read, by the general population. Many are saying 'Long live the King' (shown in Latin).

1. What does this title page tell us about how Henry VIII saw his religious role?

2. According to the title page, how freely available was the Bible in English? Can you give reasons to explain your view?

beliefs, this could be seen as an important beginning for Protestantism. However, there is no strong evidence that it had this effect. Tyndale and his ideas may have softened up the path for the Protestantism which came later in the century, but they did not cause it.

Certainly there was religious debate in England in the 1520s. The Church was not without its critics, but it would not be correct to say that the Roman Catholic faith was seriously threatened by any of these groups or individuals.

How popular was the Catholic Church in England on the eve of the Reformation?

Traditional view

The traditional view presented of the ordinary clergy (see insert on page 131), their masters, the bishops and the monks and nuns was of corruption and inefficiency. Bishops were seen as men who served the king as civil servants rather than as supervisors and trainers of their clergy. Parish priests were seen as ill educated and immoral. Monasteries were seen as rich institutions which failed to make proper use of the wealth in their care for charitable and educational purposes. The Church as a whole was seen as lacking in religious fervour, subordinate to the interests of the government. Too many of its members, be they bishops or parish priests, were felt to be **pluralists** or absented themselves too often from their place of work. Thomas Wolsey, who held many church offices, is seen as a classic example of both a pluralist and an absentee. He was, for example, Archbishop of York (and spent most of his time south at Court), papal legate, and a bishop of several areas, both in England and abroad. The religious beliefs of the Church were felt to have decayed, with too much focus on the more superstitious aspects of religion – the worship of **relics**.

Ordinary lawyers felt threatened by what they saw as the growing influence of the Church's own legal system, known as Canon Law. This dealt not only with matters such as divorces and wills, but also had a separate jurisdiction over all clergymen. The fact that the amount of business for ordinary 'common' lawyers was declining sharply during the years before 1529 may have added to their criticism. The **Hunne Case** of 1514–15 is often seen as a good example of both a grasping clergy and the depth of feeling that had grown up against the clergy. Criticism was also made of the Church spending too much time and effort on the practice of indulgences and on emphasising purgatory. The Church was also felt to be too grasping in its demands for **tithes** and the fees it charged for dealing with wills and deaths. Tax collectors are never popular.

In other words, a fairly bleak picture was traditionally presented and the conclusion drawn was that the Church was a deeply unpopular institution, which was disliked by both Court and people. It was in no position to resist the onslaught of Henry VIII, his parliament and his ministers. In addition, it was felt that there was popular support for the move towards a much more Protestant faith or at least a break from the Roman connection.

Modern appraisal

Modern research, started in particular by Christopher Haigh, indicates a very different picture. This is an unusual example of how radically an interpretation of a major event can change in quite a short space of time. It is clear now that the vast majority of the people in England at the time were content with the structure and practices of the Roman Catholic Church. They continued to leave money to the Church for good purposes and they continued to go to Church. They gave every sign of fully endorsing the burning of heretics, be they Catholic or Protestant, in the time-honoured way. There is every sign also that there was a reasonable relationship between Church, State, King, Pope and people.

Pluralists: Those who held several jobs within the Church, and got paid for them all, while not necessarily doing the work for any of them.

Relics: Religious artefacts. Examples: pieces of Christ's crown at Calvary; bones of saints and their personal possessions.

Hunne Case: Richard Hunne (died 1514) was a Londoner who refused to pay the small fee charged by the Church on the death of his child. He was sued by the Church and they won, so he sued in return under the old laws of praemunire (see page 103), which were designed to stop foreigners encroaching on English matters. Hunne was arrested by the Church authorities, and was found dead in suspicious circumstances while in Church custody. Naturally the Church was blamed for his death – whether correctly or not will never be known.

Tithes: Literally a tenth: the proportion of wealth/income/produce supposed to be given by all to the Church for its support.

There were able bishops such as Bishop Longland of Lincoln (1521–47) who resided in their dioceses (area for which a bishop was responsible) and insisted on residence of their clergy and a high standard of behaviour and training. Along with many of his contemporaries, Bishop Longland was very firm in his treatment of any new 'Protestant' ideas. There is also plenty of evidence to indicate that the monasteries performed valuable tasks in an age when there was no welfare state and no formal education system. The quality of the parish clergy was good, and detailed study of several dioceses indicates a fairly high degree of literacy, fairly moral behaviour and no sign that absenteeism or pluralism was a major issue among the rank-and-file clergy.

Certainly there was some merited criticism. Any organisation containing many thousands of employees is bound to have people who abuse their position. Geoffrey Chaucer, the great English poet of the 14th century, made fun of several clerical figures in his *Canterbury Tales*, commenting on their worldliness and lack of commitment to a properly religious way of life. (But then he made fun of people from all walks of life.) Some bishops certainly did spend too much of their time serving the king, and were seen more as civil servants than as servants of God. Given the fact that most clergy were literate and the Church offered a career to talented young men who would not have advanced elsewhere, it was long the custom for monarchs to use such men as administrators in matters of state. The greed of Wolsey and the obvious political ambitions of Bishop Stephen Gardiner gave bishops a bad name, but they were exceptions rather than the rule. Bishop John Fisher of Rochester is a good example of a Henrician bishop who worked hard to ensure that the spiritual needs of his flock were met. He set an excellent example in terms of both personal behaviour and piety to the clergy under his jurisdiction. Bishop Fisher did work particularly hard to eliminate what were the worst examples of pluralism among the clergy, that is among the 'middle ranks' – the deans and archdeacons who tended to accumulate too many ecclesiastical offices to enable them to fulfil their job of monitoring the ordinary clergy properly.

It could be argued that the monasteries were the part of the Church most open to criticism. There were examples among the **friars**, particularly the Carthusians and the Observant Franciscans, who were outstanding in their work of evangelism (trying to enthuse and convert), commitment to Roman Catholicism and caring for the needy. When Cromwell sent out his Commissioners in 1536 to investigate the monasteries they did find examples of bad behaviour and misuse of funds left for 'good' purposes, but then it is clear that to find what scandal they could was part of their instructions.

Friars: Male members of one of several Catholic religious orders.

The monasteries, with their huge resources of land and wealth, failed to play the part in educational, religious and welfare life of the country their numbers and income warranted. The abbots became too much like wealthy gentry and aristocrats. The monasteries – many of which had been founded in a very different age, where there was much greater piety and religious enthusiasm – had perhaps lost their sense of direction. There was an increasing feeling that they had become out-of-date institutions – yet very wealthy ones, as they tended to get left money or land in order that they might pray for the souls of those who wished to decrease the amount of time they had to spend in Purgatory. The ease

1. In what areas was reform needed in the Roman Catholic Church in the early 16th century?

2. 'A corrupt and inefficient organisation, seriously lacking in real religious commitment.' Discuss this view of the Roman Catholic Church in 1529.

with which Henry VIII was able to close them in the later 1530s suggests that they no longer commanded the respect or affection they had done in centuries past.

The overall impression then is of a large and powerful organisation, still fully accepted by the English people. There were justified criticisms in some areas, and the monasteries, in particular, could have done with radical reform. However, the bulk of the senior clergy and the parish priests were able men who did their job reasonably efficiently. The organisation was fairly vibrant and capable of resisting a major attack on its role and beliefs.

5.2 What were the reasons behind the religious changes 1529–1536?

A huge change took place in the formal organisation of the Church between 1529 and 1536. The supremacy of the Papacy over the Church in England was ended. The King in Parliament now assumed absolute control over all matters relating to the Church. That included matters of belief as well as organisation, although it was not clearly stated at the time. In addition, most monasteries were dissolved by 1540 (the process starting in 1536) and their land and wealth transferred to the king in one of the most remarkable administrative processes seen in England to that date. In less than a decade papal power was removed from England and a centuries-old link had come to an end.

A large number of reasons have been put forward over the years to explain this 'revolution', but there is now reasonable agreement among historians on the causes. There is also agreement that what happened in England as far as the Church was concerned was not part of a carefully planned policy to remove papal power from England and make it into a Protestant country in the way Luther had done in North Germany. It was not in the nature of Henry VIII to think long term, except possibly about the future of his dynasty, and he remained in his own eyes at least a 'good' Catholic. What happened between 1529 and 1536 was a series of measures each designed to deal with a particular problem and not really related to what happened before or after.

What were the main causes of the religious changes in England in the 1530s?

The key reasons for the break with Rome and the Dissolution of the Monasteries lay with Henry VIII himself. He felt he needed to divorce his wife, Catherine of Aragon, and the Pope failed to grant permission. Cardinal Wolsey had tried to get Henry a divorce, and his failure was a major reason for his fall from power. The only way in which Henry could get the divorce that he felt the country needed for its future security was by ending papal jurisdiction in England and transferring to the king and his ministers the ability to deal with such matters. In addition, Henry VIII had a powerful ego. He bitterly resented those who got in the way of his immediate ambitions and wishes.

The Pope had got in the way of his wishes and therefore had to be removed as an obstacle. Henry had two willing servants in this process: Thomas Cranmer, his Archbishop of Canterbury, and Thomas Cromwell who had emerged as the King's chief minister by 1532. Both of these men were highly intelligent and between them were able to offer Henry a means of getting what he wanted – a divorce from his wife. The fact that both men were Protestant sympathisers with hidden agendas of their own is why some of the actions could be seen as pro-Protestant in addition to being anti-papal. Cromwell's ability to manage Parliament, whose legislation both legalised and gave an indication of public support to the ending of papal power, was outstanding. The fact that there was limited opposition to the changes as they progressed from any social, political or economic group is also of great significance. Tudor Government was not strong enough to force more than a tiny minority into doing something they did not wish. Henry VIII's need for money played a vital part in the Dissolution of the Monasteries. The lack of any really able leaders of an opposition, either within or outside the Church, gave Henry and his ministers an easy ride. It was Henry's wish for a divorce which started the whole process.

The 'great matter': the Royal Divorce

It is not known exactly when Henry started to feel that he had to divorce Catherine of Aragon, whom he had married after his older brother Arthur had died. There is some evidence that Henry felt that she had to go as early as 1523, but it is known that he had made the decision by 1527.

The reasons are reasonably straightforward. By 1527 Catherine was aged 42 and it was extremely unlikely that she would produce another child. She had one living daughter, Mary, and had had several miscarriages. The fact that Henry had a healthy illegitimate son further convinced him that his marriage was wrong. Henry felt that he needed a legitimate male heir to succeed him and was not going to get one from Catherine. He felt strongly that leaving a daughter to succeed him would be a recipe for political anarchy and instability. There were male members of the de la Pole family (descendants of Edward IV) alive who might appear to lay claim to the throne of England and undo all the excellent dynastic achievement of his father, Henry VII. The Spanish/Imperial alliance was diminishing in importance, so the value of having the aunt of the Emperor Charles V as his wife was lessening. The marriage had a value when it was arranged 25 years earlier, but that value was gone. Also Catherine had failed in the basic duty of a royal wife – of producing a reasonable number of male heirs. The fact that Henry both liked and respected her had nothing to do with the need to provide for the dynastic security of England. There may have been additional personal reasons as well (there often were with Henry). He had fallen for Anne Boleyn, the sister of one of his former mistresses. Anne was insisting on no sex before marriage because she didn't want to join the ranks of discarded ex-mistresses. The fact that she and her family were known to have some Protestant sympathies complicates this already complex situation.

Henry VIII was convinced that he had broken the law of God in his marriage to Catherine, as she had been his brother's wife, and such marriages were forbidden in the Old Testament. The absence of a male heir, he felt, was divine punishment for such a breach of the rules. The marriage had been made possible by a papal dispensation (see page 33). Henry

---

Anne Boleyn (1507–1536)
Sent to France when she was about 12 to enter the household of Queen Claude, wife of Francis I. When she returned to England in 1522, she joined the royal court. Her older sister, Mary, became Henry VIII's mistress at about this time. When the King wanted Anne she insisted on marriage or nothing. However, she became pregnant at the end of 1532 and was secretly married to Henry in January 1533. Anne stamped her personality on the Court and government, but she failed in her main task of giving Henry a male heir. In 1536 the King sanctioned her execution on the grounds of adultery and of incest with her own brother.

naturally felt that what the Pope had made, he could unmake. So he requested a divorce. Such requests were not uncommon, and had been granted to monarchs by popes in the past in several countries.

Not unnaturally, Wolsey was expected, as Cardinal Archbishop and papal legate, to liaise with the Pope and to produce the divorce. This proved not to be easy. For a start, Catherine was strongly opposed to being discarded. For a devout Roman Catholic, such as she was, divorce was a sin and her daughter would be regarded as illegitimate. Catherine had many friends and supporters at Court and in the country. Finally, Catherine's nephew, the Emperor Charles V, had destroyed a French army in Italy and was master of Rome. The Pope was his prisoner, Charles' army having sacked the city of Rome in 1527.

Catherine, as was her right, appealed to Rome once Wolsey started to examine the case. So the whole issue had to be referred to the Pope for resolution by the end of 1527. Henry's desire for Anne Boleyn showed no signs of diminishing and she still refused to go to bed with him.

In 1528 Pope Clement VII sent Cardinal Campeggio to England to try the divorce case. Campeggio had the powers given to him actually to terminate the marriage, but he kept that information secret. His main instruction from Pope Clement was to play for time as long as was possible until the highly complex situation in Italian politics became clearer. Then the Pope might be less dependent on Charles V for the survival of the Papacy as an institution.

By 1529 Cardinal Campeggio had produced no result. The case was adjourned to Rome for a solution – a process which could take months or even years. Henry was no nearer his objective, Wolsey had fallen (partly because of this) and Henry's Court was dividing into three separate factions. The first was led by the Duke of Norfolk (Thomas Howard) and Bishop Stephen Gardiner (see page 168), conservatives who were hostile to Wolsey and opposed to any divorce. A second faction had no obvious leaders in 1529, but centred around the Boleyn family. It had key figures of the future, such as Cranmer and Cromwell, among its members. They were in favour of a radical solution to the divorce problem, beginning to argue that the question ought to be solved in England if Rome could not deliver. The third faction centred around Wolsey's replacement as Lord Chancellor, Thomas More, and bishops such as Cuthbert Tunstall and John Fisher, who were also strongly conservative and supporters of Catherine. It was into this confusing and complex situation in 1529 that a Parliament was called.

What part did Parliament play in the Royal Divorce in the years 1529–1533?

Historians, such as Geoffrey Elton in his *England under the Tudors* (1955), were to call the Parliament which met between 1529 and 1536 the 'Reformation' Parliament. It was through this Parliament that the great Acts which broke with Rome and dissolved the monasteries were passed. Some would argue that later Parliaments, perhaps those of Edward VI or Elizabeth I, deserved the title more. No one is entirely sure why a parliament was called in 1529, there is no evidence of a real agenda for it. However, what is known is that it remained in being for longer than was usual in the 16th century, having seven sessions in total – and was certainly being used by 1530 as part of a process to put pressure on the Pope to grant a divorce.

The Reformation Parliament, 1529–1536

1529   Act passed to control clerical fees to be charged for burial and probate (wills).

Act passed to end Benefit of Clergy (the right of clerics to be tried for crimes in the normal court system) for those clerics charged with robbery or murder.

Act to limit pluralism (the right of clerics to hold more than one office).

Act passed to limit clerical involvement in commerce.

1531   The whole of the English clergy were charged with praemunire (see page 103). An Act was passed which removed this charge in return for payment of a fine. The wealthiest province, Canterbury, had to pay £100,000 and the province of York £19,000.

1532   Act limiting the payment of Annates (taxes paid annually to the Pope). This was not to be enforced for one year. It was used as a threat against the Pope to grant Henry's divorce.

1533   Act in Restraint of Appeals: prevented English people appealing to Rome in legal cases.

1534   The most significant year of the Reformation Parliament. Henry VIII amends the Bishop's Book, thus declaring that people must pray to Jesus Christ not God the Father.

Parliament opened with an attack on Wolsey, the Pope's representative in England. It continued with an anti-clerical group of MPs (possibly organised and encouraged by Cromwell) setting up a committee to put forward measures which were designed as, and were seen to be, attacks on the clergy. These dealt with items such as wills, mortuary fees (charged when a person died), pluralism and non-residence. Not all of these measures were totally successful. They faced opposition in the House of Lords, with its large clerical group (bishops and some abbots had a right to sit in the Lords). However, royal pressure was used to get through some of these criticisms of the Church. There was also an attack on the power of the Pope. What proved to be particularly important for the future was the fact that Parliament was being directly involved in Church matters, and little use was made of Convocation (the Church's own Parliament). The involvement of laymen in church matters was highly significant.

With no response from Rome and with Henry himself being summoned to Rome in 1530 (an offer he declined), further pressure was now put on the Pope to grant the divorce. This pressure took two main forms: to use Parliament and to canvass the universities of Europe for their opinions on the legitimacy of the Royal Marriage. The latter plan was not totally successful, with a huge range of opinions being put forward.

Academic opinion generally believed that the case was 'won' by those who maintained the legality of the marriage. However, one group of English academics, with Cranmer being the major figure in it, produced a strong argument in 1531 saying that Henry was entitled to act on his divorce without appeal to Rome. That clearly had an impact on Henry's thinking.

Parliament continued to meet throughout 1530, as Rome remained silent on the subject of the Royal Divorce. There is evidence that Parliament was increasingly being managed by Thomas Cromwell, appointed to the Council in 1530. It has been argued that Cromwell was determined to push England away from Rome and towards Protestantism. As 1530 progressed, a charge of praemunire was laid against some of the clergy. When no response was quickly forthcoming from the Church, it was threatened that the whole clergy would be charged with this crime. In addition, a substantial amount of money was demanded from the Church (this particularly interested Henry himself) with recognition of Henry as Head of the Church in England and its clergy.

Convocation met in early 1531 to deal with this attack, and agreed to pay Henry off and accept that he was 'The Supreme Head of the Church in England and Wales … as far as the word of God allows'.

Henry had won, the Church was made to look weak, but there was still no response from Rome. In 1532 events moved to a climax. Cromwell, now on the Privy Council (see page 13), developed as a parliamentary manager. He had played a role in drafting the criticism of the Church back in 1529 and he was now to play an even more important role in the major attacks of 1532.

Was 1532 a turning point in the break with Rome?

The year opened with a major attack by the Commons on the Church, well organised by Cromwell. This was a petition to the King, formally known as the 'Supplication against the Ordinaries'. It was a very strong attack on many aspects of the Church, Canon Law and the independent power of Convocation. This was accepted by the King, indicating his support, and the clergy were required to apologise formally and to accept these criticisms in 'The Submission of the Clergy'. Lord Chancellor Thomas More, always a supporter of the old faith and its ways, soon resigned. He was replaced as the King's chief minister by Thomas Cromwell.

Annates: Payment of the first year's salary of a bishop etc. to Rome.

With Rome still unresponsive, stronger pressure was needed. So Parliament, under Cromwell's direction, produced a Bill which would cut payments to Rome by the Church. These were known as **Annates**. The measure was intended to be 'conditional' to start with, but had a sting in the tail in that if the Pope refused to accept it, then bishops would be appointed by the king without consultation with Rome. This measure did arouse a fair amount of concern in both the Commons and the Lords, which indicates that there was not a strong groundswell of opinion against the Roman Catholic Church. Although it was made clear to both Parliament and the Pope that the Bill would be forgotten if the divorce was granted, it failed to achieve its objective.

In August 1532, Archbishop Warham of Canterbury, a competent defender of the old faith, died. He was replaced by Thomas Cranmer. This was a surprising promotion, as Cranmer had been married, was a member of the Cambridge White Horse group, belonged to the Boleyn 'faction' and

1. What methods did Henry VIII use to bring pressure on the Pope to grant his divorce from Catherine of Aragon in the years 1529–1532?

2. To what extent was the year 1532 a turning point in relations between Henry VIII and the Pope?

was a prominent supporter of the King's right to a divorce. The Pope did accept Cranmer's appointment, indicative that he was perhaps sympathetic to Henry's position but was still unable to act. All these events failed to have the required impact on Pope Clement, who was still hoping that Catherine might enter a nunnery or perhaps die.

The drift continued throughout the autumn of 1532, until possibly the most significant event in the 'Reformation' process to date – Anne Boleyn gave in to the pressure from the King, slept with him and became pregnant. Henry VIII was determined that the child should not be another royal bastard and wanted the (expected and hoped for) son to be the legal heir to the throne. With Cromwell as his minister and Cranmer as his archbishop he had the men in place who were willing to assist him. By January 1533 Henry had, in his eyes at any rate, 'married' Anne and declared that Catherine was not and never had been his lawful wife. It now remained for Cromwell and Cranmer to make legal this infatuation and the resulting pregnancy.

5.3 How radical were the religious changes made in the years 1529–1536?

Between 1533 and 1534 a series of Acts of Parliament were passed which changed the relationship between the Roman Catholic Church in England and the 'Mother' Church in Rome. A centuries-old bond was dissolved. Although there were to be religious implications to these Acts of Parliament, there was not much reference to religion in the Acts themselves. The changes were all passed through Parliament. This was of considerable significance for a variety of reasons: partly as it showed there was public support for Henry's actions; partly as it gave the break with Rome more authority. Also once Parliament had become involved in one of the greatest changes for decades, it was difficult to reverse them. Parliament was on the path to increased influence. These Acts changed the status of the King and increased his power and influence over the Church. They made him master of his own house – subject it appeared to the support of Parliament. They changed the Church in England fundamentally. The implication of these Acts of 1533 and 1534 was that there was now a Church of England as opposed to a Church in England. It was no longer a part of the Roman Catholic Church centred under the authority of the Pope in Rome.

In terms of religious belief there was little difference. Those attending services would see or hear no difference. A visitor from Italy in 1534 would not notice much that was different. Services were still in Latin, in a familiar format, with priests celebrating the Mass in the traditional way. Monks and nuns were still in their monasteries and convents. However, in spite of the King's wish to remain a good Catholic, a committed Roman Catholic could see worrying signs. If so radical a change could take place so quickly, then surely other changes could follow along the lines already seen in Germany and Switzerland. The King's business was now being conducted by an outstanding administrator, Thomas Cromwell, who was known to have 'advanced' religious ideas. The new Archbishop of Canterbury, Cranmer, was another of similar views. The King himself seemed to be a Catholic, but circumstances had forced him into radical

Acts passed by the Reformation Parliament, 1533–34

The Act in Restraint of Annates

This seemed fairly unimportant: simply stopping some small payments to Rome, but built into the Act was the sole right of the King to appoint bishops – which remains to this day. The dreaded penalties for praemunire would be imposed on those who failed to obey this.

The Dispensations Act

This stopped all payments of any sort to Rome and passed to the Archbishop of Canterbury the right to deal with all requests to depart from church law.

The Act of the Submission of the Clergy

This put into statute form the earlier 'submission'. It was another example of the King and his Minister, Cromwell, getting public and statutory support for such actions. This effectively put the Crown in firm control of Convocation and prevented any sort of minor appeal, even in religious matters, to Rome. Communication with Rome was being prevented.

The Act of Succession

This ended any claim that Catherine of Aragon might have to be Henry's lawful wife, and implied that her daughter Mary was illegitimate. The marriage with Anne Boleyn was declared valid, with any children of that marriage declared to be the rightful heirs to the throne. Two vital sections to the Act were added: the first made it treason to criticise the Boleyn/Henry marriage in any way; the second required all to take an oath swearing to uphold the Act. The latter was to prove a useful weapon against opponents of the marriage, which is probably why Cromwell had it inserted.

The Act of Supremacy

Much of this Act was simply recognising in law what had already happened – that Henry had taken control of the Church in England. However, it had a wider and deeper significance. Not only did the Act formally recognise Henry as Head of the Church, it also gave him enormous influence over the doctrines and beliefs of the Church in England. He chose on the whole not to make widespread use of this power. It gave Henry VIII the power to make a layman, Cromwell, Vice-Regent and Vicar General of the Church, which meant he had more power than Wolsey had ever had (or anyone else before or since) over the Church and its property, personnel and beliefs. England, now being an 'empire', was able to make any law it wished in all areas, through the King in Parliament.

The Act for First Fruits and Tenths

This Act required the holders of all ecclesiastical posts to pass some of their income on to the King.

The Treason Act

This ended the parliamentary sessions and made it a major crime to criticise the King over what he had done to the Church. It also outlawed criticism of his marriage and succession policies.

moves and that could happen again. He was still 'The Defender of the Faith', the title granted to him by the Pope earlier for defending the faith against the attacks of Martin Luther.

The Act in Restraint of Appeals, 1533

There were several Acts of Parliament in 1533 and 1534 which dealt with the Royal Divorce and its implications. It was already established custom that such major changes should be made through Parliament and not just by a king. Issues such as where the money should now go which had been sent by the Church in England to Rome, and who should deal with church appointments needed clarifying. The first of these Acts was the Act in Restraint of Appeals of 1533. This was a radical measure, drafted by Cromwell, which laid down that in future the highest Court of Appeal in all religious matters now lay in England. There would be no outside interference in such matters. The preamble (opening statement usually containing the main ideas behind the Act) contained an interesting statement that England was 'an Empire'. This was seen by some as an indication that Cromwell was beginning to advocate the idea of an independent sovereign state – free from foreign influences. Matters like the royal divorce would now be dealt with solely in England by the English.

Excommunication: Totally cut off from the Church; destined for eternal damnation.

This led to the **excommunication** of the King by Pope Paul III by the end of the year. It did, however, enable the King to get his divorce from Catherine. Then he was able to marry Anne Boleyn before their child was born. This was the future Queen Elizabeth.

The 1534 Acts

Parliament worked overtime in 1534. There were two busy sessions and much vital legislation dealing with the Church was passed (see pages 144–5). Cromwell organised it particularly well and laid the basis for an autonomous (self-governing) Church in England. It is difficult to say which had the greater importance as all were to play an important part in the process of England becoming a Protestant country – or at least ceasing to be a Roman Catholic one. Whether all this was going too far, as far as Henry was concerned, is debatable. It is argued that much of this legislation was pushed by Cromwell. The breach with Rome seemed permanent. The ability to make major changes in belief and practice was there to be used in the future.

1. What major changes in the Church in England were passed by Parliament between 1532 and 1534?

2. To what extent was the so-called 'religious' legislation of 1533–34 concerned with purely religious matters?

The breach with Rome was passed by Parliament and was part of the law of the land. As far as Henry VIII was concerned, the matter was over. He had the wife he wished and hopefully she would produce children. Henry had enormous power over his Church, and he seemed initially content to delegate that power to Cromwell, who it is argued, made as much use of that power as he dared to advance his own ideas. Cromwell was well aware of what happened to his former master, Wolsey, so was particularly cautious in his actions. He took great care to ensure that he did not offend Henry, particularly in religious matters.

The change was legal and judicial. Much of the life of the Church continued in the way it had done for centuries, but the potential for more radical change was there. Power now lay in England, not Rome, and very much at the disposal of one individual, Henry VIII.

5.4 What was the impact of the Dissolution of the Monasteries in England?

Between 1536 and 1540 another event of major social, economic, religious and political importance took place. This was the dissolution of all the monasteries and convents in England. In effect, they were first brought under government control and then closed down. There were about 10,500 monks and nuns in some 850 institutions, although the numbers had been falling steadily. There is much debate over why this was done. Was it a simple device to loot the Church of its wealth or was it part of a concerted move towards the establishment of Protestantism in England? Others have suggested it was more a process of destroying a base from which the Pope might make an attempt to re-establish his authority in England. Added to the events of 1529 to 1534 a more anti-Catholic and pro-Protestant picture emerges. With hindsight it can appear as part of a campaign on the part of Protestant supporters in England to copy what had happened in Germany and Switzerland.

Additional questions need to be answered. Why did such a wealthy and influential institution, with a large number of personnel, gave in so easily to the Crown and allow itself to go without a fight? Did this departure without much more than a whimper indicate an institution which was fundamentally rotten or had no really useful purpose left? Or was it the victim of a carefully planned and brilliantly executed policy led by the master-schemer Cromwell? Was he the man who devised a propaganda campaign to discredit the monasteries and persuaded his catholic and conservative master to follow this path by promises of vast wealth and financial independence?

The economic impact of the Dissolution was vast and also much debated. The implications of putting huge amounts of some of the most productive land in the country up for sale was bound to be great. People could now buy land which they had not been able to in the past, and as social status went with land, then this was bound to have important social implications. It has been argued that this led to the rise of a class who were to challenge the power of both the aristocracy and the monarchy – the gentry.

Colchester Abbey church, just before the Dissolution

Preserved monastic church,
Tewkesbury, Gloucestershire

Fountains Abbey, Yorkshire: ruins

Thus political implications were involved and some historians have pointed out that because much of this formerly monastic land ended up in the hands of laymen, including such prominent conservatives as the Duke of Norfolk, many had a vested interest in ensuring that there was no return to Rome. Finally, the ending of the monasteries with their libraries and great traditions of learning and scholarship terminated what many saw as repositories of Roman Catholic learning, as centres of belief. The removal of those centres of learning and tradition was bound to have a damaging effect on the old faith.

Why were the monastries dissolved?

A variety of reasons have been suggested. What may have been Henry VIII's main motive may not have been the same one as his willing lieutenant, Thomas Cromwell. The actual idea of dissolving some monasteries was not in itself new. Wolsey had dissolved 29 of them as part of a reform and rationalisation programme in the 1520s and had used the money gained for educational purposes. No one had seen much wrong with the fact that it had diverted funds intended for one 'good' cause to another.

What was uppermost in Henry VIII's mind was the need for money, and he got huge amounts of it from the closure of the monasteries and the seizure of their vast assets. Another factor behind the closure was the image that had been presented of their corruption. There is evidence that those who Cromwell sent out to survey the monasteries had instructions to find and publicise any poor behaviour they found. They found some, but not significant amounts. Obviously those who had further progress towards Protestantism on their minds might see the monasteries as a very important part of the old Roman Catholic Church, and as such a threat. Others did not care for what had been their primary purposes, which was to say Masses for the dead, as that was seen as religiously unsound by those with Protestant ideas. It was also felt that with their huge wealth monasteries did not make the welfare and educational impact they should have done. Much of their educational work was now being done by the universities, and the friars, with their 'no fixed abode', had a better reputation for caring for the sick and the poor.

The monasteries and nunneries were accepted institutions and part of the fabric of social and economic life in the countryside, but they had few

1. **Outside London which towns had the most important monasteries?**

2. **Which town had the greatest number of houses and friars?**

3. **How useful is this map to a historian writing about the Dissolution of the Monasteries?**

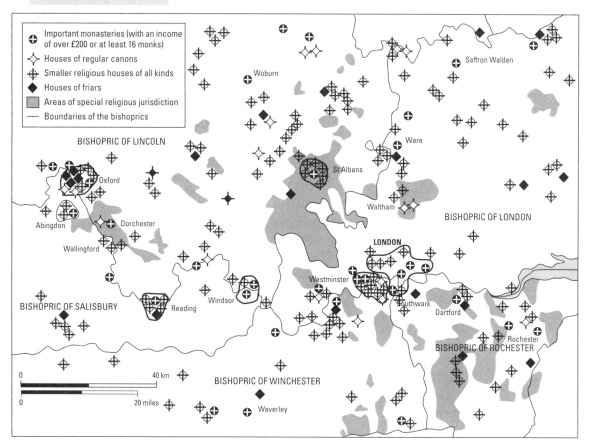

The pattern of monastic property in south-east England, 1500–30

Legend:
- ⊕ Important monasteries (with an income of over £200 or at least 16 monks)
- ◇ Houses of regular canons
- ⊕ Smaller religious houses of all kinds
- ◆ Houses of friars
- ▨ Areas of special religious jurisdiction
- — Boundaries of the bishoprics

BISHOPRIC OF LINCOLN

Oxford
Abingdon
Dorchester
Wallingford
BISHOPRIC OF SALISBURY
Reading
Windsor

Woburn
St Albans
Ware
Waltham
BISHOPRIC OF LONDON

Saffron Walden

Westminster
LONDON
Southwark
Dartford
Rochester
BISHOPRIC OF ROCHESTER

BISHOPRIC OF WINCHESTER
Waverley

0   40 km
0   20 miles

strong friends either among the laity or the non-monastic clergy. They were perhaps outdated institutions, which no longer had a clear role to play in the life of the country, and as such were an easy target for a poor king and his brilliant, Protestant minister.

How were the monasteries dissolved?

There seems, as always, to have been no clear and overall plan behind the dissolution. Henry and Cromwell seem to have agreed on it, or at least a start on it during the summer of 1535. Two major bureaucratic initiatives were started by Cromwell in the course of 1535 with regard to the monasteries. The first was a visitation, where his agents would 'visit' all monastic houses – a process similar in purpose to inspections of schools today – to check on standards. Cromwell took care with his agents here and briefed them well. Men were chosen who were not sympathetic to the monks or nuns and who were required to produce evidence which could be used against the monasteries.

The second was the 'Valor Ecclesiasticus' (literally 'The value of the Church' – see insert opposite) – a huge survey of all clerical income, which gave Cromwell and his master some idea of the Church's wealth. This was perhaps one of the most remarkable administrative achievements since the Domesday survey in the 11th century. The power to conduct such surveys had, of course, been written into the legislation of 1534 by Cromwell – yet more evidence of his superb planning and foresight. He also took the precaution of setting up a new bureaucracy under the Court of Augmentations ready to receive the wealth and land of the monasteries.

The evidence accumulated by Cromwell's visitors was duly presented to Parliament in 1536, and legislation allowing for the dissolution of monastic houses with an income of less than £200 (about 285 in all) went through. It is worth noting that income was the deciding factor here, and not spirituality or commitment to the welfare of the community. It seems that the dissolution of the smaller houses was seen as sufficient to achieve the King's purposes, and that no more was intended. It was seen as a rationalisation along the lines of Wolsey's earlier work. It was done in a civilised and caring manner, on the whole. Many of those involved left religious life permanently (which gives some indication of their fervour), some transferred to larger houses and convents, some of the abbots and older members got pensions. The only strong opposition in 1537, by the Carthusian monks, was dealt with brutally.

If Cromwell expected the process to speed up and take over the larger houses, he was wrong at first. It is clear that the Pilgrimage of Grace of 1536 (see page 154) gave him second thoughts. However, in an even more remarkable process the remaining houses were dissolved between 1537 and 1539. Little force had to be used and the Act which was passed by Parliament in 1539, dissolving the larger houses, was in fact giving legal recognition to what had already happened. A whole era of religious history, which had lasted nearly a thousand years, had come to a quiet end.

Religious houses with incomes exceeding £1,000 in the 'Valor Ecclesiasticus'

House	Order	Gross income	Net income
Westminster	Benedictine (abbey)		£2,409
Glastonbury	Benedictine (abbey)	£3,912	£3,311
Canterbury, Christ's Church	Benedictine (cathedral priory)	£3,642	£2,423
St Albans	Benedictine (abbey)	£2,909	£2,102
Reading	Benedictine (abbey)		£1,938
Abingdon	Benedictine (abbey)		£1,876
Bury St Edmunds	Benedictine (abbey)	£2,336	£1,659
York, St Mary's	Benedictine (abbey)	£2,091	£1,650
Peterborough	Benedictine (abbey)	£1,979	£1,721
Syon	Bridgettine nuns	£1,943	£1,735
Ramsey	Benedictine (abbey)	£1,849	£1,643
Winchester, St Swithun's	Benedictine (cathedral priory)	£1,762	£1,507
Gloucester	Benedictine (abbey)	£1,744	£1,419
Canterbury, St Augustine's	Benedictine (abbey)	£1,733	£1,431
Durham	Benedictine (cathedral priory)	£1,572	£1,328
Tewkesbury	Benedictine (abbey)	£1,478	£1,319
Worcester	Benedictine (cathedral priory)	£1,444	£1,296
Cirencester	Benedictine (abbey)	£1,325	£1,045
Shaftesbury	Benedictine nuns (abbey)	£1,324	£1,149
Evesham	Benedictine (abbey)	£1,313	£1,138
Ely	Benedictine (cathedral priory)		£1,084
Fountains	Cistercian (abbey)	£1,178	£1,004
Chester	Benedictine (abbey)	£1,104	£1,030
Lewes	Cluniac (abbey)	£1,091	£921
Leicester	Augustinian can. (abbey)	£1,056	£946
Norwich	Benedictine (cathedral priory)	£1,061	£871
Croyland	Benedictine (abbey)	£1,050	£947
Merton	Augustinian can. (abbey)	£1,036	£957

1. Find out the difference between an abbey and a priory.

2. Considering the purpose of the 'Valor Ecclesiasticus', how useful is the table above to a historian writing about the Dissolution of the Monasteries?

What were the results of the Dissolution?

If the intention had been to make better use of the wealth of the monasteries, then those who had that hope were to be disappointed. There was less charity and less education and only the King and the ruling elites made money. There was a massive increase in royal income and power. The traditional view was that many suffered, but the evidence would indicate that the Court of Augmentations did pay pensions to some. Most monks got jobs as ordinary parish priests, if they wished, but the nuns on the whole did badly.

The new landlords were not much different from the old and there was no radical change in the countryside. Some of the land (and the total wealth involved was over 10% of the wealth of England) went fairly quickly to key nobles such as the dukes of Norfolk and Suffolk. Whether this made them more in favour of the 'reformation' is debatable as both remained focal points of resistance to religious change in the period. Indeed, the Duke of Norfolk was to play an important part in the downfall of Cromwell in 1540.

Some of the land and wealth went to key administrators like Cromwell, but the bulk remained in royal hands, providing the monarchy with the income needed to wage war in the 1540s. A fair amount was sold off in the years 1543–47 and much of this went to those who had not been landowners before. The social and political implications of this were to be considerable in the later Tudor and early Stuart period. It is fair to say that there was little short-term or even medium-term impact, but a major one in the long term. Chronologically, the Dissolution of the Monasteries is naturally linked with the rest of the reformation process in England, but either could probably have happened without the other.

1. Why was it so easy to dissolve the monasteries?

2. 'There is only one reason worth considering for the dissolution of the monasteries, and that was Henry VIII's wish for a larger income.' To what extent do you agree with this view?

5.5 Who opposed religious change?

Given the great changes that had taken place in a short period of time, and the fact that several of the Acts of Parliament gave to the King and Parliament the ability to make even more radical changes, it is perhaps surprising that there was not more opposition to the work of Henry VIII and Cromwell. Several European countries had become involved in wars over religious change already, and the question must be asked why England did not follow this route.

As A. G. Dickens puts it, 'The opposition was not a party. It displayed all the tints of the spectrum without their coordination.' In other words, the opponents had many different views and different reasons for opposing. They came from a number of different backgrounds. With much of mainland Europe beginning to get involved in religious wars between Catholic and Protestant, which were to last for many decades, it needs to be asked why England managed to avoid the carnage which was to involve both France and the Netherlands later. There are a large number of reasons put forward, but Dickens sums it up particularly well: 'There was no one organised group, there was no leader, it came from all social groups at different times and in different ways and it seemed to have very different objectives.' Some of the protests were directed against the marriage of Henry; others against the political and judicial decisions dealing with the ending of the papal connection; others against the Dissolution of the Monasteries.

There was one major rebellion in 1536, known as the 'Pilgrimage of Grace'. It was seen as part of an anti-'reformation' protest. Close analysis of this outbreak of violence reveals it to have largely social and economic causes in spite of the religious connotations of its title. There was no coordination or consistency in the opposition. It is still surprising that it was so limited, as England had been hostile to both Lollardy and Lutheranism, and had a record of being a good 'Roman' Catholic nation.

The opposition achieved little, beyond making Henry more cautious when it came to allowing Cromwell and Cranmer free rein to add much fundamental theological change to the changes already made. The reasons for there being so little opposition when compared with other countries have been much debated, and there is no clear consensus. Some historians have argued that the most important reason was that the changes were in fact so slow and gradual, and lasted over a period of at least 40 years. Others feel that there was such a fear of a return to the faction fighting and instability of the Wars of the Roses that loyalty to the King and his succession over-rode other considerations. This was particularly important in the thinking of many conservative peers, such as the Duke of Norfolk. Some potential opponents saw the whole divorce process as a temporary breach, which would soon be patched up.

The ability of Cromwell to isolate and manage opposition is also seen as important, as is the fact that all the key legislation went through Parliament which gave it legitimacy and an appearance of consent. Effective propaganda, again mainly by Cromwell, ensured that the measures were marketed well, and opponents discredited. Royal control of the printing presses and the **pulpit** ensured that only one side was marketed. Brutality did occur and men did die, but the numbers were not great by 16th-century standards and even a king like Henry VIII, who was not naturally inclined to be merciful when crossed, appears pretty merciful when compared with his European counterparts. There was broad agreement for what he did, with some sympathy and understanding for his motives. This, coupled with a failure by many to see where it all might lead, led to the great changes of an institution which lacked strong and able supporters.

Pulpit: Place in a church from where the priest preached.

Opposition seems to have centred around certain individuals and small groups. It is a tribute to Cromwell's ability that he was able to isolate them and deal with them separately. Opposition was always dealt with very firmly.

There were individuals like Elizabeth Barton, a well-known visionary nun given the name 'the Holy Maid of Kent', who had publicly criticised the divorce, the break with Rome and the rise of some clergy with 'advanced' views. She was made to recant publicly and killed quickly in 1534 with six supporters. They were disposed of by act of attainder (see page 54) which avoided the necessity of a trial. It may have been more than a coincidence that the Oath required in the act of succession was administered and taken by the citizens of London later in the same day that they had seen the Maid and her followers publicly executed.

Some of the friars and abbots who had opposed the Act of Succession and the oaths that were involved also died, as did some who opposed the dissolution itself. It is possible that some were unfortunate in that they were executed under the Treason Laws more as a warning to others than because of the particular beliefs they held or wished to protect. About 300 men were known to have died in the period between 1533 and 1540 – appalling by present standards but insignificant by 16th-century standards – for their opposition to the changes.

Two key individuals also died. The first was Sir Thomas More – the former Lord Chancellor, talented scholar and lawyer – who had remained in office until 1532, when he resigned and was replaced by Cromwell. He had been an able royal minister, but he was unable to accept the divorce. He could have been left alone in obscurity, but Henry and Cromwell pressed him vindictively. The Act of Succession had provided no penalty for those who would not take the oath, but the Treason Act did. Sir

Engraving from Rome in 1555 showing the hanging and disembowelling of the London Carthusians in 1535. They were convicted of high treason for denying Henry VIII's royal supremacy.

1. Who opposed the religious changes during Henry VIII's reign?

2. Why was the opposition to religious change so limited?

Thomas More and another respected and able clergyman, Bishop John Fisher of Rochester, were executed. The fact that the Pope made Fisher a cardinal (the highest rank in the Roman Catholic Church under the Pope) in 1535 may well have angered Henry VIII. Firm action against even the greatest in the land may have played an important part in ensuring obedience. The bulk of the bishops seem to have accepted the change, even those like Stephen Gardiner, from the conservative wing. They saw themselves as much as royal servants as servants of the Papacy, and promotion would now be coming from London and not from Rome. Some may have wished to remain in office in order to use what influence they had to preserve the old ways as far as possible. It is easy to criticise from the comfort of a library men who chose not to take the martyr's path.

5.6 *The Pilgrimage of Grace, 1536*
A CASE STUDY IN HISTORICAL INTERPRETATION

The only serious, armed, threat to Henry VIII's government in this period came in 1536 and 1537. There were three separate incidents:

● the first in early October 1536;

● the second, and most serious, centred in Yorkshire from October to December 1536 (this is usually known as the Pilgrimage of Grace);

● the third was in the North-West of England in early 1537.

Their timing has caused them to be linked to the religious changes, and those changes have been seen as the major cause. However, this is no longer seen to be the case, although there is a link – tenuous in some cases.

Trouble first broke out in Lincolnshire in October 1536, but this was quickly repressed. About 10,000 men were involved briefly, and some of them were gentry. The King, Henry VIII, made it clear that he would not negotiate with the rebels over their demands. The rebels soon dispersed when they heard that a royal army, under the command of the Duke of Suffolk, was approaching. The demands of the rebels were various, inspired partly by the arrival in the county of Cromwell's commissioners, and partly by a visit by tax collectors in 1536. Certainly, fear of religious change was involved. The historian A. G. Dickens refers to it as a 'chaotic, ignominious and rather sordid affair, which can scarcely be dignified as the protest of a Catholic society against the Reformation'. But Anthony Fletcher and Diarmaid MacCulloch, in *Tudor Rebellions*, place greater emphasis on the 'religious' causes, pointing out the part played by the clergy in supporting the rebels at times.

Fletcher and MacCulloch go on to stress that a huge range of other factors have to be considered when looking at the causes – ranging from a personal dislike of Thomas Cromwell, a fairly standard dislike of paying taxes, bad harvests in both 1535 and 1536, to a huge range of odd myths and rumours. The threat of a royal army was sufficient to end the threat. The general consensus is that the first rebellion, in Lincolnshire, was primarily social and economic. Historians of Henry VIII, such as J. J. Scarisbrick and M. D. Palmer, stress the lack of noble participants, although the trigger was a sermon by a priest, and the Lincolnshire rising was led by a commoner (one of the common people).

C. S. L. Davies stresses that it was on the day after the Lincolnshire rising broke out that no less than three of Cromwell's commissioners were due to arrive in the area. Their tasks included collecting taxes, suppressing smaller monasteries, enforcing the Ten Articles and imposing greater supervision on the clergy. It was not so much the threat of the visits themselves that bothered people, it was more the wild rumours of what they might do. As Davies points out, the Lincolnshire petition of the time gives ammunition to those who see the rebellions caused by either religious or social or economic factors. The grievances listed on the petition specify high taxes, fear for the liberties of the Church, a fear for the monasteries, and hatred of Cromwell and Bishop Latimer as well as the **Statute of Uses**.

Statute of Uses: Law which changed the way in which property could be left in wills.

Robert Aske (? –1537)
Lawyer and gentleman. Leader of the Pilgrimage of Grace. Manipulated by Henry VIII into toning down the rebellion, but still executed in 1537.

Much more serious was the rising in the north-eastern counties of Lancashire and Yorkshire at the end of 1536. It was led by a gentleman, Robert Aske. He had conservative religious motives himself, but many of his supporters had social and economic grievances. A large and armed force assembled in the North, which was bigger than the forces Henry VIII had at his disposal. This time there were plenty gentry among the rebels. Many of them hated the recent Statute of Uses and were concerned about the economic results of the Dissolution of the Monasteries. There was also a strong personal dislike of Thomas Cromwell among the gentry, who were unused to feeling the tentacles of London's bureaucracy reaching so far and so efficiently. The masses supporting them had primarily economic grievances, but they were happy to be led by gentry who had a mix of conservative religious and social views. The articles produced by Robert Aske were a mixture of religious, social and economic demands.

Some see the Pilgrimage of Grace as part of a final fling of the Wars of the Roses. Others see it as part of a North versus South division. Of the various manifestos (printed statements) issued by Aske and his fellow rebels, there is ammunition to back almost any explanation. Enclosure (see page 111) was a factor in some areas of the country, while taxation was clearly hitting some hard for the first time. Some of the 'religious' demands seem to have been partly inspired by the clergy and monks themselves, as propaganda against the change. There were also signs of in-fighting among factions within the nobility. There is ammunition to sustain almost any argument for the causes.

Robert Aske was determined for it to be peaceful. In fact, only one man is known to have died during the course of the rebellion. Given the numbers at his disposal, Aske had 30,000 men with him at one stage. This compares with the 8,000 men that the Duke of Norfolk was able to raise against him. Aske's willingness to debate and request terms must have come as a relief to Henry VIII. The Duke of Norfolk listened to Aske's demands, but was playing for time. Execution was the inevitable fate for Aske and his principal supporters. This took place in 1537, when Henry VIII felt that the time was right and he was strong enough. No Tudor monarch could be seen to give in to rebels.

The historian A. G. Dickens, while stressing the religious motivation of Aske, writes: 'The roots of the movement were decidedly economic, its demands predominantly secular, its interests in Rome almost negligible, and its leading repressors were not Protestant merchants but the highest nobility in the land who shared its hostile views against heresy.' However, D. G. Newcombe states firmly that 'religious issues dominated the minds of those who rose'. W. J. Shiels reinforces this by writing: 'the potent force of religion sustained the rebellion'.

Biographers of Henry VIII, such as M. D. Palmer and J. J. Scarisbrick, inevitably look at the issue from the King's point of view. They support this, with Palmer writing that 'there was one common motive among all the rebels and that was a conservative desire to reverse the recent religious changes'. All point out that the Pontefract Articles of 1536 (the manifesto of the movement) have a religious focus – ranging from a desire to keep the monasteries, to reversing some (but not all) of the Act of Supremacy. Peter Ramsey, in *Tudor Economic Problems*, confirms this when he writes 'Although many hedges and fences were destroyed [as a protest against enclosure], it was chiefly inspired by the government's religious policies'. However, like one or two more recent historians, Ramsey also hints that it was possibly not so much the fear of the Dissolution itself that put people behind barricades, but a fear of what the Crown might do as the replacement landlord.

It is not difficult to find suggestions among historians of differing motivations. John Guy feels that perhaps the political and constitutional motives behind the Pontefract Articles need to be pointed out. There was a strong feeling by the lesser nobility and gentry of the North that they had not been consulted sufficiently about the huge political and constitutional changes of the previous two years. Like many other historians, John Guy mentions the fact that there had been poor harvests in 1535 and 1536. He goes on to write, 'It was neither a clash between different social groups nor a split within the governing class, but a popular rising by Northerners in general' – in other words, it might be seen more as a North/South split.

R. Rex's analysis in *Henry VIII and the English Reformation* is different. He agrees that the Pilgrimage of Grace was a huge threat to the Tudor monarchy. All these historians are agreed that this might easily have toppled Henry VIII if more senior nobles, such as the Duke of Norfolk, had joined in (and there is evidence that even the Duke of Norfolk did consider joining in). However, Rex goes on to conclude, after a survey of the huge list of social, economic, political and religious grievances, that the Pilgrimage was 'more social than religious, but it could not have held together or spread so far without the ideology of religion'. It is interesting to note that Rex, in a book on Henry VIII and the Reformation, sees the rebellions in the North more as a social and economic rebellion; while Ramsey, an economic historian, sees it as primarily religious in origin.

C. S. L. Davies adds several further twists to the tale, referring to it as 'an anachronistic, but harmless manifestation of the backward and feudalistic North'. He goes on to argue the case that much of the Lincolnshire and Yorkshire risings were the results of 'upper class promptings', with the gentry and nobility setting their own agendas and manipulating the peasantry. He goes on to say that 'quite obviously the dissolutions were not the sole, or even the main causes'. While stressing the social and economic, central versus local causes, Davies finally places stress on the peasants' fears of what might happen. He also places emphasis on the role of local faction-fighting among the noble classes. He also complicates the debate on the economic causes by pointing out that Lord Darcy – one of two major nobles who joined with the rebels – was well known as an 'enclosing' landlord.

Davies also points out that while some of the areas joining the revolt were economically backward, others were among the most economically advanced in the country. His final conclusion is that 'the defence of the Church was integrated into a more general protest'. The fact that the reaction by Cromwell and central government was to slow down the pace of religious change temporarily might indicate that contemporary officials felt that innovation in religious matters might be a cause.

A further rising in early 1537, also in the North, was hurriedly suppressed and used as an excuse for going back on the promises of reform made by the Duke of Norfolk. Robert Aske and the other rebels were rounded up and taken to London to be executed.

The Pilgrimage of Grace seems to have had little impact. It speeded up the process of Dissolution and it possibly made Henry VIII more cautious theologically. However, it is also possible that the limited nature of the rebellion and the fact it was suppressed may have actually encouraged the 'protestants' to press on.

Henry VIII was ruthless and determined. He was also used to getting his own way. Those who opposed the religious changes of the period 1529–40 all seemed to come at what had happened from a different angle. There was no leader and no real cause. Many saw the changes as temporary, or approved of some of them and not others. Also the Papacy as an institution did not command the loyalty needed to sustain a rebellion. Men were asked to compromise slowly and not make radical changes all at once. Behind the scenes there were clever men at work to ensure that all knew what fate would befall those who did oppose – such as Thomas More or Robert Aske.

1. *Make out a case for arguing that the Pilgrimage of Grace was primarily religious in origin.*

2. *Why do historians disagree so much on the causes of the Pilgrimage of Grace?*

5.7 To what extent was England a Protestant country by 1547?

This is a very difficult question to answer. It has been argued by some that England was still a fundamentally Catholic country by the death of Henry VIII, and that it was the events of the reign that followed that played the important part in making England Protestant. It can also be argued that the damage done to the Roman Catholic Church – with the Dissolution of the Monasteries and the Royal Supremacy, for example – made it more difficult to prevent the rise of Protestantism. It also made it more difficult to prevent a return to full Roman Catholicism, but that it was still possible for a return to take place.

It can also be argued that significant moves were made towards Protestantism in the last decade or so of the reign – such as the increased spread of the vernacular (English) Bible, the decline in the use of relics and in some of the appointments made to certain positions in the Church by Archbishop Cranmer. Putting some of the changes together does make it look like a significant advance towards Protestantism. However, it is also easy to identify particular items, such as the Six Articles of 1539, which make it appear that a Catholic reaction was taking place.

Events at Court also make it difficult to see what was actually going on. One year (1540), Henry is marrying a Protestant wife from Lutheran Germany, the next he is marrying a Howard who was from the deeply conservative (religiously) Howard family, led by the Duke of Norfolk. Cromwell was executed in 1540, partly for his advanced religious views, yet not long after this more than one of his conservative accusers was also in the Tower of London. The 'Catholic' Howard wife was executed, and replaced by Catherine Parr who was known for her 'Protestant' sympathies. If Henry VIII had died in 1546, then there would have been a very conservative and pro-Catholic regency council. Yet when he died in 1547 he left a group of men who imposed Protestantism with great speed.

Catherine Parr (1512–1548)
Had a classical humanist education, was a strong supporter of Humanism/ Protestantism. She had already lost two husbands when she married Henry VIII and became Queen in 1543. She survived him and married Lord Seymour of Sudeley in 1547.

This painting shows the four gospel-writers stoning the Pope. It belonged to Henry VIII, who acquired it in 1542.

What does Henry VIII's ownership of this painting tell us about his view on religion in 1542?

Coverdale's Bible, published in 1535–36, was the first completed Bible in English. It was displaced by other versions, notably the Great Bible (see page 135).

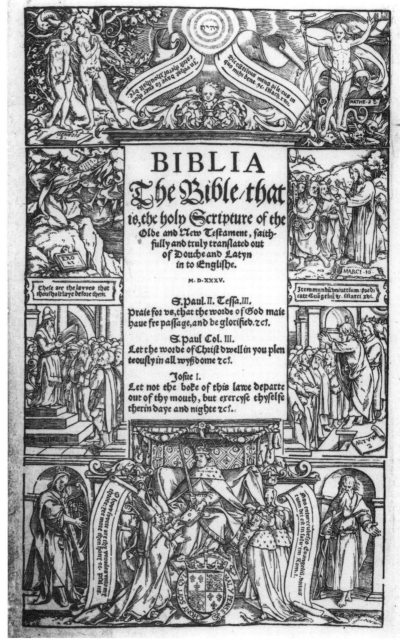

If one county, for example Kent, is looked at closely, then clear signs of a deepening Protestantism are seen; yet Lincolnshire remained Catholic to the end. In 1540 the Protestant Barnes was executed for heresy and Roman Catholics were executed for treason. The evidence is confusing. The King gave no clear direction, so no clear direction was followed. His indecisiveness and the fact that his attention was now on other matters, such as foreign wars, meant that drift was the order of the day in religious matters. Henry VIII had got his divorce, married and then had Anne Boleyn executed, received money and had a son by Jane Seymour. He had no further interest in religious change of any sort. The absence of any major change reinforces the view that the initial stages of the Reformation in the reign of Henry VIII were primarily political and

---

Religious changes 1536–1547

1538   Shrine to Thomas à Becket is destroyed – part of campaign to destroy shrines and religious images in churches.

Thirteen Articles and new set of Royal Injunctions introduced.

Cromwell made Vice-Regent in addition to position of Vicar General. This allowed him to act of spiritual and religious matters under the authority of Henry VIII.

1539   Cranmer's Great Bible in English is published.

The larger monasteries are dissolved. The last is Waltham Abbey, Essex.

Henry VIII issues the Six Articles (traditional and Catholic). The Articles support: the doctrine of transubstantiation and taking the Eucharist in the form of bread but not bread and wine; the idea that priests should not marry (celibacy). Penalties for not accepting these Articles include death by burning as a heretic.

1543   Publication of 'The Necessary Doctrine and Erudition of a Christian Man'; known as 'The King's Book'. This supported traditional Catholic beliefs.

Act passed by Parliament ending the printing of the English Bible. It also limited the use of the Bible to the more wealthy in society.

1544   All church services now in English.

1545   'King's Prymer', written by Archbishop Cranmer, replaces Catholic book of prayers for use in Church.

1546   Chantries Act abolishes chantries, but never enforced.

---

financial in motivation. When the political and financial problems were solved, Henry was content to let the Church be, and become part of the faction-fighting process between two wings at Court.

A chronological survey of the main religious events does not provide a clear picture of what Henry intended to happen. The Ten Articles of 1536 are a good example. They were a series of statements on religious belief which Henry got Convocation to accept. In some aspects – such as the fact there only seem to be three sacraments instead of the usual Roman Catholic seven – would indicate Lutheran tendencies, but the three that were there and other items covered, such as transubstantiation and prayers for the dead, were highly 'catholic'. The historian A. G. Dickens says they are a good example of 'our English talent for concocting ambiguous and flexible documents'.

The 'Bishop's Book' of the following year, 1537, can be seen in a similar light. It was written by a committee of senior clergymen in order to clarify England's theology (religious beliefs) and was seen by the King as a way of testing public opinion. Some aspects, again on the sacraments, were more conservative than the Ten Articles, but there were strong strands of Protestantism running through it which can be seen to show signs of 'reform'. The years 1538–39 produced no clarification. The Articles of 1538 can be seen as Protestant in that they were critical of so many of the old Church festivals and the obsession with relics; the order that a Bible in English should be placed in every church in the land (see photograph on page 159) would possibly indicate Lutheran leanings. The fact that Henry was considering an alliance with the Lutheran princes of Germany at the time may have helped, but the Six Articles of 1539 and the execution of Cromwell in 1540 would indicate a conservative reaction. The Six Articles were emphatically Catholic. Evangelical preaching was prohibited; clerical marriage banned, transubstantiation and confession were back in favour. The fact that Henry was tired of his Lutheran wife, Anne of Cleves, and was lured away by the young and beautiful Catherine Howard, who was part of the conservative and catholic Norfolk faction at Court may have been more important than any new theological thoughts. Henry VIII's marriage to Catherine Parr, who was known for her more Protestant sympathies, may have helped shelter Cranmer and led to the allocation of Protestant tutors to the young heir to the throne. In the 1540s the Six Articles were rigorously imposed, and radicals fled abroad (only to reappear the minute the King died in 1547).

England was still Catholic when Henry VIII died. Many of the props of the old Church had gone, such as the monasteries, and it had not been well defended. However, if Henry VIII had had a successor who was both able and determined to restore and reinvigorate the old faith in all its forms (though perhaps not as far as giving back the monastic land), then there was a good basis on which to build. As it was the rising generation at Court – such as Edward Seymour, later Duke of Somerset and John Dudley, later Duke of Northumberland – had Protestant sympathies, as did Henry's last Queen. As the heir to the throne was being educated by Protestants, then the old church was to have little chance in the future. With Cranmer left alive there was also a scholar and writer who could lay the theological basis of Protestantism to back up the political changes that were to come from Court and Parliament.

1. What evidence is there that England was still a Catholic nation in 1547?

2. How 'Protestant' a nation had England become by 1547?

Source-based question: Protestantism and Catholicism in the reign of Henry VIII

SOURCE A

The state of this our kingdom is as follows: the ceremonies are still tolerated, but explanations of them are added. These things are retained for the sake of preventing any disturbances, and are ordered to be kept up until the King himself shall either remove or alter them. Nothing has yet been settled respecting the marriage of the clergy. The mass is not asserted to be a sacrifice, but only a representation of Christ's passion. All images that are objects of worship are removed. There is a report that we are to have war with the French, Italians, Spaniards and the Scots, when this was reported to the King, he said that should not sleep at all the worse for it; and on the day after he declared to his Privy Councillors that he now found himself moved in his conscience to promote the word of God more than he had ever done before.

Letter from a group of English Protestants writing to their friends in Protestant Zurich in 1539.

SOURCE B

The King ... considering that as a result of variable and sundry opinions and the great discord and variance that hath arisen has ....
Resolved
    FIRST That the most blessed sacrament at the altar ... is present really under the form of bread and wine, the natural body and blood of our Saviour Jesus Christ
    SECONDLY That communion of both kinds is not necessary
    THIRDLY That priests may not marry
    FOURTHLY That vows of chastity ought to be observed
    FIFTHLY That it is necessary that private masses be continued
    SIXTHLY That ... confession be retained.

From an Act, abolishing the diversity of opinions, June 1539 (known also as the Six Articles).

SOURCE C

We are all of us amazed at the sight of those decrees (the Six Articles) and at the rejection of the terms of alliance between his Majesty and ourselves. We have altogether perceived a great change in England's views ... we suspect therefore, that something has blown over from France as you no longer appear to have any necessity for our alliance or even our friendship.

Martin Bucer, a German Protestant, writing to Archbishop Cranmer, Strasbourg, October 1539.

SOURCE D

Articles were decreed, commonly called the Six Articles (or the whip with six strings) in pretence of Unity. What unity followed, the groaning hearts of a great number and the cruel death of many, both in the reign of King Henry and Queen Mary ...

From John Foxe's Book of Martyrs, *1563.*

---

1. *Using the information contained in this chapter, explain the meaning of the following terms:*

a) *'mass' (Source A)*

b) *'the Six Articles' (Sources C and D).*

2. *Study Sources A, B and C.*

How far do these sources indicate that there had been a major religious change in England by 1539?

3. *Assess the reliability of all four sources as evidence for the progress of Protestantism in England by 1540.*

4. *In the light of these sources and using your own knowledge, how Protestant a country had England become by 1547?*

6 Government, politics and foreign affairs 1529–1547

6.1 Why did Thomas More 'fail' as the King's principal minister?

6.2 How able a minister was Thomas Cromwell?

6.3 Historical interpretation: Was there a 'revolution in government' in England as a result of the work of Cromwell?

6.4 Why did Cromwell fall from office in 1540?

6.5 The foreign policy of Henry VIII (1529–1547) – an expensive mistake?

6.6 How efficiently was England ruled in the final years of Henry VIII's reign?

Key Issues

- *How well served was Henry VIII by his ministers between 1529 and 1547?*

- *Was there a revolution in government led by Thomas Cromwell in the 1530s?*

- *How ably did Henry VIII deal with foreign affairs in this period?*

Framework of Events

1529	Fall of Wolsey
	Thomas More is made Lord Chancellor
	Parliament called
1530	Cromwell on the Council
	Wolsey arrested for treason; dies
1531	Cromwell on Inner Council
1532	Resignation of More
	Alliance with France
1533	Cromwell made Chancellor of the Exchequer
	Anne Boleyn marries Henry VIII
	New Council is created for Wales; peace made with Scotland
	Cromwell is made Principal Secretary
1535	Cromwell is made Lord Privy Seal and Vicar General
	Anne Boleyn is executed
1536	'Act of Union' with Wales; Act creating the Privy Council
	Pilgrimage of Grace
1537	Reconstruction of the Privy Council. Remodelling of the Council of the North
1538	10-year truce between France and Spain
	Agreement between France and Spain not to deal separately with England
	Negotiations over Anne of Cleves marriage start
	Cromwell is made Earl of Essex
	Anne of Cleves marries Henry VIII
	France and Spain fall out
	Trial and execution of Cromwell
	Gardiner starts negotiations with Charles V
	Death of Catherine Howard
	Henry VIII is declared King of Ireland
1542	Invasion of Scotland. Battle of Solway Moss

1543	Alliance with Charles V. Treaty of Greenwich with Scotland
	Marriage of Henry VIII and Catherine Parr
	War with France and Scotland
	Somerset raids Scotland
	Henry invades France
1545	Treaty of Camp
1546	Hertford–Lisle coalition at Court. Peace made
1547	Henry VIII dies.

Overview

MUCH of the focus of the years after the fall of Cardinal Wolsey tends to be on the religious changes which dominated much of the life of the country. However, there are two other areas of public life which have to be analysed in some depth, as both in their own way had real importance at the time, and in the future.

The first is the great change in the way in which the country was administered. Government had, in the past, been little more than an extension of the Royal Court, staffed by the monarch's own personal servants. What Thomas Cromwell did in the course of the 1530s was to reform the whole system of government. He made it into a far more efficient structure, capable of responding to royal wishes with speed and competence. Too often good administration had depended solely on the ability, interest or health of the monarch or minister. Cromwell created a bureaucracy which not only ensured that royal wishes were carried out correctly, that royal government was properly funded, but that England could be governed effectively if there was a minor on the throne or the monarch was abroad. He created a system which could carry on well without needing a monarch as efficient and hard working as Henry VII. This move from what had been a personal system of government to one where areas such as the administration of law and order and the collection of taxes would be carried out and properly monitored without the direct involvement of a monarch, has sometimes been called a 'revolution' in government. That definition will be debated later in this chapter.

The other main area which needs examination is the foreign policy of the period. In the 1530s foreign policy became subordinate to domestic needs, such as the Royal Divorce and the excommunication (see page 145). The result was to lower England's standing in the eyes of other European powers. It is revealing that Henry VIII would not openly join with other Protestant powers to safeguard his position against a possible invasion by France and Scotland – he was too 'Catholic' for that. The foreign policy of the last years of his reign, between 1540 and 1547, reveal a lot about Henry's personality and about England's status in Europe. They are not years of achievement, and the damage done to the economy, royal finances and relationships with other countries was immense. Henry VIII may have had a good brain and been exposed to the great humanist influences of his age, but he showed a taste for war for war's sake. The reign as a whole ought to be judged by the disasters in foreign policy in the latter years of his reign.

The wives of King Henry VIII

Catherine of Aragon
Born: 1485
Married to Henry: 11 June 1509
Children: Mary, born 1516
Fate: Divorced, 23 May 1533;
died 1536

Anne Boleyn
Born: ? 1501
Married to Henry: 28 May 1533
Children: Elizabeth, born 1534
Fate: Accused of adultery;
executed 18 May 1536

Jane Seymour
Born: 1509
Married to Henry: 30 May 1536
Children: Edward, born 1537
Fate: Died in childbirth, 1537

Anne of Cleves
Born: 1515
Married to Henry: 6 January 1540
Children: none
Fate: Divorced, 10 July 1540;
outlived Henry

Catherine Howard
Born: ? 1520
Married to Henry: 9 August 1540
Children: none
Fate: Accused of adultery;
executed 1542

Catherine Parr
Born: 1512
Married to Henry: 12 July 1543
Children: none
Fate: outlived Henry

6.1 Why did Thomas More 'fail' as the King's principal minister?

Sir Thomas More (1478–1535)

Wolsey's replacement, in so far as he was replaced as the leading minister, was Thomas More. In terms of sheer intelligence More was probably the ablest of all the men to serve Henry VIII. He was a fine lawyer and scholar and it was probably his intelligence that particularly appealed to the King. However, More was not a clever politician. A willingness to compromise was required in order to serve Henry VIII in the way he wished to be served, and More was a man of high principle and great firmness in his religious beliefs.

Thomas More had worked for the King in a variety of ways before 1529. He had undertaken some diplomatic activities on the continent for the King. He had also been Speaker of the House of Commons (always a royal nominee in those days) and a member of the King's Council. He had

A painting of Thomas More with his family, by Rowland Lockey in 1593 from an original drawing by Hans Holbein

had no major impact on government policy, but had become noted for his ability in carrying out royal wishes and in assisting the King in his attack on Luther and his Protestant ideas. Quite why he accepted the role of Lord Chancellor, given the fact that he knew the direction in which the King was moving over the Aragon/Boleyn affair, is not known. Thomas More must have realised that the Lord Chancellor would have a role in any major changes to come. Perhaps he took on the work in order to serve his own causes as well as from a wish to make himself useful to the Crown. There is some evidence to indicate that Henry VIII was aware of More's reservations about the way in which ideas on the royal marriage were going in 1529. He indicated to his Lord Chancellor that he need not be involved in such sensitive religious areas.

There is little evidence of work done by More for the King before 1529. He played an important part in the attack on Wolsey in the Parliament of 1529. There is evidence of him playing a part in attacking Protestant heretics in 1531–32. In the course of 1531 he was again involved in Parliament, putting the King's views forward in the House of Lords on the need for a royal divorce (but without much enthusiasm). There is evidence of mild opposition to the King on his part early in 1531, and the fact that he was trying to put a brake on the monarch's wish to gain a divorce was noted publicly by the end of that year. It was clear that More was deeply unhappy with the King's increasing passion for Anne Boleyn and growing determination to divorce Catherine. As a result, More resigned his office in 1532.

Thomas More, the scholar/lawyer, had too many principles for the brutal atmosphere of the Court of Henry VIII. The King required a degree of obedience in matters of conscience, of which More was not capable. More spent a good part of his retirement attacking what he saw as Protestant ideas, which did not appeal to his successor as key minister, Thomas Cromwell. In 1534 More refused to take the oath of allegiance to Henry VIII as Head of the Church, and after a year's imprisonment in the Tower of London he was executed.

1. Why did More have such a short period in office?

2. What would you see as significant about both More's rise to power, and his fall from it?

6.2 How able a minister was Thomas Cromwell?

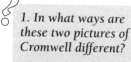

1. In what ways are these two pictures of Cromwell different?

2. What message do you think Holbein is trying to make about Cromwell's status in the left-hand picture?

Thomas Cromwell, Earl of Essex (?1485–1540)
Became a lawyer in 1523 and an MP a year later. Involved in Wolsey's Dissolution of the Monasteries in the 1520s. Cromwell became secretary to Henry VIII in 1534, and the real director of government policy. Privy Councillor in 1531; Principal Minister 1532–40. His mistake in arranging Henry's marriage to Anne of Cleves led to his being accused of treason and beheaded.

William Paget (1505–1563)
Became Principal Secretary of State in 1543. He was a first-class administrator. He was made a peer in 1550, having been a key Privy Councillor (1540–47). Paget opposed Stephen Gardiner on a range of issues. He supported the Spanish marriage to Philip II and advised Mary against executing Princess Elizabeth after Wyatt's rebellion (see page 203). His political career came to an end in 1558 when he was not invited to join Elizabeth's Council.

Cromwell is widely regarded as perhaps the outstanding servant of the Crown in the 16th century. It is a title to which quite a few men could aspire – such as Sir Reginald Bray and Sir Thomas Lovell under Henry VII, through Thomas Wolsey and William Paget under Henry VIII, to the outstanding talents of William Cecil and Francis Walsingham under Elizabeth I. Not only did Cromwell manage the most difficult of men for a decade (i.e. King Henry VIII), but he also presided over and helped organise an enormous series of changes of fundamental importance to the development of England. Whereas his predecessor Wolsey left few memorials beyond some elegant buildings, Cromwell left his mark in a number of different areas:

● He shaped the development not only of the entire system of government, but also the way in which England was administered, worshipped, paid its taxes, and was counted.

● He transformed the role of Parliament, made Wales conform more to English ways and laws, broke down the traditional independence of the North of England and started to look at ways in which trade could be developed.

● He also went a long way towards making the Crown financially independent from Parliament.

Cromwell was perhaps the only person the King regretted disposing of. Coming from a poor and comparatively low-class background, this was a remarkable achievement.

How did Cromwell rise to power?

Cromwell rose to prominence through a mix of ability, hard work, skill at collecting offices and making himself indispensable. He also had the ability to implement his master's will effectively. He proved able to tie up the many loose ends left by Henry VIII's divorce and its implications.

Little is known about Cromwell's early career, beyond the facts that he had some training as a lawyer, travelled widely and sat in the Parliament

1. Why was Cromwell able to have so great an influence on the government of England?

2. What were the limitations on Cromwell's influence?

of 1523. He was a key aide to Wolsey and played a role in the suppression of some monasteries in the 1520s. Cromwell had managed to distance himself sufficiently from Wolsey when his master fell, but he showed loyalty towards his master when others had fled. By 1530 he was a member of the Council, and over the next two years rose from being just another royal servant to being a key minister. He made enemies of those who felt they were better suited to the task, such as Stephen Gardiner and Thomas Howard, who were to play a key role in his fall in 1540.

The main reason why Cromwell rose to prominence lay in his ability to deliver what Henry VIII wanted. Not only did Cromwell have the capacity for sheer hard work, he also had the ability to manage detail while at the same time keeping a sense of vision and purpose. He had seen what happened to his former master, Wolsey, so he was well aware of the dangers of trying to develop policy on his own which did not suit the King. He put into practice what Henry VIII wanted, although inevitably he left his own mark on events. Where it might be possible to talk of 'Wolsey's foreign policy', there is little scope for referring to any of the work that Cromwell did in this way. His greatest work, in the machinery of government, was motivated by a desire to make royal government more efficient – and the focus should be on the word 'royal'. Linked in with his ability to work and his eye for detail, was his mastery of the whole machinery of government. This further enabled him to deliver what Henry VIII wished.

Cromwell collected official jobs. He managed to get a job in almost every aspect of government. He became Master of the King's Jewels in 1532, which gave him a foothold in the Royal Household. In the same year he acquired another minor post in the Court of Chancery, one of the key legal departments. He was made Chancellor of the Exchequer (a minor post then) in 1533 – but it gave him an office in the old Exchequer system of finance. Cromwell then added to this the Master of the Rolls (a major legal and record-keeping role) and Lord Privy Seal with its vital role on the Council. He also became Principal Secretary, with its access to the King and a key coordinating role. On top of that he was to become Vicar General and Vice-Regent of the Church. He was also, of course, a member of Parliament. There was virtually no aspect of English government in which Cromwell did not have some direct jurisdiction. Put together it was an amazing collection of positions and influence and enabled him to deliver with remarkable efficiency what his master wished. Often when he was transferring authority from one area of government to another, there was no opposition, simply because he was giving orders to himself.

He was the right man in the right place at the right time. His personal views would indicate that he was sympathetic to the King's wishes for a divorce. Cromwell's possible dislike of monasticism made him a willing agent in the King's desire for the cash that would come from the disposal of the monasteries.

It was not quite a master/servant relationship between Henry VIII and Cromwell, it was more of an ignorant but demanding monarch working with an agent of considerable talent and experience. Between them they had a huge impact on the direction England would go in the 1530s. It was quite a remarkable partnership.

6.3 Was there a 'revolution in government' in England as a result of the work of Cromwell?

A CASE STUDY IN HISTORICAL INTERPRETATION

Henry VIII dining in the Privy Chamber, drawing by an unknown 16th-century artist. The Privy Chamber was where the King retreated to confer with his advisers and enjoy his private life. Under Henry VII and Henry VIII the 'privy' apartments where in many respects the heart of national government.

At the same time as working on the Royal Divorce, the Church and the monasteries, Thomas Cromwell also turned his attention to the way in which England was governed. In studies of Tudor history written before 1950 (e.g. Alan Pollard's *Henry VIII*), Cromwell was not seen as having a particularly important role in the governing of England after the death of Wolsey. However, Geoffrey Elton argues in his *Tudor Revolution in Government* (and it is pretty clear in the actual title what his main idea was!) that Cromwell changed the nature and direction of the way in which England and Wales were governed so fundamentally that they amounted to a 'revolution' in government.

Elton's basic argument runs as follows. He maintains that Cromwell ended the old medieval way in which England had been governed, where the actual government of the country was little more than the monarch himself with a few servants and an itinerant court and bureaucracy with no central base. The administration of the country was performed by men who were personal servants of the monarch, in almost daily attendance. They served the king's personal needs as well as the needs of the country – in fact there was little actual difference between the two. Elton asserts that Cromwell transformed and modernised the system of government into one recognisable today. Although the purpose of government was still to reflect the will of the king, and no servant of Henry VIII would dare to think otherwise, there would be a central and well-coordinated base in the capital, London, with oversight of the local areas and proper records.

There would be a clear difference between the personal servants who organised the Royal Household with its essentially domestic needs, and those who served the King as the head of the executive of England and Wales. At the head of this more permanent and centralised administration would be the Privy Council, on which would serve the principal ministers of the day. This would include those involved in military matters, the Church, finance, law and administration. Its role would be to serve the monarch and administer the kingdom on his or her behalf if need be. Its rulings would have the force of law, and therefore it could run the country in the event of royal illness or absence abroad. It could also deal with the day-to-day administration if there was a monarch such as Henry VIII who had little interest in detail.

There were many other parts to Cromwell's work which, Elton argues, amounted to a 'revolution'. He transformed the financial administration of the country, restoring authority to the Exchequer and making the Chamber merely a small spending department which ran the Royal Household. The fact that Cromwell had a key post in the old Chamber system as well as being Chancellor of the Exchequer shows how he did this. With his key role on the Council he ensured that business was transacted there. Being Principal Secretary – with direct access to the King – he had the ability to set agendas as well as coordinate the whole business of government. Given the fact that he also had key positions in the Church (Vice-Regent etc.) and in the principal legal and record-keeping areas as Master of the Rolls, Cromwell was in himself an amazing piece of centralisation. What makes Cromwell so unusual was that he did not seem to see the collection of these offices (and presumably their salaries) as a means in themselves, but as a way to get a coordinated, centralised and efficient system of government in England.

The list of his work could go on. He was the central manager of the King's religious and divorce business in Parliament. There are many other areas of his involvement, such as in reforming the Councils of the North and Wales and in setting up new administrative systems in Wales and the North. Parts of the protests which lay behind the Pilgrimage of Grace were not only religious, but against the centralising and taxing tendencies of London (Cromwell again). He also set up completely new systems to administer monastic incomes, such as the Court of Augmentations, and the Court of First Fruits and Tenths (see page 200), which were capable of managing on their own, with their own jurisdictions and powers. Cromwell installed a new breed of efficient royal servants and revised traditional areas of government such as the Court of Wards, which dealt with the affairs of minors. The similarity with the modern government agency is strong!

Cromwell also involved himself and the government in many other areas, such as exports and imports. So it is easy to understand why Elton argues that put together his work amounts to a 'revolution'. The way in which England was administrated, who administered it and the degree of centralisation and efficiency were all remarkable. The fact that it was pushed through by one man in a short space of time (1532–40) makes it even more remarkable. As is the fact that huge religious changes were also happening in the country and the role of Parliament was altering as well. Cromwell was also to play a huge part in the lawmaking process. The nature, extent and speed would amount to 'revolutionary' changes – so Elton argues.

Elton has had many critics. Differing views were put forward by historians such as David Loades and A. G. R. Smith. The immediate attack was led by two young historians in an article in the *Past and Present* magazine (G. I. Hariss and Penry Williams' 'A Revolution in Tudor History?' Volume 25, 1963). They argue that neither in the nature nor extent did it amount to a revolution, and that too much has been attributed to Cromwell. J. J. Scarisbrick stayed out of what was becoming a debate over the definition of a word, but his comments at the end of his biography on Henry VIII are revealing:

> The England which he [Henry VIII] had led back into European affairs and exposed to the immense energies of continental Protestantism … emerged from his reign with a new political 'wholeness', thanks to the destruction of the independent Church, the final incorporation of Wales, the pruning of many liberties and refurbishing local Councils in the North and West, which lay under the surveillance of a Privy Council that, at least by the 1540s had established itself as the supreme, omnicompetent executive body. Thanks above all to Thomas Cromwell, this reign had given England much good governance. The administrative machine was much more efficient and capacious than it had ever been – as was the legal … a good deal had been done to discipline a society … to curb the peoples and their dangerous overlords in the remoter parts of the land … the growing authority of his servants in central and local government greatly strengthened the lines of force which ran between King and subject … Again, never before had England felt the power of the 'state' so widely and deeply as in the 1530s and 1540s.

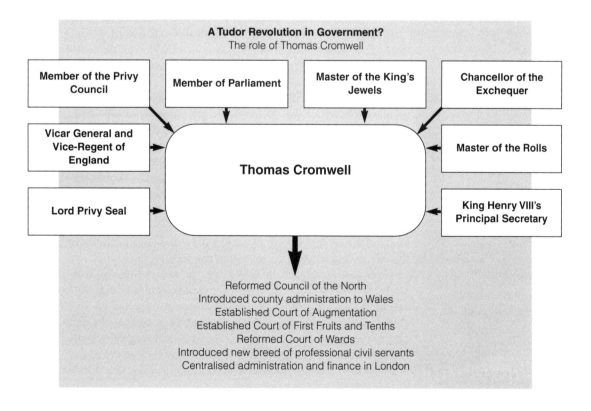

A Tudor Revolution in Government?
The role of Thomas Cromwell

Member of the Privy Council

Member of Parliament

Master of the King's Jewels

Chancellor of the Exchequer

Vicar General and Vice-Regent of England

Master of the Rolls

Thomas Cromwell

Lord Privy Seal

King Henry VIII's Principal Secretary

Reformed Council of the North
Introduced county administration to Wales
Established Court of Augmentation
Established Court of First Fruits and Tenths
Reformed Court of Wards
Introduced new breed of professional civil servants
Centralised administration and finance in London

Scarisbrick then mentions the huge work of Cromwell in the religious and administrative changes, already described, and ends with:

> … the concentrated display of the power and ubiquity (ever-present) of central authority the like of which had not been seen hitherto; and if the major administrative developments of the years of Cromwell's dominance (and after) may be better described as a return to the medieval practice of building professional, bureaucratic government outside the royal household … rather than a 'modern' event, it remains true that the consolidation of the Council and the foundation of four new financial courts gave the central government a new, firm grip on the realm.

Scarisbrick then goes on to look at the huge number of laws passed by Parliament, many of which Cromwell was directly responsible for, such as the Act of Succession of 1535.

Much of the debate centres on definitions of terms. For example, the term 'revolution' and whether what could be described as a return to older practices amounts to a revolution. No historian has endorsed Elton's ideas fully. Indeed, critics of this view – such as David Loades in his *Politics and the Nation* – argue that Cromwell was a systemiser (one who makes existing systems work) and not a creator of new structures. He made permanent a system which had been there before, at least in outline. Loades stresses that it was Stephen Gardiner who had made the role of Secretary important, particularly as a clearing house for the administration. However, Loades concedes that Cromwell was a man of considerable ability (and there is no modern historian who challenges this). It is also possible to use Loades' work to get a list of Cromwell's administrative work and achievements, especially on the changes in the financial administration of the country and with the changes in the Privy Council and the Councils of Wales and the North.

John Guy, too, argues that the Elton thesis is flawed. He feels that not nearly so much should be attributed to Cromwell, and that more credit for the changes to the Privy Council should be given to Wolsey. A careful reading of Guy's major work on this topic, *Wolsey, Cromwell and the Reform of Henrician Government*, produces a list of major changes in the whole structure of the government and administration of England put through by Cromwell, as well as references to Cromwell being an 'administrator of genius'. Guy also argues that several of the key features of the Privy Council really did not emerge until the 1540s, such as its own central headquarters, and therefore less credit should be given to Cromwell. However, it is clear from this study that the sheer pressure of events between 1536 and 1540 had made the Privy Council into an institution of huge importance and its basic shape and function was not to alter for decades. It is easy to see the debt that Queen Elizabeth I owed to the pioneering work of Cromwell in the 1530s.

Cromwell clearly changed the way in which England was governed. Students have to make up their own minds as to whether his huge work amounts to a revolution, or not. All historians are agreed on Cromwell's ability, skill and the size of his achievement as well as the quite remarkable lasting capacity of his work. England was a more efficiently governed country when he had finished, and its government was in a much stronger position to survive the strains placed upon it in the two difficult decades after his death.

1. How was Cromwell able to bring about so many changes?

2. Does the work of Thomas Cromwell in the 1530s merit the definition of 'a revolution in government'?

6.4 Why did Cromwell fall from office in 1540?

Was it a case of court faction?

As with so many of the events during Henry VIII's reign, the answer lies in the mind and attitude of the King himself. He had treated harshly ministers who had served him and his father well, as the abrupt end to the careers of Wolsey and More demonstrated. It seems remarkable that a man who had served the King so well, as Cromwell had, and who had not tried to get the personal power and wealth of a Wolsey, should also be destroyed. Cromwell had not failed the King in the way that Wolsey had over the divorce. To kill such an outstanding servant who had achieved so much seems remarkable and difficult to explain.

There is no rational explanation behind the fall of Cromwell. The simplest reason seems to be that a court faction of his more conservative opponents, such as Gardiner and the Duke of Norfolk, played on the innate fear and suspicions of the King and rushed through the disposal process before Henry quite realised what was happening. Logic should have dictated that Cromwell should be kept on as minister for several reasons. Geoffrey Elton points out that Cromwell may have made a mistake of being a part of the process which led to the arrival in England of Anne of Cleves (briefly Queen for a few months in 1540). Nevertheless, Henry should have kept him to get rid of her, as Cromwell had proved so useful in the past at disposing of wives.

Henry had become infatuated with Catherine Howard, niece of the Duke of Norfolk (no friend to Cromwell). The King's experience with Anne Boleyn indicates that infatuation led to influence. Henry was getting older, more ill and more suspicious, and readily believed the pack of lies presented to him by Cromwell's enemies. Trumped-up charges of heresy (religious crimes) were placed against Cromwell. The Privy Council – his own creation – was used against him. An Act of attainder (see page 54) was rushed through, and Cromwell was duly executed. He had become too close to religious reforming pressures so the mud could stick, although there was no evidence to link him with extreme Protestant doctrines. It seems illogical that the priest who was actually married and who was known to have radical religious ideas – Thomas Cranmer, Archbishop of Canterbury – was left alone.

Foreign policy issues may have played a part in Cromwell's fall. This was an area in which he had never involved himself much, but he certainly took some responsibility for the attempt to gain Protestant friends in Germany as possible allies against a massed Roman Catholic attack. The marriage to Anne of Cleves was part of this process – she came from a Protestant German ruling family, and when she arrived in England she was not nearly so physically attractive as her portrait had made out. Henry could not stand the sight of her, and as the French and Charles V had gone back to war, the marriage was not necessary strategically. Cromwell may have been the scapegoat here.

Perhaps the courtiers who envied Cromwell's power and achievement feared that Cranmer was harmless without Cromwell who could put through the ideas. He cannot have been too much surprised at what happened to him. After all, he had seen what had happened to both More and Wolsey and was a fairly skilled participator in the game of court politics

1. Why did Cromwell fall from power so suddenly?

2. To what extent was the execution of Cromwell just the result of 'petty court infighting'?

and faction fighting himself. Cromwell had gained many of the benefits which went with the job – an earldom (of Essex) and an income – and he could also see real achievements as a result of his work, which he knew would last. If he had been a Protestant, then he could see that fundamental moves had been made away from the Roman Catholic Church, and that significant moves towards this goal, particularly in the form of the English Bible, had been achieved. He knew the stakes of the game, and was not unduly surprised when he lost. He knew his master too well for that. He would be pleased to have known how much he was missed by his master, and Henry's anger at the way he was hoodwinked into killing the outstanding minister of his reign.

6.5 The foreign policy of Henry VIII (1529–1547) – an expensive mistake?

Overview

It is possible to divide the years after the fall of Wolsey into two periods. The first, from 1529 to about 1539, indicates that the divorce and the break with Rome was the most dominant factor in Henry's mind, and that although he did not relegate foreign affairs entirely, they were not paramount. Henry was obviously concerned with international developments – after all Catherine of Aragon was the aunt of the Emperor Charles V (King of Spain and ruler of much of what is now Germany). There was always the possibility of a catholic crusade against him. However, Charles V had his own problems with the Turks attacking his Mediterranean possessions, the Protestants in Germany and the French in Italy. The French seemed locked in permanent conflict with the Emperor, so Henry was in a position to maintain a fairly low profile as an international figure. Henry made his own policy, but Cromwell was a calming influence, and discouraged too warlike a policy

However, by the time of Cromwell's fall, Henry VIII not only felt more secure at home but had built up a sizeable war chest thanks to the Dissolution of the Monasteries. He had become increasingly worried by the possibility of France and the Emperor Charles V joining against him in a religious war to reimpose the Pope's authority. He was also in a mood to return to the more aggressive, glory-seeking days of his youth.

Henry VIII failed to achieve much by a return to war, wasted much of the financial legacy of Cromwell (as he had done with that of his father) and succeeded in making a more serious enemy of the Scots than had been the case before. There is little sign of a coherent or a rational foreign policy in what he did, and no real achievement either.

What were the main influences on Henry VIII's foreign policy between 1529 and 1540?

There is little sign of any real common sense in Henrician foreign policy in this period. Henry had plenty of expert advisers, such as Gardiner. Cromwell had travelled widely in Europe and had a real knowledge of European politics. There were signs of pressure from merchants for the state to adopt a more protective and supportive role towards them, as it had done under Henry VII, but Henry VIII's mind was on divorce and heirs. The French King, Francis I, was approached, and there was a defensive Anglo–French alliance in 1532. This was part of a process where Henry VIII was trying to get Francis I to pressurise the Sorbonne University to give favourable opinions on Henry's divorce. Francis was looking for an ally in his struggle against Charles V. Self-interest was the motive behind both men, but little of permanent value to either was achieved by this diplomacy.

There were embassies to the Protestant areas of Germany initiated by Henry (but not Cromwell) in the 1530s. With Henry refusing to make any move towards the open Protestantism of the German princes, these talks got nowhere. However, with the temporary ending of the wars between France and the Emperor in 1538, and the publication of the papal bull excommunicating Henry, both the French and Imperial ambassadors were withdrawn from London which indicated the real displeasure of both Francis and Charles. It looked as if Henry might be really threatened from abroad, and there was a need to think seriously about international relations and to win some friends.

There was major expenditure on the defences of the kingdom in 1539. The Six Articles were put through to emphasise the Catholicism of the kingdom. De la Poles, possible claimants to the throne as descendants of Edward IV, were hurriedly killed as a warning to all. Overtures were made to several Protestant European states. This led to the negotiations with several Protestant German princes, organised in a group called the Schmalkaldic League. This was designed to defend their newly acquired Protestantism against the militant Catholicism of Charles V and the Pope. It also led to the marriage of the Protestant Anne of Cleves to Henry VIII. Henry was appalled by what he saw when Anne arrived, as a picture of her sent to Henry had been flattering (see below). However, no sooner had the marriage begun than the need for it was removed. France and the Emperor returned to war against each other, and the embassy of the Duke of Norfolk to France had wooed France away from Charles V. Anne was sent back to Germany, adequately paid off for her troubles, and Henry got on with his affair with the nubile, young Catherine Howard.

Henry's foreign policy in this period achieved little. His policy was primarily reacting to events abroad, dependent on what was happening between the two European 'superpowers', France and the Holy Roman Empire, and reactive to his own immediate needs. There is no sign that Henry ever thought about the wider interests of his country, its commercial or security needs. He was prepared to put up with the 'Flanders Mare' as he called Anne of Cleves, in the interests of his country's security, but was delighted when he could follow his natural preference towards the pretty Catherine Howard.

1. What were the main influences behind English foreign policy between 1530 and 1540?

2. To what extent was English foreign policy in the 1530s influenced by the religious changes taking place?

Anne of Cleves, Henry VIII's fifth wife. This is the flattering painting by Hans Holbein which persuaded Henry to agree to the marriage.

Why did Henry VIII return to war in the 1540s?

Many of the remaining years of Henry's reign – between the fall of Cromwell and the King's death in 1547 – were dominated by war. In fact a historian will find little to write about in these years beyond battles, treaties and faction fighting at Court. There is some debate as to what Henry was actually trying to achieve in these years. A. F. Pollard, in one of the first biographies of Henry VIII, argues that Henry was primarily concerned with absorbing Scotland into England as part of a simple imperial policy, and that the war with France was secondary to this as France and Scotland were old allies. There does not seem to be much evidence for this; all the evidence points to Henry being pretty old-fashioned in his views and not having any ideas of a 'Great Britain'. R. B. Wernham, in his study of Tudor foreign policy, argues that Henry simply disliked the Scots, and his motives for fighting them were primarily defensive. The Scottish King was married to a French Queen, so in fighting the Scots Henry was just protecting his rear.

The current view, put forward by J. J. Scarisbrick, argues that Henry was primarily concerned with acquiring territory and prestige in France, and the several campaigns in Scotland were merely a means of securing his back door. For instance, James V of Scotland was always loyal to France; the Pilgrimage of Grace rebels had fled there; Cardinal Beaton (a papal agent) was there; and James had refused to turn up in 1541 to meet Henry in a way which Henry felt publicly humiliated him. All of these factors may well have added to Henry's dislike for his northern cousin. Personal irritation was always a factor in Henry's thinking.

What were the results of the wars with France and Scotland in the 1540s?

Overall the wars with Scotland were disastrous for England. War was provoked by the English in 1542, with major demands being made on the Scots which it could not possibly give in to and remain an independent sovereign state. When James V declined the terms of the 'negotiation', an English army invaded and destroyed the Scottish army decisively at the battle of Solway Moss. James V died a matter of days after the devastating defeat, leaving his one-week-old daughter, Mary, on the throne. The fact that the infant Mary had a French mother who was strongly Catholic did not help the situation. With Scotland defenceless and leaderless, Henry was in a position to make effective moves there and perhaps solve the 'Scottish problem' for once and for all.

However with Scotland always subordinate to his French ambitions, Henry rather ignored the advice given to him by his Scottish 'expert' Sir Ralph Sadler. Henry rushed through a treaty (Greenwich) in 1543, which committed his young son Edward to marrying the even younger Mary of Scotland. Without the custody of the baby girl or any guarantee that the Scots would repudiate the links with France, the treaty failed totally. Within months the Scots had repudiated it. The pro-English party of Scottish nobles, which Henry's advisers had so carefully being trying to build up, had collapsed. All the original Scottish treaties with France had been renewed. Henry VIII wasted huge resources and time achieving nothing more than creating a lasting hatred of England by many Scots.

To get revenge for this, the Earl of Hertford (later the Duke of

> **James V of Scotland (1512–1542)**
> King of Scotland from 1513, but did not assume power until 1528. Son of James IV and Margaret Tudor; nephew to Henry VIII. James allied himself with France and upheld Catholicism against the Protestants. Married Mary of Guise in 1538, and their daughter Mary Stuart became Queen of Scots when James was defeated near the border at Solway Moss in 1542, following an attack by Henry VIII's forces.

The Anglo–Scottish border region, 1540

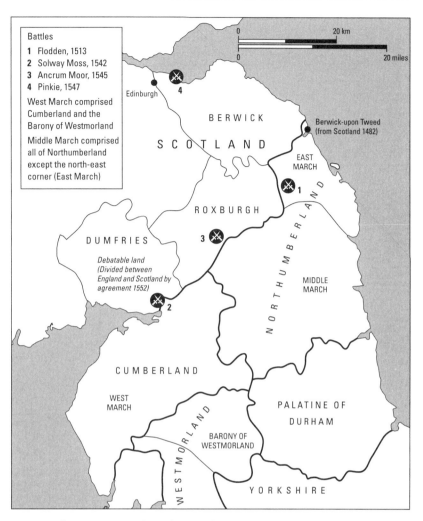

Battles
1 Flodden, 1513
2 Solway Moss, 1542
3 Ancrum Moor, 1545
4 Pinkie, 1547

West March comprised Cumberland and the Barony of Westmorland

Middle March comprised all of Northumberland except the north-east corner (East March)

Somerset) was sent north with a small army in 1544 and mounted a series of destructive raids right across the Scottish border regions. The modern tourist wishing to look at ruins can see ample evidence of Hertford's handiwork right across the Borders. The effect on the Scots was naturally to leave a legacy of considerable loathing towards the English, which was to play a major part in adding to the international difficulties of his daughter Elizabeth I later in the century. These difficulties were not really overcome until Elizabeth I had executed Mary Stuart, whom Edward VI really should have married. Beyond being a demonstration of English military competence, there are no redeeming features about the whole episode.

The wars with France produced as little as the wars in Scotland had. There appear to have been no gains and, in fact, there were serious losses. If an example of the real failings of Henry VIII as a monarch are required, then his dealings with France between 1540 and 1547 merit careful scrutiny. The contrast with his cautious father or his canny daughter, Elizabeth, could not be stronger. In all spheres – diplomatic, military, commercial, financial – the whole conflict with France seems to have been a total disaster.

There is no clear view as to why Henry VIII went to war with France. He may have felt that the honour of England had been slighted by the unsympathetic attitude of the French towards his divorce needs. It is more likely to have been simple greed. Henry no longer needed the French pension which had been a legacy from his father, and which had been important to his financial security until 1532–33. There is some sign that some key members of his Court were offended at the non-payment of their pensions by the French. On the whole the reasons may well have been trivial rather than profound. The fact that Henry felt that one of the roles of the monarch was to fight is also important. It was what monarchs in the 16th century did, in his view, and France was both the nearest and the traditional enemy.

The initial idea was for there to be a joint invasion of France by the Emperor Charles V and Henry VIII, but Charles changed his mind. Henry found himself having to invade alone, and take on the might of the larger, wealthier and more populated France. He then found that Charles had made a separate peace with the French behind his back, leaving Henry to carry on with a war on his own.

Thus Henry VIII found himself by 1545 with no allies, a serious invasion threat on his hands, with some furious Scots in his rear. The French fleet cruised blatantly up and down the Solent. The pride and joy of his fleet, his flagship the 'Mary Rose', sank in 1545, just outside Portsmouth harbour before it came anywhere near the French. Henry made peace with the French in 1546 at Camp, when he was allowed to keep his solitary gain of Boulogne, with a pension from the French King as a further face-saving device.

Close to bankruptcy, betrayed by Charles V before he had had a chance to do the same, and with no glory to report back with, Henry may well have felt humiliated. Boulogne proved expensive to maintain and there was no other item which could be seen as a gain. More than two million pounds (about 10 years' worth of normal royal income) had been spent on an exercise which achieved nothing. A huge amount of Cromwell's legacy, monastic land, had been sold. The coinage was debased, and although not realised or understood at the time, inflation was encouraged. It was a complete disaster from beginning to end, and was a particularly unfortunate legacy to leave to his children.

> 1. What were the causes and results of Henry's wars with France and Scotland between 1540 and 1547?
>
> 2. What do the wars of the last years of Henry's reign reveal about his strengths and weaknesses as a monarch?

6.6 How efficiently was England ruled in the final years of Henry VIII's reign?

In the last years of the reign, between 1540 and 1547, foreign policy dominates. This was little more than the implementation of the King's immediate wishes. There is little of significance to note on the domestic front, the dominant feature of domestic politics being the faction fighting at Court of which Cromwell's death had been a part. The historian J. J. Scarisbrick calls it the 'years of ruthless jockeying by ruthless men'. The fifth marriage of the King illustrates these years well. While Henry was still married to Anne of Cleves, the Duke of Norfolk and Bishop Gardiner (members of the more conservative religious faction) dangled the pretty and flirtatious Catherine Howard in front of the King. He duly fell for her charms. Marriage soon followed (on the day on which Cromwell was killed, ironically), but Catherine was unable to remain faithful to an ageing, frequently ill and absent king, and she was soon indicted as an adulterer. The fact that it was Cranmer, always a sympathiser of reforming religious views, who passed the information on to the King, shows the nature of faction fighting at Court, and the stakes played for. Catherine tried to defend herself on the grounds that the King was also an adulterer, but an act of attainder soon disposed of her.

Henry's final wife, Catherine Parr, was known to support humanist and possibly Protestant ideas. She certainly aided Cranmer in his protection and advancement of those with 'advanced' views. She was also partly responsible for ensuring that the education of the young heir, Edward, was entrusted to tutors known for their advanced religious views.

The Privy Council blossomed into a key administrative role, able to manage the affairs of the country without the presence of the King. However, it still saw itself as an institution which existed primarily to implement the king's wishes. However, it could manage the business of the country in his illness or absence abroad. It was as much the scene of faction fighting as it was of administration. It was vital for the future that by the time of Henry's death the Privy Council was dominated by two known religious reformers, Hertford and Dudley (later the dukes of Somerset and Northumberland respectively). Also that the Duke of Norfolk was in the Tower, being lined up for the same fate that had befallen Cromwell and Norfolk's niece Catherine.

What was the legacy of Henry VIII?

In many ways the final years, after the death of Cromwell, can be seen as a return to Henry's early years when Wolsey was the dominant influence at Court. The business of the monarch was to wage war and that seemed to be the dominating feature of these two periods. The years between seem almost an aberration. However they do balance each other out when it comes to noting the achievements of the reign. England had moved fundamentally away from Rome, and it was unlikely that it would ever return to the old relationship it had with the Roman Catholic Church in Rome. The Dissolution of the Monasteries and the subsequent alienation of so much of that land and wealth were to have profound economic, social and political implications for England. The way in which the country was governed changed for the better. The role of the State changed, it became much more intrusive in the lives of its citizens, even those who lived in areas distant from London. The development of the Navy, an area in which Henry was always interested, showed a realisation of England's potential as a maritime power. Although wasteful wars dominated too much of the reign, and they achieved little, there were lessons learnt there too. In future England tended to fight more for defensive reasons, or commercial ones. The idea of a continental empire lost its appeal.

Source-based question: Henry VIII's foreign policy

SOURCE A

The King has again applied to Parliament for a subsidy in money to fortify the frontiers of Scotland. During the debate two worthy members of that assembly were bold enough to declare openly and in plain terms that there was no need at all of such military preparations for the Scotch would never declare war or invade England without having an ally on the continent, and that the best fortifications against consisted of keeping on friendly terms with your imperial majesty. These sentiments of the two members met with the agreement of the whole of Parliament.

The imperial ambassadors to the Emperor Charles V, May 1532.

SOURCE B

'We are at war with France and Scotland, we have enmity with the Bishop of Rome; we have no assured friendship with the Emperor Charles and we have received from the … chief captain of the Protestants such displeasure that he has reason to think us angry with him … our war is harming our kingdom and all our merchants that traffic through the narrow seas … we are in a world where reason and learning prevail not and are little regarded. We have little chance of any but the worst peace.'

Bishop Stephen Gardiner to William Paget, November 1545.

SOURCE C

What precisely Henry's diplomatic intentions were during the months which ran from the conclusion of the Anglo–French treaty of 1546 to his death at the end of the following January only Heaven and Henry know. The lies, feints, the manoeuvring are so elaborate, the stealth so finely calculated, the evidence now so imperfect that perhaps half a dozen different interpretations may reasonably be put forward. But at least it does seem that, before all else, Henry was jockeying with a king of France whose every step was judged sinister and who was thought to be not only as bent on recovering Boulogne as Henry was on keeping it, but also constant menace to the successful completion of the unfinished business in Scotland.

J. J. Scarisbrick Henry VIII, *1968.*

---

1. Using the information contained within this chapter, explain the meaning of the following terms:

a) 'Bishop of Rome' (Source B)

b) 'unfinished business in Scotland' (Source C).

2. What does Source A indicate might be the nature of the relationship between Henry and his Parliaments?

3. What evidence might be seen in these sources to indicate that Henry and his subjects did not agree on the direction of his foreign policy?

4. Using the sources and your own knowledge, explain what you feel were the main motives for Henry's foreign policy.

7 'A Mid-Tudor crisis'?: the reign of Edward VI, 1547–1553

7.1 What problems did the Edwardian government inherit at the death of Henry VIII?

7.2 Why was the Duke of Somerset so unsuccessful in his attempts to deal with these problems?

7.3 How close did England come to political and social collapse in 1549?

7.4 How was the Earl of Warwick able to replace Somerset and establish himself in power?

7.5 How effective was government under the Duke of Northumberland?

7.6 What were the major religious changes introduced during the reign of Edward VI?

7.7 Historical interpretation: How popular were the religious changes of Edward VI's reign?

Key Issues

- *What problems did the Edwardian government inherit at the death of Henry VIII?*

- *How significant were the policy changes introduced during the reign of Edward VI?*

- *How successfully did Edwardian government deal with the difficulties that it faced?*

What religious and political messages are conveyed by this painting?

Framework of Events

1547 28 January: death of King Henry VIII. Edward VI is proclaimed King three days later; Duke of Somerset (formerly Earl of Hertford) is proclaimed Protector

September: Somerset invades Scotland, winning the battle of Pinkie and establishing an extensive and expensive set of garrisons

Six Articles Act and other anti-Protestant legislation are repealed. Chantries dissolved

Attack on ceremonies and images in churches

Bishop Gardiner is sent to the Tower

Enclosure Commission set up to enforce laws against enclosure

1549 17 January: Lord Seymour, brother of the Protector, is arrested and charged with high treason (executed in March)

Act of Uniformity, requiring the use of the first Book of Common Prayer

May: rioting in Somerset, Wiltshire and south-eastern counties

June: outbreak of full-scale rebellion in Cornwall and Devon

July: outbreak of full-scale rebellion in East Anglia

October: Earl of Warwick launches coup against Duke of Somerset

1550 Warwick becomes Lord President of the Council

Treaty of Boulogne surrenders the town to France

1551 April: Northumberland's final debasement of the coinage

October: Warwick is created Duke of Northumberland. Somerset arrested

1552 January: execution of Somerset

Act of Uniformity, requiring the use of the second and more Protestant Book of Common Prayer

May: marriage of Lady Jane Grey and Guildford Dudley, son of Northumberland

6 July: death of Edward VI. Northumberland attempts to replace him with Lady Jane Grey.

Overview

Edward VI as Prince of Wales

THE short reign of Edward VI was a period of uncertainty created by the speed of political and religious change taking place in a nation which was suffering from rule by an under-age monarch. The problems created by the accession of a young boy were made worse by the problems left by his father Henry VIII: an expensive and futile foreign policy, a debased coinage (see page 115 for definition), and Crown lands whose value had fallen because of the need to sell in order to finance an expensive foreign policy.

From 1547 to 1549 government was under the control of Edward Seymour (Duke of Somerset). Seymour, the King's uncle, was declared Protector and governor of the King's person by the Council. He quickly overcame his enemies on the Council, assumed control of both Council and Court, and put into effect a disastrous set of policies. These included an expensive war against Scotland, financed by debasing the coinage. It also involved the establishment of an enclosure commission. This encouraged hopes among the poor which could not be fulfilled. Finally, the government began an attack on the traditional basis of religion. All of these policies helped to cause widespread popular discontent. Moreover, the Duke of Somerset's move towards a personal style of government led to opposition from members of the Council. They resented the fact that, in increasing his own power, he was ignoring them.

The results were disastrous. In 1549 England faced a possible invasion from Scotland's ally, France. At the same time, full-scale rebellion broke out in both East Anglia and Devon and Cornwall. There was also localised rioting in many other parts of the country. The Crown's resources were spread too thinly to deal effectively with all of these problems. The Duke of Somerset's apparent indecision in the face of crisis gave his enemies the opportunity to act. In October 1549 he was brought down by a *coup d'état* led by John Dudley (the Earl of Warwick).

Coup d'état: The removal of a politician from office by force.

Dudley, though as unscrupulous a ruler as Somerset, was undoubtedly more effective. He introduced a greater degree of financial stability. He was able to follow a cheaper foreign policy by making peace with Scotland and France. The port of Boulogne was surrendered to France in return for a payment of £133,333. In domestic affairs he was able to begin far-reaching Protestant reforms, arousing less opposition than the Duke of Somerset. Dudley was more concerned, at least at first, to work through the Council. However, he did purge the Council of real and potential enemies and sought to rule through his friend at Court, Sir John Gates.

Edward Seymour (?1506–1552)

Created Earl of Hertford (1541) and Duke of Somerset (1547). He came to prominence following the marriage of his sister, Jane, to Henry VIII. He became a Privy Councillor in 1537. Edward Seymour had a successful record as a military leader, and his political prominence became more evident during the final years of Henry VIII's reign, enhanced by his status as the future king's uncle. Along with William Paget, he concealed Henry VIII's death for three days and altered the terms of the king's will to ensure that he had power as Protector. He secured the execution for treason of his brother Thomas. Incompetent in government and high-handed in his methods, he was faced with widespread rebellion in 1549. His alleged mishandling gave his enemies the opportunity to launch a *coup d'état* (see above) against him. Released from the Tower of London and restored to the Council, he plotted against his successor (the Duke of Northumberland), for which he was executed.

John Dudley, Earl of Warwick (1502–1553)
Son of Edmund Dudley (executed 1510), John was created Viscount Lisle (1542), Earl of Warwick (1547) and Duke of Northumberland (1551). A soldier, he rose to prominence through distinguished service in France. He became Lord Chamberlain early in Edward VI's reign. An ambitious man, he quickly became alienated by what he considered to be the incompetence of the rule of the Duke of Somerset. He established his credentials with his fellow councillors through his ruthless suppression of Ket's Rebellion in 1549 and successfully launched a coup against Lord Protector Somerset in October 1549. Surviving an attempted counter-coup in 1550, he became more powerful and was able to have Somerset executed in 1552. He married his son Guildford to Lady Jane Grey and attempted to use the latter to prevent the accession of Queen Mary in 1553. This attempt failed. Dudley was accused of high treason and executed.

Sir John Gates (?1504–1553)
A close ally and key 'fixer' of the Duke of Northumberland, he played a crucial role in the Royal Household as Vice-Chamberlain (1551–53). His close association with the Duke of Northumberland led to his execution when Mary I came to the throne.

By the spring of 1553 it had become obvious that the King, whose health had always been poor, was dying. His designated successor was his Catholic half-sister, Mary. The Duke of Northumberland devised a desperate plot to retain power by marrying his eldest son to Lady Jane Grey, the granddaughter of Henry VIII's sister Mary, and proclaiming her Queen. The plot failed and Mary Tudor acceded to the throne in July 1553.

7.1 What problems did the Edwardian government inherit at the death of Henry VIII?

Factional rivalry: The term 'faction' denotes a group of people getting together for a common political purpose. Often factions came together simply as a means of helping members to advance their political careers or job prospects. In this instance, however, the factions were associated with religion. Religious conservatives (see page 190) were against further religious changes, whereas evangelicals (see page 193) favoured further Protestant reforms.

Dry Stamp: This was a stamp of the royal signature. It could be inscribed on documents and then inked in by clerks. It was originally devised as a means of ensuring that Henry VIII should not be bothered with the signing of routine documents. However, it was used towards the end of Henry's reign and during the reign of Edward VI as a means of authenticating documents without the knowledge of the monarch concerned. It proved essential to the exercise of power by both Somerset and Northumberland. Its most important use was to authenticate the clauses of Henry VIII's will which were inserted after the King's death.

1. What problems did the Duke of Somerset face on assuming power after the death of Henry VIII?

2. How far were these problems caused by Henry VIII's own mistakes during the last seven years of his reign?

The flawed legacy of Henry VIII

Henry VIII's legacy to his young son Edward VI was flawed in a variety of ways. This was partly a result of the **factional rivalry** which was so marked during the final years of Henry VIII's reign. What had been at stake was control of the government after Henry's death. It was clear by the end of 1545 that Henry was dying, though it was not clear when the end would come. The Earl of Hertford and his faction were determined to be in control when the King died. They benefited from two main developments: the weakening of their opponents through the treason of the Duke of Norfolk and the Earl of Surrey; and control of the **Dry Stamp**, which Hertford's ally, Sir Anthony Denny, gained in August 1546. This allowed Denny to make documents legal without the King's knowledge and approval.

Most significantly, Denny used the stamp to 'authenticate' the King's will – after his death. Henry had altered his will in mid-December 1546, to exclude the disgraced Howards. On 26 December he left the Crown, successively, to Edward, Mary and Elizabeth. Henry created a Regency Council of 16 named members who would govern until Edward was old enough to rule himself. After his death, two clauses were added:

● One gave the Council 'full power and authority' to take whatever action was necessary for the welfare of the country during Edward's minority.

● The other allowed the Council to award any gifts that Henry had intended but had not been able to make officially.

The Earl of Hertford was able to use these clauses to secure power for himself as Edward's Protector and to reward his supporters.

It was not only Henry VIII's will which created problems. His policies in the final years of his reign proved very costly. It was during Edward VI's reign that the price for those policies had to be met. War with both France and Scotland had proved expensive. As a result, the Crown's financial position became increasingly weak, forcing Henry to sell a large proportion of the monastic lands. Henry also decided to debase the coinage. This latter policy had the effect of making inflation worse. This problem was to reach its height during the summer of 1549, when it helped to start rebellion on a massive scale. Moreover, official attitudes to religion seemed confused. Henry VIII had been content to defend the Royal Supremacy by preventing further significant Protestant reforms. On the other hand, as the historian Eamon Duffy argues in *The Stripping of the Altars*, the attack on traditional religious practices certainly continued during the early 1540s.

The problems of minority government

In addition to the difficult circumstances which were inherited in 1547, the Crown also faced the problems traditionally associated with minority rule. It was just over 60 years since the previous reign of a child, Edward V (1483). Most historians accept that Edward V died in mysterious circumstances at the hands of his uncle, Richard III, who was himself overthrown in battle two years later. There was no guarantee that Somerset's protectorship would be accepted, and there were fears about a possible breakdown in law and order. Official uncertainty was reflected in the publication in 1547 of the 'Homily on Obedience'. This had to be read by parish clergy to those who attended church. It reinforced the message that disobedience towards lawful authority offended against God's law.

Homily: A sermon prepared by others – in this case Archbishop Cranmer – which a parish clergyman could read out instead of having to write his own sermon.

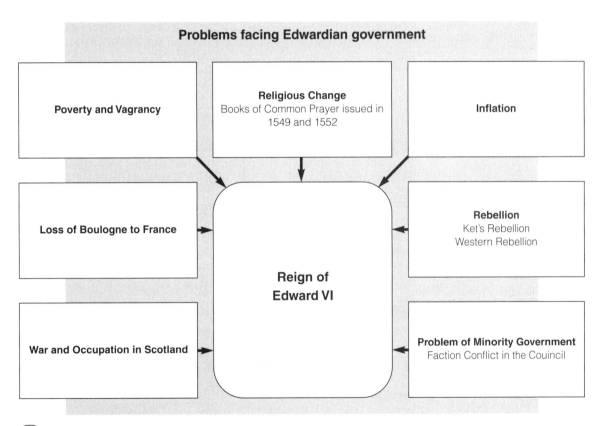

Problems facing Edwardian government

- Poverty and Vagrancy
- Religious Change
  Books of Common Prayer issued in 1549 and 1552
- Inflation
- Loss of Boulogne to France
- War and Occupation in Scotland
- Rebellion
  Ket's Rebellion
  Western Rebellion
- Problem of Minority Government
  Faction Conflict in the Council

Reign of Edward VI

Did these problems amount to a major crisis? Use the information in this chapter to find the answer.

7.2 Why was the Duke of Somerset so unsuccessful in his attempts to deal with these problems?

The scale of the problems

The scale of the problems which the Duke of Somerset inherited was vast. However, the often misguided policies which he followed from 1547 to 1549 helped to make many of these problems worse.

Foreign affairs

Somerset invaded Scotland in September 1547. He quickly won the Battle of Pinkie. He then decided on the expensive strategy of building and **garrisoning** a series of forts in the south of Scotland. In the meantime he failed to enforce a naval blockade of the Firth of Forth. This enabled the French to break the blockade, reinforce their Scottish allies and bring the young Queen Mary Stuart out of Scotland safely to France. There she would soon marry the heir to the French throne. This destroyed the political objective of Somerset's strategy and cost the vast sum of £580,393. Meanwhile, he was forced to employ over 7,000 mercenaries (see page 32) and had to face the possibility of a French invasion in the summer of 1549.

Garrisoning: The placing of soldiers in a town to protect it.

The Crown's financial position

The Duke of Somerset's expensive foreign policy was largely paid for by the debasement of the coinage, which raised £537,000 between 1547 and 1551. Other sums were raised by the dissolution of the chantries (see page 131). But the scale of Crown expenditure was so great that, even allowing for parliamentary taxation, Lord Protector Somerset was forced into land sales and borrowing.

Social and economic problems

One of the problems with debasement of the coinage was that it made an already inflationary situation even worse. The only solution, as recommended by Sir Thomas Smith, was **restoration of the coinage**. This was not possible as long as the south of Scotland was garrisoned with troops. Instead, Somerset listened to those, like John Hales, who argued that enclosure was the root cause of social problems. Enclosure commissioners were appointed, but achieved little apart from raising the hopes of the poor and upsetting landowners. With inflationary pressures once again increasing as a result of a poor harvest in 1548, the amount of unrest in the country was enormous. In the spring of 1549 rioting broke out in many parts of the country. Full-scale rebellions broke out in Cornwall and Devon in June and in East Anglia in July.

Restoration of the coinage: This was the process by which debased coins could be withdrawn from circulation and replaced by coins made from pure gold or silver.

Religion

The religious position of England was confused at the death of Henry VIII. Religious conservatism had largely been upheld since 1539, though Henry VIII had guarded the Royal Supremacy jealously. In some respects, the Protector Somerset's religious policy represented a cautious move towards a more Protestant position. Even so, there was such inconsistency in the government's position that the historian John Guy describes Somerset's religious policy as 'chaotic'. It was hardly surprising that complaints about reforms should figure so prominently in the grievances of the western rebels and that Somerset's critics complained about both the pace and the extent of the reforms he introduced.

Sir Thomas Smith (1513–1577)
A prominent humanist intellectual and close associate of the Duke of Somerset, Smith found that his policy advice on economic and financial matters was ignored by the Protector. He was the author of *A Discourse of the Commonweal of this Realm of England* (published in 1581) which was a perceptive analysis of the social and economic problems of the time. He also wrote *De Republica Anglorum*, an early Elizabethan 'textbook' on government.

William Cecil (1520–1598)
Cecil was knighted in 1553 and made Baron Burghley in 1571. Secretary to Somerset, he was briefly imprisoned after the Lord Protector's fall from power in 1549. He was restored to favour in 1550 and served the Duke of Northumberland as Secretary of State from 1550 to 1553. He was out of favour during Mary I's reign. It was Cecil who brought the news of Mary's death to Elizabeth, whom he served as Secretary of State (1559–72) and as Lord Treasurer (1572–98). He was the most consistently influential of all Elizabeth I's advisers, managing Parliament, organising the Court of Wards, being leading member of the Privy Council and offering policy advice on all issues. He was hard-working. However, his political and institutional attitudes were deeply conservative. Thus, he was unable to contemplate any changes to administrative systems, which became significantly less effective during his final years. (See photograph of Cecil on page 217.)

1. How far, and for what reasons, was the Duke of Somerset personally responsible for the failure to solve the problems which the government faced 1547–49?

2. How convincing do you find John Guy's claim that it was Somerset's style of government, as much as his policies, which brought about his downfall?

Somerset's own shortcomings

These problems were made worse not only by Somerset's style and methods of government but also by the defects in his personality. He adopted a very personalised style of government which meant that the Privy Council (see page 13), which had reasserted itself in the last years of Henry VIII's reign, was increasingly bypassed. This caused much resentment among Privy Councillors such as the Earl of Warwick and William Paget. The Duke of Somerset had his own set of advisers outside the Council, most notably William Cecil. Increasingly, the King's business became associated with Somerset's personal affairs. In the end, it was Somerset's inability to act decisively against the rebels in both East Anglia and the South West which gave his enemies the opportunity to remove him. John Guy, however, has suggested that this was a pretext: 'His autocracy [absolute government by one person] – as much as his policies – provoked Warwick's counter-coup.'

7.3 How close did England come to political and social collapse in 1549?

The year 1549 was catastrophic. The rebellions of that year were 'the closest thing Tudor England saw to a class war'. Certainly, the extent of rebellion and disorder was considerable. However, some historians, such as M. L. Bush, have claimed that government was not under immediate threat from the rebels. In any case, the leaders of the rebellions and riots had little incentive to overthrow the existing social order. In addition to the full-scale rebellions in East Anglia and the South West, at least nine other counties experienced large-scale rioting. The rebellions themselves pose two fundamental questions:

● What were their causes?

● Why did the government experience so much difficulty in suppressing them?

The causes of the rebellions

The rebellions and disorders had a variety of causes. In Cornwall and Devon, along with Buckinghamshire, Oxfordshire and Yorkshire, there was widespread resentment of the attack on popular religious practices. In

Escheator: An official who was responsible for the local collection of feudal revenues to which the Crown was entitled.

Foldcourse: In Norfolk this guaranteed the right of landowners to graze a specified number of sheep over a particular piece of land, which could belong to someone else. It was the alleged abuse of this privilege which seems to have provoked many of the rebels in East Anglia.

addition, the Cornish rebels were resentful of Protector Somerset's sheep tax, originally introduced as a means of stopping enclosure in areas such as the Midlands. In East Anglia there was widespread discontent at possible abuses in local government and of local feudal privileges associated with the **Escheator** of Norfolk, John Flowerdew. There was resentment of the harshness of the Howards as landlords, as well as resentment of abuses associated with the Norfolk **foldcourse** system. With regard to the rebels' social grievances there was, as the historian M. L. Bush claims, an attempt 'to embarrass the government by seeking to implement rather than to resist its policy'. Rebels and rioters were responding to the anti-enclosure proclamation of April 1549.

There was a common link in all the rebellions: a resentment of Crown policy or a reaction to the weak implementation of policy. Most of the disorder was affected by problems caused by the severe inflationary pressures of the spring and summer of 1549. This was made worse by government policy. The Duke of Somerset, therefore, cannot escape criticism for the outbreak of the rebellions: a consequence of his supplying the wrong solutions to problems wrongly diagnosed.

The suppression of the rebellions

Not only was Lord Protector Somerset subject to criticism by his colleagues on the Council for his role in sparking off the disorders, he was also vulnerable to criticism for his failure to deal with them effectively. In this it is possible to sympathise with his position. The authorities locally dealt effectively with outbreaks in Sussex, Yorkshire, Cambridgeshire and the Midlands, either through expert conciliation or by appropriate force. However, Somerset was let down by the gentry and aristocracy in East Anglia and the South West where matters were allowed to get worse throughout the summer of 1549.

Somerset himself was under pressure to use force. Yet there was little he could do. Although mercenaries (page 32) were employed, they had to be held in reserve to deal with the possibility of a French invasion. Moreover, Scotland was still garrisoned. The need to deal effectively with Scotland was still the central point of Somerset's strategy. The Lord Protector therefore had little option but to use delaying tactics until forces were available to him. In doing so, he left himself open to counter-accusations from colleagues like Sir William Paget who considered that he was being too lenient towards the rebels. Once forces were available, they were deployed efficiently and ruthlessly in Lord Russell's suppression of the Western Rebellion and the Earl of Warwick's suppression of Ket's Rebellion in East Anglia.

 ## Source-based questions: The downfall of the Duke of Somerset, 1549

SOURCE A

Howsoever it cometh to pass I cannot tell, but of late your Grace [Somerset] is grown in great choleric fashions, whensoever you are contraried in that which you have conceived in your head. A king which shall give men occasion of discourage to say their opinions frankly receiveth thereby great hurt and peril to his realm. But a subject in great authority, as your Grace is, using such fashion, is like to fall into great danger and peril of his own person, beside that to the commonweal.

From a letter from Sir William Paget to the Duke of Somerset, 8 May 1549.

Source-based questions: The downfall of the Duke of Somerset, 1549

SOURCE B

I know your gentle heart right well, and that your meaning is good and godly. However, some evil men list to prate here that you have some greater enterprise in your head that lean so much to the multitude …

I told your Grace the truth, and was not believed: well, now your grace seeth it, what seeth your Grace? Marry, the King's subjects out of all discipline, out of obedience, caring neither for Protector nor King, and much less for any other mean officer. And what is the cause? Your own lenity, your softness, your opinion to be good to the poor …

Society in a realm doth consist and is maintained by mean of religion and law. And these two or one wanting, farewell all just society, farewell king, government, justice and all other virtue … Look well whether you have either law or religion at home and I fear you shall find neither. The use of the old religion is forbidden by a law, and the use of the new is not yet printed in the stomachs of the 11 of 12 parts in the realm, what countenance so ever men make outwardly to please them in whom they see this power resteth. Now, Sir, for the law: where is it used in England at liberty? Almost nowhere. The foot taketh upon him the part of the head, and commons is become a king … I know in this matter of the commons every man of the Council hath misliked your proceedings, and wished it otherwise.

Remember what you promised me in the gallery at Westminster before the breath was out of the body of the king that dead is. Remember what you promised immediately after, devising with me concerning the place which you now occupy … and that was to follow mine advice in all your proceedings more than any other man's. Which promise I wish your Grace had kept.

From a letter from Sir William Paget to the Duke of Somerset, 7 July 1549.

SOURCE C

The lords and others of the King's Majesty's Privy Council, considering with themselves the great rebellion of the people in sundry parts of the realm, the great slaughter and effusion of blood that lately hath been through occasion thereof, considering also the great insolency and disobedience that yet remaineth among the King's Majesty's subjects, whereunto if speedy remedy be not provided, both his Majesty's most royal person

and the whole state might be brought into hazard and peril, and remembering withal that this and sundry other great disorders had proceeded of the ill government of the Lord Protector, who being heretofore many times spoken unto both in open council and otherwise privately, hath not only refused to give ear to their advisers, but also minding to follow his own fantasies (wherefrom all the said disorders and mischiefs hath before grown and arisen) did persist in the same …

[The Lord Protector] had suddenly raised a power of the commons to the intent, if their lordships had come to the Court, to have destroyed them, which power he had levied as well by letters whereunto he caused his Majesty to set his most gracious hand, as by a most seditious bill which he had devised for that purpose, the tenor whereof word for word followeth: '*Good people, in the name of God and King Edward, let us rise with all our power to defend him and the Lord Protector against certain lords and gentlemen … which would depose the Lord Protector and so endanger the King's royal person, because we, the poor commons, being injured by the extortionate gentlemen, had our pardon this year by the mercy of the king and the goodness of the lord protector, for whom let us fight, for he loveth … us the poor commonality of England.*'

From the Privy Council's charges against the Duke of Somerset, 6 October 1549.

---

1. Study Source C.

With reference to Source C, and to information contained within this chapter, explain the political significance during the reign of King Edward VI of the two terms highlighted in the sources.
a) Privy Council
b) Lord Protector

2. Study Sources A and B.

Compare and contrast the criticisms of Somerset's rule made by Paget in Sources A and B.

3. Study Source C.

How reliable is Source C as evidence of the reasons for Somerset's removal from office by the Privy Council?

4. Study all three sources and use information contained in this chapter. How far was Somerset responsible for his own downfall?

7.4 How was the Earl of Warwick able to replace Somerset and establish himself in power?

Religious conservatives: This term describes those who, whilst often accepting the Royal Supremacy, wished to see no further reforms to the Church of England.

Privy Chamber: This was the private quarters of the monarch. During the reign of kings, it was staffed by the Gentlemen of the Privy Chamber who were key household servants of the king and who could control access to the king's person. During the reigns of Mary I and Elizabeth I, the household servants of the Privy Chamber became women, and its political significance declined.

1. Why was the Earl of Warwick able to overthrow Somerset and establish himself in power?

2. What does the Earl of Warwick's overthrow of Somerset reveal about the weaknesses of the system of government in Somerset's time?

3. 'The Duke of Somerset deserved his fate.' How far do you agree with this statement?

The Duke of Somerset's arrogance and dictatorial manner had created many enemies among the political elite. One of the earliest enemies was Thomas Wriothesley, Earl of Southampton, who had opposed Somerset's assumption of the Protectorship. He had been removed from the Privy Council in March 1549. Though he was later re-admitted to the Council, Wriothesley clearly had a personal motive for wanting rid of Somerset. As a **religious conservative**, he had a political motive for wanting rid of him. The ambitious Earl of Warwick was anxious to replace Somerset and was looking for ways to do so. Lord Protector Somerset was also foolish enough to offend those who had been his allies. Sir William Paget and Lord Russell both criticised him for ignoring the Council's advice. Paget, in particular, had done much to establish Somerset in power. He was now bitter that Somerset had failed to keep his promise to follow his advice more than that of anyone else.

It was the failure of the Duke of Somerset to deal effectively with the rebellions which gave his opponents, led by Warwick and assisted by Paget and Southampton, the chance to act. Moreover, it was the Earl of Warwick's ruthlessness and decisiveness in suppressing Ket's Rebellion which made him a possible alternative. Somerset, sensing that he was in trouble, issued a proclamation on 5 October summoning all loyal subjects to Hampton Court to defend the king and himself against a conspiracy. He identified his enemies with those gentry who had previously been oppressing the poor. This forced his enemies to act. A few days later the Duke of Somerset was removed by a conspiracy led by an unlikely combination of radicals and conservatives which was able not only to capture the King but also to take control of the King's **Privy Chamber**.

The Earl of Warwick was left in charge. However, his position was insecure, mainly because he was not trusted by his conservative allies. Under the leadership of the Earl of Southampton, these allies conspired to remove him. Nevertheless, Warwick was able to overcome this challenge in February 1550 and was thereby able to remove the conservatives from their positions within government. One outcome of the Earl of Southampton's counter-coup was that Warwick placed himself firmly in the reformers' camp in matters of religion.

7.5 How effective was government under the Duke of Northumberland?

For many years historians considered the Earl of Warwick (or the Duke of Northumberland as he was to become in 1551) a devious and unscrupulous ruler who enjoyed little success in governing England. More recently, however, his reputation has been upgraded. Historians are now more ready to acknowledge his success in dealing with many of the problems which had affected the Lord Protector Somerset. At the same time, they accept that the Earl of Warwick was no more devious than most politicians who achieved high positions in Tudor England.

The Earl of Warwick's reputation for deviousness relates to his conduct in three crucial episodes:

● his coup against the Duke of Somerset;

- manufacturing the evidence against Somerset which justified the latter's execution;

- the scheme to alter the succession by placing his daughter-in-law Lady Jane Grey on the throne.

The American historian Dale Hoak does not blame the Duke of Northumberland. He suggests that his conduct on each of these occasions involved the realistic calculations of a tough political operator. Moreover, the first two were essential to prevent the country from once more sliding into the chaos of the Somerset period.

More importantly, Hoak argues that Northumberland was 'one of the most remarkably able governors of any European state during the 16th century'. This judgement is based on the belief that Northumberland was able to solve the problems which had been the legacy of Somerset's chaotic administration.

Improving and controlling administration

The Duke of Northumberland had noted the problems which Somerset had created for himself by giving himself the powers of Lord Protector and ignoring the Council. He was careful not to assume the title and office of 'Protector'. Instead, he was appointed Lord President of the Council and sought to exercise control through that body. This was easier to achieve once he had removed the Earl of Southampton and the conservatives, who had been plotting against him. The **Council's functions** were all firmly re-established according to a plan written by Sir William Paget. This allowed the Council to operate smoothly during the Duke of Northumberland's absences. The Secretary of State, William Cecil, played a critical role in making the changes work. The Duke of Northumberland was careful to assert his control of the Royal Household, which gave him control of the King's person. He himself was able to exploit his position as Lord Chamberlain. Moreover, Sir John Gates, his ally, became Vice-Chamberlain of the Household and had control of the Dry Stamp.

The collective approach to government did not survive the Earl of Somerset's re-admission to the Council in 1551 and his subsequent fall. Somerset could not resist the temptation to plot his enemy's downfall. His schemes were uncovered and he was arrested and executed in January 1552. According to Dale Hoak, the Duke of Northumberland's 'calculated action probably saved England the spectacle of a bloody counter-coup and the administrative chaos of a revived protectorate'. Northumberland reacted to his triumph over Somerset by removing opponents from the Council. One of his victims was William Paget, who was confined to the Tower. He created a **palace guard** to defend his interests. Thus, the Duke of Northumberland's control of both King and Council, along with Gates' possession of the Dry Stamp, ensured that Northumberland had what historian John Guy calls 'unhindered power' to act in the King's name.

Finance

The Duke of Northumberland's major administrative task was to restore the Crown's finances. By bringing the wars against Scotland and France to an end, he reduced Crown expenditure considerably. Rather foolishly, he did proceed with one final debasement, though he then abandoned the

Council's functions: The Privy Council had executive and administrative functions: for example, to issue instructions to justices of the peace, mayors and borough councils and others in authority at a local level. The judicial functions were exercised through the Court of Star Chamber (see page 18). Councillors, however, tended to see their most important task as that of advising the monarch on matters of policy.

Palace guard: The term describes a group of soldiers who owed their first loyalty to the dominant politician who employed them.

Sir Walter Mildmay (?1520–1589)

A long-standing expert in Crown finance, he was knighted in 1550. As Surveyor-General of the Court of Augmentations (1547) he was largely responsible for the recommendations on which the royal finances were restructured in 1554. By that time, however, he was out of favour. He returned to favour under Elizabeth I and was Chancellor of the Exchequer (1559–89). In religion he was inclined to puritanism and founded Emmanuel College in Cambridge in 1584.

Deflationary approach: This refers to the effects of economic and financial policies which were designed to drive down the rate of price increases.

Household: At a general level the term describes those officials and servants whose role was to ensure that the Royal Court could function effectively. At a more specific level the term describes those household officials who had access to the monarch's private apartments and who were therefore in a position in which they might have political influence.

1. *In which area of policy do you consider the Duke of Northumberland to have been (a) most effective and (b) least effective?*

2. *How far would you agree with the claim that the Duke of Northumberland's unscrupulous conduct as a ruler was necessary in order to solve the problems left by the Duke of Somerset? Give reasons and evidence to support your answers.*

practice. He entrusted the task of reorganising the Crown's finances to William Cecil and Sir Walter Mildmay. They were successful in getting extra revenue out of the Church and the King's debtors. They also adopted stricter accounting procedures in the revenue courts and were able to cut normal Crown expenditure. Moreover, Cecil and Mildmay sought to restructure financial administration, though this was not put into effect until Mary I's reign. One important consequence of Northumberland's **deflationary approach** was a reduction in the price of basic foodstuffs. This helped to ensure that some of his more unpopular policies could be pushed through with less possibility of a threat to public order.

Foreign policy

The most important factor in ensuring the Duke of Northumberland's financial success was the ending of the wars with France and Scotland. Henry VIII's capture of Boulogne in 1544 had proved a constant drain on the Crown's finances. This expenditure was ended by the Treaty of Boulogne in 1550. Though this is sometimes interpreted as a national humiliation, the Duke of Northumberland was not only able to cut his spending as a result, he also received a substantial sum (£133,333) from the French. This financial gain was aided by the abandonment of the remaining Scottish garrisons, though continued French dominance in Scotland remained a potential threat.

Northumberland's relationship with Edward VI

The standard picture of the Duke of Northumberland's relationship with Edward VI was stressed by historian W. K. Jordan who argues that the King was able to rule. By the age of 14 he had begun to dictate business to his councillors. Dale Hoak disagrees with this view. He argues that Edward was merely following the course of state business, rather than dictating it. He sees Edward VI as an 'articulate puppet far removed from the realities of government'. Moreover, the extent of the Duke of Northumberland's control over the King can be explained by his control of the **Household**. His own men were the gentlemen of the Privy Chamber who controlled access to the King.

The attempt to change the succession

Henry VIII had laid down that he should be succeeded by his son Edward. Were Edward to die without an heir, then the throne should pass to Henry's elder daughter, Mary. This created problems for the Duke of Northumberland. Most obviously, Mary remained a Roman Catholic. Whatever his own religious views, the Duke had clearly placed himself at the service of the Protestant cause. It is not clear who first thought of the plan to change the succession. It does, however, seem as if Sir John Gates was responsible for persuading the King that Mary might be removed legally from the succession and replaced by a Protestant heir.

The dying King certainly shared the objective of keeping his half-sister from the throne. Had he been likely to live longer, a parliament might have called which could have altered the succession. Instead, the King was persuaded to sign a 'Devise' to alter the succession, which was confirmed by letters signed by the Council under the Great Seal. It was only at a late stage that Sir John Gates persuaded the King to name

'A Mid-Tudor crisis'?: the reign of Edward VI, 1547–1553   **193**

Northumberland's daughter-in-law, Lady Jane Grey, as his successor. At this stage the Duke of Northumberland had the support of most of the Council. It was only when the scale of popular support for Mary was revealed that he was deserted by his colleagues. The failure of the 'Devise' made him a traitor, and he was soon to suffer a traitor's death.

7.6 What were the major religious changes introduced during the reign of Edward VI?

Religious change under Somerset

Religious developments during Edward VI's reign have often been seen as cautious and moderate reform under the Earl of Somerset and more radical changes under the Duke of Northumberland. There is some truth in this, though it is something of an over-simplification. Even so, there could be little doubt in 1547 that there would be some moves towards reform. The Earl of Somerset had allied himself with the **evangelicals** during the last few years of Henry VIII's reign. Edward VI was being given a Protestant education. Moreover, Archbishop Cranmer's biographer, Diarmaid MacCulloch, suggests that in about 1546–47 Cranmer was moving away from a Lutheran position towards a view of the **Eucharist** more commonly associated with the followers of the Swiss reformer, Huldrych Zwingli. It was reasonable to expect that there might be cautious moves in this direction. This caution was caused not only by Cranmer's temperament but also by the need not to offend the Emperor Charles V at a time when his French enemies posed a considerable threat to England.

In some respects Somerset's religious policy certainly did represent a cautious move towards a more Protestant position (see insert).

Evangelicals: This has become the generally accepted term among historians to describe those who wished to reform the doctrines and rituals of the Church in England.

Eucharist: Sacrament of the Last Supper. Martin Luther had rejected the Roman Catholic doctrine of transubstantiation (see below). Instead, he believed in the 'real presence' of Christ which could occur without any miraculous transformation of the bread and wine.

Transubstantiation: The belief that during the Eucharist the bread and the wine were transformed into the body and blood of Christ. The Roman Catholic Church had asserted this doctrine since the 13th century, but the doctrine was challenged in various ways by the Protestant reformers.

The Earl of Somerset's religious policy

- The Act of Six Articles was repealed.

- The heresy laws were repealed.

- The Act of Supremacy of 1549 required the use of the first Book of Common Prayer. This was in tune with the requirements of the reformers insofar as it was written in English. However, it was largely a direct translation by Archbishop Thomas Cranmer of traditional Catholic rites and its Eucharistic declaration could be held to imply **transubstantiation**.

- Protestant refugees from the European continent, most notably Martin Bucer, were welcomed in England.

- Priests were allowed to marry.

- There was a more tolerant attitude to the publication of Protestant texts which had been banned under Henry VIII.

- No one was executed purely on account of religion.

Huldrych Zwingli (1484–1531)
A Swiss humanist and religious reformer, Zwingli advocated more radical changes in doctrine, Church government and ritual than those advocated by Martin Luther (see below). Zwingli's doctrinal views were particularly influential on religious reform in England during the reign of Edward VI, especially his view that the Eucharist (see page 193) was essentially a commemoration of the death of Christ. Zwingli believed Luther's position on the Eucharist to be too conservative. He felt that the Eucharist was a commemoration of Christ's sacrifice. His view formed the wording of the Eucharistic declaration in Cranmer's more radical 1552 Prayer Book: 'Take and eat this in remembrance that Christ died for thee.'

On the other hand, there was a sustained attack on many traditional Catholic practices:

- The dissolution of the chantries in 1547, as well as being a money-making exercise, was an attack on the doctrine of purgatory.

- In January 1548 several **traditional religious** practices were forbidden.

- In February 1548 the Council ordered the destruction of images and of stained-glass windows depicting saints, together with the removal of wall paintings.

- The Communion service in the 1549 Prayer Book no longer permitted the **Elevation of the Host**.

It was hardly surprising that complaints about such reforms should have figured so prominently in the grievances of the western rebels. There was a belief in some quarters that religious policy was moving too far too quickly. An attempt, for example, to ban preaching in September 1548 was aimed at silencing reformers who were seen as potential trouble-makers.

Religious change under Northumberland

It was not immediately clear how religion was to be affected by the fall of the Duke of Somerset. However, Diarmaid MacCulloch is convinced of the Duke of Northumberland's genuine belief in Protestantism. His support for the radical John Hooper certainly supports this suggestion. In any case, Northumberland's defeat of the Earl of Southampton and the conservatives in February 1550 made sure that he would follow the evangelical path. That path was smoothed by the international situation. There was less need to be friendly towards the Emperor Charles V who was becoming increasingly threatened by the French. Leading English Catholics such as Bishop Gardiner and Bishop Bonner had been imprisoned, and popular Catholic opposition had been brutally suppressed in 1549. In addition, moderate continental reformers such as Martin Bucer and Peter Martyr were now working closely with Cranmer.

A range of further reforms was introduced (see insert opposite).

Traditional religious practices:
- *Candlemas*, which takes place on 2 February, celebrated the purification of the Virgin Mary. It was abolished as part of the Protestant attack on the worship of the Virgin Mary.
- *Ash Wednesday*, the first day of Lent, had been marked by the custom of sprinkling ashes on the head.
- *Lent* was traditionally a time of fasting, a tradition which was to be discouraged in Protestant practice.
- *Palm Sunday*, the Sunday before Easter, commemorated Christ's triumphant entry into Jerusalem when people 'took branches of palm trees and went forth to meet him'.
- *Creeping to the cross* on Good Friday commemorated Christ's agony in being forced to drag the cross to the place of crucifixion.

Elevation of the Host: In the Catholic version of the Eucharist, the host was the consecrated bread which became the body of Christ. By the 15th century it had become the practice to raise the 'host' so that the entire congregation could gaze upon it and receive grace.

- In 1550 altars were ordered to be abolished and replaced by communion tables.

- In the Ordinal (form of service governing the ordination of priests) of 1550 greater emphasis was placed on the priest's role as pastor and teacher.

- The 1552 Prayer Book, whose use was enforced by the Act of Uniformity, adopted a clear Zwinglian Eucharistic declaration (see page 194).

- In 1553 Cranmer produced the Forty-Two Articles which were intended to define the doctrine of the Church of England, though there was no time officially to adopt the articles before the accession of Queen Mary.

1. Which of the religious reforms introduced during the reign of Edward VI do you consider to be the most important? Give reasons to support your answer.

2. Why did the Duke of Northumberland face less opposition to his religious changes than Somerset had done?

In addition, these changes were accompanied by further attacks on the Church's financial standing and devotional role. Bishops and cathedral chapters (clergymen who managed cathedrals and distributed income) were forced into surrendering estates on poor terms:

- the charitable purposes of the dissolved chantries were not protected;

- Northumberland had plans to suppress the bishopric of Durham;

- and the regime had plans to confiscate church bells and church plate.

Such radical intentions were brought to an end by Edward VI's death and the Duke of Northumberland's fall from power. It is significant that Northumberland's more radical reforms excited far less popular controversy than the more moderate reforms of the Earl of Somerset.

7.7 *How popular were the religious changes of Edward VI's reign?*
A CASE STUDY IN HISTORICAL INTERPRETATION

How much popular support and how much popular opposition were there to the religious changes of Edward VI's reign? Before attempting to answer this it is worth asking how strong Protestant beliefs were by 1547. The historian Susan Brigden has suggested that roughly 20% of Londoners were Protestant by 1547, which means, of course, that 80% were not. The leaders of London Protestantism were a vocal lobby and were influential among the Earl of Somerset's supporters. Kent, East Sussex, Essex, Cambridge, Bristol and the East Anglian ports were other places which had secure Protestant minorities. Elsewhere it was almost non-existent. Identification with Catholicism remained particularly strong in the North, especially Lancashire, and the West.

Traditionally, most English historians have assumed that religious changes during Edward VI's reign received popular approval. They have denied that there was extensive support and sympathy for Catholicism, even in the North. Thus, in 1959 A. G. Dickens was able to claim in *Lollards and Protestants in the Diocese of York* that Yorkshire was not a hotbed of Catholicism and that even during the reign of Queen Mary 'the forest of Protestantism was spreading relentlessly across the landscape of the nation'.

Churchwardens' accounts: Churchwardens were responsible for the financial arrangements of parish churches. Hence, their accounts can often show how readily a particular parish obeyed the requirements of the Crown, for example Somerset's commissioners.

1. Why do you think that historians have differed so much in their interpretations of the popularity of religious changes at this time?

2. What problems are posed by the use of wills to show evidence of public opinion about religion at this time?

Since the 1950s historians have examined parish records closely, especially **churchwardens' accounts** and wills, to try to assess what ordinary people really believed. Churchwardens seem gradually to have put into effect the Crown's requirements regarding the destruction of old Catholic practices. However, the rapid restoration of Catholicism in 1553 suggests, as Christopher Haigh argues in *English Reformations* (published in 1993), that the old religion had substantially retained its popularity. Eamonn Duffy in *The Stripping of the Altars* (1992) argues, especially on the basis of East Anglian evidence, that many parishes continued to maintain traditional Catholic practices despite the pressures from authorities. Nevertheless, both Ronald Hutton in 'The Local Impact of the English Reformation' and Robert Whiting in *The Blind Devotion of the People: Popular Religion and the English Reformation* suggest that expenditure on church goods declined after 1540. This has led Diarmaid MacCulloch in *The Later Reformation in England, 1547–1603* to suggest that 'already in the 1540s the old world was losing its enchantment'. If this was so, however, both J. J. Scarisbrick in *The Reformation and the English People* and Christopher Haigh argue that it was largely an understandable popular reaction to the destructive attitudes of the Crown.

The evidence from wills has been much debated, though these can be difficult to interpret. Many wills have not survived. Most people did not leave wills in any case, and the declaration in the preamble (in this instance, the preface to a will) might well reflect the views of the person drawing up the document as much as the person making the will. Nevertheless, the evidence from wills is important because they are one of the few sources which reveal public, as opposed to official, attitudes. A. G. Dickens was one of the first historians to use this evidence systematically. He argues that traditional preambles to wills in Yorkshire and Nottinghamshire started to disappear soon after the Injunctions of 1538; Kent straight away and East Sussex and Huntingdonshire from the mid-1540s also show a decline in traditional preambles. However, Christopher Haigh, among others, questions whether this actually means enthusiasm for Protestantism. By 1549 only 8% of Kentish wills had a recognisably Protestant preamble. In Suffolk the figure was much higher, at 27%, for the whole of Edward VI's reign. Before 1550 there were only two Protestant preambles in wills from the city of York and only one from the whole of south-west England – both areas which had risen in rebellion against the religious policies of the Crown.

8 'A Mid-Tudor crisis'?: the reign of Mary I, 1553–1558

8.1 Why was Mary I able to establish herself on the throne so quickly and decisively?

8.2 What were the key features of government during Mary I's reign?

8.3 How important to Mary I's reign was her marriage to Philip of Spain?

8.4 How popular were the religious changes of Mary I's reign?

8.5 How successful was Mary I's reign?

8.6 Historical interpretation: Was there a 'mid-Tudor crisis' during the reigns of Edward VI and Mary I?

Key Issues

- *What were the key political and administrative changes of the reign of Mary I?*

- *How popular were the religious changes introduced by Mary I?*

- *How successful was Mary I's reign?*

Framework of Events

1553	6 July: death of Edward VI; Lady Jane Grey proclaims herself queen; Mary asserts her right to the throne
	18 July: Northumberland's fleet mutinies
	19 July: Mary is officially proclaimed Queen
	Duke of Northumberland is executed
	Repeal of Edwardian religious laws
1554	January: marriage treaty with Spain; Wyatt's Rebellion
	February: execution of Lady Jane Grey
	July: arrival in England of Philip of Spain; marriage of Philip and Mary
	November: Reginald Pole arrives as papal legate
	Heresy laws revived
	Restructuring of Crown finances re-establishes Exchequer dominance
1555	January: Act restoring papal supremacy
	February: beginning of heresy persecutions; burning of Hooper, Latimer and Ridley
	Pole appointed Archbishop of Canterbury
	Beginning of naval rebuilding programme
	Poor harvest
1556	January: Philip becomes King of Spain
	Burning of Cranmer
	Another poor harvest
	Beginning of epidemic of 'sweating sickness'
	Plans for full recoinage drawn up but not implemented
1557	Stafford conspiracy
	War with France, which has papal support
	Pole deprived of legateship and under investigation in Rome for heresy
	Continuation of 'sweating sickness' epidemic
1558	Loss of Calais
	Militia system reformed
	New Book of Rates
	November: death of Mary.

Overview

AFTER having seized the throne through her decisive actions in July 1553, Mary I's principal aims were to restore the Catholic religion and to secure its continuance through marriage to Philip, son of Charles V (King of Spain and Holy Roman Emperor). The 'Spanish' marriage proposal caused some opposition within the Council and provoked a rebellion in Kent in January 1554. In the short term, it was possible to restore most aspects of the Catholic faith, which was widely welcomed in most parts of England.

However, Mary was unable to secure the restoration of most of the property which the Church had lost since the break with Rome. Also, her reputation suffered because of the ferocity with which the revived heresy laws were implemented from 1555. The restoration of Catholicism could only prove short term because her marriage was to prove childless. In the end, she was forced to accept that she would be succeeded on the throne by her Protestant half-sister Elizabeth.

Her last years were affected by increasing personal despair, by the devastation caused by poor harvests and an influenza epidemic, and by involvement in a futile war with France which resulted in the loss of Calais. On the other hand, her reign continued the sound administrative reforms begun by the Duke of Northumberland. However, it was Elizabeth I who was to prove to be the principal beneficiary of the re-organisation of the navy in 1557, the 1558 revision of the Book of Rates and the passing of the Muster Act in the same year.

8.1 Why was Mary I able to establish herself on the throne so quickly and decisively?

Mary Tudor (1542–1567)
daughter of Henry VIII and
Catherine of Aragon

Edward VI's health, always delicate, began to deteriorate seriously early in 1553. In order to preserve both his own power and the Protestant faith, the Duke of Northumberland attempted to secure the succession for his daughter-in-law, Lady Jane Grey, in place of Edward's half-sister, Princess Mary.

The first step in order to ensure the success of this plan was for Northumberland to arrest Mary, thereby preventing her from rallying her supporters personally. He failed. On 6 July Mary, who was travelling to Greenwich to see the dying Edward, either guessed the Duke of Northumberland's intention or was alerted to it. She immediately took flight into East Anglia, reaching her manor at Kenninghall in Norfolk.

The consequences of the Duke of Northumberland's failure to arrest the princess were made worse by the decisiveness of Mary's response. On 9 July she styled herself Queen, and asserted her right to the throne to the Privy Council (see page 13 for definition). At the same time, she notified individuals and towns throughout the country of her intention. She quickly gathered supporters from all social classes and about 14 July she moved south from Kenninghall to Framlingham in Suffolk. By this time several towns, including Norwich, had proclaimed Mary Queen. The situation seemed critical to the Duke of Northumberland. He felt it necessary to set out with a small number of troops to East Anglia. From Northumberland's point of view, this was a gamble. His ruthless suppression of Ket's Rebellion had made him unpopular in East Anglia. Having left London, he was no longer in a position to keep his councillors in line. In his absence, their collective nerve cracked and Sir William Cecil was commissioned by several colleagues to make a declaration of loyalty to Mary.

The Duke of Northumberland had reached East Anglia by 16 July, hoping to cut Mary off from her supporters outside East Anglia. He had also sent six ships to cut off a potential retreat from Great Yarmouth. Unfortunately for Northumberland, Mary's devoted follower, Sir Henry Jerningham, had brought about a mutiny in the Fleet. This suggests that support for Northumberland was fragile. Moreover, his power base in London had crumbled. By 19 July Mary had been officially proclaimed Queen and the Duke of Northumberland had little choice but to accept the situation. Mary was able to progress in a more leisurely fashion through her newly-acquired kingdom, arriving in London on 3 August.

The only successful Tudor rebellion had been brought about by a combination of factors:

- Mary's decisiveness;

- her popular support compared with Northumberland's unpopularity. This was founded, in part, on respect for the traditional succession and devotion to the Catholic faith;

- the Duke of Northumberland's enforced absence from the capital which left him unable to intimidate his fellow councillors.

> **Sir Henry Jerningham (? –1571)**
> A member of the 'Kenninghall faction' of keen personal supporters of Mary, he was a Privy Councillor and Vice-Chamberlain of the Household during Mary I's reign. He was removed from office on the accession of Queen Elizabeth I.

8.2 What were the key features of government during Mary I's reign?

The quality of government in Mary I's reign has often been criticised by historians. In 1910 Alan Pollard claimed that Mary's regime was weak and unproductive and that both royal and ministerial leadership were held responsible for this. More recently, Geoffrey Elton claimed in 1977 that Mary lacked political skill. However, it can also be argued that some developments in government in Mary I's reign helped lay the foundations for the apparent success of the Elizabethan state.

Privy Council

A. F. Pollard and other critics of Marian government assumed that the Privy Council was too large and faction-ridden to be able to function effectively. This does seem to be an over-simplified view, but it is supported by the way in which Mary's crucial decision to marry Philip of Spain was arrived at. There was no attempt to discuss the matter formally in Council. The first that some councillors knew about it was when the decision was communicated to them at a council meeting.

On the other hand, the Privy Council's supervision of routine administration was reasonably effective. Mary was sensible enough to ensure some administrative continuity by appointing some councillors who had served Edward VI effectively. They were prepared to show the same loyalty to her. These included Sir William Paget, William Paulet (Marquis of Winchester) and Sir William Petre. Bishop Stephen Gardiner, having been released from the Tower of London, returned to the Council. None of these men, however, was part of Mary's intimate circle. This mainly

> **William Paulet (?1485–1572)**
> First Baron St John, first Earl of Wiltshire and later first Marquis of Winchester (1550). One of the key financial officers of Tudor England, he was appointed Comptroller of the Royal Household (1532), Treasurer of the Household (1537), Chamberlain of the Household (1543), Master of the Household (1545), and Lord President of the Council (1546). He was subsequently appointed Lord Treasurer in 1550, in which office he served three monarchs – Edward VI, Mary and Elizabeth. In his own phrase he was 'sprung from the willow not the oak' and was thus able to survive the frequent changes of regime which occurred in the 1550s.

Sir William Petre (?1505–1572)
Appointed Secretary of State in 1543, he remained in office until 1566. Like Paulet, he was one of a number of officials who provided administrative continuity during the mid-Tudor period.

Kenninghall faction: This describes a group of courtiers who were intensely loyal to Princess Mary. They served Mary at her estate at Kenninghall in Norfolk, assisted her assertion of her right to the Crown and continued to serve her, not entirely successfully, as privy councillors.

Sequester: A term which implies the legal seizure of an individual's assets or offices.

Court of Augmentations: This Court was set up in 1537 to administer the lands and property which had, or would, come into the hands of the Crown as a result of the Dissolution of the Monasteries. Its name derived from the fact that it was intended to deal with the 'augmentation' (i.e. growth) in the Royal revenue.

Court of First Fruits and Tenths: Before the break with Rome, first fruits and tenths had been payable to the Pope. This Court was set up to administer first fruits and tenths now that they had become payable to the Crown.

comprised those from the **Kenninghall faction** who had remained devoted to her during Edward VI's reign. Their role in the Council was limited. Moreover, the number of working councillors was relatively small and cohesive. They provided skilful administration, often in committees to which the working councillors were attached.

A further administrative reform occurred in 1555 when Philip II of Spain was partly responsible for setting up an 'inner' council of nine members which combined working administrators – such as Paget and Petre – with a nucleus of clergymen, such as Bishop Gardiner and Archbishop Heath. The historian Robert Tittler believes that, though this inner council did not always function effectively, it did 'strengthen the concept of conciliar committees'. These were evident in the last years of the reign when the war against France was a pressing issue.

The role of Parliament

Cooperation rather than conflict usually characterised the relationship between Crown and Parliament during Mary I's reign. There was, of course, some serious opposition to key aspects of the Crown's religious policy. About 80 MPs opposed the repeal of the Edwardian religious legislation. This attitude was clearly based on principle. Parliamentary concern for property rights was sufficient to ensure defeat for the Crown's original intentions on two occasions. In 1554, to ensure the passing of the bill repealing all anti-papal legislation passed since 1529, the Crown was forced to guarantee the continuation of lay ownership of former church lands. In 1555 a bill to **sequester** the property of Protestant exiles abroad was defeated in both the House of Commons and the House of Lords. Parliament also refused to comply with the Crown's full demands for taxation.

The Lords and Commons, working together, attempted to limit Philip of Spain's role. For example, in 1554 they rejected a bill to include Philip's name in the protective clauses of the treason laws. In 1555 they prevented his coronation as King. After Wyatt's Rebellion in 1554, they rejected the Crown's proposals to exclude Elizabeth from the succession. On the other hand, there is little to suggest that there was systematic opposition to the Crown. There was much cooperation, especially in respect of social and economic legislation, and a willingness on both sides to seek compromise when possible. Mary I did not press for Philip's coronation or the exclusion of Elizabeth from the succession when the scale of parliamentary opposition to these issues became apparent.

Revenue administration

The Duke of Northumberland had set up a commission to investigate ways of reforming the administration of Crown finances. It had not proved possible to implement the recommendations before the death of Edward VI and the fall of the Duke of Northumberland. However, Mary and her councillors were sensible enough to implement the changes in 1554. As a result, Lord Treasurer Winchester took over to the Exchequer both the **Court of First Fruits and Tenths** and the **Court of Augmentations**. This arrangement, which lasted for the rest of the Tudor period, introduced more efficient augmentation methods into the Exchequer. In the process, the status of the Lord Treasurer was increased and there was an increase in the revenue from Crown lands.

Another important administrative development, from which Elizabeth benefited, was the introduction in 1558 of a new Book of Rates. The existing customs rates were hopelessly outdated. The revaluations were significant, with additional duties being placed on the import of non-essential goods. This was to increase customs revenues substantially and no significant amendments were introduced throughout the reign of Elizabeth. Indeed, Alan Smith argues that the Marian financial reforms 'were fundamental for Elizabeth's solvency [financial security] and thus for the Elizabethan achievement as a whole'.

Recoinage

The full-scale recoinage which took place early in Elizabeth's reign (1560–61) was based almost entirely on plans drawn up by Mary's officials between 1556 and 1558 to deal with the problem that substantial numbers of debased coins were still in circulation. The implementation of the plans had been put off because of extreme difficulties: war, disease and harvest failure. It is clear, according to C. E. Challis, that 'Elizabeth could never have tackled the problem of the coinage either as quickly or as effectively as she did had it not been so thoroughly aired amongst government officials in the immediately preceding years'.

Naval and militia reforms

The Marian government successfully undertook a complete reorganisation of the administration and finances of the navy. Six new ships were built, and many other ships were repaired. An annual sum of £14,000 was allocated to the navy in peacetime, a figure which was reduced by Queen Elizabeth to £12,000. Naval finances were to be administered by a naval treasurer, Benjamin Gonson, who was answerable to Lord Treasurer Winchester. This was a system which worked very effectively.

Musters: This term denotes the bringing together for inspection of men eligible for military service, together with their arms.

There was a clear need to reform the methods by which troops were raised. The old methods were obsolete (out of date). The chosen solution was for Acts of Parliament to create a national system of **musters**, with penalties established for absence from musters and for corrupt administration, and to modernise the system for the provision of weapons. Despite their limitations, these Acts undoubtedly improved the previous situation.

Support for boroughs

Robert Tittler argues that there was 'conscious support' for towns during the period 1540–58. This support was most marked during the reign of Queen Mary and formed a 'relatively perceptive urban outlook' which tried to ensure stability by assuring strong local government in towns. Part of the Crown's response to the difficulties faced by towns was to issue charters of incorporation which confirmed existing rights or conferred new rights on towns and enabled them to act as corporate and permanent bodies in law. This was seen as essential for a variety of reasons, not least because the religious changes of the Reformation period had destroyed most of those institutions which had organised poor relief in towns. In most cases, of course, Mary and her Council were responding to proposals from the towns themselves. This was not in itself unusual. What was distinctive about the Marian response was the move towards a uniform standard for the structure and powers of town councils.

1. How convincing is the claim that the achievements of Marian government were more important than its failures?

2. In what respects did Elizabeth I directly benefit from changes which had been introduced in Mary's reign?

Poverty and poor relief

The Marian government became particularly active in this area, partly as a response to the scale of problems which were experienced in the final years of the reign. These were marked by the social problems associated with high taxation to pay for war, epidemic disease on a vast scale and harvest failure. Laws against grain hoarders were strictly enforced, and local initiatives against grain hoarding were supported. Justices of the peace (see page 13) were appointed as overseers of the poor in Yorkshire, and the laws encouraging the conversion of pasture land to tillage (crop cultivation) were more severe than previous anti-enclosure laws.

8.3 How important to Mary I's reign was her marriage to Philip of Spain?

The marriage negotiations

After coming to the throne Mary was anxious to marry as soon as possible. It was essential to secure an heir to preserve Catholicism in England and, because of Mary's age (she was 37 in 1553), time was getting short. Moreover, Mary, whose life had been characterised by unhappiness and isolation, was anxious to secure what she saw as the comforts of marriage.

This immediately raised the question of whom she should marry. There were few English candidates – Edward Courtenay, a great-grandson of Edward IV, seemed the most suitable. His candidacy was supported by the Chancellor, Stephen Gardiner. There were, however, problems. Marriage to an Englishman would increase the status of that person's family and perhaps increase factional conflict. (The activities of the Seymour family between 1536 and 1552 provided a recent precedent for such fears.) Also, Courtenay was personally unsuitable. A virtual prisoner since the age of 12, he had few social graces and quickly became the victim of cruel courtly humour.

Given the lack of appropriate English suitors, it was obvious that Mary would need to look for a foreign prince. By far the best qualified person for the role was the recently widowed Prince Philip of Spain: he was a relative, he was Spanish, a good Catholic and Mary trusted his father, Charles. Philip, on the other hand, was unenthusiastic about marrying his older cousin, though his father was keen about the prospects of the match at a time when he needed English support because of Habsburg–Valois hostility.

Charles V's ambassador, Simon Renard, presented an official proposal of marriage on 10 October 1553. By the end of the month the offer had been accepted, though there had been little in the way of formal consultation between Mary and members of her Council. In some cases, the first the councillors knew was when the decision was formally communicated by Mary to the Council on 8 November. Some of Mary's advisers – most importantly Paget – enthusiastically supported the Spanish marriage. The one exception was Stephen Gardiner, who continued to argue for the Courtenay match even when Mary had already dropped the idea.

Philip II of Spain (1527–1598)
– a painting by Titian, sent to England to be shown to Mary Tudor before the Spanish marriage

The proposed marriage created immediate problems for Mary. The negotiation of the marriage settlement took place over the following month, both sides being conscious that the marriage might not meet with popular support. To counteract this possibility, strict limitations were placed on Philip's role and influence in England. Though he was permitted to hold the title of King, he was to enjoy none of the prerogatives (see page 61 for definition) which normally went with the title. His followers were to be prevented from holding public office in England. If there were no children or if Mary were to die before Philip, he and his heirs would have no further claim to the English Crown.

Reactions to the marriage proposal: Wyatt's Rebellion, 1554

The marriage proposal did not have the desired effect of making the general public accept the marriage. There was an immediate outcry, and a royal proclamation had to be issued to deal with opposition. More seriously, rumours were circulating of plots involving a marriage between Edward Courtenay and the Princess Elizabeth as a starting point for creating a Protestant succession. More seriously still, the marriage settlement provided opponents of Mary with a motive to start a full-scale rebellion.

It was intended that four linked risings should take place in March 1554: one in Devon led by Courtenay or Sir Peter Carew; one in Leicestershire led by the Duke of Suffolk, father of Lady Jane Grey; one in the Welsh borders led by Sir James Croftes; and one in Kent led by Sir Thomas Wyatt. News of the plot leaked out in January, forcing the rebels into a premature uprising. In the event, only the Kentish rebels were able to raise a substantial force. There appears to have been little popular support for a rising. According to historian David Loades, this can be explained by a number of factors:

- Opposition to the Spanish marriage, though widespread, was not strong enough to provoke popular rebellion.

- Too many of the rebel leaders had had close connections with the unpopular Duke of Northumberland.

- Protestant religious leaders were too cautious to become involved.

Wyatt was able to raise about 3,000 men. The rebels' closeness to London meant that Mary's control was seriously threatened, especially given the weaknesses of the Crown's own forces. Though Wyatt came close to success, his venture failed. This was due partly to Mary's resolve, partly to his own indecisiveness, but most of all because the City of London decided not to support him. Wyatt's way into London was blocked and the rebellion collapsed on 7 February after a virtually bloodless encounter at Temple Bar, where the authorities had barred his entry to the City of London.

Mary adopted a more lenient approach to the rebels than had been adopted either in 1536 or in 1549. About 90 of Wyatt's supporters were executed. Mary's half-sister, the Princess Elizabeth, was arrested on 9 February. The evidence of her involvement in the plot was circumstantial. More importantly, both Stephen Gardiner and William Paget were interested in Elizabeth's survival. Gardiner, who had been given the job of investigating the conspiracy, was still close to Edward Courtenay. Therefore, any attempt by him to emphasise Elizabeth's guilt would undoubtedly have revealed Courtenay's own level of involvement, thereby undermining Gardiner's own political position at Court. Paget was playing a different game. He saw Elizabeth as the long-term heir. On the other hand, Lady Jane Grey, entirely innocent of any involvement in the plot, was sacrificed as a result of her father's treason and executed.

What were the political consequences of the marriage?

The rebellion made Philip more reluctant to marry his cousin. Much to the annoyance of both his father and the Imperial ambassador, Simon Renard, he delayed his departure for England as long as possible. By the time Philip arrived in England on 20 July, the political situation in England had been transformed. Philip's chief English supporter, Paget, had fallen from favour, and his old opponent, Gardiner, had re-established himself as the Queen's leading councillor. Moreover, it meant that Paget's ally, Renard, was not as closely in touch with key developments as previously. Though the Queen's attitude to Philip had not changed, he found that his reception at Court was less friendly than might have been the case earlier.

The wedding took place on 25 July 1554. Mary liked Philip immensely. The latter, though naturally shy, tried to make a good impression. The atmosphere, however, quickly soured for Philip as both English and Spanish courtiers complained about the suspicion and coldness of relationships at Court. Nevertheless, Philip remained at Court to do his duty as both husband and king. There were regular rumours to suggest that he had fulfilled his primary function, that of fathering an heir. Unfortunately for Mary, these all proved to be false.

Even worse, the marriage brought England firmly into the Habsburg–Valois dispute in Europe. The resumption of hostilities in Europe had coincided with the election in May 1555 of an anti-Spanish and pro-French pope, Paul IV. This left the devoted Catholic Mary at loggerheads with the Papacy during the remaining years of her reign. European conflict resumed when Philip's trusty military commander, the Duke of Alva, invaded the Papal States (area of central Italy under the Pope's control) in September 1556. Pope Paul IV retaliated by cancelling Archbishop Pole's commission as a papal legate (see page 84). This had a disastrous effect on Pole's authority within the English Church. The Pope also ordered Pole back to Rome to face heresy charges. This forced Mary into the position of declaring that, if Pole were indeed a heretic, he would face charges in an English court, rather than a papal court. In the process, Mary was forced to adopt a legal position similar to that of her father, Henry VIII, immediately prior to the break with Rome.

These disasters were made worse by the English performance in the war against France. War had been declared on 7 June 1557. A reluctant Council was pushed into conflict by the 'invasion' of Scarborough by Humphrey Stafford, a Protestant exile supported by Henry II of France and Pope Paul IV. At first, English participation in the war went well. French shipping was cleared out of the Channel – a strategy which protected Philip's supply lines to the Netherlands. However, the English garrisons around Calais were forced to surrender by the end of January 1558. The threat of a Scottish invasion was so great that the Privy Council was prevented from undertaking any action to recover Calais. The port of Calais had long been a financial burden to the English. Its loss might

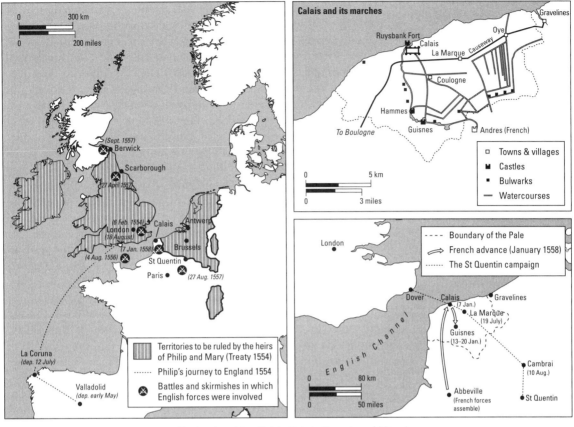

England and the Calais Pale in the reign of Mary I

1. What political problems within England did the Spanish marriage create for Mary?

2. To what extent was Mary's authority undermined by the hostility of Pope Paul IV?

therefore have been seen as a blessing. Mary did not take this view. The loss of Calais was a great psychological blow which further undermined her already fragile health.

In the end, Mary's marriage to Philip had brought few benefits. Philip himself continued to be regarded with suspicion by many of Mary's councillors. He made little attempt either to impose himself on English politics or to identify with the interests of his English subjects. The marriage never produced the hoped-for heir. This ensured that the succession would pass to Mary's Protestant half-sister, Elizabeth. Finally, England's involvement on the Habsburg side in their conflict with France proved very costly both in terms of finance and of prestige.

8.4 How popular were the religious changes of Mary I's reign?

Responses to Mary's accession

It is undeniable that Queen Mary's accession was, on the whole, greeted favourably by the English people. This popularity, it was argued, was a reflection of the regard that the English people had for the legitimate succession of Henry VIII's daughter. Recently, however, Christopher Haigh has argued in *English Reformations: Religion, Politics and Society under the Tudors* that the scale of Mary's popularity reflected the considerable devotion to the

Catholic faith still held by most English people. This claim has to be tempered by evidence of opposition to Mary, even within East Anglia.

Indeed, popular support for Mary was quick to appear. For example, on 12 July 1553 – a mere two days after Jane Grey had been proclaimed Queen – Richard Troughton of South Witham, Lincolnshire, was proclaiming that 'the duke [Northumberland] had made himself strong, for he had gotten the Tower and all the ordnances of artillery, and all the treasure into his hands', but derided him claiming 'fie [exclamation of disgust!] of money, in comparison to men's hearts'. Mary, as Christopher Haigh argues, 'was swept to power by a revolution'. In East Anglia it was ordinary people who had first joined her cause. She was proclaimed Queen in Buckinghamshire, Oxfordshire, Northamptonshire and the North. The Earl of Oxford was forced by his household servants into declaring for Mary. A naval squadron, sent by the Duke of Northumberland to the Norfolk coast to prevent Mary's escape, mutinied.

The Duke of Northumberland marched into East Anglia after Mary. In his absence, the rest of the Council realised the game was up and deserted him. On 19 July Mary was proclaimed Queen in London. The '**Te Deum**' was sung in St Paul's Cathedral in London, and in Grantham in Lincolnshire. There was massive popular rejoicing in many parts of the country, such as York and the small Shropshire town of Bridgnorth. Christopher Haigh suggests that much of this represented the releasing of pent-up opposition to the introduction of the 1552 Prayer Book and the confiscation of Church goods.

The restoration of the 'old religion' was anticipated in many parts of the country. For example, at Melton Mowbray in Leicestershire the altar was immediately rebuilt and Masses were said. In Yorkshire Masses were held from the beginning of August. Even in London, where Protestantism was well established, parishes rushed to turn back the clock. An altar was set up in one church on 23 August; **Requiem Masses** were heard at St Helen's in Bishopsgate, London. Churchwardens' accounts show that Latin service books were being bought quickly. Where possible, altar stones were restored. Altars, images and crucifixes were set up and traditional processions began again.

It is important to remember, as a Yorkshire priest Robert Parkyn put it, that 'all this came to pass without compulsion of any Act, statute, proclamation or law'. Almost all such actions were technically illegal. Nevertheless, evidence from churchwardens' accounts suggests that parishes were quite happy to go to the expense of re-equipping their churches for Catholic services, despite the drain on scarce financial resources which this represented. Examples of such payments can be seen in Sherborne in Dorset and St Martin's in Leicester.

It should not be assumed, of course, that such charges were universally accepted. There was trouble, for example, in places as widely separated as Crowland (Lincolnshire), Poole (Dorset), Adisham (Kent) and in various parts of London, Essex and Norfolk. However, almost everywhere there were realistic programmes of restoration undertaken with enthusiasm. There was a willingness to raise large sums of money very quickly.

Mary's restoration of Catholicism and her treatment of Protestants

Mary has long been criticised for her treatment of Protestants. Much of this criticism rests on the assumption that England was already, by 1553,

'Te Deum': A traditional Catholic form of service, usually sung in order to thank God for the successful outcome of a momentous event.

Requiem Masses: These are masses which are performed on behalf of the dead.

a substantially Protestant nation. Certainly in 1552–53 the Duke of Northumberland and Thomas Cranmer had pushed through a radical religious settlement. The reign of Edward VI saw much Protestant propaganda. Continental reformers such as Martin Bucer and Peter Martyr had been active, and there had been many converts among the ruling and educated classes.

How much Protestantism was there?

- Evidence of wills, though disputable, suggests some growth in Protestantism.

- 80 MPs voted against the repeal of the Edwardian religious laws. This suggests a sincere support for Protestantism among many members of the governing classes.

- There were 800 Protestants drawn from among the relatively wealthy and well-educated who spent the reign in exile in such centres of Protestantism as Geneva, Strasbourg and Frankfurt.

- Almost 300 Protestants – ranging from Archbishop Cranmer to humble folk – were willing to die for their faith during Mary I's reign.

- There is evidence of Protestant motives among Wyatt's followers in Kent.

- There is evidence of popular Protestantism in London, Kent, East Sussex and parts of East Anglia.

This is clear evidence of support for Protestantism. This was particularly true in the South East of England, though the extent of popular Catholicism was undoubtedly much greater.

Is this woodcut propaganda against Mary I or is it an accurate representation of what took place? Give reasons to support your answer.

Bishop Bonner, one of Mary I's Catholic bishops, whipping a Protestant. This woodcut is taken from John Foxe's *Book of Martyrs.*

Mary I's religious objectives at the start of her reign were quite simple:

● to re-assert Catholic doctrines and practices;

● to re-establish a Catholic church hierarchy (structure).

Mary asserted that all of the anti-Catholic laws which had been passed during the reigns of Henry VIII and Edward VI were invalid. However, **statute law** had become so influential that Mary had no alternative but to get Parliament to reverse the religious laws, thereby admitting the jurisdiction of statute laws in matters relating to religion. Thus, in 1553 all of the religious laws passed during Edward VI's reign were repealed. In 1554 the heresy laws were re-enacted, and in 1555 all anti-papal Acts passed since 1529 were repealed.

Reginald Pole, Mary's father's second cousin, had been appointed Archbishop of Canterbury. He was a man of considerable vision and ability. Efforts to restore Catholicism might well have succeeded had more time been available, though responsibility for this must be shared by Mary, Pole and Pope Julius III (reign: 1550–55). They hesitated about establishing the most appropriate way of restoring England to the Catholic fold. A few monasteries were restored. However, too many men of property had benefited from the dissolution to enable this to happen more frequently. Heretics (see page 124 for definition) and married clergy were punished. Some able bishops, such as Thomas Watson and Richard Pate, were appointed.

Almost 300 heretics were burnt. Some of Mary's victims were important members of society. These included Archbishop Thomas Cranmer, bishops Latimer, Ridley and Hooper and several other prominent clergymen. Most of the victims were humble folk, like Derek Carver who was a Brighton brewer. There are some hints of increasing popular concern at the scope and extent of the burnings. The policy certainly failed to destroy Protestantism. In some continental countries a similar policy succeeded. Its failure in England might reflect lack of time rather more than the extent of popular feeling. Certainly, the policy did nothing for Mary's subsequent reputation which was thoroughly blackened in the Elizabethan bestseller, John Foxe's *Book of Martyrs* (published in 1563).

Statute law: Laws passed by Act of Parliament and recognised as the supreme form of law. They are more powerful than precedent or royal proclamation.

1. What problems faced the Marian regime in trying to re-introduce Roman Catholicism to England?

2. On what grounds might it be possible to argue that the restoration of Roman Catholicism would have been successful if Mary I and Reginald Pole had lived beyond 1558?

Cardinal Reginald Pole (1500–1558)
His mother, the Countess of Shrewsbury, was of the House of York – so Reginald was born of royal blood. He was educated for the priesthood, but was forced into exile when he opposed Henry VIII's divorce. From 1532 he lived in Italy. He became a cardinal and twice narrowly missed being elected Pope. On Mary I's accession he was appointed papal legate to England. Mary made him Archbishop of Canterbury. He did his best to restore Catholicism to England, but was hindered by lack of time and money. In 1557 his legateship was taken away by Pope Paul IV but Mary refused to let him go back to Rome. Pole continued as Archbishop of Canterbury until his death a few hours after the Queen's in November 1558.

Source-based questions: Popular reactions to the burning of Protestants in Mary's reign

SOURCE A

The people of this town of London are murmuring about the cruel enforcement of the recent acts of Parliament on heresy which has now begun, as shown publicly when a certain Rogers was burnt yesterday. Some of the onlookers wept, others prayed God to give them strength, perseverance, and patience to bear the pain and not to recant, others gathered the ashes and bones and wrapped them up in paper to preserve them, yet others threatening the bishops. The haste with which the bishops have proceeded in this matter may well cause a revolt.

From a letter from Simon Renard, Imperial Ambassador, to Philip II of Spain, 5 February 1555.

SOURCE B

[Rogers] was brought towards Smithfield, saying the psalm 'Miserere' by the way, all the people rejoicing at his constancy, and thanked God for the same. And there in the presence of both sheriffs and many people the fire was put unto him, and when it had taken hold both upon his legs and shoulders, he, as one feeling no smart, washed his hands in the flame, as though it had been in cold water. And lifting his hands unto heaven, not removing the same until such time as the devouring flame had consumed them, most mildly this happy martyr yielded up his spirit into the hands of the heavenly Father. A little before his burning his pardon was brought if he would have recanted, but he utterly refused it. He was the first of all the blessed martyrs that suffered in the reign of Queen Mary. His wife and children met him by the way as he went towards Smithfield, but he cheerfully took his defence of the gospel of Christ.

From Acts and Monuments *by John Foxe, 1563.*

SOURCE C

Title page of John Foxe's Acts and Monuments of the English Church *(1570 edition):*

'A Table Describing the Burning of Bishop Ridley and Father Latimer'.

---

1. Study Sources A and B.

How far do Sources A and B agree about the popular response to the execution of Rogers?

2. Study Source A.

Why might Source A be regarded as particularly valuable evidence about the response of public opinion to the execution of Rogers?

3. Study Sources B and C.

On what grounds might one be sceptical about the reliability of Sources B and C as evidence of public responses to the Marian burnings?

4. Use all of the sources above and the information in this chapter.

On what grounds might the policy of burning heretics be seen to have failed?

8.5 How successful was Mary I's reign?

Traditional interpretations of Mary's reign have been dominated by a 'Protestant' view of English history which viewed this period as a brief but unfortunate interlude in a national triumph, begun by Henry VIII and completed by Elizabeth I. Such views derived originally from John Foxe's *Acts and Monuments of the English Church* (known more familiarly as Foxe's *Book of Martyrs*), published in 1563. It culminated in the historian A. F. Pollard's 1910 view that Mary's reign achieved nothing. More recently, Geoffrey Elton claimed in 1977 that Mary lacked political skill and was completely unsuited to the exercise of political power.

It is possible, however, to judge both Mary and her reign more positively. Firstly, we can identify a range of achievements. It has been argued that her religious reforms would have borne fruit had she and Pole survived long enough to see the reform established. The task facing Mary and Reginald Pole was enormous. There was a need to sift out Protestant clergy whom they thought were unreliable and re-establish Catholic bishops who would be capable of implementing the reforms which they considered necessary. Many of their approaches to religious policy anticipated the reforms which would later be established by the Council of Trent. Pole, for example, was anxious to establish seminaries for the training of priests; attempts were made to improve church administration, and six new religious houses were founded by the Crown. Traditional Catholic doctrines and practices were, according to David Loades, given 'a new lease of life'. Progress was also made in restoring church buildings. However, three main factors prevented the success of the religious policy:

- the deaths of Mary and Pole in November 1558;

- Pope Paul IV's withdrawal of the legatine commission from Pole which made it much more difficult for the Cardinal to implement his policies;

- the counter-productive nature of the policy of burning heretics. As David Loades has noted, 'quite suddenly what had appeared to be a discredited ... movement had become a cause that brave men would die for and testify to in the face of death'.

In other respects, Marian government did have some useful reforms to its credit. For example, the militia and naval reforms, changes in financial administration and proposals for recoinage all assisted significantly the successes of Elizabethan government. Moreover, Mary's government showed considerable strength in being able, as David Loades argues, to enforce its will effectively. The Council performed its duties thoroughly. Mary was able to enforce her will over her marriage, the restoration of Catholicism and the declaration of war. Government continued to operate with some effectiveness despite the problems created by harvest failures and large-scale epidemic disease.

Perhaps the least contentious judgement of Mary's reign has been made by Robert Tittler. Despite the achievements of the first years of her reign, the final two years were 'dominated by a host of setbacks': disease, famine, excessive persecution of heretics and disasters in the French war. Mary herself was conscious of her failure, recognising the lack of a Catholic heir. She hoped that Philip would be 'a brother or member of

1. On what grounds might it be possible to argue that Mary Tudor had a successful and productive reign?

2. How convincing is the claim that it was only during Elizabeth I's reign that Mary's successes became evident?

this realm in his love and favours' and vainly hoped that her executors (people appointed to carry out her will) would look after the interests of the religious houses which she had founded. There would certainly be no continuation of the Marian regime after her death, either in religion or in political decision making. On the other hand, many of the successes of Elizabethan England owed their origins to decisions or preparations undertaken during Mary's reign. In that sense, if in no other, her reign should be accounted a success.

8.6 Was there a 'mid-Tudor crisis' during the reigns of Edward VI and Mary I?

A CASE STUDY IN HISTORICAL INTERPRETATION

The concept of the 'mid-Tudor crisis' is founded on the assumption that the years from 1547 to 1558 were a third-rate and unproductive interlude between the important reigns of the two 'big' Tudors, Henry VIII and Elizabeth I. The concept was implicit in the writings of influential historians in the earlier years of the 20th century, such as A. F. Pollard and S. T. Bindoff. The concept was expanded in 1973 by W. R. D. Jones who argued that the reigns of Edward VI and Mary I were a period of great religious disruption, large-scale disorder and rebellion. There was inefficiency and sterility in government and administration, massive social and economic problems and a disastrous foreign policy.

Why did the concept of a 'mid-Tudor crisis' receive so much support from historians? Undoubtedly, part of the reason for this lies in the enormity of the reputations of Henry VIII and Elizabeth I. They both enjoyed long and dramatic reigns. Each of their reigns witnessed fundamental changes to England. Henry VIII accomplished the 'break with Rome' and presided over the emergence of Parliament as a key institution. Elizabeth I ensured the permanence of a Protestant religious settlement. These were important considerations to historians writing within an Anglican and Protestant tradition which saw the Church of England as having a key role in creating a distinctive English culture. Moreover, historians writing at a time when the British Empire was at its height could identify both with Henry's aggressive attitude towards the French and with Elizabeth's heroic defeat of the Spanish Armada. Furthermore, both Henry, with his six marriages, and Elizabeth, whose personality had been emphasised by the 'Gloriana' image, were colourful characters who could appeal equally to historians and their readers.

The two 'little' Tudors seemed colourless in comparison. Edward VI was a young boy who was simply manipulated by his protectors, the naïve liberal Earl of Somerset and the dishonest and corrupt Duke of Northumberland. Mary, at best, was a simple-minded women completely dominated by her husband, Philip of Spain. At worst, she was the monster depicted by John Foxe in his *Book of Martyrs* – an evil woman who took a sadistic delight in the suffering which she inflicted on the Protestant martyrs. Foxe was largely responsible for creating a picture of Mary which lasted down the centuries because it fitted the prejudices of a confident, Protestant and imperial power which viewed Catholicism as the product of an alien culture. (The influence of Foxe's perspective on attitudes in the 18th century has recently been emphasised by Linda Colley in her book *Britons*.) In these circumstances, therefore, it was hardly surprising that the period from 1547 to 1558 was marked by so many disasters.

More recently, the concept has been severely criticised – particularly in *The Mid-Tudor Polity* (1980), edited by Jennifer Loach and Robert Tittler, and by David Loades in *The Mid-Tudor Crisis, 1545–1565* (1992). All of these historians have written under the influence of detailed research undertaken in both national and local archives, which were not available when Jones was writing. Among works dealing with national politics, they have been indebted to:

- Dale Hoak, whose *The King's Council in the Reign of Edward VI* (1976) has stressed the efficiency of conciliar government under the Duke of Northumberland;

- the late Jennifer Loach, whose *Parliament and the Crown in the Reign of Mary Tudor* (1986) stresses the continuing importance of Parliament in Mary's reign.

In terms of local studies they are particularly indebted to Diarmaid MacCulloch's *Suffolk and the Tudors* (1986). This emphasises not only that the county of Suffolk was heavily involved in rebellion in 1549, but that it recovered remarkably quickly from the experience.

Historians such as Loades, Loach and Tittler have stressed that there was much creativity in the period. Government, particularly under Northumberland and Mary whose reputations have been revised upwards, continued to be effective. There was much continuity in religious beliefs and there were some foreign policy successes. Moreover, those features which were presumed to be particularly distinctive about the reigns of Edward VI and Mary could be found at times during the reigns of Henry VIII and Elizabeth I. For example, the most serious rebellion of the period was the Pilgrimage of Grace in 1536; the greatest foreign policy crisis of the period came with the Spanish Armada in 1588; and the social and economic problems of the late 1590s matched those of the late 1540s. Such comments are not intended to under-estimate those difficulties which occurred during the reigns of Edward VI and Mary I. The year 1549 was a time of extreme difficulty. Northumberland's plan to alter the succession in 1553 might have succeeded had Mary not been so resolute and Wyatt came close to taking London in 1554.

What was really significant about the reigns of Edward VI and Mary I was what did *not* happen. Parliament's status was not destroyed, the Royal Supremacy was not overthrown during Edward's reign, and England during Mary's reign retained its independence from Habsburg Spain. Most importantly, perhaps, England did not fall victim to the faction-ridden civil wars which afflicted France from the 1560s.

Though David Loades considers the term 'mid-Tudor crisis' as 'artificial and in many ways unhelpful', it does offer a way of approaching study of a complex and eventful few years. It is certainly possible for history students to examine a range of relevant evidence about government, economy, society, rebellions and religious changes in order to draw their own conclusions.

1. How appropriate is the term 'Mid-Tudor crisis' to describe the reigns of Edward VI and Mary I?

2. Why have historians differed in their views on the reigns of Edward VI and Mary I?

9 English government under Elizabeth I, 1558–1603

Key Issues

- How effective was the conduct of central government in Elizabethan England?

- How effective was the conduct of local government in Elizabethan England?

- How convincing is the claim that the quality of English government declined significantly during the later stages of the reign of Elizabeth I?

9.1 How important to Elizabeth government was the role of the Queen?

9.2 How important to Elizabethan government was the Royal Court?

9.3 Was the Privy Council an effective instrument of government?

9.4 Historical interpretation: How important was Parliament to the functioning of Elizabethan government?

9.5 What were the distinctive features of Elizabethan local government?

9.6 How successful was Elizabethan government?

Philip and Mary are accompanied by Mars, the god of war. Elizabeth is accompanied by symbols of peace and prosperity. What political messages does the painting convey? How effectively did it get its message across?

'The Family of Henry VIII: an Allegory of the Tudor Succession', which was painted in around 1572

Framework of Events

1558	November: Elizabeth succeeds to the throne and appoints William Cecil Secretary of State; Marquis of Winchester remains Lord Treasurer.
1559	Passing of Acts of Supremacy and Uniformity
1560	Robert Dudley emerges as the Queen's favourite
	Recoinage begins
1562	Queen catches smallpox and almost dies
1563	Differences between Queen and Parliament over succession
1564	Robert Dudley is created Earl of Leicester
1566	Differences between Elizabeth and Parliament over marriage and succession
1568	Arrival in England of Mary Stuart, who had abdicated from the throne of Scotland; kept under 'house arrest' by Elizabeth
1569	Plot to marry Mary Stuart to the Duke of Norfolk
	October: Norfolk sent to Tower
	Rising in the north led by the Earls of Northumberland and Westmorland
	December: collapse of Northern Rebellion
1570	February: final defeat of northern rebels in Cumberland
	August: release of Duke of Norfolk
1571	April–May: difficulties between Elizabeth and Parliament over succession
	William Cecil is raised to the peerage as Lord Burghley
	September: Duke of Norfolk is implicated in Ridolfi Plot against Elizabeth and re-arrested
	Treasons Act makes it high treason to deny the Royal Supremacy
1572	March: death of Lord Treasurer Winchester
	June: execution of Norfolk
	May–June: further difficulties between Elizabeth and Parliament over succession
	July: Burghley is appointed Lord Treasurer
	Reform of poor law, providing system for relief of the deserving poor
1573	Sir Francis Walsingham is appointed Secretary of State
	Creation of 'trained bands' – armed and trained local militias
1576	Peter Wentworth's parliamentary speech extolling freedom of speech; Wentworth imprisoned in Tower of London by order of Parliament
	Poor Relief Act – stocks of raw materials to be provided throughout the country to give work to unemployed
1579	Privy Council advises Queen against proposed marriage to Duke of Alençon
1581	Parliament increases recusancy fines to £20 per month
1583	Throckmorton Plot
1584	Differences between Queen and Parliament over succession
1585	Act of Parliament against Jesuits and seminary priests
1586	January: Star Chamber decree tightens censorship of press
	Babington Plot
	November: both Houses of Parliament petition Queen for execution of Mary Stuart
1587	February: execution of Mary Stuart
	Cope's Bill and Book
	March: Wentworth makes another parliamentary speech in favour of freedom of speech
	April: Sir Christopher Hatton is appointed Lord Chancellor
1588	September: defeat of Spanish Armada
1590	Death of Walsingham
1591	Death of Hatton
1593	Peter Wentworth is arrested for raising in the House of Commons the issue of the succession
1596	Sir Robert Cecil is appointed Secretary of State
1597	Monopolies a key issue in parliamentary session
	More comprehensive Poor Law enacted

1598	August: death of Burghley
1599	Lord Buckhurst is appointed Lord Treasurer; Robert Cecil appointed Master of the Court of Wards
1600	June: Earl of Essex is condemned to lose all of his offices and imprisoned at the Queen's pleasure (released in August)
1601	January: failure of Essex Rebellion
	February: execution of Earl of Essex
	Revised Poor Law enacted
	November: Elizabeth makes 'Golden Speech' to House of Commons
1602	Cecil begins secret correspondence with James VI of Scotland to prepare him for the succession to the English throne
1603	March: death of Elizabeth I.

Overview

THE reputation of Elizabeth I stands very high among English monarchs. Her virtues have not only been emphasised in scholarly and popular biographies but also in the cinema and on the television screen. The foundations of this reputation lie in the:

● glittering nature of the Elizabethan Court;

● development of English literary and musical culture;

● defeat of the Spanish Armada;

● successful re-creation of the Church of England and in the skill of Elizabeth's image makers.

How much of this image survives a study of Elizabethan government and administration? On the one hand, there existed a government founded on the principles of economy, peace and caution. It was headed by an intelligent monarch advised by a group of perceptive and hard-working ministers. On the other hand, the Queen could be shrewish (wicked), and her desire for economy often lapsed into meanness. For example, she deliberately starved the Church of resources by refusing to make appointments to bishoprics (office of bishop). The conservatism of the administration ensured that few substantial changes aiming to make government more efficient were introduced, thereby storing up trouble for Elizabeth I's successor.

On the whole, historians of Elizabethan England have tended to emphasise the former rather than the latter. Only Christopher Haigh has been prepared to emphasise the negative side of Elizabeth's reign. It is undeniable that for much of Elizabeth's reign England was provided with cheap but effective government, characterised by what the historian Penry Williams calls 'the informal cooperation and goodwill of the great men of the localities' (1995). Until the late 1580s taxes remained low. Social stability was maintained through the development of a successful and long-lasting system of poor relief. Most importantly, peace was largely maintained at a time when much of western Europe was faced by turmoil and violence. Despite its faults, there was much to be admired in the Elizabethan system of government.

9.1 How important to Elizabethan government was the role of the Queen?

Though the image of Tudor monarchs was bolstered through propaganda, few English people in the 16th century seriously questioned the right of the monarch to rule. Elizabeth I was clearly aware of this from the start of her reign. The Spanish ambassador, the Count of Feria, noted as early as December 1558 that Elizabeth was 'incomparably more feared than her sister and gives her orders and has her way as absolutely as her father did'. Elizabeth herself was keen to reinforce the message that she was her father's daughter, telling Parliament in 1559 that 'we hope to rule, govern and keep this our realm in as good justice, peace and rest, in like wise as the king my father held you in'. Clearly, Elizabeth intended to govern in line with the popular image of her robust and ruthless father, Henry VIII.

This was no easy task. She had to overcome the prejudice against female rulers, which had been reinforced by the disasters of the later stages of Mary's reign. Also, she had to overcome the popular stereotype of women, which emphasised their physical, intellectual and emotional inferiority to men. Even as devoted a servant as William Cecil was occasionally annoyed by what he perceived to be her feminine weaknesses. He moaned in 1560, for example, that a diplomatic dispatch from Paris was 'too much for a woman's knowledge'.

The Queen, nevertheless, enjoyed much power. In particular, it was the right of the monarch to exercise the prerogative powers of the Crown:

Proroguing: The right of the monarch to suspend parliamentary sessions until further notice.

● calling, **proroguing** and dissolving Parliament;

● declaring war and making peace;

● appointing and dismissing ministers and judges;

● determining the monarch's own marriage and naming a successor.

Elizabeth defended these rights robustly. These remained key issues throughout the reign. She was first urged to name a successor during the 1559 Parliament. The lack of a named successor seemed particularly acute in 1562 when Elizabeth became dangerously ill from smallpox. In the early stages of her reign there were two possible successors. According to Henry VIII's will, which the Queen had the power to set aside, the succession should have passed to Lady Catherine Grey, younger sister of Jane Grey. From the point of view of some of Elizabeth's ministers, Catherine had the advantage of being a Protestant. Unfortunately for Catherine, however, that was the only advantage she possessed. Elizabeth had little time for her relative whom she imprisoned in the Tower in 1561 after her secret marriage to the Earl of Hertford.

The strongest claimant on dynastic grounds was Mary, Queen of Scots – the granddaughter of Henry VIII's sister, Margaret. The possibility of Mary's succession alarmed many of Elizabeth's ministers, on account of her Catholicism and her close connections with the French Court. (See the discussion of Elizabethan foreign policy on pages 263–292.)

In the circumstances, therefore, it was understandable that the Privy Council should have urged marriage on the Queen. The Council's tactic was to petition Elizabeth to marry and, when that failed, to use Parliament as a means of raising public concern about the succession. In 1563 both Houses of Parliament petitioned the Queen to marry; the

Francis Bacon (1561–1626)

Politician, philosopher and essayist. He was nephew of Elizabeth I's adviser, William Cecil (Lord Burghley), but turned against him when Burghley failed to provide Bacon with patronage (see page 58). Bacon studied law at Cambridge University from 1573, was part of the English embassy in France until 1579 and became MP in 1584. He helped to secure the execution of the Earl of Essex as a traitor in 1601. Bacon was knighted on the accession of James I in 1603, becoming the first Baron Verulam in 1618 and Viscount St Albans three years later. Soon after becoming Lord Chancellor in 1618, Bacon confessed to bribe-taking, was fined £40,000 (later remitted by the king), and spent four days in the Tower of London.

Francis Walsingham (1532–1590)

As Secretary of State (1568–90) Walsingham was primarily responsible for foreign affairs. Like the Earl of Leicester he was a firm supporter of a 'Protestant' foreign policy. Walsingham organised a large and effective secret service operation which was responsible for uncovering many Catholic priests.

Queen responded by saying that she had vowed to remain unmarried but would settle the succession at an appropriate time.

By 1566, when Elizabeth's refusal to name a successor was regarded by her subjects as irresponsible, the situation had become even more bad-tempered. The failure to name a successor, in the event of the Queen's premature death, would cause much innocent blood to be spilt. Elizabeth I's response to such criticism was to prohibit Parliament from further discussion of the issues. Nevertheless, marriage and succession were to remain areas of contention between Queen and Parliament for much of the reign, especially at the time of her on–off courtship with the Duke of Alençon in 1579. Even as late as 1601 she refused to confirm to Parliament the name of her successor.

Did Elizabeth trust her ministers?

In general, the Queen did trust her ministers and seldom interfered in day-to-day administrative matters. Occasionally, however, she involved herself directly in the decision making processes: often frustrating her ministers by delaying key decisions as long as possible, especially in foreign affairs; or annoying them because of the scale of her interference, spectacularly so in 1593 when she rejected the pressure of both the Cecil and the Essex factions to appoint Francis Bacon as Solicitor General. One historian, Alan Smith, has suggested that royal interventions were beneficial; the Queen could 'keep the Crown's servants on their toes'.

Naturally, this contrasted with the view of the Crown's servants who frequently complained to each other about Elizabeth I's methods. On one occasion Francis Walsingham wrote to William Cecil (Lord Burghley) that 'I would to God her Majesty could be content to refer these things to them that can best judge of them as other princes do'. In 1575 Sir Thomas Smith complained that 'this irresolution doth weary and kill her ministers, destroy her actions and overcome all good designs and counsels'. Moreover, the Queen was good at blaming others if things went wrong. For example, in 1588 Lord Burghley wrote to Francis Walsingham that 'all irresolutions ... are thrown upon us two in all her speeches to everybody'.

On the whole relations between the Queen and her principal ministers were cordial and productive. As Alan Smith has pointed out, 'the Queen depended in some measure upon her councillors for advice, ... (but) she alone made the final decisions'. He argues that 'in the last analysis credit for the triumphs of the period must therefore go to Elizabeth herself'. By the same criterion, she must also accept responsibility for the mistakes and for the flawed inheritance which she passed on to James I.

William Cecil, Lord Burghley (1520–1598)

1. What do you regard as being the most important of the Queen's roles in government?

2. To what extent did Elizabeth I rely on her ministers to make key decisions?

9.2 How important to Elizabethan government was the Royal Court?

Painting entitled 'Eliza Triumphans, 1600'

What impression of Queen Elizabeth and her courtiers is this painting intended to convey?

The Royal Household: a survey

The Royal Household was divided into two parts. One part was purely functional: the Household proper supplied the physical needs of the Court, such as food, drink and transport. The other part, the Royal Court, was as vital politically during Elizabeth I's reign as it had been during the reigns of her predecessors. The Royal Court existed wherever the Queen might be at a particular time, irrespective of whether she was resident in one of the royal palaces or in the great house of one of her wealthy subjects whilst undertaking a royal progress.

The Court had two main areas: first, the Presence Chamber, to which access might be gained relatively easily by subjects with the right connections. This was where the monarch was seen occasionally. Admission to the Privy Chamber, the private rooms of the monarch, was strictly guarded.

This whole area was controlled by the Lord Chamberlain. Elizabeth I revived the practice of appointing only great nobles to the post. Her first two appointees were Charles, Lord Howard of Effingham, and the Earl of Sussex. Under Henry VIII and Edward VI the monarch's principal attendants were the Gentlemen of the Privy Chamber. These courtiers had come to exercise considerable political influence, as the intimate body servants of the king. Under Mary I and Elizabeth I these functions were

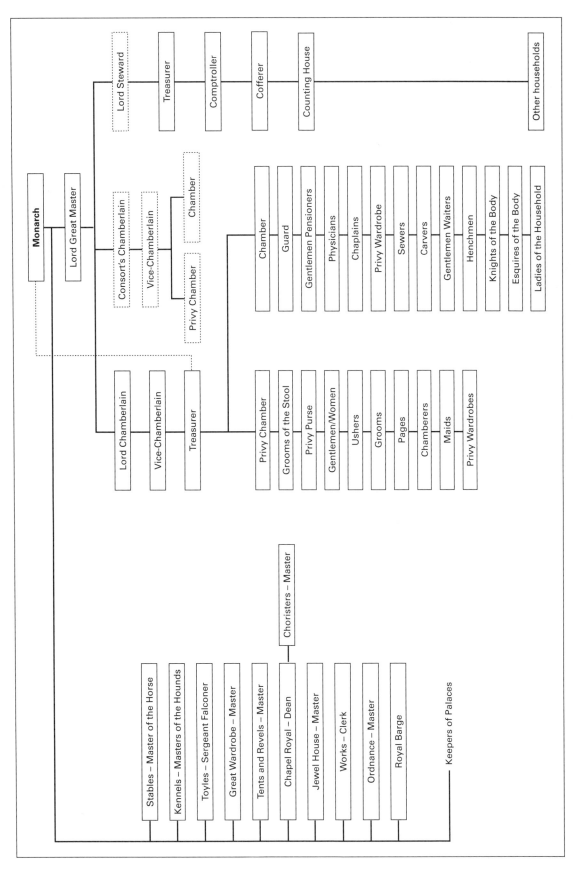

The Royal Household

Robert Dudley (1532–1588)
Created Earl of Leicester, Dudley was a Privy Councillor and favourite of the Queen. He strongly favoured a 'Protestant' foreign policy, which sometimes brought him into conflict with the more cautious Lord Burghley, with whom he was in competition for the distribution of patronage. Despite the closeness of his personal relationship with Queen Elizabeth, he rarely exercised the same influence over policy making as did Burghley. His conduct as commander of the English forces in the United Provinces in 1586–87 severely offended the Queen.

Christopher Hatton (1540–1592)
A courtier and favourite of the Queen, who was reportedly impressed by Hatton's shapely legs. Hatton, despite being a somewhat lightweight figure, was appointed Lord Chancellor. Allegedly pro-Catholic in his sympathies, he nevertheless took a key role in bringing Mary, Queen of Scots to trial.

Queen's Champion: This post was based on the practice of medieval chivalry. It was invented by Sir Henry Lee who appointed himself the Queen's Champion. He represented the Queen's honour at Accession Day Tilts and other tournaments. The whole thing reinforced the 'Gloriana' myth.

Accession Day Tilts: These were jousting tournaments which were staged annually on the anniversary of the Queen's succession (17 November 1558). These tournaments were open to the public.

Masques: Court productions involving music, dancing and acting.

Astraea: Astraea was a virgin goddess who returned to Earth to proclaim a new golden age. It was easy for Elizabethan writers to draw parallels between Astraea and Queen Elizabeth.

undertaken by the ladies of the bedchamber. As a result, the political significance of the Privy Chamber was much diminished. The ladies of the bedchamber could exercise little political influence in their own right and the role of the gentleman of the Privy Chamber became less significant. Even so, presence at Court could be crucial to political success. Thus, in the early 1590s the Earl of Shrewsbury, who was not a regular courtier, lost a battle for control in Nottinghamshire to the Stanhope family, who were strongly represented at Court. A few years later, Robert Cecil secured crucial promotions while his rival, the Earl of Essex (see page 287), was absent on foreign expeditions.

On the other hand, the ceremonial aspects of courtly life became even more important. According to historian Christopher Haigh, the rituals of court life were used as techniques of political control. Elizabeth deliberately politicised her Court by making courtiers – such as Robert Dudley (Earl of Leicester), Christopher Hatton and Robert Devereux (Earl of Essex) – into politicians. She also turned her politicians – such as Lord Burghley – into courtiers. In the process, politics became a full-time business in which personal relationships at Court were crucial. Ritual aspects were emphasised, especially from the 1570s when the **Queen's Champion**, Sir Henry Lee, devised the **Accession Day Tilts**. Not only did the tilts enable the Queen to be accessible to her subjects, it also meant that she could become the focus of the affection and flattery of her young courtiers.

The Queen was also the public focus of the Court during royal progresses which took place in over half of the summers of Elizabeth I's reign. Though geographically restricted to the South, south Midlands and East Anglia, the progresses were, nevertheless, important. They enabled the Queen to be seen by ordinary subjects as well as the nobility and gentry. In Christopher Haigh's view they represented 'major public relations exercises', but there was more to them than that. According to the historian David Loades, the progresses showed that Elizabeth I had a 'genuine rapport with her people, which was demonstrated repeatedly in different circumstances'.

The Court was also the focus of more private rituals. Court **masques** were used to reinforce the Queen's 'Gloriana' image, originally derived from Edmund Spenser's poem *The Faerie Queene*. The cult of the goddess **Astraea** was publicised. Such rituals bound Elizabeth's courtiers more closely to her through ties of loyalty and obedience. Some historians – for example, Frances Yates and Roy Strong – have argued that these images were an essential part of the Elizabethan propaganda. However, the private and sophisticated nature of much of the ritual had little effect on the wider public.

How important was political patronage to Elizabethan government?

Queen Elizabeth lacked a civil service, paid local officials and an army. It was therefore difficult for Elizabethan government to enforce its will. In the circumstances, the Crown was forced to depend on two features to secure its authority: the exploitation of the mystique of monarchy and the capacity of the Crown to reward the governing classes by the distribution of office and wealth. It was this distribution of office and wealth which formed the patronage system (see page 58). No Tudor government could be effective without organising its patronage rationally. The governing classes who benefited from this distribution of patronage were few in number.

The historian W. T. MacCaffrey estimates that no more than about 2,500 men took a serious interest in political matters at any one time during Elizabeth I's reign. MacCaffrey believes that Elizabeth 'kept a firm and economical hand' on patronage. The value of honours was maintained by keeping grants of peerages and knighthoods to a minimum. More frequent were grants of office. These were eagerly sought, not only because they often conferred honour and prestige on the recipient, but also because usually there were assets to be exploited. Fees from offices were almost always inadequate. Therefore, corruption became an essential part of the system as officers sought to exploit their offices for maximum profit. MacCaffrey estimates that at least 1,000 'gentlemen-placemen' held office at any one time during Elizabeth I's reign; in other words, a considerable proportion of the political nation depended on royal patronage for some part of their livelihood.

This system, and the potential for profits and political advancement, led to intense competition for advancement. For much of Elizabeth I's reign such competition was organised through competing **patrons**, with the Queen ensuring that there was more than one route to advancement. The main route for most of her reign was through Lord Burghley, though other potential patrons – such as Robert Dudley, Christopher Hatton and Francis Walsingham – also carried influence. Lord Burghley's importance rested on his political closeness to the Queen. It also depended on his control of offices, such as the Lord Treasurership and mastership of the Court of Wards, which gave him direct control over a large number of appointments. However, he also had a wider role as confidant to a large number of the governing class. He smoothed over family quarrels. He assisted such fallen aristocrats as the Countess of Westmorland. He promoted the interests of colleagues such as the Earl of Huntingdon and Sir Francis Knollys. He secured appointments to bishoprics and other church offices, and appointed members to the regional councils. Much of this work was accomplished through the efforts of Burghley's own patronage secretary, Sir Michael Hickes, who was responsible for processing the many requests for advancement which Burghley received.

Despite his predominance, Lord Burghley did not seek to control patronage completely. In the final years of Elizabeth I's reign, however, the situation changed. This was partly a reflection of the fact that Burghley outlived all of his contemporaries and therefore became predominant in his final years. It also reflected the less subtle approach adopted by his son, Robert, to the distribution of patronage as his political importance rose during the 1590s. Most importantly it reflected, in the view of historian Alan Smith, the response of the ambitious Earl of Essex to being

Patrons: Those who could offer jobs, promotions or favours to other individuals.

Sir Francis Knollys (?1514–1596)

A gentleman-pensioner at the Court of Henry VIII, Knollys came to political prominence under the Protector Somerset. A strong Protestant who was exiled during Mary's reign, Knollys' career benefited from his marriage to Queen Elizabeth's cousin, Catherine Carey. Under Elizabeth he became Vice-Chamberlain of the Household. He spoke regularly in the House of Commons, where he took a strongly anti-Catholic line. He was also a known defender of puritan preachers as well as a critic of Church courts.

Monopoly: See page 115 for definition. In Elizabethan times the Earl of Essex, for example, had the monopoly on the import of sweet wines. In other instances the granting of a monopoly was a way of rewarding merit. For instance, the composers William Byrd and Thomas Tallis had the monopoly for sale of music paper.

1. What was the political importance of the Royal Court during Elizabeth I's reign?

2. How did the system of patronage work during Elizabeth I's reign?

3. Why, and with what political consequences, did the system break down during the 1590s?

denied what he considered to be his rightful place as the predominant dispenser of patronage. In contrast, Christopher Haigh considers that the main responsibility for the situation lay with the Queen herself. She had presided over an ageing administration which had concentrated power in too few hands. In the process government had become 'the tool of a single and unscrupulous faction'. The charismatic Earl of Essex became the natural focus for the discontented and excluded.

By September 1599, however, when the Earl of Essex left his post in Ireland without the Queen's permission and burst unannounced into her bedchamber, any hopes placed in him were doomed. He was stripped of his offices, banished from Court and, in September 1600, he was financially ruined when Elizabeth refused to renew his **monopoly** on the import of sweet wines. In desperation Essex thought about launching a *coup d'état*, the object of which was the removal of his enemies rather than the deposition of the Queen. Unfortunately for the Earl of Essex, his plans were not sufficiently thought through. In any case, his purposes had been rumbled by Robert Cecil. His disastrous rising on 8 February 1601 was prompted by a visit from four privy councillors whom he took hostage. Then the Earl of Essex tried to raise the City of London in his cause. The attempt was doomed to failure and within 12 hours Essex and his supporters were forced to surrender. Within two weeks the Earl of Essex was executed.

For much of Elizabeth I's reign the patronage system, however corrupt it might seem by modern standards, nevertheless played its part in helping to ensure reasonably effective government. The collapse of the system in the 1590s heightened discontent among the governing classes, reduced the quality of government and forced the Earl of Essex's rebellion.

Source-based questions: Patronage and corruption in Elizabethan government

SOURCE A

Mr Hickes. Our very hearty commendations remembered. Understanding by the bringer hereof … your readiness and willingness in preferring and furthering such petitions and suits as the last [law] term he had cause for us in our names to prefer to the right honourable our very good lord the Lord High Treasurer of England [Lord Burghley], we have therefore thought it our part not only to yield unto you our hearty thanks for the same, but also earnestly to desire continuance of that your great courtesy and friendship, for which you shall be assured both to find us thankful and also ready to the uttermost of our powers to do any pleasure to you or any your friends as opportunity anyway may serve … .

Letter from the Mayor and Burgesses of Hull to Sir Michael Hickes, private secretary to Lord Burghley, 28 April 1590.

SOURCE B

Right honourable,

Your Lordship having always been an especial patron to the see [bishop's office] of Durham, wherein it has now pleased God and Her Majesty to place me, though unworthy, and myself reaping the fruit of your Lordship's extraordinary furtherance in obtaining the same, and seeking by all good means, but contrary to my expectation, not finding any office or other particular presently void, either fit for me to offer your Lordship or sue for your Lordship to receive at my hand, I have presumed in lieu thereof to present your good Lordship with a hundred pounds in gold, which this bringer will deliver to you.

Letter from Dr Toby Matthew, Dean of Durham, to Lord Burghley, thanking him for his promotion to the bishopric of Durham, April 1595.

Source-based questions: Patronage and corruption in Elizabethan government

SOURCE C

Viewed as a system of political patronage, Elizabethan government shows certain defects. It lacked adequate safeguards against a free-for-all scramble for spoils. In some measure Burghley's ceaseless supervision staved off the worst abuses, but this was a protection which waned with the ageing statesman's health and strength. The nature of the prizes encouraged a reckless competition … They were, first of all too small, … and the incumbent was driven to increase his income by any means open to him … Second, the terms of appointment were in many cases ill-defined … and this encouraged the office-holder to exploit his opportunities, often to the detriment of both Crown and subject. Third, the private exploitation of political advantage created a vast 'black market' in which political influence and favour were increasingly bought and sold. Like most black markets it raised prices; the heavy cost of political success made each participant more ruthless in the exploitation of whatever advantage he possessed. … Lastly, the poverty of the Crown drove it to make unwise concessions to suitors for favour or place. Grants of monopoly … were tempting to the Crown because they offered an increase in income for no outlay. But grants of this speculative type … [resulted in] angry resentment on the part of subjects …

Yet in judging the regime as a whole, high praise must be given for the transformation of English political habits which was accomplished during these years. By the end of the reign Englishmen were turning away from their bad old habits of conspiracy and treason … Under … Burghley and his royal mistress they had learned the peaceful, if sometimes corrupt, habits of a new political order.

From 'Place and Patronage in Elizabethan Politics' by W. T. MacCaffrey in Elizabethan Government and Society: Essays presented to Sir John Neale, *edited by S. T. Bindoff, J. Hurstfield and C. H. Williams, 1961.*

SOURCE D

[Essex] desperately turned his mind to a coup in the autumn of 1600. When Elizabeth refused to renew his patent of sweet wines in September, his credit structure collapsed. She had effectively condemned him to a life of poverty, nor would she answer his appeal for an audience … Creditors were pressing for payment and starting to arrest his servants who had stood surety for him. Yet Essex's motivation went beyond this. A faction leader who was denied access to the monarch was in an untenable position: the earl saw himself as compelled to act because his court opponents had exploited their 'corrupt' monopoly of power.

From Tudor England *by John Guy, 1988.*

---

1. Study Source C.

With reference to Source C and the information contained in this chapter, explain the meaning of the two terms highlighted in the context of the political system as it operated during the reign of Elizabeth I.

a) 'a system of political patronage'

b) 'grants of monopoly'.

2. Study Sources A and B.

What is revealed in Sources A and B about the nature and effectiveness of Lord Burghley's role as a political patron?

3. Study Sources C and D.

To what extent does Source D's comments about the Earl of Essex contradict the claim made in Source C that 'by the end of the reign Englishmen were turning away from their bad old habits of conspiracy and treason'.

4. Study all four sources and use information contained in this chapter.

To what extent might it be argued that the Elizabethan system of government was both corrupt and inefficient?

9.3 Was the Privy Council an effective instrument of government?

The Privy Council had emerged during Henry VIII's reign as the 'select ruling board' of the realm. It had several functions. It advised the monarch on policy, and carried out decisions. It had a broad responsibility for administration and public expenditure. It coordinated the work of agencies of government. Finally, it exercised some judicial functions. Under the terms of his will, Henry VIII appointed 16 privy councillors. This number had grown under Mary I. One of Elizabeth's first actions was to limit the size of the Privy Council to 19 members. In the process she removed many who had been owed their position on account of their household service to Mary.

In political terms Elizabeth had largely recreated the Privy Council which had existed under the Duke of Northumberland. She had rehabilitated those, like William Cecil, who had been out of favour under Mary. In cases such as Robert Dudley, she appointed the sons of those who had served in the previous 'Protestant' administration. Relatively few great nobles served on Elizabeth I's Privy Councils and she only ever appointed one clergyman, Archbishop Whitgift.

The Council was a professional and largely cooperative body which was small enough to deal with business efficiently. In the words of Christopher Haigh, it was 'dangerously weak and narrow in its membership'. Regional magnates and the old nobility were largely ignored. This might have contributed to the outbreak of rebellion in 1569. Few councillors – of whom Sir Christopher Hatton was one – exercised real influence unless they were committed Protestants.

The main functions of the Council were to discuss matters of state and to present advice to the Queen. It is not always easy to reconstruct these functions. The bulk of remaining evidence comprises formal decisions, often relating to fairly trivial matters. As a result, there are few indications of the political debates which were conducted within the Council. The main areas of disagreement within the Privy Council tended to concern foreign policy. Disputes occurred between the Earl of Leicester and Francis Walsingham, on one hand, and between Leicester and Lord Burghley, on the other. The Earl of Leicester wanted a foreign policy to support Protestant interests abroad; Lord Burghley, although a committed Protestant, placed English national interests first.

Reconstructing the Council's administrative functions is more straightforward. The Council instructed a whole range of institutions and individuals, such as lords lieutenant, justices of the peace, sheriffs, subsidy commissioners and borough councils. Often, such instructions concerned the enforcement of law and order, including laws against riot, vagrancy and illegal alehouses. The Council also attempted to enforce regulations regarding wages and prices. It could also enforce the spending of public money. However, among its most important administrative tasks were the continued enforcement of the 1559 religious settlement and overseeing arrangements for national defence.

Towards the end of Elizabeth I's reign the Privy Council was often meeting six times a week. By the 1590s the Privy Council had become a more organised body than it had been 50 years earlier, even though its functions had not changed. However, two important questions need to be asked about the Privy Council during the reign of Elizabeth I:

● How effectively did it fulfil its functions?

● How important was the Privy Council in deciding government policy?

How important was the Privy Council in deciding government policy?

Regarding the Council's effectiveness, John Guy, in particular, takes an optimistic view. Tudor governments, of which the Privy Council was the most important part, 'got things done'. Regarding the latter question, it was sometimes possible for the Council to persuade the Queen to take a policy decision against her better judgement, but only at some risk. For example, at the beginning of the reign, by threatening to resign William Cecil was able to force the Queen to follow the advice of most of the Council by intervening in Scotland. However, there were also instances when the Queen chose to ignore the advice of the Council. This happened in 1562 and 1566 when the Council urged marriage on the Queen. Moreover, it took ten months following the assassination of William the Silent on 10 July 1584 for the majority of the Council to persuade the Queen that England should intervene directly in the Netherlands on the side of the Dutch rebels. The Privy Council, in the words of historian Penry Williams, 'could and did reach conclusions upon policy, but the final decision rested with the Queen, who seldom attended meetings and might easily ignore their conclusions'.

On the other hand, on one notable occasion the Council was able to act collectively in a way which it knew was against Elizabeth's wishes. It sent the warrant for the execution of Mary, Queen of Scots without telling the Queen until they had confirmation that the execution had taken place. Elizabeth was furious, declined to see Lord Burghley for a month, refused normal relations with the Council for four months and had Secretary of State William Davison arrested. There was to be no repetition of such behaviour.

1. How important was the Privy Council in deciding government policy?

2. How effective was the Privy Council in fulfilling its functions?

9.4 How important was Parliament to the functioning of Elizabethan government?
A CASE STUDY IN HISTORICAL INTERPRETATION

For a long time there were two competing interpretations of the nature and significance of Elizabethan Parliaments. On the one hand, it was assumed that Parliament was a subordinate body to an autocratic state (i.e. control was in the hands of a single person). On the other hand, it was assumed that Parliament had evolved from being an under-developed institution in the later medieval period to maturity under Elizabeth I. Such views are particularly associated with A. F. Pollard and his distinguished student, Sir John Neale. This historical interpretation suggests that an important theme in English history was the rise in political importance of Parliament, dating from the later Middle Ages, and the decline in the power of the monarch. In accepting this Neale also followed the argument put forward in 1924 by the American historian Wallace Notestein that parliament's political victory over the monarch can be traced to the 1590s, when the House of Commons won the political initiative at the expense of a tired and increasingly incompetent government. John Neale believed that Elizabeth I's reign helped to establish England as one of Europe's most important states. Christopher Haigh describes Neale as putting forward a 'romantic and nationalist' view of Elizabeth I's reign.

Neale argued that there was a new desire among the gentry to become members of the House of Commons. Members of Parliament were becoming better educated and were increasingly able and willing to challenge the control exercised on Parliament through privy councillors and the Speaker. In addition, many such members were Puritans who were using Parliament as a way to bring about radical change to the Church of England.

Neale's views reflected the 'Whig Interpretation of History'. It placed parliamentary developments in Elizabeth I's reign in a historical framework which emphasised the importance to English history of the emergence of the House of Commons as the dominant political and constitutional force in English history. Neale was writing at a time (the 1950s) when not only did the House of Commons enjoy more prestige than it does now but Britain was still perceived in some quarters as a world power. It was not surprising that his views should have come under attack with the decline in the political importance of the House of Commons and Britain's decline as a major power.

The most serious attack on Neale came from Geoffrey Elton. Writing in 1984, Elton argued that Neale had both over-estimated the importance of the House of Commons and under-estimated the importance of the House of Lords. In making this last point, Elton was heavily influenced by the work of the American historian Norman Jones, in particular his *Faith by Statute* (published in 1982). This emphasised the degree of Catholic opposition to the 1559 religious settlement in the House of Lords. Furthermore, Geoffrey Elton challenged Neale's claims about the greater assertiveness and anti-government attitudes of the House of Commons and its 'puritan' members. One such member, Thomas Norton, was identified by M. A. R. Graves as being in reality a client and business organiser for Lord Burghley rather than an opponent of the Crown, as Neale had claimed. The 40-strong 'Puritan Choir', which Neale had identified as being important in expressing anti-government attitudes, never existed. Elton claims that 'the members of that "choir" formed no party and few of them were Puritans'. However, more recently D. M. Dean has claimed that the Puritans were 'an extremely active and well-organised lobby', though one which did not adopt an anti-government position.

Given the nature of such arguments and counter-arguments, it is important to establish what can be accepted with confidence about parliaments in the Elizabethan era. The diagram (see page 227) provides a pictorial representation of the points of contact in the English government under Elizabeth I. Study it closely before reading on.

1. In what ways was Parliament important to the functioning of Elizabethan government?

2. Why have historians differed in their interpretation of the use and function of Parliament in Elizabeth I's reign?

Parliament, therefore, served many uses and functions. It is important, however, to recognise that the most eminent of recent Tudor historians, Geoffrey Elton, argues that politically it was 'only a secondary instrument to be used or ignored by agencies whose real power base and arena of activity lay elsewhere – at Court or in Council'. On the other hand, another 'revisionist' historian, M. A. R. Graves, has put forward the view that Parliament was an 'important but irregular part of Elizabethan government'. The relationship between Crown and Parliament was based on cooperation. Most parliamentary business took place without fuss. At other times, 'Queen, Council, Lord and Commons managed to work through political crises together'.

Government of Elizabethan England

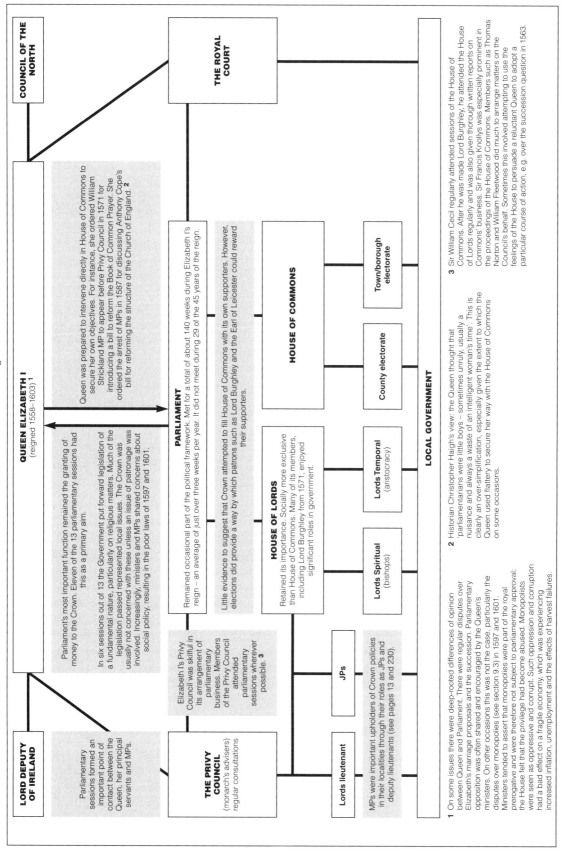

LORD DEPUTY OF IRELAND

Parliamentary sessions formed an important point of contact between the Queen, her principal servants and MPs.

COUNCIL OF THE NORTH

QUEEN ELIZABETH I (reigned 1558–1603) [1]

Queen was prepared to intervene directly in House of Commons to secure her own objectives. For instance, she ordered William Strickland MP to appear before Privy Council in 1571 for introducing a bill to reform the Book of Common Prayer. She ordered the arrest of MPs in 1587 for discussing Anthony Cope's bill for reforming the structure of the Church of England. [2]

THE ROYAL COURT

Parliament's most important function remained the granting of money to the Crown. Eleven of the 13 parliamentary sessions had this as a primary aim.

In six sessions out of 13 the Government put forward legislation of a fundamental nature, particularly on religious matters. Much of the legislation passed represented local issues. The Crown was usually not concerned with these unless an issue of patronage was involved. Increasingly, ministers and MPs shared concerns about social policy, resulting in the poor laws of 1597 and 1601.

PARLIAMENT

Remained occasional part of the political framework. Met for a total of about 140 weeks during Elizabeth I's reign – an average of just over three weeks per year. It did not meet during 29 of the 45 years of the reign.

Little evidence to suggest that Crown attempted to fill House of Commons with its own supporters. However, elections did provide a way by which patrons such as Lord Burghley and the Earl of Leicester could reward their supporters.

HOUSE OF LORDS

Retained its importance. Socially more exclusive than House of Commons. Many of its members, including Lord Burghley from 1571, enjoyed significant roles in government.

HOUSE OF COMMONS

Lords Spiritual (bishops)

Lords Temporal (aristocracy)

County electorate

Town/borough electorate

LOCAL GOVERNMENT

THE PRIVY COUNCIL (monarch's advisers) regular consultations

Elizabeth I's Privy Council was skilful in its arrangement of parliamentary business. Members of the Privy Council attended parliamentary sessions wherever possible. [3]

Lords lieutenant

JPs

MPs were important upholders of Crown policies in their localities through their roles as JPs and deputy lieutenants (see pages 13 and 230).

1 On some issues there were deep-rooted differences of opinion between Queen and Parliament. There were regular disputes over Elizabeth's marriage proposals and the succession. Parliamentary opposition was often shared and encouraged by the Queen's ministers. On other occasions this was not the case, particularly the disputes over monopolies (see section 9.3) in 1597 and 1601. Ministers tended to assert that monopolies were part of the royal prerogative and were therefore not subject to parliamentary approval; the House felt that the privilege had become abused. Monopolists were seen as oppressive and corrupt. Such oppression and corruption had a bad effect on a fragile economy, which was experiencing increased inflation, unemployment and the effects of harvest failures.

2 Historian Christopher Haigh's view: the Queen thought that 'parliamentarians were little boys – sometimes unruly, usually a nuisance and always a waste of an intelligent woman's time'. This is clearly an over-simplification, especially given the extent to which the Queen used flattery to secure her way with the House of Commons on some occasions.

3 Sir William Cecil regularly attended sessions of the House of Commons. After he was made Lord Burghley, he attended the House of Lords regularly and was also given thorough written reports on Commons' business. Sir Francis Knollys was especially prominent in the proceedings of the House of Commons. Members such as Thomas Norton and William Fleetwood did much to arrange matters on the Council's behalf. Sometimes this involved attempting to use the feelings of the House to persuade a reluctant Queen to adopt a particular course of action, e.g. over the succession question in 1563.

9.5 What were the main features of Elizabethan local government?

In a society where communications were as difficult to maintain as they were in Elizabethan England, it was essential for central government to maintain a range of networks by which the localities could be governed.

Regional government

A series of institutions was maintained to oversee government in key regions. This was particularly important at the English frontier with Scotland. Not only was Scotland a foreign power, the border area was also notorious as a centre of rustling (cattle stealing) and other forms of banditry. To minimise the scale of the problems which this might involve, the Crown had created three marches – border areas each under the control of a warden. By the time of Elizabeth I's reign, the government had abandoned the idea of giving such posts to the local nobility. There was too much danger of their becoming over-mighty subjects (see page 43 for definition). Instead, the wardens were either reliable nobles with estates in other parts of the country or loyal gentry from the localities whose advancement depended on Crown favour. A similar system applied on the Welsh border. There, however, the situation was different. Since 1536 an English-style shire administration had been imposed upon Wales which had, in effect, been incorporated into the English state.

In the case of both Wales and the North, a further tier of regional government was provided by the Councils. The Council in the Marches of Wales had some jurisdiction over Shropshire, Worcestershire, Herefordshire, Gloucestershire and, until 1569, Cheshire. However, its main function was as a regional law court. The Council of the North had a mixed history during the first few years of Elizabeth I's reign. It established considerable prestige and influence under the presidency of the Earl of Huntingdon (1572–96), although even then the extent of its control outside Yorkshire remained rather sketchy.

Lords lieutenant

Deputy lieutenants: Normally drawn from amongst the leading gentry of a county, deputy lieutenants were appointed by lords lieutenant to assist them in their duties.

It was the Duke of Northumberland who had originally established the idea that a lord lieutenant should be appointed in each county 'for the levying of men and to fight against the King's enemies'. After his fall from power, lords lieutenant were appointed only occasionally. From 1585, in the light of worsening relations with Spain, lords lieutenant were appointed in every shire. They were assisted in their work by **deputy lieutenants** and by muster captains and muster masters who offered professional assistance in the training of local militias. The other duties of the lord lieutenant included raising money, keeping watch over Roman Catholic **recusants** and generally supervising county affairs.

Recusants: A term which was used from around 1570 onwards to describe those English Catholics who refused to attend Church of England church services. When convicted they could receive heavy fines and the loss of property. 'Recusant' comes from the Latin word for 'refuse'.

Assize judges

Assize Courts: These were courts which tried the most serious cases at a local level. The Assize judges visited each county twice a year to hear the cases.

England was divided into six circuits, each of which was visited twice a year by professional judges who sat in the county towns to hear both civil and more serious criminal cases. The **Assize Courts** helped the central government maintain contact with the regions. Liaison between judges and justices of the peace (JPs) could be developed through the Assizes.

England in the 16th century

Sheriffs

The sheriff held the oldest royal office in each county. Though the role was less significant than it had been during the Middle Ages, the sheriff still had some important functions. For example, he presided over county elections, collected certain revenues and presided over executions. The responsibility which the sheriff traditionally exercised in respect of the maintenance of law and order was passing to the justices of the peace.

Justices of the peace (magistrates)

By Elizabeth I's reign justices of the peace had become the central figures in local government. They had a dual role: they maintained law and order at a local level; and had also become the linchpins of administration at county level. Their wide-ranging duties included:

- presiding over the Quarter Sessions (courts of law dealing with offences committed within the county and meeting four times in the year);

- examining suspects;

- arresting rioters;

- dealing with the increasing number of administrative matters which were becoming their responsibility under new legislation;

- and often being the recipients of orders and requests issued by the Privy Council.

Membership of the magistrates' bench became, during Elizabeth I's reign, one of the key measures by which the social position of a gentleman could be assessed. This represented a considerable advantage to the Crown. It meant that there was never a shortage of volunteers for what was often a difficult task, which was always unpaid. Certainly the task of JPs was considerably more complicated by the end of the 16th century. They were given administrative responsibilities under no fewer than 176 new Acts of Parliament. Most importantly, the Poor Laws recognised their very important position within local administration.

Church Courts

Operating under the authority of the bishop, these courts exercised a range of functions which are nowadays the responsibility of the secular (not concerned with religion or the Church) courts. Their areas of authority included matrimonial disputes, disputes over wills and sexual misconduct. These cases brought them frequently into contact with local populations and increased the extent to which the Church could function as an agent of social control.

Local officials

Local government in the Elizabethan era could not function effectively without the cooperation of local officials. Each division of a county had a high constable who acted as a link between the county administration and the parishes. Parish constables, elected annually by ratepayers, were the link between their village community and superior officials. They were

1. Draw a diagram showing how Elizabethan local government was organised.

2. Which do you consider was the most important office in Elizabethan local government, and why?

responsible for such tasks as arresting vagrants (tramps or beggars), supervising alehouses, repairing the highway and maintaining the village stock of weapons and armour.

Corporate boroughs

Administrative systems in the towns differed from those which existed in the counties. Corporate boroughs were self-governing towns where control was vested in the aldermen and councillors. They could establish their own by-laws, administer the town's corporate property, and carry out the instructions of central government. The mayor and senior aldermen, in addition, often sat as justices of the peace within the confines of the town.

9.6 How successful was Elizabethan government?

In addition to assessing the overall quality of Elizabethan government, it is also necessary to examine the claim that Elizabethan government became less effective during the last third of the reign. The most critical of Elizabeth I's recent historians, Christopher Haigh, has described the Queen in the 1590s as 'politically bankrupt'.

For much of her reign Elizabeth I had clearly been successful, when judged by the standards of her time. Before 1585 she largely avoided wars. As a result, the revenue demands which her administration imposed were relatively modest – until the second half of the 1580s. There were no serious hints about problems with taxation, which was not used, even as an excuse, by the rebels of 1569.

Queen Elizabeth I was fortunate also in the quality of her ministers, such as Lord Burghley, Francis Walsingham and Walter Mildmay. (Sir Christopher Hatton was arguably less effective.) Lord Burghley, in particular, had a huge capacity for work, overseeing many aspects of government and handling royal patronage with skill. Mildmay, as the long-serving Chancellor of the Exchequer, was Burghley's chief assistant in financial matters. He handled his responsibilities with great skill and discretion. Walsingham, as Secretary of State, did have his differences with Lord Burghley over foreign policy. Along with the Earl of Leicester, he usually favoured a more openly 'Protestant' (and expensive) foreign policy. Nevertheless, he worked effectively with Lord Burghley for much of his time in office.

Relations with Parliament were usually good. However, there were disputes over marriage and the succession – when parliamentary opinion was often closer to that of the Privy Council than the Privy Council was to the Queen. These good relations were reinforced by the skill of parliamentary managers such as Mildmay, Norton and Fleetwood. It is also important to note that most MPs knew that there were certain boundaries which they could not cross in expressing their opinions. The nature of that boundary was expressed by Mildmay in 1576 when he commented:

Licentious speech: In this context Mildmay was referring to those who were going too far in criticising the Queen.

'we must not forget to put a difference between liberty of speech and **licentious speech**, for by the one men deliver their opinions freely but with this caution, that all be spoken pertinently, modestly, reverently and discreetly. The other, contrariwise, uttereth all impertinently, rashly, arrogantly and irreverently, without respect of person, time or place.'

As Christopher Haigh has pointed out, such limitations on the manner of debate caused far less trouble than the Queen's use of the prerogative (see page 61) to prevent debate on issues which she considered too sensitive, such as the Church of England.

It is more difficult to estimate the effectiveness of local government. In contrast to Spain, for example, the Crown had no properly paid officials who could be relied upon to run the localities. Instead, there was a reliance on unpaid volunteers. This worked well up to a point. The office of justice of the peace gave its holder considerable local prestige. This meant that JPs usually worked hard to follow orders from the Privy Council or to enforce laws passed by Parliament. There is little evidence to suggest that JPs abused their position when conducting their office. They were often selective in the approach to their duties. In the words of Penry Williams, 'the main burden of county government was carried out by a few devoted and conscientious men: model officials or tiresome busybodies depending on one's point of view'. Nevertheless, there is evidence of selectivity of approach. In Lancashire, for example, there is little to suggest that the JPs ever did much to enforce legislation against Catholics. In largely Catholic Lancashire that might not have been too much of a shock. Yet a similar situation happened in Suffolk, which was much more strongly Protestant and where Catholic influence remained among the JPs until the late 1580s. At the more humble level of constable, there was much hard work and a genuine attempt to cope with the demands of the office.

There is evidence to suggest that, certainly in the first 30 years of the reign, government was conducted with effectiveness at both national and local level. This was certainly not the case during the latter stages of the reign when a combination of factors placed immense strain on the Elizabethan system of government. The patronage system broke down in the hands of Robert Cecil. The ageing Queen was becoming, in the words of Alan Smith, 'irascible [angry and bad-tempered] and embittered'. Many of her most trusted ministers – Lord Burghley, Thomas Hatton and Sir Francis Knollys – died during the 1590s. The long-lasting war with Spain created immense financial pressures. At a local level, officials found it increasingly difficult to cope with the financial and administrative demands which government was making. To make matters worse, these pressures coincided during the second half of the 1590s with a massive series of social strains. A series of harvest failures created food shortages which, in turn, increased the pressures of inflation. Moreover, many parts of the country were affected in 1597 with a severe outbreak of plague.

At the heart of many of these administrative problems lay the government's conservatism. There was no willingness, either in Elizabeth or among her ministers, to change methods of government in the light of changing political and financial circumstances. Historians whose views on the reign are as contrasting as those of Alan Smith and Christopher Haigh share this view of the disastrous final years. To the former, Elizabethan government in the 1590s 'was bankrupt of new ideas in a changing world'; to the latter 'her reign had been 30 years of illusion, followed by 15 years of disillusion'. Admittedly, Elizabethan England had largely avoided the conflicts which had afflicted neighbouring France. Moreover, the Spanish threat had been safely overcome. By 1603, however, few people were prepared to give the Queen much credit for these successes. She had reigned too long, and the succession of King James was widely welcomed.

1. What evidence would you put forward (a) to support and (b) to disprove the claim that Elizabethan government up to 1588 was successful?

2. 'Thirty years of illusion, followed by 15 years of disillusion.' How far does the evidence which you have read in this chapter support this claim?

10 Religion in Elizabethan England

10.1 What were Elizabeth I's personal religious beliefs?
10.2 Historical interpretation: The Elizabethan Church Settlement
10.3 How far were Catholics a threat to Elizabeth I?
10.4 How successful was Elizabeth in dealing with the Catholic threat?
10.5 Why did Puritanism develop in Elizabethan England?
10.6 What impact did Puritanism have on the Elizabethan Church?
10.7 How strong was the Church of England in 1603?

Key Issues

- How radical was the Elizabethan Church Settlement of 1559 to 1563?

- How far were Catholics a threat to Elizabeth I?

- What impact did Puritanism have on Elizabethan England?

Framework of Events

Papal Bull: Decree issued by the Pope.

1558	November: Elizabeth I becomes Queen, at the age of 25
1559	15 January: Elizabeth displays her displeasure at the elevation of the host at communion in the Royal Chapel
	March–April: Conference between Catholic and Protestant theologians at Westminster
	May: Acts of Supremacy and Uniformity become law
	July: Royal Injunctions on religious beliefs
	Matthew Parker becomes Archbishop of Canterbury
1563	Convocation approves the Thirty Nine Articles (of faith)
1566	Vestiarian Controversy over the wearing of vestments by Elizabethan clergy
1568	William Allen founds the Catholic college at Douai (Netherlands) to train priests for the mission to England
	Mary Stuart arrives in England from Scotland
1569	Rebellion of the Northern Earls begins
1570	Rebellion ends in failure. **Papal Bull** of Excommunication against Elizabeth I
	Thomas Cartwright delivers spring lectures at the University of Cambridge on the organisation of the Church
1571	Ridolfi Plot by Catholics
1572	Duke of Norfolk executed for treason. Thomas Cartwright, John Field and others begin a campaign to reform the Elizabethan Church along Genevan lines
1574	Seminary priests begin arriving in England from Douai
1575	17 May: Matthew Parker dies; replaced as Archbishop of Canterbury by Edmund Grindal
1576	December: Queen orders Archbishop Grindal to suppress prophesying
1577	May: Grindal suspended as Archbishop and placed under house arrest
	John Aylmer, Bishop of London, placed at head of Ecclesiastical Commission to suppress prophesying
	November: execution of Cuthbert Mayne, seminary priest
1579	English College founded in Rome under the supervision of the Jesuits

1580	Edmund Campion and Robert Parsons (Jesuits) arrive in England
1581	Parliament passes legislation against Catholics, seminary priests and Jesuits
1583	Parsons and Campion implicated in Throckmorton [Guise] Plot against Elizabeth. Grindal dies and is replaced as Archbishop of Canterbury by John Whitgift
	Beginning of concerted attack on Presbyterianism
1584	Bill and Book proposals by Presbyterians in Parliament
1585	Act against Jesuits and Seminary Priests
1586	Babington Plot against Elizabeth which implicates Mary Stuart
1587	Mary Stuart is executed
	Anthony Cope MP re-introduces Bill and Book proposal in Parliament
1588	Spanish Armada
	John Field and Earl of Leicester die
	Martin Marprelate Tracts published
1589	More Martin Marprelate Tracts
1590	Thomas Cartwright brought before Court of High Commission
1591	Royal Proclamation against Jesuits
	Hacket Affair
1593	Act against Seditious Sectaries
	Execution of Separatists: Barrow, Greenwood and Penry
1594	William Allen dies
1598	Height of Archpriest Controversy within English Catholicism
1602	Royal Proclamation against Jesuits
1603	Thirteen Seminary priests accept Elizabeth as head of state.

Overview

WHEN Elizabeth I became Queen in 1558 England had gone through over 25 years of religious change. The 'National Catholicism' of her father, Henry VIII, was followed by more radical religious reform under her half-brother, Edward VI. In the five years before the start of her reign her half-sister, Mary I, had attempted to re-establish England as a Catholic country.

When Elizabeth I ascended the throne it seemed clear to contemporaries that further religious change was inevitable. Elizabeth was regarded as illegitimate by Catholic Europe. Also, she had been educated by Protestants such as Roger Ascham. However, any change in England's religious position was affected by a number of factors.

Firstly, England was still an ally of Catholic Spain in its war with France. When Elizabeth became queen England had lost Calais – its last possession on the continent. The monarch also feared invasion from France's ally, Scotland. Any radical change in the religion of the country could have had a major impact on England's position in foreign affairs. Throughout the early years of Elizabeth I's reign the issue of religion was linked closely to foreign affairs. This was most apparent in the issue of the succession to the throne. The strongest claimant, on the death of Elizabeth, was Mary Stuart (Mary, Queen of Scots). Until her execution in 1587 Mary Stuart created major political and religious problems for Elizabeth I.

Secondly, although Elizabeth was unlikely to keep England a Catholic country it was unclear what type of Protestantism she would adopt. In mid-16th century Europe Protestantism took a variety of forms. In the German part of the Holy Roman Empire and in Scandinavia Lutheranism was dominant (see insert on page 236). However, there were other forms of Protestantism. Originating in

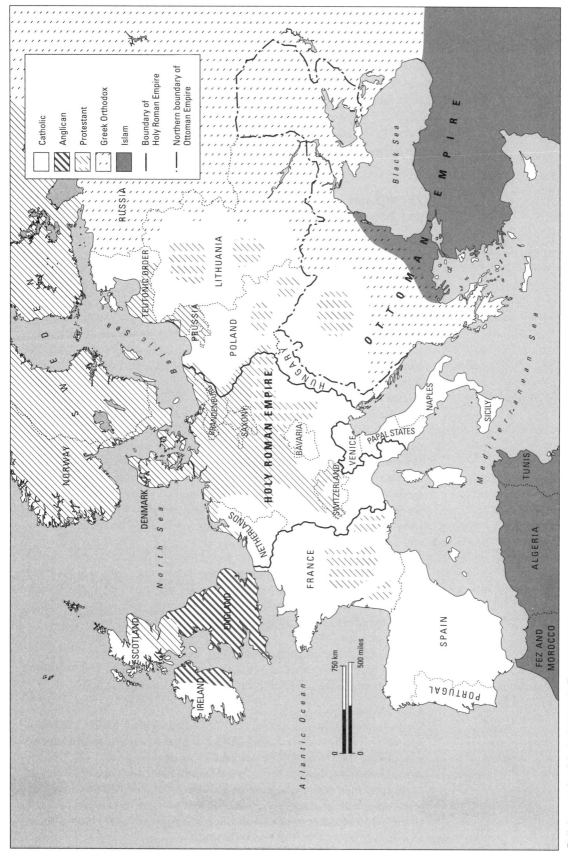

Religious and political divisions in Europe, 1559

Switzerland was Zwinglianism (see insert). Also, centred on Switzerland, was Calvinism (known as Presbyterianism in Scotland) which adopted different beliefs and church organisation. When the Marian exiles returned from the continent they did not all have the same religious beliefs.

Religion and religious affairs were a dominant theme in Elizabethan England. Religious issues have involved controversy and debate between historians. Did the religious settlements of 1559 to 1563 reflect Elizabeth I's own religious views? Why did Catholicism survive in Elizabethan England? How extensive was support for puritan ideas during the reign?

The differences between Catholicism, Lutheranism, Calvinism and Zwinglianism

Catholicism

In structure, the Catholic Church is a hierarchy with the Pope as Head of the Church. He ruled an area of central Italy known as the Papal States. The Pope is elected by the College of Cardinals for life. Once elected, the Pope has the power to appoint Cardinals, Archbishops and Bishops throughout the Catholic Church. The Church is divided into provinces, under the control of an archbishop. Within a province, a diocese is administered by a bishop. The lowest level of administration is a parish, administered by a priest. In addition to the 'secular' clergy (bishops, priests etc.) are 'regular' clergy. These are monks and nuns who live in monasteries and convents respectively. They performed a variety of tasks such as helping the poor and education.

Catholics believe that, in authority, the Pope is a direct descendant of St Peter. The most important ceremony is Mass, which was said in Latin. All Catholics were expected to go to Mass on Sundays and some Holy Days. The central feature of Mass is communion. Catholics believe in the doctrine of transubstantiation. This means that during communion the bread and wine, although never changing appearance, becomes the body and blood of Jesus Christ.

Catholics also believe in saints. In addition to Sunday worship, there are also Holy Days which commemorate the lives of saints (e.g. St Peter and St Paul) or important events such as Christmas and Good Friday. Catholic churches usually have statues of saints and Jesus. The altar, where the priest celebrates Mass, is adorned with candles and a cross (see picture on page 244).

Catholics believed there were seven sacraments – Baptism, Penance, Communion, Confirmation, Marriage or Holy Orders and Extreme Unction (which was given if it was felt someone was about to die).

Lutheranism

This Christian religion began in the Holy Roman Empire in the 1520s and spread to Scandinavia. In organisation, Lutheran Churches were Erastian. This meant the Head of State was also Head of the Church. The Church was also episcopalian – that is, it was administered by bishops who, in turn, appointed ministers (parsons). In religious belief, Lutherans placed great emphasis on the study of the Bible. Therefore, Lutherans believed there were two sacraments – Baptism and Communion – because these were mentioned in the New Testament. Lutheran Church services contained Bible reading and communion. However, Lutherans believed in consubstantiation. This doctrine stated that the bread and wine at communion did not become the body and blood of Jesus Christ. Instead there was a 'spiritual' presence of Christ. Lutherans also believed clergymen should wear simple vestments (clerical clothes).

Zwinglianism
Named after Huldrych Zwingli (1484–1531), the Swiss Protestant reformer. Zwingli believed that only Jesus Christ could be head of the Christian Church. Like Lutheranism, they placed great emphasis on the Bible as the source for religious belief. On the issue of communion, Zwinglians believed the service was merely a memorial service to remember the Last Supper. They also rejected other Catholic beliefs, such as masses for the dead and the use of religious statues and paintings in churches.

Calvinism
Named after John Calvin (1509–64), the French Protestant reformer. Although Calvin was French-born, the centre of Calvinism was Geneva in Switzerland. Calvinists believed in a church structure which was very different to Catholicism and Lutheranism. In Calvinism there were no bishops. Instead the church was made up of independent groups (congregations) led by elders. The Elders chose the clergyman, known as a minister.

Calvinists accepted Lutheran ideas such as the belief that you could get to Heaven by faith (belief in God) alone. However, they also believed in predestination. This stated that God had already chosen those who would get to Heaven. This denied the idea of free will to be good or commit sin, which Catholics believed. On the issue of communion, Calvinists' belief was somewhere between the Lutheran and Zwinglian view. In Scotland and England Calvinists were known as Presbyterians.

Like Lutherans and Zwinglians, they believed clergymen should wear simple vestments (clerical clothes).

10.1 What were Elizabeth I's personal religious beliefs?

On 5 February 1550 the Protestant Bishop John Hooper wrote to the Swiss Protestant reformer Bullinger concerning the religious beliefs of the future Elizabeth I: 'She not only knows what the true religion is, but has acquired such proficiency in Greek and Latin that she is able to defend it.' This view of the personal religious beliefs of Elizabeth I has not always been accepted by historians. Alan Pollard, in his *History of England* (published in 1919), claimed that Queen Elizabeth I was 'indifferent to religion'. In the 1950s, Sir John Neale took the view that Elizabeth planned to return England to the religion of her father's day, a form of National Catholicism.

However, there is sufficient evidence to suggest that Elizabeth I was both religious and interested in Protestantism. The political faction which surrounded her mother during the early 1530s had Lutheran sympathies. Also,

These two illustrations of Queen Elizabeth I were made during her reign. The first (left) shows Elizabeth on her accession to the throne. The contemporary engraving (right) was made later in her reign.

1. What image of Elizabeth I are these pictures trying to portray? Give reasons to support your answer.

2. How useful to a historian are these portrayals of Elizabeth I?

her education by Roger Ascham and in the households of Sir Anthony Denny and Queen Catherine Parr was grounded in the 'new religion'.

It is now accepted that Elizabeth was a sincere and committed Protestant. As Christopher Haigh notes in his biography of Elizabeth I written in 1988: 'There can be little doubt of Elizabeth's personal Protestantism.' But what type of Protestantism did Elizabeth follow? The American historian Winthrop Hudson believes that she did not wish to re-establish the National Catholicism of her father or Lutheranism. In his view, Elizabeth favoured the Zwinglian (see insert on page 237) model of 'pure' religion, which was indicated in the 1559 version of the Book of Common Prayer.

Yet there is evidence to suggest that Elizabeth was a political realist. She was aware that her religious beliefs differed from other rulers, both Catholic and Lutheran. She was also aware of the difficult position England faced in foreign affairs. The idea of a coalition of Catholic forces, under the leadership of Spain and France, against England was a concern throughout her reign.

England in 1558 was a country with a large proportion of its population still Catholic. It was also a country where there were many different types of Protestant ideas and beliefs. Therefore, Elizabeth adopted religious policies which were aimed not to drive Catholics into outright opposition to her regime. Throughout her reign Elizabeth restrained Protestant preaching of a radical type. She did not persecute Catholics unless they offered a direct threat to her rule. She was reluctant to support Protestant rebels abroad.

Was this conservatism in religion merely a tactic to prevent threats to her rule at home and abroad? There is evidence to suggest that these views also reflected Elizabeth's own personal religious beliefs. For instance, throughout her reign she had a deep dislike of clerical marriage. She also insisted on the use of a cross and candlesticks on the altar of the Royal Chapel. According to the historian Patrick Collinson in *Windows in a Woman's Soul: Questions about the Religion of Queen Elizabeth I*: 'It remains possible that the Elizabethan compromise of Protestantism was a concession not only to the conservative prejudices of Elizabeth's subjects but to her own feelings.'

This view is of considerable importance in any historical interpretation of the religious nature of the Elizabethan Settlement of 1559.

The organisation of the Church of England during the reign of Elizabeth I

The Head of the Church

At the top of the Church structure was Queen Elizabeth I. Under the 1559 Act of Supremacy Elizabeth was the Supreme Governor of the Church of England. The Church organisation of Elizabethan England can be regarded as Erastian, that is both political and religious power belonged to the ruler. Some contemporaries believed that the control of the Church by the State was shared between monarch and Parliament. This was based on the belief that the Church Settlement of 1559 was a joint act by Queen and Parliament. Queen Elizabeth I believed that the monarch alone had control. She merely used Parliament to introduce these changes. Throughout her reign Elizabeth I consistently opposed any attempt by Parliament to debate the Church Settlement.

The province

England and Wales were divided into two provinces: Canterbury and York, each under the control of an Archbishop. If you look at the map on page 240 you will see that Canterbury was much larger. Because it covered the southern and central parts of England and Wales it was richer and politically more important. The Archbishop of Canterbury had a residence in London, at Lambeth Palace, across the River Thames from Whitehall and Parliament.

Each province had a convocation, an assembly of clergy who could discuss church matters. With a strong Catholic influence at the beginning of her reign, it is not surprising that Elizabeth used Parliament rather than Convocation to pass the religious settlement.

The English and Welsh dioceses during Elizabeth I's reign

The diocese

There were 27 dioceses in England and Wales. In charge of each diocese was a bishop who was appointed by the Queen. The bishop had several duties, including ordaining parsons (vicars and other members of the clergy without special rank) and consecrating churches. He was also responsible to the Queen for making sure the clergy followed the Act of Uniformity and Royal Injunctions of the Elizabethan Church Settlement.

The bishop's own church was a cathedral which was usually administered by a dean. Deans were also appointed by the Queen.

The parish

This was the smallest unit of Church organisation. During Elizabeth I's reign there were approximately 10,000 parishes in England. In each parish there was meant to be a clergyman – a parson. Other names for the clergy of a parish were vicar or rector. In the early part of Elizabeth's reign there was a shortage of suitably qualified clergy. The parson was responsible for the spiritual welfare of his congregation. In return, he received an income partly from

'Elizabeth's view of religion was based on political considerations.'

'Elizabeth was a committed Protestant.'

Using the information is this section, which view do you regard as the most accurate?

Give reasons to support your answer.

tithes (taxes, usually in the form of goods and produce) and partly from renting out land owned by the parish. To assist the parson were two churchwardens who were appointed by the parson and the parishioners for a term of one year. Their main task was the repair and upkeep of the church.

10.2 *The Elizabethan Church Settlement*
A CASE STUDY IN HISTORICAL INTERPRETATION

The Elizabethan Church Settlement, which formed the foundations of the Church of England, was established in the years 1559 to 1563. It was laid down mainly by the Parliament of 1559 which passed four Acts relating to religion:

● an Act of Supremacy, dealing with church organisation;

● an Act of Uniformity which dealt with religious belief;

● and two acts dealing with church property: the Act of Exchange allowed the Queen to use revenues from dioceses if there was a vacancy for a bishop; the other Act restored to the monarch money derived from the **First Fruits and Tenths** which Elizabeth's elder sister, Mary I, had restored to the Church during her reign (1553–58).

First Fruits and Tenths: A tax paid by clergymen to the monarch. They had to pay all of their first year's income and 10% of every other year's income.

In addition to these Acts, the Settlement also involved Royal Injunctions, introduced in July 1559, which filled in much of the detail of religious practice not covered in the Act of Uniformity. In 1563 Convocation (the Church assembly), rather than Parliament, produced the Thirty Nine Articles. These contained the main statements of belief of the Church of England. Parliament approved the Articles in 1571 with the passage of the Subscription Act.

Since the establishment of the Church Settlement, historians have differed in their interpretation of the motives of Queen Elizabeth and the nature of the religious changes that were made.

Why have historians differed in their interpretations of the Church Settlement?

Contemporaries of Elizabeth I – like John Foxe who published *Acts and Monuments* in 1563 – believed that Elizabeth had pushed through Parliament a Protestant religious settlement against the opposition of Catholics. There is evidence from her first months as queen that she was a committed Protestant, which tends to support this view. At the Christmas Mass of 1558 Queen Elizabeth I made a public display of walking out when Bishop Oglethorpe decided to raise the host (the bread used during the religious service). This action showed her disapproval of the Catholic church service.

On 27 and 28 December 1558 Elizabeth issued proclamations that religious books, such as the Bible, and prayers, such as the Lord's Prayer, should be said in English rather than Latin. Early in the following year she refused to attend the procession of monks participating in the Opening of Parliament. On 1 February 1559 the Privy Council ordered the English ambassador to Pope Paul IV to return to England. Finally, Elizabeth allowed William Bill, Queen's Almoner and known Protestant, to make the first official sermon at St Paul's Cross, outside St Paul's Cathedral in London. When Bishop Christopherson, the Catholic bishop of Chichester, criticised William Bill's sermon on the following Sunday, he in turn was criticised by the Queen and placed under house arrest.

Together with her background and education, these acts strongly suggested that Queen Elizabeth I wished to have a Protestant religious settlement. The so-called compromise or *via media* (middle way) nature of the changes of 1559–63 suggest that the Queen was prevented from achieving her aims by conservative catholic forces in Parliament and by Convocation. However, there was the hope felt by Protestants in England that, at last, they had a monarch who would introduce the 'new religion'. Therefore, the views of Foxe and other historians, such as William Camden, were affected by this belief.

This view of the Settlement was challenged by Sir John Neale in a series of books published in the 1950s. In *Elizabeth I and her Parliaments, 1559–1581* (published in 1953), Neale argued that the Settlement was the result of a conservative Queen forced into a more radical Religious Settlement by a group of radical protestants in the House of Commons – the so-called 'Puritan choir.'

Neale came to this view for several reasons. Firstly, he placed considerable weight on the international situation in 1558–59. When Elizabeth came to the throne in November 1558, England was still at war with France. The government did not possess the revenue to continue fighting. Therefore, Elizabeth had to follow a conservative religious policy in order not to upset Catholics at home or abroad. The Treaty of Cateau-Cambrésis, which ended the war with France, was not signed until 2 April 1559.

Secondly, Neale believed that a significant body of opinion in the House of Commons supported a radical religious settlement. This group was led by Sir Francis Knollys and Sir Anthony Cooke. Sir John Neale noted that approximately one-quarter of the 404 members of the House of Commons acted together to force a reluctant Queen towards Protestantism.

However, Sir John Neale's interpretation has been criticised by several historians. Geoffrey Elton in an essay on Parliament, published in 1984, believes Neale's methods of working out the religious views of MPs to be incorrect. According to Elton:

> With good grounds, leading members of the House [Commons] were identified as Puritans, so that what leading members did became Puritan activities, and when something happened that might be connected with reformist views in religion the notional Puritan group was alleged to be behind it. In fact, members of that 'choir' formed no party and few of them were Puritans.

In addition, Neale's view can be criticised for giving the House of Commons more influence than it in fact possessed in 1559. Because the Commons became a dominant force in early Stuart England, its role in the Church Settlement of 1559 has been overstated. According to M. A. R. Graves, historian of Elizabethan parliaments, the actions Neale thought came from a group of radical Protestant Members of Parliament were actually the work of William Cecil and the Privy Council, following the wishes of the Queen.

The historian who, more than any other, led the criticism of Sir John Neale's view is Norman Jones. In *Faith by Statute: Parliament and the Settlement of Religion in 1559* (published in 1982). Norman Jones argues that Elizabeth I and her advisers established a religious settlement which reflected their own religious views. Opposition to this settlement came from Catholics in the House of Lords, not radical Protestants in the House of Commons.

Jones believed that Elizabeth planned to re-establish Royal Supremacy over the Church and to reintroduce the Book of Common Prayer of 1552. The main opposition to these proposals came from Catholic Bishops in the House of Lords. As an example, on 21 February 1559 a religious Bill was presented to the House of Lords which, if enacted, would have made Elizabeth supreme head of the Church with a Protestant form of religious worship. By the time the Bill had been debated, the Lords had decided that Elizabeth might become supreme head, if she wished, but they would not accept the responsibility of giving the title to her. The Lords also amended radically the proposals for changing religious worship. As Jones noted in his essay 'Elizabeth's First Year' in Christopher Haigh's *The Reign of Elizabeth I* (1984): 'By 23rd March the Queen and Cecil, having badly miscalculated the strength of resistance to religious change in the Lords, found themselves in a difficult position.'

Only after recalling Parliament after Easter and imprisoning some Catholic Bishops did a new Act of Uniformity pass the House of Lords, by three votes. It became law on 8 May 1559. In the vote all the Catholic Bishops in the Lords voted against. Convocation also opposed the changes.

Although the Settlement of Religion passed by Parliament in 1559 contained elements of compromise, it was a compromise close to the Queen's original view. Throughout the rest of her reign, Elizabeth I was unwilling to allow Parliament to discuss the Religious Settlement. This suggests her general satisfaction with what was produced between 1559 and 1563.

What religious changes were made by the Elizabethan Church Settlement?

The Act of Supremacy, May 1559
In *The Royal Supremacy in the Elizabethan Church*, historian Claire Cross states that 'One of the main functions of the First Parliament of Elizabeth was to re-establish formally the Queen's authority over the English Church'. Unlike her father, Elizabeth was not proclaimed 'supreme head'. Instead she became 'supreme governor'. This form of words was aimed to please both Catholics and the more extreme Protestants who disliked the idea of a woman taking on such an important religious position.

The Act also required all the clergy to take an oath recognising the Royal Supremacy over the Church. This gave Elizabeth the opportunity to remove Catholic clergy who refused the oath. Apart from Bishop Kitchen of Llandaff and the Bishop of Sodor and Man, all the Catholic Bishops

---

1. *Explain in what ways historians have differed in their interpretation of the reasons behind the Elizabethan Church Settlement.*

2. *What reasons can you give to explain why John Foxe, John Neale and Norman Jones have provided different historical interpretations of the Church Settlement?*

1. *Using the information contained within the illustrations below, explain how a Catholic Church service differed from the Protestant service towards the end of Edward VI's reign.*

2. *Use the information from this chapter. The Elizabethan Church Settlement introduced a new form of church service. How far did it differ from the two church services shown below?*

1 Wall painting
2 Server
3 Surplice
4 Rood screen
5 Sanctuary lamps
6 Cross with statue of St John (left) and Virgin Mary (right)
7 Missal
8 Reredos
9 Hanging tabernacle
10 Chalice
11 Chasuble
12 Alb
13 Priest
14 Rushes strewn on floor
15 Altar
16 Stained-glass window

Catholic form of worship and vestments during the reign of Mary I (1553–58)

1 'Eagle' lectern for Bible
2 Surplice
3 Scarf of black silk
4 Priest
5 Wall tablets containing the Ten Commandments
6 Plain glass in window
7 Royal coat-of-arms
8 Pulpit for preaching
9 Book of Common Prayer at north end of table. The priest stands there at communion service
10 Ordinary bread
11 White linen cloth
12 Flagon of wine

Protestant form of worship and vestments towards the end of the reign of Edward VI (1547–53)

Matthew Parker (1504–1575)
Educated at the University of Cambridge and ordained a priest in 1527, Parker became chaplain to Anne Boleyn and a supporter of Lady Jane Grey. He lost his religious position under Queen Mary. Regarded as a moderate Protestant.

refused. With existing vacancies, this enabled Elizabeth to appoint 25 bishops although she seemed in no hurry to fill them all. However, she did appoint Matthew Parker as Archbishop of Canterbury, John Jewell for Salisbury, Edmund Grindal for London and Cox for Ely.

When the oath was issued to the lower clergy only 4% refused to take it – about 200 in all, in the period November 1559 to November 1564.

The Act also required a visitation (tour) of the Church nationwide. The first visitation began at the end of June 1559, to administer the Oath of Supremacy and to deliver the new Royal Injunctions on Religion. For this purpose a commission of clergy and laymen was created – the Court of High Commission. The commission was used to locate and prosecute people with Catholic sympathies.

The Act of Uniformity, May 1559
This Act dealt with religious beliefs. It made attendance at church on Sundays and Holy Days compulsory. There was a fine of 12d [5p] for non-attendance. This money was to be used to aid the poor.

The most controversial part of the Act centred on the new Book of Common Prayer. This book was based on the Edwardian Books of Common Prayer of 1549 and 1552 but there were significant differences. Most notable was the wording to be used during a communion service, which was a combination of words from the 1549 Book followed by words from the 1552 Book. When a parson gave the bread to a person taking communion, the parson was meant to say the words from the 1549 Book: 'The Body of Our Lord Jesus Christ, which was given for thee, preserve thy body and soul unto everlasting life.' This was to be followed by words from the 1552 Book: 'Take and eat this in remembrance that Christ died for thee, and feed on him thy heart by faith with thanksgiving.' This formula of words was a masterstroke of compromise because it contained the possibility of pleasing Catholics and Lutherans, who believed in the spiritual presence of Christ at communion, and the Zwinglians who regarded communion as merely a way to remember the Last Supper.

The Act of Uniformity also allowed crosses and candlesticks to be placed on the communion table and laid down regulations for the type of clothes worn by clergymen. The dress regulations led to the Vestiarian Controversy of 1566.

The Royal Injunctions, July 1559
These Injunctions were drawn up by William Cecil. Numbering 57 in all, they filled in much of the detail about the day-to-day organisation of the Church not contained in the Act of Uniformity. In many ways they were similar to the Injunctions issued in 1538 by Thomas Cromwell and by Protector Somerset in the 1540s. Their aim was to ensure a uniformity of religious practice. For instance, preaching was to be licensed by a bishop. Once licensed, preachers had to preach once a month. Another injunction stated that all books and pamphlets had to be licensed by the Court of High Commission or a council of bishops. Every church was ordered to display a Bible in English and every parson was expected to instruct young members of a parish to know the Lord's Prayer, the Catechism (a book containing the main religious beliefs) and the Ten Commandments.

Some aspects of the Royal Injunctions pleased Protestants – such as the injunction to close shrines and outlaw pilgrimages. However, other injunctions – such as the use of a wafer as a host at communion, like the Catholic

Mass, instead of bread as laid down in the 1552 Book of Common Prayer – disappointed them. They were also disappointed by the removal of the Black Rubric of the 1552 Book which forbade kneeling at communion. The act of kneeling, to Protestants, symbolised the 'real' presence of Christ at communion. What also disappointed radical Protestants were the injunctions concerning the wearing of vestments (clerical clothes) and the injunction preventing the further destruction of altars.

Although more extreme Protestants may have been displeased by several Royal Injunctions, it seems clear that they represented the religious views of Elizabeth I. The one area which did not conform to this view was the injunction which allowed clerical marriage, something Elizabeth always disliked. However, any future wife of a clergyman had to be interviewed first by a bishop and two justices of the peace to ensure she was of a suitable moral standard.

The Thirty Nine Articles, 1563–1571

While the Royal Injunctions dealt with the day-to-day administration and organisation of the Elizabethan Church, it took until 1563 for the doctrine (religious beliefs) of the Church to be produced. Instead of using Parliament, Elizabeth allowed Convocation to deal with this matter.

The Thirty Nine Articles (of faith) owed much to previous pronouncements, such as the Forty Two Articles from the reign of Edward VI. Introduced by Convocation in 1563, they became law when Parliament passed the Subscription Act in 1571. Historian Susan Doran, in *Elizabeth and Religion* (1994), states that the Thirty Nine Articles were 'something of a hybrid, containing features that were Lutheran, Zwinglian and Calvinist'. For instance, Article XVII stated that 'Predestination to Life is the ever-lasting purpose of God, whereby he hath constantly decreed by his counsel, secret to us, to deliver from curse and damnation those whom he hath chosen in Christ out of mankind'. The wording seems to go against the views on predestination held by Calvinists and contains words and phrases that could be acceptable to both Lutherans and Zwinglians.

On the issue of Communion Article XXVIII stated: 'The Body of Christ is given and taken in the Supper [communion] only after an heavenly and spiritual manner. And the mean whereby the Body of Christ is received and eaten [the wafer or host] in the Supper is Faith.' This formula of words denied the 'real' presence of Jesus Christ in the communion service, which was central to Catholic religious beliefs. Instead it was similar to the Lutheran belief of consubstantiation (the spiritual, not real, presence of Christ).

Financial aspects of the Settlement

When Elizabeth I became Queen, the monarchy was in deep financial crisis. This was mainly as a result of the French War. Like her father, Elizabeth used her religious settlement to provide the Crown with much needed revenue. One of her first actions was to take under royal control the church taxes of First Fruits and Tenths. Although Henry VIII had taken these taxes from the Church, Mary I had returned them. This 1559 Act allowed Elizabeth much needed revenue without increasing taxes on the laity (non-clerical population).

More controversial was the Act of Exchange, also passed in 1559. This Act was passed after much debate, because it involved the transfer of property. It gave Elizabeth the right to take over property once held by bishops. It also stopped bishops from making money from renting out land for more than 21 years, except to Elizabeth herself. The result of this Act of Exchange was to take considerable wealth away from the Church. It also allowed Elizabeth and her government to put pressure on bishops by threatening to use parts of the Act against them. This ensured that the bishops followed Elizabeth's wishes in religion. It was not surprising that this Act was passed against protests from the newly appointed Protestant Bishops.

Conclusion

According to Christopher Haigh, in his biography of Elizabeth published in 1988:

> The ecclesiastical decisions of 1559–1563 seemed to make no coherent sense, and the 'Elizabethan Settlement' had, apparently, settled nothing. But to the surprise of everyone except the Queen, the uneasy compromise was maintained and Elizabeth tried to freeze her Church in the form it had reached by 1563.

It is true that the religious beliefs contained in the settlement included elements of Lutheranism, Zwinglianism, Calvinism and Catholicism. However, the Thirty Nine Articles remain, to this day, the basis of doctrine for the Church of England. The organisation of the Church owed much to the Catholic model, with a hierarchical structure where power came from the top downwards from the Queen, through the bishops to the clergy.

On matters of administrative control and finance, the Church was firmly under the control of the monarchy. The Settlement could, therefore, be described as 'Erastian', with the State controlling both political and religious life. In this sense, it had more in common with the Lutheran churches in the Holy Roman Empire. However, the precise nature of state control of the Church was not accepted by everyone. The historian Claire Cross, in her study of the Royal Supremacy and the Elizabethan Church, believes that the term 'Erastian' could be used in two ways. One body of thought saw the Church Settlement as a joint act by Queen and Parliament. Elizabeth viewed it differently. She saw the Church Settlement as created by her using Parliament.

The religious changes of 1559–63 were clearly Protestant but not enough to alienate totally Catholics at home and abroad. Both Philip II of Spain and the Pope hoped that England and Elizabeth would return to the Catholic fold. However, to many, the Settlement was not Protestant enough. Throughout the rest of Elizabeth I's reign, and beyond, radical Protestants attempted to introduce more 'protestant' reforms, to make the Church of England a church of the 'godly' rather than a church born out of compromise.

1. What parts of the Elizabethan Church Settlement could be described as:

a) Catholic

b) Lutheran

c) Zwinglian

d) Calvinist?

Give reasons to support your answers.

2. The Elizabethan Church Settlement has been described as an 'Erastian' Church Settlement.

a) Explain the meaning of the term 'Erastian'.

b) Explain the ways in which the Church Settlement was 'Erastian'.

10.3 *How far were Catholics a threat to Elizabeth I?*

At the beginning of the reign most people in England were still Catholic. In a study of wills at the beginning of Elizabeth I's reign, *The Stripping of the Altars*, Eamon Duffy has shown that Catholic beliefs were held by large sections of the population. Therefore, Elizabeth and her Protestant supporters were faced with a difficult task in implementing the Religious Settlement.

Elizabeth also found herself facing a difficult situation in foreign affairs. In 1558 England was an ally of Catholic Spain against France and Scotland. Once it was seen that England had left the Catholic fold to become a Protestant country, Elizabeth expected opposition from across the Catholic world. Throughout her reign there was a fear of foreign Catholic intervention in English affairs. The most serious threat came from Mary Stuart, who possessed the strongest claim to the English throne on the death of Elizabeth. As Queen of France, then Scotland, Mary acted as a potential leader of English Catholicism against Elizabeth. This problem became serious following Mary's decision to leave Scotland to find exile in England in 1568 – until Mary's execution in 1587.

How strong was English Catholicism from 1558 to 1568?

Popes during Elizabeth I's reign	
1556–59	Paul IV
1559–65	Pius IV
1565–72	Pius V
1572–85	Gregory XIII
1586–90	Sixtus V
1590	Urban VIII
1590–91	Gregory XIV
1591	Innocent IX
1592–1605	Clement VIII

At the beginning of the reign, the main opposition came from the Catholic Bishops in the House of Lords. As the study of the Church Settlement illustrates it was this group, rather than a band of radical Protestants in the House of Commons, who provided the main obstacle to the passage through Parliament of the Religious Settlement.

In the first decade of her reign Elizabeth has been credited with adopting a moderate policy towards Catholics. This was due, in part, to the international situation where Elizabeth had to maintain English independence in a western European world dominated by France and Spain. It was also due to Elizabeth I's inability to enforce her religious settlement in all parts of the country. For instance, in Lancashire and Sussex the local gentry were Catholic, which protected Catholics from the effects of Elizabethan laws against them.

Although the period 1558–68 saw little persecution of Catholics, they, in turn, seemed to lack leadership and direction in how to deal with the new religious situation. There was a clear lack of papal leadership. It was not until 1562 that Pope Pius IV made a statement prohibiting Catholics from attending Anglican services. However, this papal statement was not made known to English Catholics until 1566. This lack of action was partly due to Philip II's ability to persuade the Pope that England could be won back to Catholicism by peaceful means, through diplomacy. The Pope even had hopes that Elizabeth might attend the Council of Trent. It was only after the election of a new pope, Pius V, in 1566 that papal opposition to Elizabeth became more hostile.

What reasons can you give to explain the lack of opposition from Catholics towards Elizabeth's religious changes, in the years 1558–68?

To what extent was the Rebellion of the Northern Earls a Catholic revolt against Elizabeth's religious changes?

Mary Stuart arrived in England from Scotland in 1568. As the person with the strongest claim to the throne on Elizabeth's death she was the focus for a series of plots and conspiracies against Elizabeth. The Rebellion of

The area of the Northern
Rebellions, 1569–70

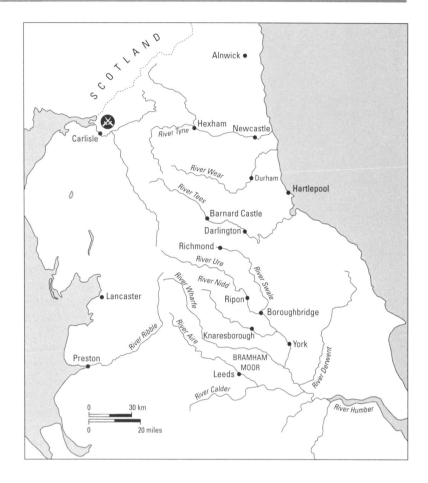

the Northern Earls could be regarded as one example of Catholic
opposition to the Elizabethan Church Settlement. There is considerable
evidence to support this view.

It has been claimed that the Northern Earls (Northumberland and
Westmorland) planned to overthrow Elizabeth and replace her with Mary

The Pope excommunicates
Queen Elizabeth I in 1570

*1. What message is
this illustration trying
to make about the role
of the Pope in the
Rebellion of the
Northern Earls?*

*2. How reliable is this
contemporary
illustration to a
historian writing about
the Rebellion of the
Northern Earls?*

Stuart who was to marry the Duke of Norfolk. The Rebellion began when both earls were ordered to go to London to face charges on this matter.

In *Tudor Rebellions*, Anthony Fletcher and Diarmaid MacCulloch identify strong Catholic influence in the people who launched the revolt. For instance, Richard Norton, sheriff of Yorkshire, had taken part in the Pilgrimage of Grace in 1536; while other agitators for rebellion, such as Thomas Markenfeld and Dr Nicholas Morton, had visited Europe and had become enthusiasts of the Catholic Counter-Reformation before returning home in 1568.

The proclamations made by the rebels also had a strong Catholic content and during the rebellion several actions by the rebels displayed their religious views. For instance, on entry into Durham on 14 November 1569 the rebels carried a banner displaying the Five Wounds of Christ. When the rebels arrived at Durham Cathedral they celebrated the Catholic Mass and destroyed any evidence of Protestantism.

Finally, to coincide with the Rebellion the Pope was to issue a decree (a papal bull) declaring Elizabeth I excommunicated from the Catholic Church. This was to encourage Catholics in England and Europe to take up arms against Elizabeth. However, the Papal Bull, *Regnans in Excelsis*, was issued on 22 February 1570 – after the Northern Rebellion had collapsed.

Overall, the Rebellion of the Northern Earls lacked organisation and direction. It began in early November 1569, the main rebellion being over by Christmas. However, in January 1570 another rebellion took place. Lord Dacre raised 3,000 troops before he was defeated in the battle of Naworth, near Carlisle. Many rebels escaped to Scotland – such as the Earl of Northumberland who was later handed back to the English in 1572 to be executed at York. Although Elizabeth ordered the execution of 700 of the rebels, only 450 suffered that fate.

However, the Northern Rebellion cannot be seen as purely religious in origin. In the spring of 1569 the Earl of Leicester and the dukes of Norfolk and Arundel attacked Cecil's anti-Spanish foreign policy. However, of greater importance was the opposition of the northern nobility to the increasing central control exercised by Elizabeth's chief minister, William Cecil, over northern England. This was most apparent in Cecil's interference in the Council of the North (see Chapter 9). According to historian Lawrence Stone, in *The Crisis of Aristocracy*, the rebellion was 'the last episode in 500 years of protest by the Highland zone [The North] against interference from London'.

1. What evidence is there to suggest that the Northern Rebellion was caused by opposition to Elizabeth's religious changes?

2. How far was the Northern Rebellion a Catholic revolt against Elizabeth?

10.4 How successful were Elizabeth's policies in dealing with the Catholic threat?

What policies did the government introduce to deal with Catholics?

From the beginning of the reign the government introduced a variety of policies to ensure that Catholics conformed to the new religious settlement. In the Act of Supremacy all clergy, and subsequently professions such as schoolmasters, had to take the Oath of Supremacy recognising Elizabeth as Supreme Governor. Anyone who held that the Pope was still

Head of the Church in England lost property for the first offence. For a second offence, the person lost all his property and was imprisoned. In the case of a third offence, the person concerned faced execution.

The Act of Uniformity placed a fine of 12d [5p] on anyone who failed to attend church on Sundays and Holy Days. The Act also placed penalties on clergymen who failed to follow the 1559 Book of Common Prayer. Clergymen failing to follow the terms of the Act faced six months' imprisonment and the loss of one year's income for a first offence, one year's imprisonment for a second offence and life imprisonment for a third offence.

Although the penalties contained in the Elizabethan Church Settlement Acts of 1559 seem harsh by today's standards, they were not seen that way by contemporaries. In particular, the Acts did not provide the opportunity for the creation of martyrs who died for the Catholic cause.

However, the events of 1569–71 forced the government into a harsher policy towards Catholics. The Rebellion of the Northern Earls was quickly followed by the Papal Bull of Excommunication. In 1571, the Ridolfi Plot was uncovered. This planned for a rising of English Catholics, supported by the Duke of Alva's Spanish troops based in the Netherlands. The plot aimed to depose Elizabeth I and place Mary Stuart on the English throne. It was uncovered by Francis Walsingham's secret service. The Duke of Norfolk was executed for treason in March 1572 and the Spanish ambassador was expelled.

The Parliament of 1571 not only approved the Thirty Nine Articles of 1563, it also passed three Acts aimed at English Catholics. The Treason Act re-enacted the terms of the 1534 Act, making it high treason for anyone to write that Elizabeth I was not the lawful queen. Another law made it a treasonable offence to bring Papal Bulls into England. A further Act made it an offence to leave England without permission for more than six months. Anyone found guilty was to lose all their lands.

However, these policies did not have the effect of ending plots against Elizabeth or attempts to sustain and spread Catholicism. In 1574 seminary priests from Douai in the Netherlands began arriving in England.

A contemporary woodcut of the Ridolfi Plot against Elizabeth I. On the left, Catholic noblemen and Catholic priest are plotting against the Queen. On the right, the Earl of Northumberland is being executed for treason.

1. What message is this woodcut trying to make about those who were involved in the Ridolfi Plot?

2. How far can this woodcut be regarded as a piece of government propaganda?

Jesuits: Catholic order of priests founded by St Ignatius Loyola in 1534 to fight against the Reformation. From 1540 the Jesuit Order came under the direction of the Pope. Jesuits were highly intelligent, well-educated priests. Their religious education lasted seven years. The Jesuit Mission to England aimed to convert all England back to Catholicism.

From 1580 **Jesuits** began their mission to win England back to Catholicism. From 1581 to 1584 the Throckmorton, or Guise, Plot involved planned invasions of England from Scotland and then the Netherlands in attempts to establish Mary Stuart on the throne. In 1585 the MP Dr Thomas Parry was convicted for planning to murder Elizabeth. In the following year, Anthony Babington of Derbyshire also planned to murder Elizabeth and release Mary Stuart from house arrest. Finally, in 1588, 'the Enterprise of England', the Spanish Armada, planned an invasion of England from the Netherlands.

The events of the 1570s and 1580s meant that policy towards Catholics was interlinked with policy towards Mary Stuart and foreign policy. These ultimately involved war with Spain from 1585. The parliaments of 1581 and 1585 wanted to take harsh measures against Catholics. Even though the Queen intervened to reduce the severity of proposals, two important laws were passed. The Act to Retain the Queen's Majesty's Subjects in their True Obedience and the Act against Seditious Words and Rumours were aimed at the arrival of priests from the continent. Under these Acts the Jesuit Edmund Campion and two missionary priests, Alexander Bryant and Ralph Sherwin, were executed in December 1581.

In 1585, in response to the influx of more Catholic priests from the continent, Parliament passed an 'Act against Jesuits, seminary priests and such other disobedient Persons'. This made any Catholic priest guilty of treason. Of the 146 Catholics executed between 1586 and 1603, 123 were convicted using this Act.

Further legislation passed in 1587 and 1593 increased fines for non-attendance at Anglican church services (recusancy) to the point where Catholic recusants were forced to stay within five miles of their homes. This prevented recusants moving to a different area to avoid paying fines. In addition, Royal Proclamations in 1592 and 1602 established commissioners to find Catholic priests, in particular Jesuits.

Government policy against Catholics, although initially mild, became increasingly harsh as Catholic issues became involved with foreign policy and the arrival of priests from the continent. In *English Catholicism 1558–1642* (published in 1984), Alan Dures notes that 'by 1603 the rigours of Elizabethan government policy had eliminated Catholicism within the Elizabethan church, so that Catholicism was now a distinctive, separated religion'.

Given government opposition, why did Catholicism survive?

1. What events prompted the Elizabethan government to take actions against Catholics?

2. What do you regard as the main Catholic threat to Elizabeth? Give reasons to support your case.

How important were seminary priests and Jesuits in the survival of Catholicism?

The English who remained Catholic after 1558 took many forms. The most important were members of the gentry and their dependants, what Alan Dures has termed 'seigneurial' Catholicism. This group helps explain why Catholicism was strong in certain parts of the country, such as Lancashire and Sussex. The Catholic gentry possessed the political power in a locality to hide priests and protect Catholics from paying recusancy fines.

Another group, identified by historian H. G. Alexander in *Religion in England 1558 to 1662*, were composed of 'young men, many of whom were younger sons of traditional Catholic families; though unlike their fathers, they had left home to seek wealth either in London or military service'. Individuals such as Anthony Babington (**Babington Plot**) came from this

Babington Plot (1586): This was a Catholic plot discovered by Sir Francis Walsingham. Anthony Babington and his accomplices planned to murder Elizabeth, free Mary Stuart and then make her Queen. This action was supported by Catholic troops from the continent. Mary Stuart's involvement in the Plot led to the decision to execute her in the following year.

group. There were also scholars who came to Catholicism through accepting its theology (religious beliefs). Jesuits like Edmund Campion and other Oxford-educated scholars come into this group.

Finally, there still existed in England 'peasant' Catholicism among the rural poor. Eamon Duffy in *The Stripping of the Altars* supports the view that the 'Old Religion' persisted amongst this group. The Jesuit Thomas Stanney noted the existence of this group in his tour of Hampshire, in about 1590.

During the first 15 years of Elizabeth's reign, the Catholic population was leaderless with little contact with Counter-Reformation Catholicism on the continent. However, from 1574 links were established. In 1568 William Allen founded a college (seminary) for training priests for missionary work in England. The first four seminary or missionary priests arrived in England in 1574. By 1580 the numbers had risen to approximately 100.

In 1580 Robert Parsons and Edmund Campion were the first Jesuits to arrive in England. The Jesuits were highly educated and highly motivated Catholic priests who aimed to win England back to Catholicism. These groups of priests worked closely with the Catholic gentry during their mission.

Much historical controversy has surrounded the role of seminary priests and Jesuits in the survival of English Catholicism. In a series of works, including *Elizabethan Catholicism* and *The English Catholic Community, 1570 to 1850*, John Bossy argues that the seminary priests and Jesuits were a major success in guaranteeing the survival of English Catholicism. Once the old Marian priests had either died or been forced to submit to the new religious changes through government policy, it was the missionary priests who kept Catholic communities alive.

However, the role of these priests has been criticised more recently by Christopher Haigh in *The Church of England, The Catholics and the People* (1984). He takes the view that the mission to England was not very effective. This was in part due to the geographical distribution of missionary priests. Most worked in the South East. For instance, in 1580 half the missionaries were in Essex which had a relatively small Catholic community. Haigh contends that the priests should have operated in the North where most English Catholics lived. He also believes that too much emphasis was placed on looking after the Catholic gentry to the detriment of other sections of the Catholic community.

Although Haigh's views widened the historical debate on this issue, they seem unduly harsh. The missionaries arrived at ports close to the part of the continent where they had been trained – ports such as Dover and Rye, in Sussex. Many chose to operate close to London because the capital was an obvious focal point for activity.

Finally, the support of the Catholic gentry was of considerable importance to the survival of missionary priests. Without their support it would have been difficult for them to avoid capture by the Elizabethan authorities. Also if Catholicism was ever to be restored as the religion of England, gentry support was vital.

How strong was English Catholicism by 1603?

At the time of Elizabeth I's death, Catholicism survived in England, in spite of government action. Between 1581 and 1603, 180 Catholics were

---

Cardinal William Allen (1532–1594)
Educated at Oxford University; left England for ever in 1565. In 1568 he founded Douai College in the Netherlands to train seminary priests for the Catholic mission to England.

Edmund Campion (1540–1581)
One of the first Jesuits to reach England in 1580. Campion spent his time supporting Catholicism in Lancashire. He was arrested and executed for treason in 1581. Was made a saint in the 20th century.

1. What actions did seminary priests and Jesuits take to win support for Catholicism?

2. How important were seminary priests and Jesuits to the survival of Catholicism during Elizabeth I's reign?

executed for treason, 120 of them priests. Also, by 1603, the Catholic community was served by around 400 seminary priests and 12 Jesuits in England. Catholicism remained particularly strong in counties such as Lancashire where it was supported by much of the county gentry.

It is difficult to know precisely the size of the Catholic community. One method of calculating the number of Catholics would be to find out how many were fined for being recusants. Recusancy increased during Elizabeth I's reign. For instance, in the East Riding of Yorkshire there were 40 adult recusants and 70 others who refused to take communion in the period 1570 to 1578. This number had risen to approximately 200 recusants by 1590. However, this method is unreliable for several reasons. Firstly, the increased number of recusants might be due to an improvement or a greater willingness by the authorities to seek them out. Secondly, in areas of the country where Catholic gentry still possessed political power, the number of recusants may not have reflected the true size of the Catholic community. This may have been due, in part, to a reluctance to convict potential recusants because of the heavy penalties facing recusants towards the end of Elizabeth I's reign.

Although Catholicism survived as a separate religion, it was not united. Beginning in 1594 a split became apparent between the seminary priests and the Jesuits, the so-called Archpriest Controversy. This was brought about, in part, by the uncertainty following the death of William Allen in October 1594. The issue came to a head in 1598 when George Blackwell was appointed Archpriest (chief priest) for England by Rome. Although not a Jesuit, Blackwell worked closely with them. The opponents of this development, known as Appellants, appealed to Rome against this appointment.

The issue highlighted a major difference of opinion about the nature of English Catholicism. The Appellants saw a direct link between the pre-Reformation English Church and the Catholic community of the 1590s. Their aim was to make Catholicism a tolerated religious minority. In contrast, the Jesuits wished to see a full restoration of Catholicism in line with the major developments in the Counter-Reformation in Europe.

In the final year of Elizabeth's reign, 13 Appellants had talks with the Government and were willing to sign a declaration recognising Elizabeth as Queen and refusing to support any Catholic invasion of England.

1. What problems did the English Catholic community face during the 1590s?

2. 'The threat posed by Catholics to the Elizabethan Church was grossly exaggerated.'

Using the evidence contained in this chapter, how far do you agree with this statement?

10.5 Why did Puritanism develop in Elizabethan England?

Who were the Puritans?

One of the biggest problems facing historians in their study of Protestantism in Elizabethan England is to find an acceptable definition of the term 'puritan'. At the time 'puritan' was used as a term of abuse for those Protestants who criticised the Church Settlement. Therefore, 'Puritans' contained Protestants who possessed widely differing opinions. Some merely disliked certain aspects of the Royal Injunctions or the Thirty Nine Articles. Others were critical of the Church structure. Although they never formed a unified group there were organised groups who could be described as 'Puritans', such as Presbyterians. Patrick Collinson has quoted a 16th-century writer who described puritans as 'a hotter type of Protestant'. In this sense a puritan could be described as a Protestant who did not regard the Church Settlement as the final reform of the Church. Although it is difficult to generalise, Puritans tended to come from the educated elements in society, such as lawyers, merchants and skilled workers. By the end of Elizabeth's reign, Puritanism was strongest in London, the South and the Midlands. It was weakest in the North and Wales. Puritans wanted a 'godly' or 'pure' church stripped of all unnecessary ceremonial. They placed great emphasis on studying the Bible and preaching. In religious belief they accepted the Calvinist views on predestination (see insert on page 237).

There has been some debate among historians about whether or not Puritans and puritan ideas helped develop the capitalist economic system. At the beginning of this century the German sociologist Max Weber, in *The Protestant Ethic and the Spirit of Capitalism,* believed there was a direct link between radical Protestantism and capitalism. However, the historian M. M. Knappen in *Tudor Puritanism* (1939) believed that Puritans were suspicious of capitalist methods and were very traditional in their views on economic matters.

When did Puritans begin to criticise the Church Settlement?

Although Puritans were unhappy about certain aspects of the Acts of Supremacy and Uniformity in 1559, the first major conflict with the government occurred in 1566 over the wearing of vestments – the Vestiarian Controversy. However, dissatisfaction among Puritans had already surfaced at Convocation in 1563, during the production of the Thirty Nine Articles. Puritans attempted to include in these Articles the reduction of Holy Days, the end of the use of the sign of the cross at baptism and a simplification of the vestments worn by a parson. These proposals were defeated by one vote.

In 1566 the Archbishop of Canterbury, Matthew Parker, issued his Book of Advertisements. These were designed to ensure conformity of practice within the Church of England. Although the Advertisements dealt with a variety of matters such as preaching licences, the main issue was the vestments worn by the clergy. Parker insisted clergy wear a surplice and the cope (cloak). All Anglican clergy were asked to make a pledge to conform. However, 37 clergy in the diocese of London refused to obey. These were suspended from office and ultimately some were deprived (sacked) from their positions.

The Puritans who opposed the wearing of Anglican vestments had influential supporters. Two heads of Oxford colleges – Laurence Humphrey of Magdalen and Thomas Sampson of Christ Church – together with support from continental reformers Martin Bucer and Peter Martyr, regarded the Anglican vestments as too similar to Catholic vestments. However, the issue was not simply one of wearing vestments. It was also an issue of authority and obedience. Queen Elizabeth and Archbishop Parker were determined to establish uniformity even though it created opposition from Puritans. Although the vast majority of Anglican clergy conformed in 1566, the issue remained throughout Elizabeth's reign. For instance, some of the London clergy who defied the Advertisements held services at the Plumbers' Hall, London until discovered by the sheriff's officers in June 1567.

---

1. What reasons can you produce to explain why Puritanism developed during the reign of Elizabeth I?

2. Why have historians found it difficult to produce a precise definition for Puritanism during the reign of Elizabeth I?

---

1. Which parts of the Elizabethan Church Settlements did Puritans dislike?

2. What reasons can be given to support Puritan opposition to parts of the Elizabethan Church Settlement?

10.6 What impact did Puritanism have on the Elizabethan Church?

Why did Presbyterianism become a major issue in the 1570s?

Thomas Cartwright (1535–1603)

A Puritan who helped found the Presbyterianism movement in England. Spent time abroad, including being minister to English congregation in Antwerp in the Netherlands. Imprisoned by Elizabeth I for his extreme views on several occasions.

John Field (1545–1588)

A leader of the Presbyterian movement. Co-author with Thomas Wilcox of *the Admonition of Parliament* of 1572 which put forward the demand for radical religious change. His death in 1588 was a major blow to the Presbyterian cause.

---

1. Why did Presbyterianism develop in England in the 1570s?

2. Why did Presbyterianism survive in spite of Elizabeth I's opposition?

On the continent Calvinism was spreading from Geneva to France, the Netherlands and the British Isles, in particular Scotland. The British variant of Calvinism was termed Presbyterianism. This proved to be the first serious challenge to the Church Settlement from Protestants. The central issue was an attack on Church organisation and involved considerable activity in the House of Commons. In the development of this movement two individuals stand out: Thomas Cartwright and John Field.

The Presbyterian movement received national recognition in 1570 through Thomas Cartwright's Spring Lectures at the University of Cambridge. He openly criticised the organisation of the Elizabethan Church into archbishops, bishops, parsons and deacons. In defence of his views he used the example of the early Christian Church which is described in the Acts of the Apostles (in the Bible). In its place Cartwright suggested the use of a Presbyterian form of Church government which had been established in Geneva by John Calvin and by John Knox in Scotland. Instead of a hierarchy with the Queen as Supreme Governor, the Church would comprise separate congregations each led by lay elders who, in turn, chose a minister.

Cartwright's views caused so much concern that he was removed from his professorship in December 1570 by John Whitgift, the University Vice-Chancellor. Cartwright's views found sympathy in the House of Commons, where William Strickland attempted to launch a parliamentary campaign in the 1571 Parliament in favour of Presbyterianism. He introduced a Bill which met several Puritan objections to the Church Settlement. He wished to reform the 1559 Book of Common Prayer in a more radical way. He wanted to see the introduction of private baptism, a change in clerical vestments and an end to kneeling at communion. Puritans also attempted further reform in the 1572 Parliament. On both occasions, intervention by government prevented progress. In 1571 Strickland was imprisoned for his efforts. The next year, the Queen sent an instruction to Parliament preventing the introduction of religious bills not approved by the Bishops.

Outside Parliament, a group of Presbyterians led by John Field and Thomas Wilcox kept up their campaign by producing a manifesto called 'The Admonition of Parliament' which called for changes in Church government and religious practice towards a Calvinist model. For his efforts Field received one year's imprisonment. In spite of the efforts of these individuals, Presbyterianism would not have developed without important political support. They received sympathetic support from Ambrose Dudley (Earl of Warwick), Henry Hastings (Earl of Huntingdon) and Francis Russell (Earl of Bedford). The most important support came from Robert Dudley (Earl of Leicester) and Sir Francis Walsingham. To them, and other political sympathisers, the main threat to the Elizabethan Church Settlement came from the Catholic community and the development of the Counter-Reformation in Europe. The massacre of French Protestants, in Paris, on St Bartholemew's Day (24 August 1572) emphasised this fear.

What impact did Presbyterianism have in England in the 1570s and 1580s?

Even though Presbyterianism was supported by influential members of the aristocracy, its impact was limited by official opposition from Elizabeth and the government. Until his death in 1575, Archbishop Parker attempted to enforce the Church Settlement. Thomas Cartwright was forced into exile in 1573. Parker also used his power to interrogate clergy in London who were thought to be sympathetic to Presbyterianism. Several were subsequently imprisoned. Also, Presbyterianism had a narrow power base. It was centred on towns, many in the South East. With its emphasis on scripture reading, it was also limited to the educated classes.

Following Parker's death, Edmund Grindal was appointed Archbishop of Canterbury in 1576. It seemed that Presbyterian ideas would now receive more sympathy from the Elizabethan Church leadership. Grindal had a reputation for wishing to heal divisions within the Church and to introduce further reforms. Petitions were made to Parliament urging more radical Protestant reform.

Of greater significance was the development of **prophesying**. Elizabeth I saw these meetings of parsons as opportunities for Puritans to spread their views on the Church and wished to suppress them. This led to a clash between monarch and the Archbishop of Canterbury. Grindal was bold enough to write to the Queen stating: 'Bear with me ... if I choose rather to offend your earthly majesty than to offend the heavenly majesty of God. Remember Madam, that you are a mortal [human] ... Although ye are a mighty Prince, yet remember that he which dwelleth in heaven is mightier.'

Grindal's action led to his suspension as archbishop in 1577 and his forced confinement in his home. He remained suspended until his death in 1583. His duties as archbishop were performed by commissioners appointed by the Queen. Grindal was replaced by John Whitgift. Although he believed in Calvinism, Whitgift's elevation to the position of archbishop launched a concerted attack to enforce support for the Elizabethan Church Settlement. In October 1583 he ordered all clergy to subscribe to three articles:

- to recognise the Queen as Supreme Governor;

- to use the 1559 Book of Common Prayer, and no other;

- to conform to the Thirty Nine Articles of 1563–71.

This led to a backlash. Over 400 clergy refused to subscribe to the three articles. Influential lay supporters such as Lord Burghley (William Cecil) and the Earl of Leicester came to their aid. Following a petition to the Privy Council by 38 Kentish gentry concerning the lack of preaching in their county, Whitgift modified his second article. Clergy were now required to agree to use the 1559 Prayer Book. As a result, most of the 400 clergy agreed to subscribe. In early 1584 Whitgift introduced 24 articles to be answered under oath. The aim was to isolate and then prosecute the leaders.

In spite of Whitgift's efforts, Presbyterianism retained influence in the country. Under the leadership of John Field, Presbyterians began a concerted attempt to force through religious reform. H. G. Alexander in *Religion in England 1558 to 1662* describes the development as 'the first really effective pressure group in parliamentary history'.

Edmund Grindal (1519–1583)
Like Matthew Parker, Grindal was educated at Cambridge University. He was chaplain to Edward VI. Spent Queen Mary's reign in exile before becoming Archbishop of York in 1570 and Archbishop of Canterbury in 1576. Grindal was suspended from duty from 1577 by Elizabeth I over prophesying.

Prophesying: Described by historian Patrick Collinson as 'universities of the poorer clergy', prophesying or exercises were meetings of lower clergy (parsons) to discuss religious topics. These meetings usually occurred with the approval of the local bishop.

John Whitgift (1530–1604)
Like Parker and Grindal, Whitgift was educated at Cambridge University, where he became Master of Pembroke and Trinity colleges and Professor of Divinity. He served as Bishop of Worcester before becoming Archbishop of Canterbury in 1583.

In the parliament of 1584–85 Presbyterians attempted to introduce a 'Bill' and a 'Book'. The Bill aimed to introduce a new form of Church government based on ministers and lay elders. The Book aimed to introduce a set of religious beliefs based on the English edition of the Genevan Prayer Book. This parliamentary action was supported by extensive petitioning of Parliament on the issue from Presbyterians around England. These attempts failed. The failure reflects the power of the Queen and the Privy Council to control developments in Parliament.

The final parliamentary attempt to alter the Church Settlement came in 1587 by a Member of Parliament, Anthony Cope. This proposal was more radical and coincided with the uncovering of the Catholic Babington Plot. The suggestion that the Elizabethan Church adopt the Genevan Prayer and abolish all the existing regulations and laws of the Church alienated moderate Puritans and ensured that Cope's attempt at reform through Parliament would fail. Cope and four other Puritans were arrested and imprisoned in the Tower of London for their criticism of the Church Settlement.

The impact of Presbyterianism should not be seen simply through its effect on the hierarchy of the Church or through parliamentary support. In the country at large the Classical Movement (from the Latin *classis* meaning group) developed in the 1580s. Beginning in the late 1570s members of the clergy began to meet in groups or classes to discuss religious matters of common interests, such as the Book of Common Prayer. According to M. A. R. Graves and R. H. Silcock in *Revolution, Reaction and the Triumph of Conservatism*, 'at their most developed they virtually set up local Presbyterian churches'. The example most quoted by historians was at Dedham, in north Essex, where they met on a monthly basis from 1582 to 1587.

The year 1588 can be regarded as the high-water mark of Elizabethan Presbyterianism. John Field, its most effective organiser, died. One of the group's most influential supporters at Court, the Earl of Leicester, also died in that year. Sir Francis Walsingham died in 1590. By the beginning of the 1590s Whitgift faced little opposition from the Privy Council for his attacks on the Presbyterians. Also the threat from Catholic Europe seemed to be reduced following the execution of Mary Stuart in 1587 and the defeat of the Spanish Armada in the following year.

However, the decline of Presbyterianism was partly self-inflicted. The publication of the Martin Marprelate Tracts in 1588 and 1589 (seven in all) isolated the more radical Puritans from moderates. Published anonymously, these tracts (pamphlets) were an extreme attack on the structural organisation of the Elizabethan Church. Even Thomas Cartwright was shocked. They gave Whitgift and the government the opportunity to launch a concerted attack on the Puritan press. Secret printing presses were discovered by government officials led by Richard Bancroft. Using the Courts of High Commission and Star Chamber, Puritan leaders were arrested and interrogated.

Matters went from bad to worse with the Hacket Affair. Hacket, a Presbyterian leader, proclaimed himself the new Messiah (promised deliverer) in 1591. Although Hacket died in November 1591, the credibility of Presbyterianism was compromised. By 1593 the Presbyterian movement in England was effectively leaderless and clearly in decline. By 1603 the movement comprised around 300 clergy and some 75,000 lay members.

1. What actions did the government take to limit the influence of Presbyterianism?

2. Why did Presbyterianism decline so rapidly after 1588?

How did Puritanism develop in the 1590s? The problem of Separatism

The Separatists, also known as Brownists, were an extreme group of Puritans who believed the creation of a truly reformed Protestantism could only take place outside the Church of England. In some ways the Separatists provide the link between Elizabethan Puritanism and the revolutionary Puritanism of the 1640s.

The first Separatist Church was founded by Robert Browne in Norwich, in 1581. Shortly afterwards the congregation moved to Middleburg in the Netherlands.

As a movement Separatism attracted only a small minority of Puritans. In 1593 Walter Ralegh believed that there were between 10,000 and 12,000 Separatists in England. However, its radicalism made it seem a major threat to the Elizabethan Church. As a result, the 1593 Act against Seditious Sectaries was aimed at groups such as the Separatists. In that year Separatist leaders Henry Barrow, John Greenwood and John Penry were executed. Government action did not destroy Separatism but it did force most of the remaining Separatists into exile in the Netherlands.

Conclusion

By the close of Elizabeth's reign Puritans had failed in their attempts to bring radical reform to the Elizabethan Church Settlement. However, the Church of England possessed a majority of clergy who supported the Calvinist idea of predestination but who rejected the Church organisation associated with Geneva. The Lambeth Articles of 1595, drafted by Cambridge academics, contained a strong Puritan theology. Although never officially adopted, they did reflect the religious beliefs of Whitgift. The issue of religious belief within the English Church would continue into the next century with the growing conflict between Puritans and those who adopted views of a more 'catholic' nature, the Arminians.

Although Separatists were small in number, why did the government fear this movement more than Presbyterianism?

1. By 1603 how strong was Puritanism in England?

2. Using the information from the section explain how far Puritanism posed a threat to the Elizabethan Church Settlement in the years 1558–80 or 1580–1603.

10.7 How strong was the Church of England in 1603?

By 1603 the Elizabethan Church seemed firmly established as the religion of the vast majority in England. Catholicism, which had been the religion of most of the population, had been reduced to a sect. In counties such as Lancashire Catholicism was able to muster support across the population. In most of the rest of the country it had become the religion of a small number of gentry.

The Elizabethan Church also survived the varied assaults of Puritans. What seemed to many Protestants as the first steps towards the creation of a 'godly' church at the beginning of the reign had an air of permanence by the end. Elizabeth I had consistently opposed discussion and reform of the Settlement in Parliament. MPs such as Strickland and Cope who attempted to challenge this position quickly found themselves under arrest.

In Elizabeth's drive to maintain the Settlement she had made John Whitgift Archbishop of Canterbury (1583–1604). This proved to be effective in enforcing uniformity. Whitgift was made a Privy Councillor in 1586. His use of the Courts of High Commission and Star Chamber effectively silenced the Presbyterian movement. However, the failure to allow further reform did create problems for Elizabeth's successors. Both James I and Charles I faced the increasingly militant demands of Puritanism in the first half of the 17th century.

Elizabeth's impact on the Church went beyond enforcing the Acts of Supremacy and Uniformity. Using the financial aspects of the Settlement, such as the Act of Exchange, she was able to milk the Church of revenue, thereby undermining the authority of her bishops. According to Penry Williams in *The Later Tudors, 1547–1603*, 'by about 1580 the established Church had won control of the commanding heights of society'.

Did the Elizabethan Church provide the trained Protestant clergy to make the Settlement effective at parish level? In her attempts to enforce uniformity, Elizabeth I had thwarted attempts to develop preaching, such as her attacks on prophesying. Nevertheless, important development did take place. Patrick Collinson in his study *The Elizabethan Puritan Movement* (1967) notes that two new Cambridge colleges were established during the reign (Sidney Sussex and Emmanuel) to train clergy. By 1603 the Church had made moves towards providing an all-graduate clergy.

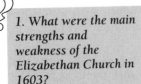

1. What were the main strengths and weakness of the Elizabethan Church in 1603?

2. How successful was Elizabeth in dealing with the threats posed by Catholics and Puritans to the Church Settlement?

? *Source-based question: Catholics and Elizabeth I*

SOURCE A

This very woman, having seized on the kingdom, and monstrously usurped [taken illegally] the place of supreme head of the church in all England, and the chief authority and jurisdiction thereof, hath again reduced the said kingdom into a miserable and ruinous condition, which was so lately reclaimed to the Catholic faith and a thriving condition. We seeing that wicked actions are multiplied one upon the other, as also the persecution of the faithful groweth every day heavier by the means of Elizabeth.

We do, out of the fullness of our apostolic power, declare Elizabeth as being a heretic and favourer of heretics. Moreover we do declare her to be deprived of her pretended title to the kingdom aforesaid [England].

We command all and every noblemen, subjects, people that they not obey her or her orders and laws.

From The Papal Bull of Excommunication [Regnans in Excelsis] issued by Pope Pius V, 22 February 1570 against Elizabeth I.

SOURCE B

28 November 1574: The Queen has appointed commissioners who are examining the principal Catholics, bishops and others … the substance of their examination being as follows:

If they recognise the Queen as head of the Church of England. To this they have all replied to the same effect, although examined separately, they they did not, and that the Supreme Pontiff [the Pope] is head of the Universal Church and the vicar of our Lord Jesus Christ. They were then asked if they recognised the Queen as sovereign, to which they replied they did. They were then asked if the service in use in churches here, by order of the Queen was acceptable to God. They replied that it was not. It was performed outside the unity of the Church and [against] its sacred doctrine.

Each one had to sign his name to his confession for the information of the Queen and Council. People expect that severity will come of this.

From The Calender of State Papers edited by M. Hume. Elizabeth I enforces support for her position as Supreme Governor of the Church of England, 1574.

Source-based question: Catholics and Elizabeth I

SOURCE C

The government's first line of defence against Catholics at home lay in the ecclesiastical courts, whose proceedings reveal wide resistance to the settlement from an early date: there were many charges of recusancy and of refusal to take communion. However, the ... courts were inadequate to deal with the task of enforcing conformity. Many officials were sympathetic to the Catholic cause; the courts themselves were too heavily loaded with other business to deal with recusancy; and when they did act they were able to inflict only negligible punishments. The work of the ecclesiastical commissions established early on in London and York was more impressive: with spiritual and secular members, a brisk procedure, and the power to fine and imprison, they were able to bring effective pressure to bear.

From The Later Tudors: 1547–1603 *by Penry Williams, 1995.*

1. *Study Source C.*

Using the information contained in this chapter on Elizabethan Catholicism, explain the meaning of the two terms highlighted in Source C.

a) 'ecclesiastical courts'

b) 'recusancy'

2. *Study Source A.*

How, by its use of language and style, can you tell this is an official pronouncement by the Pope?

3. *Study Sources A and B.*

How far do these two sources agree on why Elizabeth I should be opposed by English Catholics?

4. *Study Sources A, B and C and use information from the section on Elizabethan Catholicism.*

'The Government faced major problems in trying to make English Catholicism accept the Elizabethan Church Settlement.'

On the evidence of the three sources, and information from this chapter, how far do you agree with this statement?

Elizabethan foreign policy

11.1 What problems did Elizabeth face at the beginning of her reign, 1558–1564?

11.2 How far did England's relations with France change in the years 1564–1603?

11.3 How did Scotland affect Elizabethan foreign policy?

11.4 Why did England go to war with Spain from 1585?

11.5 How important were voyages of discovery and colonisation during Elizabeth I's reign?

11.6 How did Ireland affect Elizabeth's foreign policy?

11.7 Historical interpretation: Who made Elizabethan foreign policy?

Key Issues

- *Did Elizabeth I follow a consistent foreign policy?*

- *How far did England's relationship with France and Spain change during Elizabeth's reign?*

- *What impact did Scotland and Ireland have on Elizabeth's foreign policy?*

Framework of Events

1558	April: Calais surrenders to the French
1559	January: Philip II of Spain proposes marriage to Elizabeth
	April: Treaty of Cateau-Cambrésis with France
1560	February: Treaty of Berwick between Scottish Protestants and England
	July: Treaty of Edinburgh leads to English and French withdrawal from Scotland
1562	September: Treaty of Hampton Court with French Protestants
	November: Shane O'Neill Rebellion in Ireland
	December: John Hawkins leads slaving expedition to west Africa
1563	July: Treaty of Amboise leads to Warwick surrender at Le Havre
1564	April: Treaty of Troyes with France: Calais stays French
1567	February: Lord Darnley, Mary Stuart's husband, is murdered
	May: Mary Stuart marries Earl of Bothwell, Darnley's murderer
	June: Battle of Carberry Hill, Scotland: Mary Stuart defeated
	July: Mary Stuart abdicates in favour of her son, now James VI of Scotland
1568	May: Mary Stuart defeated in Battle of Langside by Earl of Moray. Mary then flees to England
	September: clash between English and Spanish at San Juan de Ulloa (Ulua)
	November: Spanish bullion ships (the Genoese Loan) arrive in Plymouth and Southampton
1569	June: Irish rebellion in Munster
1570	February: Papal Bull of Excommunication against Elizabeth I
	Butler of Ormond Rebellion in Ireland
1572	March: Elizabeth refuses to allow Dutch 'sea beggars' to land in England
	April: Treaty of Blois with France
	August: St Bartholomew's Day Massacre of Protestants in Paris
1574	May: Elizabeth renews Treaty of Blois
1579	July: Desmond Rebellion in Ireland begins (ends in 1580)
	Marriage negotiations between French Duke of Alençon and Elizabeth

1580	September: Francis Drake completes circumnavigation of the world.
	Union of Spain and Portugal under Philip II
1581	March: Irish rebellion in Munster (ends in 1583)
1583	February: failure of marriage negotiations with Duke of Alençon
1584	January: expulsion of Spanish ambassador
	June: assassination of William the Silent
	Treaty of Joinville between Philip II and French Catholic League
1585	May: English ships in the Atlantic seized by Spain
	English colony established in North America
	August: Treaty of Nonsuch with Dutch rebels
	October: Mary Stuart is declared guilty of treason
1587	Febraury: English troops surrender to Duke of Parma in Netherlands
	Execution of Mary Stuart
1588	July: Spanish Armada is defeated
1589	July: failure of Drake's armada against Spain
1591	August: Earl of Essex lands at Dieppe with English army to aid
	Henry IV of France
1592	January: Earl of Essex is recalled from France
1593	Henry IV of France converts to Catholicism
1595	January: beginning of Tyrone Rebellion in Ireland
	August: Drake and Hawkins lead expedition to the West Indies
1596	October: fears of Spanish invasion of England and Ireland
1598	August: Battle of Yellow Ford in Ulster: Tyrone defeats English
1599	September: truce in Ireland between Earl of Essex and Tyrone
1600	Founding of East India Company
1601	July: fear of Spanish invasion of England
	December: Battle of Kinsale: Tyrone is defeated by English army under
	Mountjoy
1603	March: Elizabeth I on her death bed announces James VI as her
	successor.

Overview

ELIZABETH I's reign of 45 years covered some of the most momentous events in English history. In the Oxford History of England volume *The Reign of Elizabeth* (first published in 1936), the historian J. R. Black states: 'Few rulers have impressed themselves so forcibly on the memory and imagination of the English race as Queen Elizabeth I.'

The defeat of the Spanish Armada in 1588, the establishment of the first English colonies in North America and the extension of English influence over Scotland and Ireland, all laid the foundations for the rise of Britain as a major power by the early 18th century. How successful was Elizabeth I's foreign policy?

The reign began with England at war with France. It ended with England at war with Spain. The reign also began with English military intervention in Scotland. It ended with English military intervention in Ireland. The war with France meant that Elizabeth began her reign with major financial problems. Lack of finance affected Elizabeth's foreign policy throughout the reign. In the final decade of her reign, with military involvement in Ireland and France and war with Spain, England again faced major financial and economic problems.

Elizabeth's reign coincided with the Catholic Counter-Reformation. Throughout her reign Elizabeth feared a Catholic Crusade by France and Spain against England. Towards the end of the 17th century England became a major European power. However, in the period 1558 to 1603 England was a second-rate power compared with both Spain and France. In the late 16th century France had a population around four times larger than England's. Spain controlled the Netherlands, Franche-Comté and extensive territories in both Italy and the New World (see map opposite). Fortunately for Elizabeth, France was affected by Wars of Religion from 1562 to 1598, which limited the threat from there. Spain faced a major revolt in the Netherlands after 1566. The Spanish also had to face periodic threats from Ottoman Turkey, such as the siege of Malta in 1565. Both of these problems involved considerable expenditure by the Spanish.

The Netherlands or Dutch Revolt proved to be the issue which led to a war between England and Spain from 1585 to 1604. The Netherlands (United Provinces) were an extremely important area for England for a number of reasons. Firstly, Antwerp was the centre for the sale of English wool and cloth, both of which were of great value to the English economy and the prosperity of Antwerp (see Chapter 12).

Secondly, the Netherlands occupied an important, strategic position from which an invasion of England could be launched. It was only 30 miles (48 km) from Dover and about 100 miles from the Thames estuary. For both reasons Elizabeth I was determined that the area should not fall under the direct control of either France or Spain. It has been the subject of debate among historians whether or not Elizabeth followed a consistent foreign policy. On the issue of the Netherlands Elizabeth supported the idea of Netherlands self-government throughout her reign.

An issue which lasted throughout Elizabeth's reign was the succession to the throne. From the moment Elizabeth became queen it was expected that she would marry and have children. However, Elizabeth never married. This had important consequences for foreign affairs. During the period 1559–87 the problem of Mary Stuart's claim to the throne raised major problems concerning religion and relations with both France and Scotland. Elizabeth also used the prospect of marriage as a diplomatic weapon to further English interests. At various times she engaged in marriage negotiations. In the 1560s the Habsburg Archduke Charles was a possible husband. In the 1570s Elizabeth actively sought French suitors, for diplomatic reasons – in the form of the Duke of Anjou and the Duke of Alençon. By the end of the 1580s Elizabeth was beyond 'marriageable and child-bearing' age.

Faced with warfare and military intervention on the continent, and Scotland and Ireland, England's military power changed considerably. The English army was improved through the creation of trained bands of soldiers. The lord lieutenant of each county was given the responsibility of raising the **militia** and providing military training. Although these forces were never seriously tested through invasion, Elizabeth I's reign witnessed this important development. Of greater importance was the development of the English navy into an ocean-going force. Although the number of ships over 100 tons only grew from 22 in 1558 to 29 in 1603, the improvement in the quality of English ships and gunnery was considerable. The war with Spain after 1585 was fought not just in the Netherlands but across the Atlantic to the New World.

Elizabeth I's reign also saw an increase in voyages of exploration. Although not as impressive as either Portuguese or Spanish expeditions, the search for the **North West Passage** and the establishment of settlements in Virginia (North America) laid the foundations for British control of North America by the mid-18th century.

Duke of Anjou (1551–1589)
Henry, Duke of Anjou, was the second son of Catherine de Medici. He was involved in marriage negotiations with Elizabeth I in 1569. Became Henry III of France in 1574. Assassinated in 1589.

Duke of Alençon (1554–1584)
Francis, Duke of Alençon, was the youngest son of Catherine de Medici. When Henry III became King of France in 1574, Francis became the Duke of Anjou. He was involved in marriage negotiations with Elizabeth I from 1572–76 and 1578–84. Led French armies into the Netherlands in attempts to take Antwerp for the Dutch rebels. His last attempt, in 1583, ended in disaster.

Militia: Part-time armed force raised in each county, usually when there was fear of invasion. The lord lieutenant had the responsibility of raising and organising the militia.

North West Passage: It was believed that it was possible to sail north of Canada in order to get to Asia. This was not possible due to ice fields.

Closer to home, Elizabethan policy towards Scotland and Ireland increased English control over the British Isles. Much discussion among historians about the aims of English policy in these two areas has taken place in recent years (see *Tudor Ireland* by Steven Ellis). However, what is clear is that the results of English involvement led to substantial change. Following Elizabeth's death, England and Scotland possessed the same monarch – James VI and I. Also by 1603 the Gaelic Chieftains of Ireland had been defeated. In 1605 'the Flight of the Earls' saw the leaders of Gaelic Ireland leave for the continent.

A number of important questions have been asked about foreign policy during Elizabeth's reign. Did England follow a consistent policy? Who controlled or influenced English policy? Was it Elizabeth I? Or was it politicians such as William Cecil (Lord Burghley) or the Earls of Leicester or Essex? What is clear is that foreign policy was conducted at a time when communications were very poor by modern standards? Letters to and from the continent could take weeks, if not months, to arrive. Knowledge of what was happening on the continent was also poor. Only a few ambassadors existed at the major courts in Europe by the late 16th century. Therefore, decision making was based on limited knowledge by a small group of individuals.

Europe in 1580

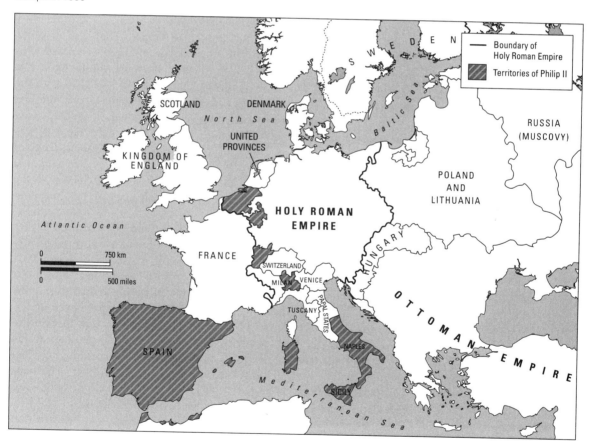

11.1 *What problems did Elizabeth face at the beginning of her reign, 1558–1564?*

When Elizabeth became Queen, England was at war. As part of an Anglo–Spanish alliance, England had gone to war with France in 1557. Although the war was brought to an end in 1559, because both France and Spain were financially incapable of continuing the struggle, the war will be remembered in England for the loss of Calais. As the last remnant of England's once-mighty possessions in France Calais's loss was more symbolic than material. The war also proved to be very expensive. As one contemporary, Sir John Mason, noted: 'our state can no longer bear these wars'.

Although Elizabeth was willing to delay the peace agreement until she retrieved Calais, her ally, Philip II of Spain, wished to end the war. Therefore, in April 1559 the Treaty of Cateau-Cambrésis ended the Habsburg–Valois wars. France retained Calais for a period of eight years. After that date it had to be handed back to England.

Crown: A unit of currency. Worth about one-quarter of a pound (sterling).

If France failed to do this, they would have to pay England 500,000 **crowns**. Unfortunately for Elizabeth I her military intervention in France, during the First War of Religion (1562–64) broke the 1559 Treaty. Although English monarchs continued to call themselves kings of France until 1802, Calais was never recovered.

Elizabeth's problems were not limited to France. They also involved France's ally, Scotland. Britain's 'northern kingdom' had been allied with France against England in the 'Auld Alliance' since the Middle Ages. The link between England's two opponents came closer in July 1559 with the death of the French King Henry II during a tournament to celebrate the Treaty of Cateau-Cambrésis. His successor was Francis II, aged 15, who was married to Mary Stuart, Queen of Scotland. Although Francis II was legally king, real political power in France was held by Francis, Duke of Guise, who was the brother of Mary of Guise, Regent of Scotland (see family tree on page 272). The death of Henry II also coincided with the revolt of the Lords of the Congregation which started the Protestant Reformation in Scotland.

In the years up to 1564 England intervened militarily in both France and Scotland. The intervention in France proved to be a failure, while military intervention in Scotland was successful. On 20 September 1562 England signed the Treaty at Hampton Court (sometimes termed the Treaty of Richmond) to assist French Protestants (Huguenots) during the First War of Religion in France. This intervention may have been undertaken for religious reasons. The newly-crowned Queen was involved in re-establishing the Protestant faith in England. It might seem logical that she should aid fellow Protestants in France. However, throughout her reign Elizabeth was reluctant to support rebels against legitimate monarchs. This was due, in part, to her own feeling of insecurity. She was regarded throughout Catholic Europe as the illegitimate child of Henry VIII and Anne Boleyn. One of Elizabeth's priorities in the early part of her reign was to establish her position as monarch.

A more plausible reason for Elizabeth's military intervention was to exploit divisions in France between Catholic and Protestant in order to try to secure the return of Calais. The 1562 Treaty stated that England would give the Huguenot leader, Louis de Bourbon Condé, a large loan of

140,000 crowns and 3,000 English troops under the command of the Earl of Warwick, brother of Robert Dudley, to garrison the port of Le Havre. The loan would be repaid once Calais was returned to England. However, military intervention failed. The Earl of Warwick's troops suffered from plague while garrisoning Le Havre. English intervention also coincided with the end of the First War of Religion. A combined assault on Le Havre by French Catholics and Protestants captured the port on 26 July 1563. By the Treaty of Troyes (April 1564), England gave up all rights to Calais which had been contained in the Treaty of Cateau-Cambrésis.

English defeat in France contrasted with success in Scotland. Scotland's alliance with France had always posed a major threat for England. For instance, while Henry VIII was at war with France, in 1513, the Scots attempted an invasion of northern England. Fortunately, an English army under Catherine of Aragon routed the Scots at Flodden. In 1559 French influence over Scotland was at its height. Mary of Guise was the Regent of Scotland. The French Queen was Mary Stuart. One thousand French troops were garrisoned in Leith, the seaport for Edinburgh, with a French expeditionary force of a further 9,500 ready to be sent to Scotland.

The politician most responsible for England's subsequent policy towards Scotland was William Cecil, the Secretary of State. Cecil feared a Catholic crusade against Protestant England, led by France. He was able to persuade fellow members of the Privy Council and the Queen to send financial aid to the Scottish Protestants. In 1559 England sent £5,000 in aid. The most important part of English policy was the decision taken on 16 December 1559 to send an English fleet, under Sir William Wynter, to the Firth of Forth to intercept the French expeditionary force. Fortunately for Wynter the French fleet was severely damaged in a storm off the Netherlands.

In February 1560, the second part of English policy was completed with the signing of the Treaty of Berwick with the Scottish Protestants. Under the treaty Elizabeth offered the Scottish Protestants her protection. The Treaty was followed by military intervention: 8,000 English troops under Lord Grey entered Scotland and marched on Leith. The subsequent Treaty of Edinburgh, signed in July 1560, was the crowning triumph of Cecil's policy. Both French and English troops were withdrawn from Scotland. Mary Stuart recognised Elizabeth as Queen of England and freedom of worship was allowed.

Elizabeth was not particularly happy with the Treaty of Edinburgh. She had hoped for the return of Calais. She was also concerned that she was being seen to assist rebels against a fellow monarch. However, the treaty protected England against attack from Scotland and helped to establish Protestantism there.

The military interventions during the early years of the reign illustrate important aspects of Elizabethan foreign policy. England did not possess the military power to recover Calais. The temporary religious divisions in France gave Elizabeth a 'window of opportunity'. Once this division was over, English military intervention was doomed. In Scotland, Cecil's swift actions and poor weather conditions in the North Sea brought French intervention in Scotland to an end. Through supporting Scottish Protestantism Cecil had created a pro-English force which would lead eventually to the union of the two kingdoms on Elizabeth's death.

1. What were the reasons for English military intervention in both France and Scotland?

2. Why do you think England was successful in its policy towards Scotland and unsuccessful in its policy towards France?

11.2 How far did England's relations with France change in the years 1564–1603?

What factors affected Anglo–French relations?

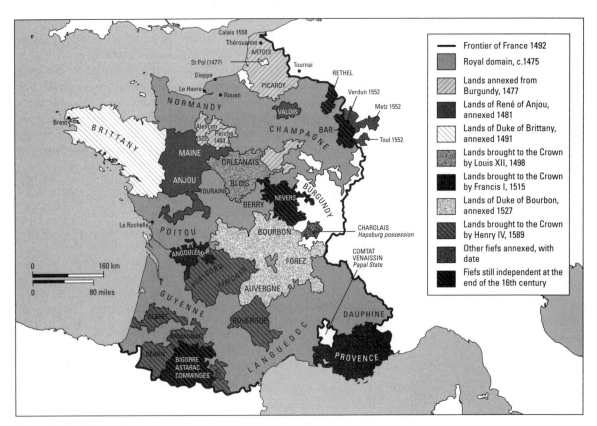

——	Frontier of France 1492
	Royal domain, c.1475
	Lands annexed from Burgundy, 1477
	Lands of René of Anjou, annexed 1481
	Lands of Duke of Brittany, annexed 1491
	Lands brought to the Crown by Louis XII, 1498
	Lands brought to the Crown by Francis I, 1515
	Lands of Duke of Bourbon, annexed 1527
	Lands brought to the Crown by Henry IV, 1589
	Other fiefs annexed, with date
	Fiefs still independent at the end of the 16th century

France in the 16th century

France had been England's traditional enemy in western Europe since the 14th century. During the early Tudor period England had been at war with France on several occasions during the reign of Henry VIII and towards the end of Mary I's reign. The early years of Elizabeth I's reign can be seen as the end of one era of Anglo–French relations. The Treaty of Troyes of 1564 brought to an end the English ambition to re-establish territory in France.

English monarchs such as Henry VIII had sought to gain territory in France. English monarchs also feared attack from France or from France's traditional ally, Scotland. Fortunately for Elizabeth I France was involved in a series of religious civil wars from 1562 to 1598 which limited its ability to exercise political influence outside its own territory. On one side of the conflict were French Protestants (Huguenots). On the other side were Catholics who wished to eradicate Protestantism in France. This group was led by the Guise family. There was also a group of moderate Catholics who wished to rule France but were also willing to allow Protestants freedom to practise their religion. These were termed the 'politiques'. The most notable was Catherine de Medici, who ruled France as Regent during the 1560s and early 1570s. Anglo–French relations were affected greatly by this intermittent religious warfare.

During Elizabeth I's reign Anglo–French relations were also affected by events in the Netherlands. The English desire to keep the Netherlands independent from direct French or Spanish control was an important principle of English policy throughout the reign. The Netherlands were important to England both as a major export market for woollen goods and because it was regarded as a possible base for the invasion of England.

The issue of the Catholic Counter-Reformation was also important. A constant nightmare for Elizabeth I was the creation of a Catholic Alliance of France and Spain against England. In this respect the secret Treaty of Joinville of 1584 between the French Catholic League and Spain was a turning point in Elizabethan foreign policy. It was of considerable importance in forcing England into a war with Spain and English military intervention in the Dutch Revolt.

Why did Anglo–French relations change in the years from 1564?

Duke of Alva (1507–1582)
Born Fernando Alvarez de Toledo. Spanish soldier and statesman. Governor of the Netherlands 1568–73. He was sent at the head of a large Spanish army to suppress revolt against Philip II's rule. Founded the Council of Troubles (known as Council of Blood) which condemned thousands to death without right of appeal. Replaced by the moderate Luis de Requesens in 1573 when Philip II wanted to adopt a more conciliatory policy.

Following the Treaty of Troyes of 1564 Anglo–French relations remained relatively friendly. However, with the outbreak of the disturbances in the Netherlands in 1566 and the worsening of relations between England and Spain from 1568, Elizabeth attempted to improve relations with France. The major Elizabethan fear was the presence of a large Spanish army under the Duke of Alva in the Netherlands.

One ploy which was adopted effectively by Elizabeth for much of her reign was to use the prospect of marriage for diplomatic reasons. In 1569 Elizabeth began a series of marriage negotiations with Henry, Duke of Anjou (second son of Catherine de Medici). When it seemed that these negotiations were faltering, a second set was begun between Elizabeth and Catherine's youngest son the Duke of Alençon. Although marriage never occurred, the two monarchies signed the Treaty of Blois in 1572. The Treaty committed the two countries to military and naval assistance if either were attacked by a third country (i.e. Spain). England and France also agreed to help bring peace to Scotland which was experiencing civil disorder. It also gave England certain economic advantages concerning the export of English cloth.

Admiral Coligny (1519–1572)
Declared conversion to Protestantism in 1559. Leading Huguenot during the 1560s. In 1572 Catherine de Medici formed plot with the extreme Catholic Duke of Guise to assassinate Coligny. Assassination attempt failed on 22 August 1572. Led to Massacre of St Bartholomew's Eve when Coligny was murdered (24 August 1572).

The Treaty of Blois was almost stillborn. Firstly, the leading Huguenot, Admiral Coligny, persuaded King Charles IX to send a French army into the Netherlands to aid the Protestant rebels against Spain. This action raised major fears in England about French intentions in the Netherlands. Of greater significance was the Massacre of St Bartholomew's Eve on 24 August. In the following month 13,000 Huguenots were massacred by the Catholic Guise faction. The incident plunged France into another war of religion until 1577. Elizabeth I and her government were deeply alarmed by French Catholic aggression. It coincided with the Ridolfi Plot by Catholics against Elizabeth in England (see Chapter 10). Although Elizabeth was against formal intervention in France, she did allow English volunteers to assist the Huguenots in the defence of the port of La Rochelle, in 1573. In spite of these difficulties, the Treaty of Blois was renewed in 1574.

Anglo–French relations in the years to 1584 were affected mainly by the deterioration in England's relations with Spain, in particular, the presence of a large Spanish army in the Netherlands. Given Elizabeth's reluctance to aid rebels against a ruling monarch and England's limited financial and military resources, English policy aimed at inducing France to intervene against Spain. After 1578 Elizabeth again used the diplomatic ploy of marriage negotiations, this time with the Duke of Anjou's younger brother, the Duke of Alençon. Although Elizabeth was personally keen on marriage, the negotiations came to nothing.

Having failed to achieve French support through one plan, Elizabeth tried another. English aid was offered to the Duke of Anjou to launch an attack on the Netherlands. Already in 1578 Anjou had attacked the Spanish in the southern Netherlands but without success. In September 1580, in the Treaty of Plessis le Tours, the Dutch rebels offered Anjou **sovereignty** over the Netherlands. Although the English provided over £60,000 in aid to the Duke of Anjou, his lack of military ability led to defeat at Antwerp in 1583. His death in 1584 effectively ended English attempts to use French military intervention against the Spanish in the Netherlands.

> **Sovereignty**: The legal claim over territory.

The turning point in Elizabethan relations with France came in 1584. The rise of the French Catholic League and its treaty with Spain at Joinville convinced Elizabeth that a Franco–Spanish Catholic Crusade against England was becoming a possibility. Elizabeth now accepted the idea of military intervention in the Netherlands through the Treaty of Nonsuch the following year. She also accepted the need to oppose the Catholic League in France by supporting Henry of Navarre, who became Henry IV in 1589. In that year England sent 4,000 troops to aid Henry at Dieppe. In 1591 a further 3,000 troops were sent to Rouen. Finally, between 1591 and 1595 an English military force was maintained in Brittany at considerable expense. The aim of this policy was to help secure Henry IV's hold on the French throne. It was also used to deny the Spanish control of the French ports of St Malo, Brest and Dieppe.

Throughout the period 1564 to 1603 English policy towards France was dominated by concerns over national security. Either the French were to be used against the Spanish in the Netherlands or they were to be supported to prevent the Spanish, or their French allies in the Catholic League, controlling the Channel ports. However, the need to prevent France and Spain becoming allies against England in a Counter-Reformation Crusade was the main concern. The Treaty of Joinville of 1584 stands out as a significant event in changing the course of English foreign policy not only towards France but also Spain and the Netherlands. By 1603 Anglo–French relations had changed considerably since 1558. France was no longer seen as the major threat to English national security. Both England and France, under Henry IV (1589–1610), had come to fear Spain.

11.3 How did Scotland affect Elizabethan foreign policy?

How important was the issue of national security?

Scotland affected Elizabethan policy in a number of ways. Firstly, since the Scottish war of independence in the early 14th century, Scotland and France had periodically formed the 'Auld Alliance' against England. In the 16th century the two nations had been at war during the reigns of Henry VIII and Edward VI. So, by the start of Elizabeth I's reign Scotland was an important factor in English national security. The issue of national security was made worse in 1558–60 by the presence of Mary of Guise as Queen Regent of Scotland and the presence of French troops in Scotland. However, English military intervention ended when the Treaty of Edinburgh in 1560 brought French involvement in Scotland to an end.

How did the issue of religion affect Anglo–Scottish relations?

Another factor affecting Anglo–Scottish relations after 1558 was religion. Elizabeth I's accession to the throne coincided with the start of the Scottish Reformation. In 1557 the Band of the Lords of the Congregation was formed between leading noblemen sympathetic to Protestantism. It was formed under the leadership of Lord James Stuart (Mary Stuart's half-brother) and the Earl of Argyll. In 1559 John Knox, the Calvinist Protestant, returned to Scotland. These two developments led to the rise of Protestant opposition to the rule of the Catholic Mary of Guise. English military intervention which led to the Treaty of Edinburgh gave vital support to the establishment of Scottish Protestantism. The Treaty guaranteed freedom of religious worship. On 20 December the first General Assembly of the Protestant Church of Scotland met in Edinburgh.

Elizabeth and her advisers realised that the success of the Protestant nobility helped to guarantee pro-English rule. However, as Susan Doran states in *England and Europe 1485–1603* (published in 1986):

> Elizabeth, after 1560, consistently demonstrated a marked reluctance to give financial and military aid to the Protestant pro-English party in Scotland. Only extreme pressure from her Council or men on the spot could induce her to give it limited support in 1570, 1571 and 1572. These were times when the threat of French intervention seemed to be greatest.

Esme Stuart (?1542–1583)
Created Earl of Lennox in 1581. Responsible for execution of Earl of Morton for latter's role in the murder of Lord Darnley. Esme was expelled from Scoland in 1582 for attempting to invade England to release Mary Stuart.

This policy of non-intervention was most apparent during the civil war (1565–68) between the supporters of Mary Stuart and her Protestant opponents. Also, Elizabeth did not intervene when the pro-English Earl of Morton was overthrown by Esme Stuart in the years 1579–81 even though Esme Stuart was regarded as a possible agent of the Guise faction in France. There is evidence that English money aided Protestant conspirators who kidnapped James VI of Scotland in the Ruthven Raid of August 1582. It is not clear whether Elizabeth was aware of this development.

However, Anglo–Scottish relations were improved greatly by the Treaty of Berwick in July 1586 between Elizabeth I and James VI. Under the treaty, James VI was to receive an annual pension of £4,000 from England ensuring his political independence from France. Both signatories agreed to assist each other if either were attacked by a third power. Also, both parties agreed to maintain the religion followed in each state (i.e. Protestantism). Although the succession to the English throne was not mentioned, James VI's claim was not ruled out.

How did Mary Stuart affect Anglo–Scottish relations?

Mary Stuart, Queen of Scots, had a considerable impact on Elizabeth's reign, both in foreign and domestic policy, from 1558 to her execution in 1587. In 1559, as the wife of the French king, Francis II, Mary was seen as a threat to national security as a possible agent of France. As a Catholic Queen of Scotland, in the 1560s she posed a threat to the pro-English party of Scottish Protestants. However, Mary's main impact on Elizabethan history was her role in the question of the royal succession.

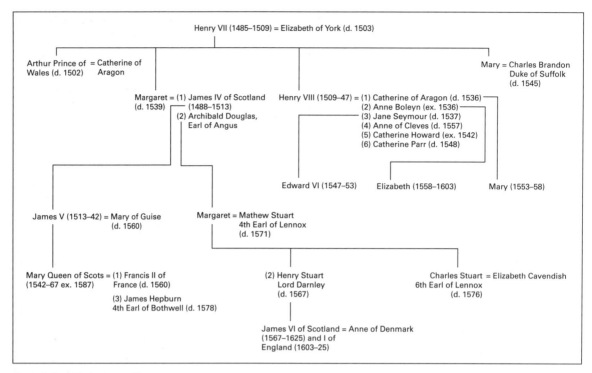

The relationship between Mary Stuart, Henry VIII and Elizabeth I

1. Using the family tree above, explain the relationship between

a) Mary, Queen of Scots and Elizabeth I

b) Mary, Queen of Scots and Lord Darnley, her second husband.

2. If you were a Catholic, why do you think Mary, Queen of Scots had a stronger claim to the English throne than Elizabeth I? Give reasons to support your answer.

The issue of the royal succession was a dominant theme throughout Elizabeth's reign. When she became Queen, in 1558, it was expected by virtually all her contemporaries that she would marry. The issue of the succession became extremely important in 1562 when Elizabeth almost died from smallpox. In spite of its importance, Elizabeth I consistently refused to allow the issue to be discussed publicly or in Parliament.

Early in the reign Elizabeth's infatuation with Robert Dudley (created Earl of Leicester in 1564) caused considerable disquiet among her advisers. This concern reached its height in 1560 when Dudley's wife, Amy Robsart, died in mysterious circumstances. Fortunately, Elizabeth did not marry Dudley. Instead, up to the mid-1580s, Elizabeth used the prospect of marriage for diplomatic purposes.

In the 1560s Archduke Charles Habsburg, the younger son of the Holy Roman Emperor, was considered. Differences over religion brought this potential match to an end. Also in the 1560s was the possibility of marriage to a Scot, James Hamilton. Son of the Earl of Arran, Hamilton was in line of succession to the Scottish throne. However, by 1566 he had become mentally unbalanced. The most important use of marriage negotiations involved the sons of the French Regent, Catherine de Medici, the dukes of Anjou and Alençon (see section 11.2) during the period 1569–84.

The main succession issue involved Mary Stuart. She had a very strong claim to the English throne (see family tree). From 1568, when she fled from Scotland to England after military defeat in a civil war, Mary became the centre of intrigue involving Spain and English Catholics. From 1568 to 1587 she was under 'house arrest' in England, mainly in Staffordshire. In 1569 the Rebellion of the Northern Earls aimed to re-establish Catholicism. Mary Stuart was to replace Elizabeth as Queen. In 1571 the Ridolfi Plot aimed to murder Elizabeth and replace her with Mary. In 1583 the Throckmorton or Guise Plot aimed to achieve the same result. Finally, the Babington Plot of 1586 showed a clear link between Mary and the conspirators in an attempt to replace Elizabeth with Mary as the start to the return of England to Catholicism. In 1587 Elizabeth I finally gave her permission to issue an execution warrant against Mary.

A central question which has always occupied historians is why Elizabeth showed a reluctance to take action against Mary Stuart, in the years 1568–87. Mary was clearly a major threat to Elizabeth. As long as Mary lived she was to be the focus of plots by English Catholics and the Spanish against Elizabeth.

Most importantly, Elizabeth I was reluctant to take action against fellow monarchs. Elizabeth's claim to the English throne was disputed by many Catholic monarchs in Europe. If Elizabeth had agreed to the execution of Mary Stuart she would undermine her own position. It would have given English Catholics more justification to remove Elizabeth.

Linked to this first factor was the fear of French and Spanish reaction to the execution of Mary Stuart. The Catholic Crusade of France and Spain against England could have become reality as a result of Elizabeth's own actions. It was only after the 1584 Treaty of Joinville (see section 11.2) and the 1585 Treaty of Nonsuch that Elizabeth was finally persuaded to take action. In the Babington Plot, Sir Francis Walsingham had intercepted the correspondence between Anthony Babington, an English Catholic, and Mary. Babington was acting as a go-between for the Spanish who planned to release Mary Stuart from house arrest through the use of a Spanish army. It was only after July 1586, when Mary had written expressing her approval of the plot, that Elizabeth allowed the trial of Mary to take place. In October 1586, at Fotheringay Castle in Northamptonshire, Mary was tried for 'imagining and encompassing Her Majesty's death'. She was found guilty by a court of 30, comprising members of the House of Lords, the Privy Council and judges. Even though Elizabeth I was petitioned by Parliament to execute Mary she did not herself take action. Although Elizabeth signed the death warrant on 1 February, it was the Privy Council – in particular Burghley and Walsingham – who sent the death warrant to Fotheringay Castle where Mary was executed on 8 February 1587.

Following the execution, Mary was given a royal funeral and Elizabeth talked of putting members of the Privy Council on trial for murder. She refused to see Burghley for weeks after the execution. The Secretary of State, William Davison, who took the death warrant to Fotheringay Castle, was imprisoned for a while in the Tower of London. The execution caused considerable disquiet in western Europe. It helped to cement the alliance between the French Catholic League and Philip II. However, England was already at war with Spain and Mary's death removed a major internal threat to Elizabeth. After 1587 English Catholics were reluctant to see Elizabeth replaced by a Spanish queen.

1. In what ways did Scottish issues affect England during Elizabeth I's reign?

2. Explain why Mary Stuart was a major problem for Elizabeth I in the years 1558–87. In your answer consider the following issues:

a) national security

b) religion

c) relations with France and Spain.

(You may wish to consult Chapter 10 on religion in Elizabethan England.)

3. What do you regard as the most important issue affecting Anglo–Scottish relations during Elizabeth I's reign? Give reasons for your answer.

11.4 Why did England go to war with Spain from 1585?

The dominant theme in Elizabethan foreign policy was Anglo–Spanish relations. From 1585 to 1604 England was at war with Spain. This war centred on the Spanish military presence in the Netherlands. However, the war also involved conflict at sea and in the West Indies. Anglo–Spanish conflict played a part in the Tyrone Rebellion in Ireland and military intervention in France, both during the 1590s.

For much of the early Tudor period England and Spain had been on friendly terms. In 1489 Henry VII had signed the Treaty of Medina del Campo with Spain (see Chapter 2). The marriage of Catherine of Aragon to Henry VII's sons Arthur and Henry brought the Tudor and Habsburg dynasties closer together. In 1554 Mary Tudor married Philip II of Spain. This dynastic link involved England directly with a war against France between 1557 and 1559. Therefore, on the accession of Elizabeth I, England and Spain were military allies. The history of Elizabeth's early reign is the gradual deterioration of relations between England and Spain to the point where both nations believed war was unavoidable by 1585. Why did Anglo–Spanish relations deteriorate in the years 1558–85?

Why were the Netherlands an important issue in Anglo–Spanish relations?

The Netherlands during the War of Independence

When Charles V, the Holy Roman Emperor, abdicated in 1555 he divided his lands. Ferdinand became Holy Roman Emperor and ruler of the Habsburg lands of Austria and Bohemia. Philip II of Spain became ruler of the Habsburg lands in Italy, Franche-Comte and the Spanish lands in the Americas. He also became ruler of the Habsburg lands in the Netherlands.

The Netherlands were extremely important to England. On the issue of national security the Netherlands were regarded as the natural invasion route from the continent to England. Using ports such as Antwerp, a continental army was only a day's sailing from the coasts of Essex and Kent. Throughout Elizabeth I's reign England had followed a policy which attempted to prevent either France or Spain gaining control of this area. Charles V, although ruler of the Netherlands, had allowed the area considerable self-government. Philip II attempted to gain more direct control of the area from the 1560s. Spain's military presence posed a direct threat to English national security. In many of the Catholic plots against Elizabeth – such as the Babington Plot of 1586 – Spanish military assistance from the Netherlands was seen as vital for success.

Iconoclastic Fury of 1566: Outbreak of anti-church riots in the southern Netherlands. Characterised by the destruction of church statues and images.

The Netherlands were also important because of the outbreak of the Dutch Revolt in 1572. Anti-catholic disturbances had occurred in the southern Netherlands in 1566, an event known as the **Iconoclastic Fury**. However, after 1572, the Spanish faced open revolt from the provinces of the northern Netherlands. To Philip II and many Englishmen the Dutch Revolt was an important aspect of the conflict between Catholic and Protestant. Within the English Court and Privy Council influential members, such as the Earl of Leicester and Francis Walsingham, pressured Elizabeth to take action to assist the Protestant rebels.

Finally, the Netherlands were extremely important for English overseas trade. Antwerp was the European base for the Merchant Adventurers (see page 46). This organisation had control over the export of English woollen cloth. In his study of economic and social history, *The Age of Elizabeth, 1547–1603* (published in 1983), the historian D. M. Palliser notes:

> The bulk of English exports consisted of wool and woollen cloth. For example, in the year ending Michaelmas [Autumn] 1565, for which figures survive, cloth accounted for 78% of all exports, and wool ... and textiles of all kinds for over 90%.

It was because of the area's economic importance that successive English governments attempted to stay friendly with the Habsburg rulers of the Netherlands.

Embargo: Order preventing foreign ships entering or leaving ports.

When England's export trade in woollen goods to the Netherlands was interrupted, it caused economic hardship to both areas. In 1563–64, 1568–73 and 1586–87 an **embargo** was placed on English exports to Antwerp. This involved attempts to find alternative outlets. In 1564 the port of Emden, just outside the Netherlands, was chosen. In the late 1560s cloth exports were redirected to Hamburg. However, the cloth embargoes came to show how important the Netherlands were to the English wool trade.

Why were the years 1568–1573 a turning point in Anglo–Spanish relations?

During the first decade of Elizabeth I's reign Anglo–Spanish relations were relatively friendly. Philip II hoped to keep England as an ally against

Valois France. He helped to influence the Pope not to excommunicate Elizabeth I in 1558. To the Pope she was the illegitimate child of an unauthorised marriage. In addition, Philip II made the offer of marriage to Elizabeth in 1559. She declined. However, throughout the period up to 1568 Philip held out the hope that Elizabeth might return to Catholicism.

Elizabeth also wanted to maintain Anglo–Spanish friendship. In the early part of her reign Elizabeth still regarded France as the main threat to national security. Also as she established her regime Elizabeth could not afford to become involved in conflict overseas. The lack of finance was to be an important constraint on an active foreign policy throughout her reign.

There were signs of future Anglo–Spanish hostility in the years 1562–64. The individual mainly responsible for this development was Cardinal Granvelle, Philip II's chief minister in the Netherlands alongside the Regent, Margaret of Parma. Granvelle believed Elizabeth I was involved in an international conspiracy in favour of Protestants. She supported the Lords of the Congregation in Scotland in 1560. She also signed the Treaty of Hampton Court of 1562 with French Protestants. In 1563 Elizabeth I allowed England to be a base for Protestant **privateers** to attack French Catholic shipping. In November 1563 Cardinal Granvelle placed an embargo on all English exports to Antwerp from London. He used the outbreak of plague in London to justify his actions. However, in December 1564 normal relations with the Netherlands were resumed following Granvelle's dismissal. This development was aided by the Spanish ambassador to the English court, from 1564 to 1568, De Silva.

There were a number of reasons why Anglo–Spanish relations deteriorated so rapidly after 1568. The most important reason was the appearance of a Spanish army of 10,000 in the Netherlands from August 1567, under the Duke of Alva. The army was increased later to 50,000. Philip II had sent the army into the Netherlands to quell the disturbances, which had begun in 1566. Such a large military force was seen as a threat to the national security of both England and France. The issue was made worse by Alva's 'Council of Blood', which executed leaders of the disturbances such as the Counts of Egmont and Hoorn. To Elizabeth I and her advisers, if Alva was successful in defeating Protestantism in the Netherlands he might consider defeating 'heresy' in England.

Anglo–Spanish relations were also adversely affected by events within England. The arrival of Mary Stuart from Scotland in 1568 provided English Catholics with a figurehead. The following year saw the outbreak of rebellion in northern England which coincided with the Pope's decision to excommunicate Elizabeth in the Papal Bull *Regnans in Excelsis*. In 1571 the Ridolfi Plot was uncovered. All these events suggested that there was an international Catholic conspiracy against Elizabeth which involved the Spanish king.

Conflict over the West Indies and the New World also contributed to conflict. The main culprit was John Hawkins. In 1562–63, 1564–65 and 1567–68 Hawkins led three expeditions to west Africa to purchase slaves for sale in Spain's New World territories. These acts broke the Spanish control of trade with its own colonies. Hawkins' final voyage ended in a major Anglo–Spanish clash at San Juan de Ulloa (sometimes spelt Ulua) in September 1568, off Mexico. Most of the English fleet was captured or

Privateers: Pirates. Privateers sometimes received Letters of Marque which allowed them to fight for a country. Any ship they captured could be sold for profit.

sunk. Many English sailors were captured. Both monarchs were determined not to allow Hawkins' expeditions to disrupt Anglo–Spanish relations. However, the issue of the Genoese Loan of 1568 did bring a rapid deterioration in relations. Historians have long debated who was responsible.

In November 1568 five unarmed Spanish ships carrying silver bullion (400,000 florins, equivalent to £80,000) to pay Alva's army in the Netherlands were forced by bad weather and fear of pirates to sail into Plymouth and Southampton. The Spanish ambassador to the English court, Don Guerau de Spes, obtained permission from William Cecil to transport the bullion overland to Dover where it was to be transported to the Netherlands. The bullion came from Genoese bankers who were loaning the money to Philip II. Technically, the loan was not made until the bullion arrived in Antwerp. In December 1568 Elizabeth took over the Genoese loan for herself. The event led to the seizure of English ships and goods in the Netherlands and the re-introduction of an embargo on English trade.

This issue had a major impact on Anglo–Spanish relations. According to historian Charles Wilson, in *Queen Elizabeth and the Revolt of the Netherlands*, the actions of Elizabeth and Cecil were regarded as 'costly and senseless'. However, the blame for the incident may lie elsewhere. G. D. Ramsay, in *The Foreign Policy of Elizabeth I* (1984), claims that: 'In little more than three months de Spes, through sheer bungling, managed to wreck the ancient Tudor–Habsburg alliance.'

According to Ramsay, de Spes acted before any action by Elizabeth to take over the loan. Cecil had met de Spes on 21 December 1568 to discuss who owned the loan. De Spes jumped to the wrong conclusion that Elizabeth had already decided to seize the loan. He wrote to instruct the Duke of Alva to seize English ships and goods, which he did on 28 December. Elizabeth I retaliated by banning all Spanish trade with England. De Spes was dismissed from the English Court in December 1571. This led England to seek a defensive alliance with France – the Treaty of Blois in 1572. Elizabeth I also began marriage negotiations with the Duke of Anjou, Catherine de Medici's son.

Attempts were made to mend Tudor–Habsburg relations. In 1573 the Convention of Nymegen reopened English trade with the Netherlands. In 1574 the Convention of Bristol attempted to limit English raids on the West Indies. Elizabeth also expelled Dutch pirates (the 'Sea Beggars') from English ports, as part of the reconciliation process with Spain. However, the Sea Beggars attacked and captured the Dutch port of Brill (see map on page 274). This action led to the reopening of armed conflict in the Netherlands which would eventually lead England into war with Spain.

The years 1568–74 are a turning point for several reasons. After 1574 England adopted a foreign policy position where it was independent from both Spain and France. Although in defensive alliance with France during the 1570s, England remained concerned about the action of what were seen as western Europe's two major military powers. From 1574 England's fear of Spain and concern over Spanish control of the Netherlands would lead a reluctant Queen towards war.

Why did England go to war with Spain in 1585?

Throughout the remainder of the late 1570s and early 1580s Elizabethan foreign policy was concerned primarily with developments in the Netherlands. The failure to pay the large Spanish army there led to the sack of Antwerp (The Spanish Fury) of 1576 which forced all 17 provinces of the Netherlands into open revolt.

Under the leadership of Don John and, from 1578, the Duke of Parma (Alexander Farnese), the Spanish began to win back territory in the southern Netherlands. Elizabeth I's main aim was to remove the Spanish army and return the Netherlands to self-government.

During this period Elizabeth attempted to mediate between the two sides. This policy achieved temporary success with the Pacification of Ghent of October 1578. This called for the expulsion of all foreign troops. However, Philip II rejected the idea.

Elizabeth I also attempted to use foreign troops to aid the rebels. In 1578 she attempted to get John Casimir of the Palantine to lead an army of mercenaries (page 32). This failed to occur. Finally, she hoped to use the Duke of Anjou to lead a French army against Spain. These attempts also proved unsuccessful in 1578 and 1581.

English policy was hampered by division in the Privy Council. The Earl of Leicester and Francis Walsingham were in favour of direct English intervention in support of the rebels. The Earl of Sussex was against forcing Spain into open warfare.

The decisive year in moving England towards direct intervention was 1584. The assassination of William the Silent in Delft removed the main leader of the Dutch rebels. In France the Duke of Anjou died, removing the chance of French military intervention. Then, in December 1584, the Treaty of Joinville was signed between Philip II and the French Catholic League. Not only did it seem that the Dutch rebels would now be defeated, it also raised the prospect of a Franco–Spanish Catholic Crusade against England.

These developments led directly to the Treaty of Nonsuch in June 1585 between England and the Dutch rebels. Under the Treaty England would provide an army of 6,000 under the command of the Earl of Leicester. This treaty was a milestone in Elizabethan policy. Having tried to avoid war with a major power throughout her reign Elizabeth, at last, committed England to a war with Spain. The Treaty of Nonsuch is also significant as it was signed with a rebel force against a legitimate monarch. By siding with the Dutch Elizabeth I had gone against a major principle which she had been following during her reign.

Why were the Spanish willing to go to war with England in 1585?

Elizabeth I was not the only monarch who wished to avoid war. Philip II was also wishing to avoid open conflict with England. During his reign Philip II had to face open revolt in the Netherlands. He also had to fight the Ottoman Turks in the Mediterranean. Both conflicts would cost considerable amounts of money. Once Elizabeth had signed a treaty with the Dutch rebels, Philip had little choice but to go to war.

There were other reasons. Philip II also hoped that Catholicism could be restored in England. In this aim he hoped to see Mary Stuart replace Elizabeth as Queen. On a number of occasions – such as the Rebellion of

---

Alexander Farnese, Duke of Parma (1546–1592)

Italian, former ruler of state of Parma in Italy. Farnese was one of Philip II's most able military commanders. He became commander of the Spanish army in the Netherlands in 1578, at the age of 32. Helped recapture of territory captured by the Dutch Rebels, the most notable being the port of Antwerp in 1585. The Spanish Armada of 1588 was meant to transport his army across the Channel to invade England. From 1590 the Duke of Parma fought in the French Wars of Religion on behalf of the Catholic League.

the Northern Earls 1569–70, the Ridolfi Plot and the Babington Plot – attempts were made to achieve this end. However, once Mary Stuart was executed in February 1587, this hope came to an end.

Philip was also concerned about the possibility of a new outbreak of conflict with France. For much of the period 1515–59 France and Spain had been at war. The French Wars of Religion, which began in 1562, weakened France militarily. Also the rise of French Protestantism encouraged the Catholic Guise faction to seek allies in their fight against 'heresy'. The Treaty of Joinville of December 1584 provided Philip II with a French alliance.

Finally, with the death of the King of Portugal in 1580, Philip II became ruler of Spain and Portugal. It placed at his disposal a large ocean-going fleet which would give him the military capability of fighting England.

How did the war between England and Spain develop in the years 1585–1604?

England's war with Spain involved armed conflict in the Netherlands, in the New World and in Ireland. However, the most notable event of the conflict was the Spanish Armada of 1588.

The Earl of Leicester's military intervention in the Netherlands created many problems for Elizabeth. In January 1586 Leicester accepted the title of Governor-General of the Netherlands. This suggested that the Dutch were independent from Spain. This went against Elizabeth's aim of regaining Netherlands self-government under Philip II.

The Earl of Leicester proved to be inept as a military commander. The English army had no real experience of continental warfare. It also suffered major supply problems. Nevertheless, Leicester's intervention helped prevent the Duke of Parma over-running the provinces of Holland and Zeeland. Although Leicester was recalled in November 1586, he returned again in June 1587 with an army of 5,000 to prevent the Duke of Parma from taking the ports of Sluys and Flushing. The failure to capture a 'deep-water' port had important repercussions for the Spanish Armada.

The 'Enterprise of England', or Spanish Armada, has captured the imagination of generations. The 'defeat' of Europe's most powerful nation and the prevention of invasion are seen as one of Elizabeth I's greatest triumphs. However, in the conditions at the time, the success of such an expedition was unlikely. The initial plan was for the Armada to leave Spain and link up with Parma's army in the Netherlands. Then an invasion of England, supported by English Catholics, would take place. Philip II had hoped that the mere presence of such a large fleet would act as a deterrent to Elizabeth and force her to make peace with Spain. The choice of the Duke of Medina-Sidonia as commander is a case in point. He lacked experience of such a venture and asked Philip not to be appointed.

The geography and wind patterns of the English Channel also played their part. The English Channel is shaped like a funnel (see map on page 280). Once the Spanish fleet had entered the Channel, it became increasingly difficult to turn back if something went wrong. Secondly, the prevailing winds blow from the south west forcing the Spanish to the north east. In the naval fighting in the Channel the English Navy with superior long-range gunnery, kept the Spanish from landing. The turning point came with a **fireship** attack on the Armada as it lay at anchor off

Fireship: A ship laden with firewood. It was set alight and floated towards enemy shipping.

The route of the Spanish
Armada, June–September 1588

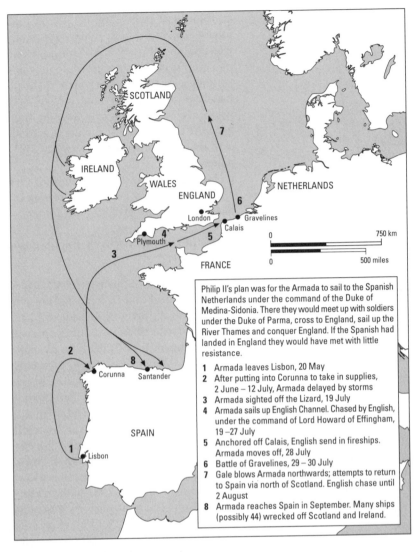

Philip II's plan was for the Armada to sail to the Spanish
Netherlands under the command of the Duke of
Medina-Sidonia. There they would meet up with soldiers
under the Duke of Parma, cross to England, sail up the
River Thames and conquer England. If the Spanish had
landed in England they would have met with little
resistance.

1 Armada leaves Lisbon, 20 May
2 After putting into Corunna to take in supplies,
 2 June – 12 July, Armada delayed by storms
3 Armada sighted off the Lizard, 19 July
4 Armada sails up English Channel. Chased by English,
 under the command of Lord Howard of Effingham,
 19 –27 July
5 Anchored off Calais, English send in fireships.
 Armada moves off, 28 July
6 Battle of Gravelines, 29 – 30 July
7 Gale blows Armada northwards; attempts to return
 to Spain via north of Scotland. English chase until
 2 August
8 Armada reaches Spain in September. Many ships
 (possibly 44) wrecked off Scotland and Ireland.

> Using the map and
> information contained
> within this chapter,
> why do you think the
> Spanish Armada of
> 1588 failed in its
> objective?

Gravelines. Any attempt to land on the Netherlands coast was thwarted
because of shallow seas and dangerous sandbanks. Once the Armada had
passed the Straits of Dover it had to go 'north about' the British Isles to
return to Spain. Most Armada ships were lost in rough seas off Scotland
and Ireland.

The Armada episode of 1588 was not the only attempt to launch a
seaborne attack during the war. In 1596 and 1597 Philip II planned
further armadas. This time the Spanish attempted to land in Cornwall and
Ireland. However, rough seas prevented Spanish success. The Spanish did
land an expeditionary force at Kinsale in Ireland in 1601. This was forced
to surrender, at Kinsale, after a siege by the English under Lord Mountjoy.

The English also undertook naval expeditions. In 1589 Francis Drake
failed in an attempt to launch a naval attack on Spain. However, the
English were more successful in sending expeditions to Dieppe and
Brittany in France in the 1590s (see section 11.2).

Warfare was not confined to Europe. The English and Spanish fought
an ocean-going naval war across the Atlantic and in the New World. The
most notable success was Drake's attack on the Spanish naval base of

1. What were the main issues affecting relations between England and Spain in the years to 1585?

2. Why can the years 1568–74 be seen as a turning point in Anglo–Spanish relations?

3. Who do you regard as most responsible for the worsening of Anglo–Spanish relations in the years 1558–85: England or Spain? Give reasons for your answer.

Cadiz in 1587 which disrupted preparations for the Spanish Armada. Throughout the war Drake, Richard Hawkins and other 'Elizabethan sea-dogs' attempted to disrupt the movement of Spanish colonial trade. By the time of Elizabeth I's death England's involvement in the war must be seen as successful. The main foreign policy objective was national security. This was secured. Although the Spanish had not subdued the northern Netherlands, they had regained effective control of the south. Secondly, the accession of Henry IV in France and the Edict of Nantes in 1598 (order issued by French King Henry IV granting Huguenots the right to worship) had brought to an end the possibility of a Franco–Spanish Catholic Crusade.

In organising national defence, major improvements had taken place in both the English army and navy. The creation of trained bands and the work of lords lieutenant had improved military defence greatly. In naval terms, the improvement in ship design and the administration of the Admiralty created a fleet which could operate across the Atlantic as well as in the narrow seas around the British Isles.

According to historian Alan Smith in *The Emergence of the Nation State* (published in 1984):

> There is no doubt that the Anglo–Spanish War of 1585–1604 was a decisive event in the struggle of Counter-Reformation Catholicism to suppress the Reformation. Elizabeth's intervention in the Netherlands and later in France made sure that neither Catholicism nor Spain would win a complete victory.

1. What information about the nature of warfare in the reign of Elizabeth I does this woodcut reveal?

2. How useful is this woodcut to a historian writing about warfare at sea in the late 16th century? Explain your answer.

A contemporary woodcut of warfare at sea

11.5 How important were voyages of discovery and colonisation during Elizabeth I's reign?

The 16th century was a period of exploration and colonisation by western European states. In the lead were the Portuguese and Spanish. Both states established vast new territories in the Americas. England, on the other hand, had become involved in exploration on a limited scale. In the reign of Henry VII the Genoese explorers, Sebastian and John Cabot, had discovered Newfoundland. In the reign of Mary I, Sir Hugh Willoughby and Richard Chancellor had discovered a sea route north of Scandinavia to Muscovy. During Elizabeth I's reign, Francis Drake made a circumnavigation of the globe between 1577 and 1580. However, the main direction of English exploration involved attempts to discover a North West and a North East Passage to Asia. In 1580 Arthur Pett and Charles Jackman tried to build on the work of Willoughby and Chancellor in an attempt to go north round Europe to Asia. Trying to find a North West Passage, Martin Frobisher and John Davis attempted to discover a route west of Greenland and north of Canada. In 1576 and 1578 Frobisher made three voyages, without success. He was followed by John Davis in 1585 and 1587. Any study of a world map will show that both westward and eastward attempts to find sea routes to Asia were impracticable.

A dominant factor behind exploration was the development of trade. This became important with the disruption of overseas trade with the Netherlands. Following Willoughby's and Chancellor's voyage, the Russia or Muscovy Company was created by royal charter in 1555. To exploit trade with Spain and its empire, a Spanish Company was formed in 1577. In 1581 Elizabeth I allowed the formation of the Turkey Company to trade with the Muslim Ottoman Empire. This company was later merged with the Venice Company to form the Levant Company. In 1600 the East India Company was formed to exploit trade with the East Indies (modern-day Indonesia).

Even with these developments, by the time of Elizabeth I's death, English overseas trade was still dominated by woollen exports through Antwerp in the Netherlands. Over 70% of exports took this route, although English merchants were beginning to trade directly with Germany, Spain and the Baltic. The development of Baltic trade was increasing with English trade usually in profit. The English did not make much impact on Mediterranean or New World trade, however.

1. What changes took place in English overseas trade during Elizabeth I's reign?

2. Do you regard the search for new trading opportunities and colonisation as important developments during Elizabeth I's reign? Give reasons to support your answer.

Attempts at colonisation were associated with the war with Spain. The first English colonies on the continent of North America were established in 1585 and 1587. The individual most responsible was Sir Walter Ralegh. The two colonies were located in Virginia (America). Both failed due to food shortages. In the case of the second colony, no trace was ever found of the 150 original colonists. It was not until the establishment of Jamestown, Virginia, in 1607, that a permanent English colony was established.

To most Elizabethans the idea of colonisation did not mean establishing settlements in North America. For the majority, colonisation involved establishing estates in Ireland. English involvement in Ireland was an important development during Elizabeth I's reign. The 1587 English colony in Virginia involved 150 colonists. By 1598 over 5,000 English settlers had begun to colonise the province of Munster in Ireland.

11.6 How did Ireland affect Elizabethan foreign policy?

A survey of Ireland in 1558

English involvement in Ireland can be traced back to 1189 when the only English Pope, Adrian, granted Henry II the Lordship of Ireland. In 1541 the English link with Ireland was strengthened when Henry VIII was declared King of Ireland. However, English influence in Ireland was limited by the accession of Elizabeth I.

The area of greatest English influence was the Pale, an area around Dublin (see map on page 284). This area was inhabited mainly by English-speaking people who regarded themselves as English. English law was in operation here. The area also had its own Parliament but since the reign of Henry VII Poynings Law was in operation. This declared that the Irish Parliament was subject to the English Parliament. The government of the Pale was under the control of a Lord Deputy, appointed by the English monarch.

In the north east of Ireland, in the county of Antrim, Scottish settlers had established a colony. The settlers were Presbyterian (Calvinist) Protestants (see Chapter 10). Most of the rest of Ireland was controlled by Anglo–Irish (The Old English) noble families. The Fitzgeralds were earls of Kildare and earls of Desmond. They controlled large areas of Leinster and Munster. The Butlers of Ormond also had large estates in Leinster and Munster. During the Yorkist (1469–85) and early Tudor period these earls were used to control Ireland on behalf of England.

When English governments attempted to alter this arrangement, conflict usually took place. In 1533–34 the Kildare Rebellion affected much of eastern Ireland when Thomas Cromwell attempted to replace Lord Kildare as Lord Deputy with an Englishman, William Skeffington. The Rebellion was also caused by Irish opposition to the introduction of Protestantism.

In west Ireland and within the area controlled by the Anglo–Irish families lived Irish clans. Both the Anglo–Irish and the Irish clans (families) spoke Gaelic Irish. In addition, the Irish clans possessed a different kind of land tenure which followed Brehon Law, not English law. Irish clans chose their chieftains and land was owned collectively by all the clan. Clans such as the McCarthy More and McCarthy Reagh lived in west Cork. The area beyond the River Shannon (Connacht and Clare) was dominated by Irish clans.

In 1560 Elizabeth I was declared Supreme Governor of the Church of Ireland. However, Protestantism had made little impact in Ireland outside the Pale. The majority of the Irish remained Catholic. During Elizabeth I's reign, Ireland would be an area where the conflict between Catholic and Protestant would take place. In 1579 troops financed by Pope Gregory XIII landed at Smerwick in Kerry. In 1601 Spanish troops landed at Kinsale in Cork, to aid the Tyrone Rebellion.

What policies did Elizabeth's predecessors follow to increase English control of Ireland?

During the reign of Henry VIII a new policy was used to increase English control. Under Lord Deputy Sir Warham St Leger and his 'right-hand' man, Thomas Cusack, the policy of 'surrender and regrant' was introduced in the

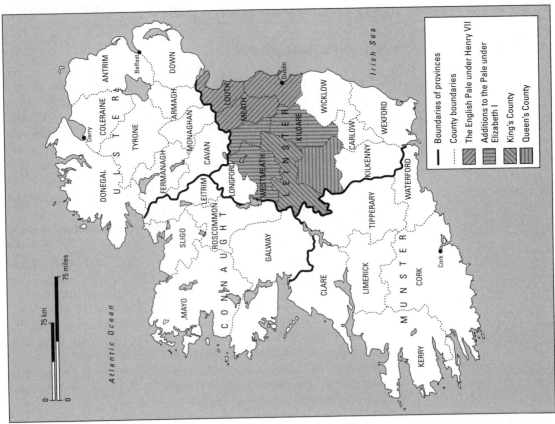

Ireland in the reign of Elizabeth I

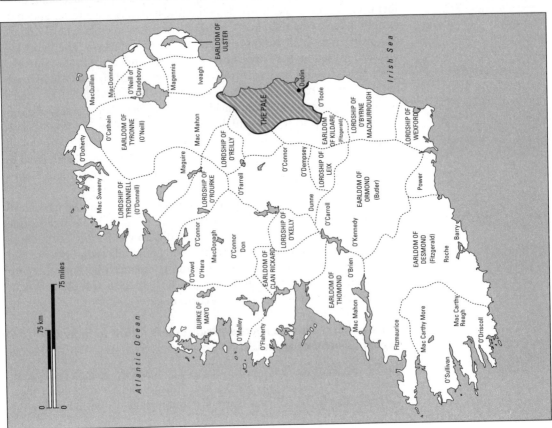

Ireland in about 1530

A contemporary illustration of a Gaelic Irish chieftain eating a meal

1. **What evidence is there in this illustration to suggest that the Gaelic Irish were regarded as uncivilised by the Elizabethan English?**

2. **Compare this illustration with the engraving of the Earl of Essex (page 287). Which do you regard as more useful to a historian writing about Elizabethan England? Give reasons to support your answer.**

Primogeniture: Land law in operation in England and Wales which allows the eldest son to inherit all land and property on the death of a father.

1540s. Under this policy Gaelic chieftains would surrender their clan titles and then receive English titles. Land law for the clan would change from Brehon Law to the English law of **primogeniture**. For instance, in 1543 the O'Brien chieftain was given the title of Earl of Thomond and Burke became Earl of Clanrickard. However, this policy was abandoned in 1556 by Thomas Radcliffe (Earl of Sussex) who was Lord Deputy from 1556 to 1560 and Lord Lieutenant from 1560 to 1564.

The Earl of Sussex adopted a more aggressive policy, which sought to increase English control through colonisation. Two areas in central Ireland, termed King's and Queen's Counties, were created from the Gaelic counties of Offlay and Leix. But it wasn't until 1563 that settlers began to arrive in this area. However, the colonies did not prove popular. The Earl of Sussex also aimed to limit the power of the main Anglo–Irish chieftains such as Kildare and O'Neill.

What policies did Elizabeth follow towards Ireland in the years to 1567?

For the first 20 years of her reign Elizabeth I's government followed the policies laid down by the Earl of Sussex and followed by his successor, Sir Henry Sidney. This policy led to open rebellion by the Anglo-Irish and Irish. Unfortunately, the policy failed to take into consideration the finance and military support to make it a success.

The most immediate problem facing Elizabeth I was Shane O'Neill's rebellion in Ulster which had begun shortly before her accession to the throne. Shane had rebelled because the title of Earl of Tyrone had been given to his illegitimate half-brother, Matthew. The Earl of Sussex failed to defeat Shane O'Neill militarily. His army was insufficient for the task. Also the Irish adopted a guerrilla warfare style campaign. By 1563 a treaty was signed between Elizabeth and O'Neill giving the latter effective control over Ulster. However, Sir Henry Sidney was more successful. In 1566 he raided Ulster and captured several O'Neill strongholds. Sidney's presence encouraged others to stand up to the O'Neill's. Shane became involved in a feud with a lesser Irish clan in Ulster, the O'Donnells of Tyrconnell (modern-day Donegal). Having suffered defeat at the battle of Farsetmore in 1567, Shane was killed by the MacDonalds, Scottish settlers in Antrim.

The removal of Shane O'Neill gave Elizabeth the opportunity to follow a policy which was a central feature of her Irish policy: colonisation.

How successful was the policy of colonisation in Ireland?

From 1569 English policy involved the encouragement of settlers (The New English) with grants of land. These plantations would provide the basis for future English control. Although the Dublin Parliament were generally against this policy, grants of land were made to Sir Peter Carew and Sir Warham St Leger in Munster. In 1571 Sir Thomas Smith was granted land in east Ulster (modern-day Down).

The immediate effect of this policy was to spark off rebellion in Munster by Butler and James Fitzmaurice Fitzgerald. Although the rebellions were put down by 1572, Fitzmaurice returned with foreign troops in 1579–82 to lead another rebellion with the support of the Earl of Desmond. Only after this rebellion was defeated did the 'plantation' of colonists in Munster begin to take place in any numbers, many to lands confiscated from the Earl of

Tudor plantations in Ireland

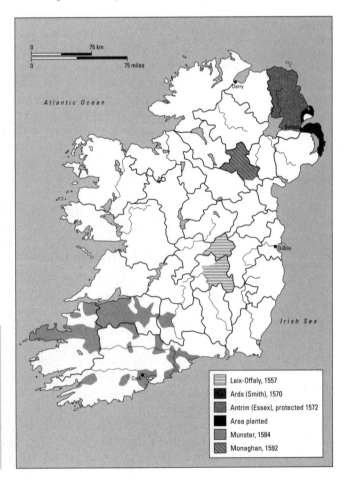

Leix-Offaly, 1557
Ards (Smith), 1570
Antrim (Essex), protected 1572
Area planted
Munster, 1584
Monaghan, 1592

Use the information in this section. How far was there a connection between the plantation of English colonists in Ireland and Irish revolts against English rule?

Desmond. Although 15,000 colonists were intended for Munster, by the end of the century only 4,000 had taken residence.

How serious was the Tyrone Rebellion of 1595–1603?

In *Tudor Ireland*, the historian Steven Ellis states that English policy towards Ireland can be seen as a failure. Indeed, Elizabeth I's policies for much of her reign were not successful. Her government failed to provide the Lord Deputy and the English administration in Dublin with sufficient resources to make her policies a success. The plan to increase control through colonisation was of limited success in Munster and failed to develop in Ulster. This policy created resentment among the Anglo-Irish, which resulted in intermittent rebellion.

The most serious problem Elizabeth faced came during the latter part of her reign. The Tyrone Rebellion almost brought English rule in Ireland to an end. Its defeat, ironically, led to the Tudor conquest and control over the whole island. This was achieved at considerable financial expense and major military involvement.

The rebellion came when Hugh O'Neill (Earl of Tyrone) was able to gain effective control over Ulster. He arranged a marriage alliance with his traditional enemies the O'Donnells of Tyrconnell. Then, following the death of Turlough O'Neill, Hugh became undisputed leader of his clan. He also possessed considerable military might. According to historian Penry

---

Hugh O'Neill, Earl of Tyrone (?1540–1616)
Second son of Matthew O'Neill. Created Earl of Tyrone in 1584. Became chief of the O'Neills in 1595. With Owen Roe O'Donnell, he led Irish opposition to English rule. Following defeat at Kinsale (1601–02), Hugh O'Neill fled Ireland. Died in Rome.

Robert Devereux, 2nd Earl of Essex (1566–1601) from a contemporary engraving by Robert Boissard

1. What message is this engraving trying to give about the Earl of Essex as a military commander?

2. Use the information contained within this chapter. How far do you think the Earl of Essex was an effective military commander?

The most noble ROBERT Earle of Essex and Ewe, Earle Marshall of England Viscount Hereford and Bourgchier, Lord Ferrers of Chartle L. Bourgchier and Louayn and her Maiesties lieutenant and Gouernour generall of the Kingdome of Irland. 1600.

Williams in *The Later Tudors*, 'He [O'Neill] posed a greater threat to the English presence in Ireland than any Irish lord of the century.' O'Neill commanded an army of 1,000 cavalry and 5,000 infantry which included 4,000 musketeers. He also sought military aid from Spain. Only bad weather in 1597 prevented a Spanish armada landing in Ireland.

O'Neill's Rebellion took place during the war with Spain and during a period of considerable economic hardship in England brought on by successive harvest failures in the mid-1590s (see Chapter 12).

O'Neill had several spectacular military successes over the English. In the battle of the Yellow Ford, in 1598, he defeated an English army of 4,000. The victory allowed O'Neill and his allies to occupy most of Connacht and Leinster. It also forced Elizabeth I to take more effective action. Her government raised an army of 17,000. Unfortunately, she chose the Earl of Essex to lead it. In 1599 his campaign against O'Neill ended in disaster. His army suffered military defeat and mass desertion forcing the Earl of Essex to demand a truce from O'Neill. Essex's defeat and his loss of prestige at Court led to an attempted coup which led to his execution in 1601.

Fortunately for Elizabeth the appointment of Charles Blount (Lord Mountjoy) to the position of Lord Deputy in 1600 proved a turning point in English fortunes. With an army of 13,000, he outnumbered and outmanoeuvred O'Neill. The decisive engagement came at Kinsale where Mountjoy defeated O'Neill and a Spanish expeditionary force in December 1601. The defeat brought to an end the resistance of Gaelic Ireland to English rule. O'Neill and other Gaelic chiefs left Ireland for Spain in 1605 (the Flight of the Earls).

The Tyrone Rebellion illustrated a major problem for English policy. Only with major financial and military resources could England gain effective control over Ireland.

1. What were the main aspects of Elizabethan policy towards Ireland?

2. How did Elizabethan policy towards Ireland differ from her predecessors?

3. Why do you think it took so long for English control of Ireland to take place during Elizabeth I's reign?

11.7 *Who made Elizabethan foreign policy?*
A CASE STUDY IN HISTORICAL INTERPRETATION

Historians such as William Camden, J. E. Neale and A. L. Rowse tended to see the reign of Elizabeth I as an age of greatness where England began to establish itself as a leading power in western Europe. However, when Elizabeth became Queen in 1558 she possessed little knowledge or understanding of foreign affairs. An important question which is posed by historians of the Tudor period is: Who made Elizabethan foreign policy?

Part of the problem is the limited amount of primary evidence available to the historian. The main sources of information are:

● State Papers and correspondence between the Queen and her principal advisers. However, these are limited in coverage.

● treaties and correspondence between England and foreign powers;

● reports by ambassadors, either English ambassadors abroad or foreign ambassadors at the English Court. However, there are questions of reliability concerning these reports.

Throughout her reign Elizabeth found it difficult to find suitable individuals to act as ambassadors. John Man, the English representative at the Spanish

Court until 1567, was a noted anti-Catholic who regarded the Pope as Antichrist. Also George Gilpin, who was once secretary to the Merchant Adventurers, was likely to issue reports which reflected his economic interests. Similarly, the quality of foreign representatives at the English Court was open to question. Don Guerau de Spes, the representative of Spain from 1568 to 1571, was unfamiliar with England. He reported to Philip II that the Principal Secretary, William Cecil, was a 'bare-faced' heretic. The most reliable foreign reports were those of the Venetian representative to the Doge (ruler) of Venice.

Foreign policy was traditionally controlled by the monarch. Throughout her reign Elizabeth I played a full and active role in foreign affairs. Her employment of the prospect of marriage to a foreign prince is a case in point. However, the day-to-day running of foreign affairs was handled by her Principal Secretary. Until 1572, foreign affairs were handled by William Cecil. He played a major role in deciding policy towards Scotland in the years 1558 to 1560. From 1573 to 1587 Sir Francis Walsingham filled this role, although Cecil still possessed influence in foreign affairs. During the latter part of Elizabeth I's reign, foreign affairs were again handled by William Cecil (now Lord Burghley). After his death, they were handled by his son Robert Cecil.

The Principal Secretary received reports from English agents and representatives abroad. Apart from formal representatives at some of the leading European Courts, reports were received from English ships, trading companies such as the Muscovy Company and the Merchant Adventurers and English agents such as the one placed at St Jean-de-Luz on the border between France and Spain. Problems of communication made a regular flow of quality information difficult.

Outside the formal structure dealing with foreign affairs there were other influences. For instance, throughout her reign Elizabeth faced the problem of Court faction. Considerable debate took place on the issue of the Dutch Revolt between Cecil, who favoured a cautious approach, and the Earl of Leicester who wanted more intervention to support fellow Protestants. Similar splits over foreign affairs appeared in the 1590s between Robert Cecil and the Earl of Essex.

Occasionally, the full Privy Council was consulted about foreign affairs. In *The Making of Elizabethan Foreign Policy 1558–1603*, R. B. Wernham notes that Elizabeth did this in December 1559 before intervening in Scotland, in June 1565. She also consulted the Privy Council about English policy towards the marriage of Mary Stuart to Lord Darnley and over Dutch policy following the assassination of William the Silent.

Elizabethan Parliaments played a very limited role in foreign affairs. This was due in part to the little amount of time Parliament was in session during Elizabeth's reign. However, Parliament did discuss the issue of the succession in 1566 and Mary Stuart in 1572.

Considerable debate has taken place between historians about the aims and objectives of Elizabethan foreign policy, in particular concerning policy towards the Netherlands. In *Tudor Foreign Policy*, P. S. Crowson states that 'the 45 years of Elizabeth's reign was a time of pessimism, of insecurity and of agonising national danger under the overshadowing power first of France and then of Spain'.

Given England's limited financial and military resources compared to these two states it would seem that Elizabeth would want to avoid conflict in foreign affairs. In *Queen Elizabeth and the Revolt in the Netherlands*, Charles Wilson believes that Elizabeth adopted a very reactive foreign policy. She merely reacted to events without having any overall aim or objective. For instance, Wilson believes Elizabeth suffered from an irrational fear of France which did not take into account the disruption caused by the French Wars of Religion. The clearest example of Elizabeth's lack of policy was her handling of the Netherlands issue. Wilson regards her policy as a failure.

On the other hand, R. B. Wernham, in *Before the Armada*, believes Elizabeth had clear aims and objectives. On the issue of the Netherlands, Wernham identifies three aims:

- to remove the Spanish army;

- to prevent France gaining control of the Netherlands;

- to return the Netherlands to self-government which it had experienced under Charles V.

However, given its limited military and financial resources, England was restricted in what it could do in foreign affairs.

Perhaps Elizabeth I's foreign policy was not quite 'an age of greatness', as seen by William Camden in 1617 (where he subtitled his *Annales* 'The True and Royall History of the famous Empresse Elizabeth, Queene of England, France and Ireland … of Divine Renown and Happy Memory') and some later historians. However, Elizabeth I had to operate with the constraints of finance and resources permitted for a nation of three million in a western Europe dominated by France and Spain in the era of the Catholic Counter-Reformation. As the R. B. Wernham notes in *The Making of Elizabethan Foreign Policy*: 'National policy … was shaped quite as much by circumstances as by the will of the Queen or the persuasions of her privy councillors or the interests of commerce or the pressures of religion.'

If the main aim of foreign policy is to protect national security and to prevent invasion then Elizabeth's foreign policy was a success.

1. Draw a chart showing the factors which influenced Elizabethan foreign policy.

2. What problems have faced historians in their attempt to understand who made English foreign policy during the reign of Elizabeth I?

3. Why do you think historians have disagreed about Elizabeth I's policy towards the Netherlands?

? *Source-based questions: The trial and execution of Mary Stuart*

SOURCE A

By the time that Anthony Babington's plot to assassinate Elizabeth was spawned, Walsingham's network was complete. He wrote to Leicester, 'If the matter be well handled, it will break the neck of all dangerous practices during her Majesty's reign.'

When Mary endorsed the planned murder in a dictated letter (17 July 1586), she was trapped. The Babington conspirators were tried and hanged, but Elizabeth agonised even more over Mary's execution than she had over Norfolk's after the Ridolfi Plot.

Since the Tower was considered insufficiently secure and too close to London, Mary was sent to Fotheringay Castle, where her trial formally began on 14 October 1586. Her judges were a committee of nobles, privy councillors, and leading judges appointed under the terms of the Act for the Queen's Safety. Although Mary objected that she was a queen and thus not subject to English common law, she was persuaded that she damaged her reputation by refusing to defend herself. She denied any complicity in attempted assassination, but by virtue of her letter to Babington she was plainly guilty.

From Tudor England *by John Guy, 1988*

Source-based questions: The trial and execution of Mary Stuart

SOURCE B

Her Majesty in not executing justice upon the Scottish Queen shall foster and nourish that only hope which the Catholics have to re-establish their religion within this realm. The Scottish Queen's life cannot stand with Her Majesty's safety and quiet estate of this realm, being as she is the only ground of all practices and attempts both at home and abroad.

Mercy and Pity is nothing else but cruel kindness; but in the Scottish Queen experience teaches that the more favour she receives the more mischief she attempts.

What dishonour were it, in sparing the life of so grievous an offender, to hazard the lives of so many thousands of true subjects, being left to so malicious a woman.

Argument, urging the execution of Mary Stuart, put forward by Sir Christopher Hatton, a Privy Councillor, during 1586–87.

SOURCE C

Ambassadors from France and Scotland presented themselves at court with vigorous pleas and petitions for clemency, which could not be ignored. It was only too apparent that the affairs of Mary Stuart were inextricably bound up with the general European situation. To endanger the completed alliance with Scotland or the goodwill of France, at a time when the great duel with Spain was looming over the horizon, was a heavy price to pay for ridding England of the enemy within the gate. In January 1587 the intercession of France was largely nullified [cancelled out] by the discovery (or was it an invention?) of a fresh plot against the queen's life, emanating, it was said, from the French embassy in London. A 'great fear' swept over the country. It was reported that the Spaniards were at Milford, that Mary had escaped, that the northern counties were in revolt, that the capital was on fire. Elizabeth was heard to murmur the words 'Aut fer, aut fer; ne feriare, feri' [suffer or strike; in order not to be struck]. On 1 February she signed the death-warrant.

From The Reign of Elizabeth *by J. S. Black, 1936*

SOURCE D

[Mary Stuart] was a free and absolute Princess and had no superiour but God alone. They said, she was Queen Elizabeth's very near Kinswoman, who made her a large Promise, on the Word of a Prince, of all Courtesie and kind Hospitality, as soon as she arrived in England, being thrown out of her Kingdom by her rebels. Yet on the contrary had kept her still in prison, and violated the sacred rights of hospitality; that she could not be otherways reputed than as a prisoner taken in war. She could not commit treason, because she was no subject, and Princes in equal degree have no power or sovereignty over one another. Moreover, that it was never heard of, that a Prince should be subjected to the Stroke of an Executioner.

From A History of the Most Renowned and Victorious Princess Elizabeth, late Queen of England *by William Camden, 1615*

---

1. With reference to Sources C and D, and to information contained within this chapter, explain the meaning of the two terms highlighted in the sources:

a) 'the completed alliance with Scotland' (Source C)

b) 'a free and absolute Princess and had no superiour but God alone' (Source D).

2. Study Sources A and B.

How far do these sources agree on the reasons why Mary Stuart should be tried and executed?

3. Study Sources B and D.

How useful are these sources to a historian writing about the issue raised by the trial and execution of Mary Stuart?

4. Study all four sources and use information contained within this chapter.

'The problems Mary Stuart created for Elizabeth I can only be understood if they are seen as part of England's relations with France and Spain.'

Assess the validity of this statement.

Social, economic and cultural history in the reign of Elizabeth I

12.1 What changes took place in the size and structure of population?

12.2 Historical interpretation: How far did society change during Elizabeth I's reign?

12.3 How successful was Elizabeth's government in dealing with the problem of inflation?

12.4 How did Elizabethans deal with the issues of poverty and vagrancy?

12.5 How far did trade and industry change during Elizabeth I's reign?

12.6 Were there any changes in the pattern and development of agriculture?

12.7 How important were developments in English culture during Elizabeth I's reign?

Key Issues

- *In what ways did society change in Elizabeth's England?*

- *How successful was Elizabethan government in dealing with social and economic problems?*

- *How far did industry, trade and agriculture change during Elizabeth's reign?*

Framework of Events

1560	December: recoinage begins
1561	October: recoinage completed
1563	Statute of Artificers regulates conditions of employment for most of the working population
	Act for the Relief of the Poor (Beggars Act)
	Embargo on English woollen trade with the Netherlands (ends 1564)
1568	Embargo on English woollen trade with the Netherlands
1572	Act for the Punishment of Vagabonds and for the Relief of the Poor and Impotent
1576	Act 'for the setting of the poor on work and for avoiding of idleness'
1587	Christopher Marlowe writes *Tamburlaine*
1588	William Shakespeare begins writing plays. The first plays include *Henry VI*, *Richard III* and *Love's Labours Lost*
1589	Edmund Spenser begins writing *The Faerie Queene*
1593	Outbreak of plague
1594	Shakespeare begins writing *A Midsummer Night's Dream*
	First of four years of poor harvests
1596	Shakespeare begins writing *Merchant of Venice* and *Henry V*
1597	Shakespeare's play *Romeo and Juliet* is published
	Act for the Relief of the Poor; Act for the Punishment of Rogues, Vagabonds and Sturdy Beggars
1598	Outbreak of famine due to four years of poor harvests
	Act on Husbandry and Tillage to stop depopulation in the countryside
1599	Shakespeare begins writing *Julius Caesar*
	Globe Theatre built
1600	Formation of East India Company
	Fortune Theatre opens in London
	Ben Jonson's *Every Man out of his Humour* is published
1601	Poor Law of 1597 reissued in modified form
	Shakespeare's *The Merry Wives of Windsor* is published

Overview

THE reign of Elizabeth I was a period of change in social and economic history. During the last half of the 16th century England experienced a rapid rise in population from three to four million. This rise placed considerable pressure on agriculture to produce enough food for this expanding population. By the time of Elizabeth's death in 1603 the food resources of the country were not sufficient to meet demand.

England was an overwhelmingly agricultural country. The vast majority of the population lived in villages. However, cities and towns did grow in size. The largest city by far was London. In fact London contained two cities: the City of London was the commercial and business centre of the country; the City of Westminster contained the Parliament building and the Palace of Whitehall, making it a centre of government. Town growth occurred not only because of a rise in population but also because of migration from the countryside.

The social structure of Elizabethan England was dominated by the aristocracy. Over the past 50 years historians have debated the importance of the aristocracy. Some have put forward the view that the importance of the aristocracy was in decline. It was faced with the rise in importance and size of the gentry (see page 111).

Elizabeth I's reign was affected by a number of social and economic problems. The problem of rising prices (inflation) affected the early years of her reign and the 1590s. Elizabeth's government overcame the first period of inflation but not the latter. In addition, both central and local governments had to deal with the issue of poverty and vagrancy. During the reign many laws were passed at national and local level which dealt with these problems. By 1603 the idea that central and local government had a responsibility for helping the poor was firmly established.

Agriculture did not experience great change in Elizabeth's reign. This part of the economy was dominated by sheep farming and the production of wool. Wool and woollen cloth dominated overseas trade. These commodities were exported to Antwerp, in the Netherlands. However, this trade was disrupted on a number of occasions by the outbreak of conflict in the Netherlands against Spanish rule.

Cottage industry: Industry where manufacturing occurs in individual's households. Also known as 'putting out'. Householders would acquire raw materials from a central location, manufacture in their own homes and then return the finished work.

Industry was also dominated by the woollen and textile industry. Most industry was on a small scale, with **cottage industry** predominating. During Elizabeth I's reign this industry experienced change. The New Draperies were producing lighter, cheaper cloths for internal trade and export.

Perhaps the most enduring development in the social history of Elizabethan England was the development of drama and poetry. The reign has been described as the 'Age of Shakespeare'. Although the 'Bard of Avon' was the most notable literary figure, others such as the playwright Ben Jonson and the poets Edmund Spenser and John Donne played an important part in the development of English literature.

12.1 What changes took place in the size and structure of the population?

How much did population increase?

During the reign of Elizabeth I the population of England increased considerably. In the 1550s the population had reached approximately three million, rising to around four million by the time of Elizabeth's death in 1603. In this period population growth was limited by two factors. Just before the start of Elizabeth's reign there was a major outbreak of influenza which increased the death rate. In the mid-1590s England suffered from four bad harvests in a row. By 1597 many parts of the country were facing an acute food shortage leading, in some cases, to famine.

The centre for population was the South East and the Midlands. By far the largest city was London. By 1603 it had a population of 130,000–150,000. This made it one of Europe's largest cities, alongside Paris and Naples. To illustrate the size of London in comparison to other English cities, the second largest city in Elizabethan England was Norwich with a population of only 15,000. Other regional centres were Newcastle, Bristol, Exeter and York. Apart from London, there were only 18 towns with populations over 5,000. Around 90% of Englishmen and women lived in villages.

Historians of Elizabethan England have found it difficult to find accurate information on population structure and growth. The most useful sources of information are parish registers. These contain information on baptisms, marriages and funerals. However, they do not contain information about child death shortly after birth as this was before a baptism was seen as necessary.

The main reasons for the increase in population during the Elizabethan period was a rise in fertility and a fall in the death rate. Between 1561 and 1600 the death rate averaged 25 per 1,000. The birth rate averaged 34.5 per 1,000 between 1561 and 1586, falling slightly to 32 per 1,000 by 1600. According to the historian A. G. R. Smith in *The Emergence of A Nation State: The Commonwealth of England 1529–1660*: 'The late Elizabethan era was "a golden period of low mortality" in which the expectation of life at birth exceeded 40 years, a figure not reached again until the 19th century.'

How was Elizabethan society structured?

In studying the structure of Elizabethan society historians have been fortunate that three worthwhile contemporary studies exist. Sir Thomas Smith wrote *De Republica Anglorum* in the 1560s but it was not published until 1583. William Harrison wrote a *Description of England* in the 1570s. Finally, Thomas Wilson wrote *The State of England anno domini 1600*. Each of these studies provides the historian with an insight into the organisation of society at different times in Elizabeth I's reign.

According to William Harrison, English society could be divided into four groups: gentlemen, citizens or burgesses, yeomen and artificers or labourers. Those individuals in the group entitled 'gentlemen' occupied the top section of society. This group included the monarch, the aristocracy and the gentry. To Sir Thomas Smith, Queen Elizabeth was 'the head, and the authoritie of all thinges that be doone in the realm of England'.

Below the monarch came the major landowners of England, the aristocracy, who had the right to sit in the House of Lords. According to the historian D. M. Palliser, the aristocracy numbered 57 at the start of Elizabeth's reign, falling slightly to 55 by time of her death. Families such as the Howards, Percys and Stanleys were members of the aristocracy.

The other group which formed Harrison's category of 'gentlemen' were the gentry. This term has caused problems for historians as it is open to a number of definitions. Suffice to say that the gentry were landowners who did *not* have the right to sit in the House of Lords. They comprised knights of the shires and individuals who could call themselves 'esquire'. The historian Lawrence Stone, in *The Crisis of the Aristocracy*, claims that there were 600 knights in Elizabethan England in 1558. This number fell to 550 by 1603. Esquires were described by Thomas Wilson as those 'gentlemen whose ancestors are or have been knights, or else are the heirs of their houses'. Wilson believed that the combined numbers of knights and esquires in England numbered 16,000 in 1601. This seems a rather high figure.

Elizabethan costume (from left to right): a wealthy merchant; a noble lady; a middle-class lady; a young squire

1. In what ways does the costume of the middle-class lady differ from the noble lady?

2. How do the costumes shown in the illustration help to emphasise the differences in wealth and social structure in Elizabethan society?

Freehold: Ownership of land or property where the owner possesses complete control, including the right to decide who owns the property on their death.

Elizabeth I's England was a predominantly rural society. Therefore, below the 'gentlemen' in order of social importance were yeoman farmers. This group was made up of those who held land by **freehold** to the value of 40 shillings [£2]. However, with inflation in the Tudor period, this definition lost its value. Yeomen were independent farmers who owned their land. Their farms varied in size dependent on the region and type of agriculture. Fifty acres [20 hectares] was an approximate size of a yeoman farm.

Tenants-at-will: Occupant of land or property with no right of control. Could be forced to hand back land or property without forewarning.

Typhus: A contagious disease associated with poor levels of hygiene and poor diet.

Below yeoman farmers came husbandmen. These were farmers who held small amounts of land by various methods of tenure. Some were freeholders. Others were merely **tenants-at-will**. However, the overwhelming majority of the rural population were cottagers or day labourers. These individuals rented small cottages and worked for others. With low wages and poor diet it was this class who were most vulnerable to diseases such as influenza and **typhus**. During the periods of poor harvests in the 1590s many suffered badly. In some parts of the North West many suffered starvation and famine.

1. What reasons can you give to explain the rise in population during Elizabeth I's reign?

2. William Harrison divided Elizabethan society into four groups: gentlemen, citizens or burgesses, yeomen and artificers. How accurate do you regard his description as being?

Townspeople in Elizabethan England comprised only a small proportion of the population. Throughout the reign towns grew, mainly due to migration from the countryside. In towns at the top of the social ladder were burgesses and merchants. This group not only possessed the most wealth but also occupied the key positions in town government. During the last half of the 16th century, the legal and medical professions became more important in town life.

Beneath these groups came the artificers or skilled craftsmen. This group comprised craftspeople such as masons, tailors, butchers and carpenters. The Statute of Artificers of 1563 laid down that craftsmen had to complete a seven-year apprenticeship before qualifying. The Act also laid down the rates of pay to be received within each craft. At the bottom of the social scale came casual labourers. This group was usually made up of migrants from the countryside. It was also the group who, in hard economic times, provided the main source of vagrants and beggars.

12.2 How far did society change during Elizabeth I's reign?
A CASE STUDY IN HISTORICAL INTERPRETATION

There has been considerable debate among historians about the nature and extent of change in Elizabethan society. Rising prices, a growing population and major changes in landownership brought about by religious upheaval resulted in social change. How great was this change? Which groups, in society, were most affected?

Was there a crisis of the aristocracy?

In 1941, in an article in *Proceedings of the British Academy*, the historian R. H. Tawney stated that the ownership of property had seen major changes in the century before the outbreak of the Civil War in 1642. He believed that the old-fashioned, large-scale landowners, the aristocracy, had begun to decline in importance. Increasingly, a new class of landowners, the gentry, was rising in both wealth and social importance.

In 1948, Tawney's views were taken up by Lawrence Stone. In a historical article in the *Economic History Review* entitled 'The anatomy of the Elizabethan aristocracy', Stone accepted the view that the aristocracy had declined in importance. However, he believed this was due mainly to over-expenditure on their part. He stated that over 60% of the aristocracy were facing financial ruin by the time of Elizabeth's death.

Then in 1953, in an article in the *Economic History Review* entitled 'The gentry, 1540–1640', Hugh Trevor-Roper (later Lord Dacre) criticised Stone's view. He believed that Stone had wrongly interpreted historical evidence on the amount of debt owed by the aristocracy. He also stated that instead of a rise in the importance of the gentry, there had been a 'massive decline' in what he called the 'mere' gentry. These were small-scale landowners. Trevor-Roper believed these had suffered economic decline due to rising prices (inflation). He pointed out that some members of the gentry rose in importance. These were usually courtiers or merchants who were involved in monopolies (page 115) at the end of Elizabeth I's reign.

By 1959 Trevor-Roper's views were under attack from Perez Zagorin in an article entitled 'The social interpretations of the English Revolution' in

Copyholders: A form of land ownership where a person leases land but over a long period. The copyholder could pass on the lease to his/her children.

1. From the evidence contained in this section, do you think the aristocracy declined in power and influence during Elizabeth's reign? Give reasons for your answer.

2. Why do you think historians have differed in their views on the aristocracy and gentry in Elizabeth's England?

Study the information contained in the table on the right.

1. In which decade did nominal wage rates rise the most for:

a) skilled workers

b) unskilled workers?

2. In which decade was the gap between nominal wages and real wages at its greatest for:

a) skilled workers

b) unskilled workers?

Can you give a reason why this gap may have arisen?

3. During Elizabeth I's reign did the standard of living rise or fall for skilled workers and unskilled workers in London? Give reasons for your answer.

the *Journal of Economic History*. Zagorin's main concern was the lack of important links in Trevor-Roper's argument. He felt Trevor-Roper had made a rather dubious link between gentry who owned small farms and estates and the effects of rising prices. In 1961 J. R. Hexter in *Reappraisals in History* made an important observation on Trevor-Roper's views. Hexter pointed out that in his attempt to explain the outbreak of civil war in the 17th century Trevor-Roper had tried to prove that the gentry had risen in importance at the expense of the aristocracy, thereby providing a strong economic reason for that conflict.

In 1983 the economic historian D. M. Palliser, in *The Age of Elizabeth*, points out that the gentry did increase in wealth and number during the reign of Elizabeth I but not necessarily at the expense of the aristocracy. New lands had become available following the dissolution of the monasteries and chantries (page 131). There was also a rising population. Therefore, greater wealth could be earned from agriculture. Therefore, the proportion of landed wealth owned by the gentry increased. This trend was made worse by Elizabeth I's reluctance to increase the number of lords.

In *The Later Tudors*, published in 1995, Penry Williams believes that the evidence available suggests that landowners did prosper, in particular after 1570. However, he states that not all landowners were successful:

> Revenues had to be raised to meet inflation and this might be difficult for landlords with estates largely held by **copyholders**. By and large the adjustment seems to have been hardest for the lesser (mere) gentry, who lacked the reserves to meet periods of crisis.

Did the standard of living fall for skilled and unskilled workers in London?
A STUDY IN STATISTICAL EVIDENCE

Nominal[†] and real wage[*] rates in London 1550–1599

Decade	Nominal rates of pay		Real rates of pay	
	Skilled [artificers]	Unskilled [artificers]	Skilled	Unskilled
1550–59	148	159	70	75
1560–69	173	200	78	90
1570–79	189	200	79	84
1580–89	200	200	79	84
1590–99	209	222	67	71

[†] 'Nominal wages' refers to the amount of money received.

[*] 'Real wages' refers to the amount of goods money will buy. Real wages fall in times of price rises (inflation).

The numbers in the table are index numbers based on the base decade of the 1460s.

Therefore, 1460s = 100.

Example: the nominal rate of pay for skilled workers in the 1550s is 148. This means that nominal wages were 48% higher than in the 1460s.

12.3 How successful was Elizabeth's government in dealing with the problem of inflation?

A general rise in prices, known to economists as inflation, affected Elizabeth I's reign at her accession and in the 1590s. The issue was seen as sufficiently important to be included on Elizabeth's tomb in Westminster Abbey, London. Her ability to end the inflation at the beginning of her reign was placed alongside other achievements, such as the establishment of the Church of England and the defeat of the Spanish Armada.

What caused inflation in Elizabethan England?

In 1549 *A Discourse of the Common Weal of this Realm of England* was published. It is most probably the work of Sir Thomas Smith who later wrote a survey of Elizabethan England. In this pamphlet he laid the cause of inflation at the door of the debasement of the coinage (page 115) during the last years of Henry VIII. The proportion of gold and silver in coins was secretly reduced in 1542–44. A public debasement followed in the year 1544–45.

Clearly, the reduction of bullion in coins did lead to a rise in prices. This can be explained through the 'Quantity Theory of Money'. Irving Fisher, an economist, put forward this view in 1919. It stated that an increase in the supply of money into an economy can lead to a general rise in prices. The theory is explained through the use of a formula:

$$MV = PT$$

(M is the supply of money. V is the velocity (or speed) with which this money circulates within an economy. P is the price level. T is the number of transactions involving the use of money in an economy.) It is accepted by monetarist economists that V and T remain relatively constant. Therefore, any increase in M leads to an increase in P. This causes inflation.

The need to debase the coinage was due to the high cost of warfare during the last years of Henry VIII's reign and the rule of Protector Somerset. For instance, the approximate cost of Henry's wars of the 1540s was £3.6 million. Unfortunately, taxation produced only £1 million. Even the sale of monastic lands only brought in £1 million. Therefore, there was a shortfall of £1.6 million. This gap was to be closed by issuing more coins from the same limited amount of gold and silver available.

Although the Quantity Theory of Money helps explain why inflation occurred at the start of Elizabeth's reign, it does not explain why inflation returned in the 1590s. By the last decade of Elizabeth's reign the rise in population meant that demand was outstripping food resources. This was combined with a series of poor harvests, beginning in 1594, which meant demand greatly exceeded supply. The considerable rise in the price of a staple food, such as corn, helps explain why inflation reappeared.

However, R. B. Outhwaite in *Inflation in Tudor and Early Stuart England* states that 'we must avoid making population pressure do all the work' in explaining the inflation of the 1590s. Inflation affected all of western Europe, not just England. One factor which helps explain western European inflation is the importation of large amounts of silver from Spanish mines in the New World, such as Potosi in Peru. This increased the supply of money. There were also increased government costs resulting from war with Spain and rebellion in Ireland. These helped increase demand for goods, thereby forcing up prices.

1. What reasons can you give to explain why inflation occurred in Elizabeth I's England?

2. What policies did Elizabeth I's government take to control inflation?

3. How successful was Elizabeth I's government in dealing with inflation during her reign?

What actions did Elizabeth's government take to deal with inflation?

In December 1560 the government ordered that all debased money be returned. This was replaced by new coins containing more silver, thus returning the quality of coinage to the position it held before the debasement of 1542–44. The recoinage was completed by October 1561. This policy had the effect of limiting the money supply and re-establishing public confidence in the coinage. Fortunately for Elizabeth I her stocks of silver were increased by the acquisition of the Genoese loan in 1568 (see Chapter 11).

The government also attempted to limit demand through controlling wages. The Statute of Artificers of 1563 set wage limits for skilled workers. Unfortunately, the reappearance of inflation in the 1590s meant that the standard of living of these workers fell as the cost of living rose.

12.4 How did Elizabethans deal with the issues of poverty and vagrancy?

In an article in *The Reign of Elizabeth I* entitled 'Poverty and Social Regulation in Elizabethan England' Paul Slack stated: 'After the Anglican Church, the English poor law was the most long-lasting of Elizabethan achievements.'

During Elizabeth I's reign a long list of Acts were passed to deal with poverty and vagrancy. In 1563, 1572, 1576, 1597 and 1601 Parliament introduced laws which lasted, with minor alteration, until 1834. The twin issues of poverty and vagrancy did not only interest central government. Many towns dealt with these issues through local laws. Norwich, Ipswich and Cambridge were three East Anglian towns which introduced laws dealing with the poor. Policy at national and local level had to deal with two problems. Firstly, how should the government punish and deter vagrants and beggars? Secondly, what should they do to help 'the deserving poor' such as orphans, the elderly or the infirm?

A contemporary woodcut illustration of beggars. The title reads (from left to right): 'Beggers Bush', 'A Maundering [travelling] Begger' and 'A gallant Begger'. The two people under the 'begger's bush' are physically handicapped.

1. What message is this woodcut trying to convey about beggars in Elizabethan England?

2. Use the information in this section. How did Elizabethan government attempt to deal with the types of beggar shown in the woodcut?

What were the causes of poverty in Elizabethan England?

In a study on poverty and vagrancy in Tudor England (published in 1994), the historian John Pound notes various reasons to explain poverty. He states that the rise in population (43% between 1550 and 1600) helped put pressure on limited food resources. This was most important during the 1590s. In addition, harvest failure created famine or near-famine (dearth) conditions. The worst decade for these problems was the 1590s. However, there were poor harvests earlier in the reign, such as 1556 and 1586. As a result, dearth conditions existed across England in 1555–57, 1586–87 and 1596–97.

Another cause of poverty was the outbreak of illness, including plague. The reign began with the effects of the influenza epidemic, which had affected the end of Mary's reign. There was also a smallpox epidemic in 1562 which almost took the life of the Queen. Throughout the reign there were severe outbreaks of plague in towns. The plague outbreak in London in 1563 accounted for the deaths of over 20% of the city's population. There was also epidemics in 1583–86 and 1590–93.

The enclosure and engrossing of land (see pages 111–19) in the past has been blamed for creating poverty in the countryside. However, by the start of Elizabeth I's reign the enclosure of common land had passed its peak. It was only during the crisis of the 1590s that the issue of **husbandry and tillage** was again regarded as a major economic problem. In 1598 Parliament passed the Act on Husbandry and Tillage which attempted to retain tillage, and with it employment, in the countryside.

Husbandry and tillage: Husbandry refers to pastoral farming, tillage refers to arable farming.

The problem of inflation also caused poverty through the rise in the cost of living. During Elizabeth I's reign the Statute of Artificers had placed an upper limit on the wages of skilled workers. At the same time, the standard of living of most town workers fell as a result of rising prices. Unemployment in towns was also made worse by the embargoes on wool exports to the Netherlands in 1563–64, 1568–73 and in the 1580s.

Finally, the end of warfare placed large numbers of soldiers and sailors in a position of poverty. For instance, after the cancellation of an attack on Portugal in 1589, large numbers of discharged soldiers and seaman roamed the southern counties of Kent and Sussex.

Who were the poor?

According to the historian A. L. Beier about half the population of Tudor England were unable to support themselves. These included those members of society who were incapable of work, such as the very young or very old. Also included were the infirm, such as the blind or physically disabled. It also included widows – a social group who found it very difficult to find work. During periods of harvest failure and depressions in the cloth trade, the numbers would be increased with the inclusion of families who merely fell 'on hard times'. These groups comprised 'the deserving poor'.

Poverty was at its greatest in towns. In a census in Norwich, made in 1570, the poor comprised approximately 25% of the population (500 men, 850 women and 1,000 children). Added to this list were the 'undeserving poor' who were seen as a threat to social order. They included rogues and villains who made a living from crime. There were also beggars. Former soldiers and sailors were often reduced to begging or a life of crime. This group was feared, in particular, because they were usually armed. Finally, this group would also include migrants who would leave their own area to look for work. Cities such as London and Norwich had large numbers of migrant workers.

Under the terms of the 1576 Poor Law Act a third category of poor was created: the deserving, able-bodied unemployed. These were given the opportunity to work in return for some **poor relief**.

Poor relief: Giving assistance to the poor. This could be money, housing or work.

What actions were taken to deal with poverty and vagrancy?

The actions by the national government in Elizabethan England to deal with these issues stand as a major example of government intervention to maintain social control and order.

A major theme of government policy was to deter and punish the undeserving poor. The 1563 Act continued the policy begun earlier in the Tudor period of whipping able-bodied beggars. This was followed, in 1572, by an Act for the Punishment of Vagabonds and for the Relief of the Poor. This was the harshest law of Elizabeth I's reign. It was passed following the Rebellion of the Northern Earls (1569–70). The government feared more outbreaks of disorder. This Act declared that all vagabonds above the age of 14 were to be whipped and burned through the right ear unless some honest person took them into **domestic service**. The Act also allowed for imprisonment for a second offence for vagabondage and the possibility of execution for persistent offenders. Any children of a convicted beggar were to be placed in domestic service. Ear-boring and execution were not removed until 1593.

Domestic service: Work in a household which usually involved cooking, cleaning etc.

A vagrant being whipped through the streets of a town. In the distance (left) is the gallows – a reminder of what might happen to the vagrant.

1. Use the information in this section. Which Acts of Parliament encouraged the treatment of vagrants shown right?

2. Study the two illustrations on vagrancy and beggars (here and on page 299). Why do you think these two woodcuts were produced in Elizabethan England? You might consider the audience for each illustration.

A more enlightened approach was put forward in the 1576 Act for the setting of the poor on work, and for avoiding idleness. For the first time towns were required to give the unemployed some work. This would involve setting up stocks of wool and other commodities for the poor to work on. If any member of the poor would not work then they were to be placed in a local prison. The prison would be financed from a local tax, the rates.

However, during the economic crisis of the 1590s Parliament was forced into passing harsher laws against the 'undeserving poor'. In 1597 the Act for the Punishment of Rogues, Vagabonds and Sturdy Beggars was passed. The Act demanded that all counties and cities should have local prisons to house these groups. In addition, anyone caught offending for the first time was to be whipped and then sent back to the parish of their birth. Those individuals who continued to re-offend were to be sent to the **galleys**, or could be executed.

Galleys: A type of warship with sails and oars. Large numbers of oarsmen were required. Once sent to the galleys, offenders were rarely freed.

In addition to deterring the undeserving poor, the Elizabethan government extended the power of the central government on matters relating to helping the poor. The 1563 Act declared that anyone who refused to pay for the aid of the poor could face imprisonment. It also introduced fines from £2 to £20 for officials who failed to organise help for the poor. The 1572 Act established, for the first time, a national poor law rate (tax). This Act was a turning point in helping the poor. For the first time towns were given the responsibility for providing work for the able-bodied unemployed.

Finally, the 1597 Act for the Relief of the Poor laid the foundations for the poor law for the next 250 years. It declared that each parish should appoint an 'overseer of the poor'. This official had the task of finding work for the young unemployed. He also had to hand out help to the 'deserving poor'. The Act also gave overseers the right to take away goods and property from anyone who refused to pay taxes to aid the poor.

Apart from Acts of Parliament the central government took other actions to aid the poor. The Privy Council made efforts to increase the food supply during periods of food shortage. In 1576 it ordered the government of the City of London to buy corn. It also intervened to prevent the export of corn during the 1590s.

Town governments also played a major part in providing assistance for the poor. The historian D. M. Palliser notes that, by 1569, the East Anglian town of Ipswich had established a compulsory poor tax, a school for the young poor, a local house of correction and a hospital for the poor. England's second city at the time, Norwich, followed with a detailed town plan to deal with poverty and vagrancy in the 1570s. In London five hospitals were established, including the Bethlehem hospital for the insane, the Bridewell for vagrants and Christ's for orphans.

An important source of aid for the poor came from private charity. The most important groups to provide aid were merchants and tradesmen. Aid was usually made in a bequest in a will.

How successful were government actions?

The fact that the 1597 and 1601 Poor Law Acts remained in force for over 250 years is a measure of their success. By the time of Elizabeth I's death central government had accepted the responsibility of providing a minimum level of subsistence for the poor. In addition, one of the main aims of the Poor Law was to prevent major disturbances and outbreak of disorder by the poor. Even though Elizabeth's reign saw periods of great food shortages, there were no major disturbances. As historian Penry Williams states in *The Tudor Regime*: 'Even the combination of war and harvest failure in the 1590s produced no serious eruption by the dispossessed.'

However, John Pound takes a more moderate view on the effect of government action in *Poverty and Vagrancy in Tudor England*. He believes that contemporaries exaggerated the problem. He notes that 'both poverty and vagrancy were fairly well contained, and to say that either created a dangerous national situation would be to strain the evidence'.

1. What caused poverty and vagrancy in Elizabethan England?

2. What actions were taken to help the deserving poor and deter vagrancy?

3. How successful were government policies in dealing with poverty and vagrancy?

Source-based questions: The Poor Law

SOURCE A

With us the poor is commonly divided into three sorts, so that some are poor by impotency [not through their own fault], as the fatherless child, the aged, blind, lame, and the diseased person that is judged to be incurable: the second are poor by casualty, as the wounded soldier, the decayed householder, and the sick person visited with grievous and painful disease; the third consisteth of thriftless poor, as the rioter that hath consumed all, the vagabond that will abide nowhere but runneth up and down from place to place, and finally the rogue and the strumpet [prostitute].

From A Description of England *by William Harrison, 1577.*

SOURCE B

Names of the Poor to be Reviewed Weekly in St Peters of Southgate

Richard Rich of the age of 35 years, a husbandman which worketh with Mrs Cattrell and keepeth not with his wife and helpeth her little. And Margaret his wife of the age of 40 years she spins and Joan her daughter, of the age of 12 years, that spins also. Peter Browne a cobbler [shoemaker] of the age of 50 years and hath little work. And Agnes his wife of the age of 52 years that worketh not, but have lain sick since Christmas. She spins having three daughters, the one of the age of 18 years, the other of the age of 14 years, the which all spin when they can get it, but now they are without work.

From The Norwich Census of the Poor, *1570.*

SOURCE C

And when the number of the said poor people forced to live upon alms [charity] be by that means truly known the said justices, mayors, sheriffs, bailiffs and other officers shall within like convenient time devise and appoint, within every their said divisions, meet and convenient places by their discretions to settle the same poor people for their habitations and abidings, if the parish within which they shall be found shall not or will not provide for them; and shall also within like convenient time number all the said poor people within their said several limits, and thereupon set down what portion the weekly charge towards poor relief and sustentation of the said poor people will amount unto within every their said several divisions and that done, they ... shall by their good discretion tax and assess all and every the inhabitants, dwelling in all and every city, borough, town, village, hamlet and place known within the said limits, to such weekly charge as they and every of them weekly contribute towards the relief of the said poor people.

From An Act for the Punishment of Vagabonds and for the Relief of the Poor and Impotent, 1572.

---

1. Study Sources A and B.

In which 'sorts' of poor, mentioned by Harrison in Source A, would you place the people mentioned in Source B? Give reasons to support your answer.

2. Study Source B.

How useful is this source to a historian writing about the poor in Elizabethan England?

3. Study Source C.

How, by its use of language and style, is it possible to tell that this is an official document?

4. Study Sources A, B and C and use information from the chapter.

How were the poor (mentioned in Sources A and B) dealt with by central and local government during Elizabeth I's reign?

12.5 How far did trade and industry change during Elizabeth I's reign?

Were there any major changes in the pattern of trade?

A popular view of Elizabeth I's England is that trade went through consider-able change. The foundation of the Muscovy, Levant and East India companies seem to support this view. However, the vast majority of trade during Elizabeth's reign was internal or coastal. Goods were transported within England either by road or navigable river. In addition, a coastal trade along the east coast brought bulky goods such as coal from Newcastle and the North East to London. Internal trade by road employed the extensive use of packhorses. Packhorse routes through the Lake District and across the Pennines linked Westmorland with Cumberland (both these counties are now in Cumbria) and Durham, and Lancashire with Yorkshire.

On the navigable rivers small commercial craft brought cities such as York into contact with Hull and trade with the continent. Merchants from York were able to transport woollen cloth and lead down the rivers Ouse and Humber to Hull. In return, they transported fish and coal back to York.

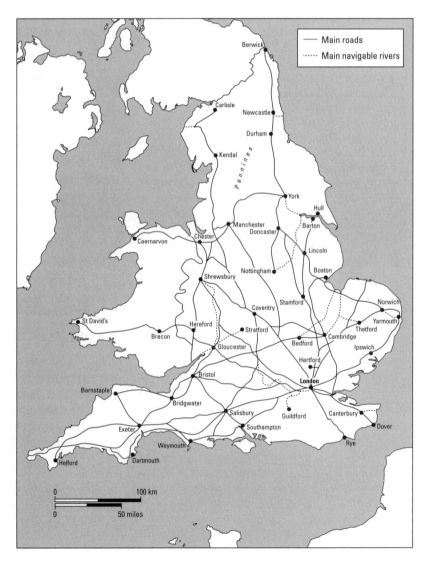

Main roads and navigable rivers in England, 1600

1. Describe the pattern of trade with the Baltic and Mediterranean areas as shown in the map.

2. How far was English trade with the Baltic different from English trade with the Mediterranean? Give reasons to support your answer.

In external trade the main commodities were woollen cloth and goods to the Merchant Adventurers' staple in Antwerp, in the Netherlands. (For a fuller coverage of the Netherlands trade see Chapter 11.) During Elizabeth I's reign the Netherlands trade was interrupted by trade embargoes on English goods made in 1563–64, 1568–73 and 1586–88. These embargoes forced English merchants to seek out new outlets for English woollen goods. Emden in East Friesland and Hamburg in north Germany were both chosen for short periods during these embargoes.

Although the trading companies to the Levant and the East Indies were to play an important role in English trade in the 17th century, they had little impact on Elizabethan trade.

Trade in the Baltic and the Mediterranean during Elizabeth I's reign

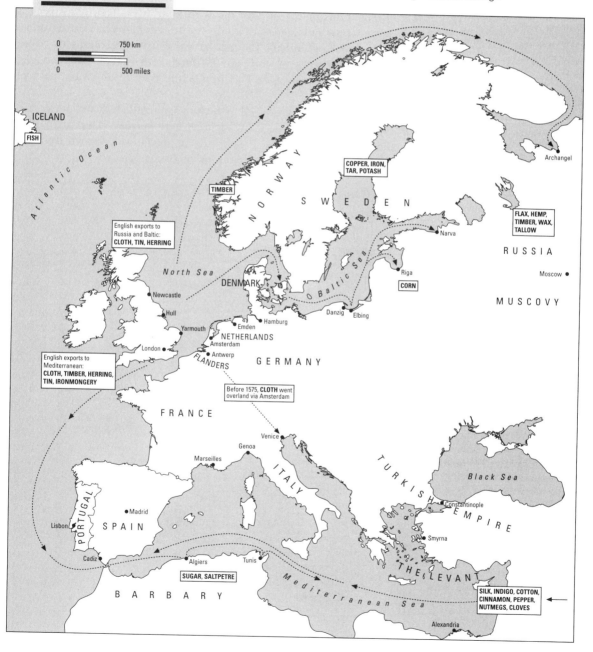

What changes took place in industry?

Compared to areas such as the Netherlands, England was a backward, undeveloped country in industry. The vast majority of industrial concerns were family businesses. The business was managed and operated by a craftsman (artificer) who was involved directly in the manufacturing process. Craftsmen were organised into craft guilds. These guilds had the purpose of setting standards for the quality of work and wage rates. The 1563 Statute of Artificers contained detailed information about wage rates and the supply of labour in each craft. In any large town a wide variety of crafts could be found, such as bakers, tailors, weavers, shoemakers and carpenters. In the countryside an important craftsman was the blacksmith.

England produced a wide variety of goods and materials during Elizabeth I's reign. These included iron, coal and lead. However, the most important industry by far was the textile industry. This industry was located near the raw material (wool). It also required water power and a plentiful source of workers. Production was usually decentralised – work was 'put out' to workers who manufactured cloth in their own cottages. The industry was centred on East Anglia, the West Country and parts of west Yorkshire.

The main products produced by the English textile industry at the start of Elizabeth I's reign were broadcloths and kerseys. The latter were smaller and lighter fabrics. Usually the products were known from the place of manufacture such as 'Tauntons' or 'Bridgwaters'.

1. Describe the nature and location of industry shown in the map of industry in Elizabethan England.

2. Use the information in this chapter. Why was the woollen industry located in East Anglia, west Yorkshire and the West Country?

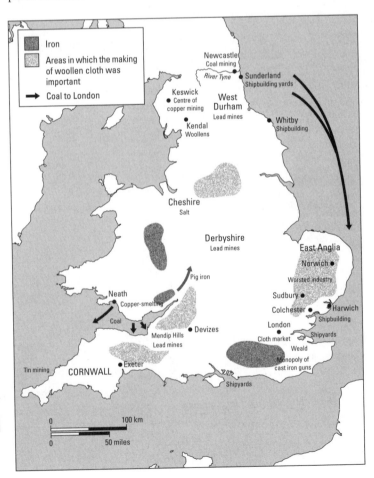

Industry in Elizabethan England

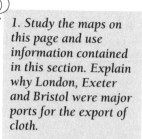

1. Study the maps on this page and use information contained in this section. Explain why London, Exeter and Bristol were major ports for the export of cloth.

2. Explain the pattern of broadcloth exports in the graph.

3. Use information in this chapter and in Chapter 11. Why was there a major fall in the export of broadcloths in the 1560s and 1570s?

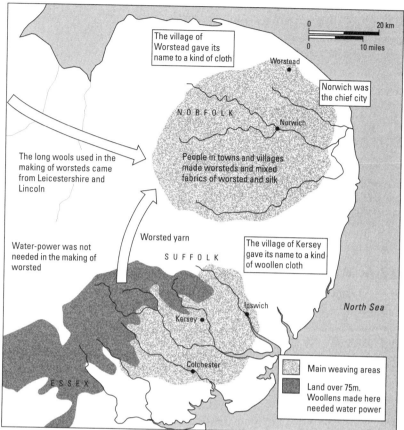

The village of Worstead gave its name to a kind of cloth

Norwich was the chief city

N O R F O L K

The long wools used in the making of worsteds came from Leicestershire and Lincoln

People in towns and villages made worsteds and mixed fabrics of worsted and silk

Water-power was not needed in the making of worsted

Worsted yarn

S U F F O L K

The village of Kersey gave its name to a kind of woollen cloth

North Sea

E S S E X

Main weaving areas

Land over 75m. Woollens made here needed water power

The woollen industry in East Anglia

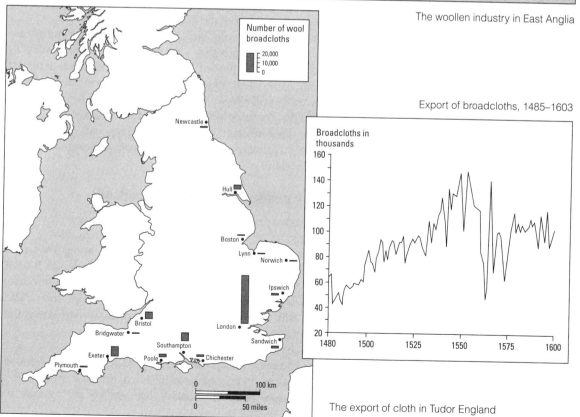

Number of wool broadcloths

20,000
10,000
0

Export of broadcloths, 1485–1603

Broadcloths in thousands

The export of cloth in Tudor England

Long-stapled wool: Long wool which could be combed instead of carded before conversion into yarn. Carding was a more expensive process involving a wire brush or teezels.

1. *Explain the pattern of trade during Elizabeth I's reign.*

2. *How far did trade and industry change during Elizabeth I's reign?*

A major change took place in the textile industry from the 1560s onwards with the development of the 'New Draperies'. These were cheaper and lighter cloths. This new development was due, in part, to a scarcity of wool. These new fabrics were made from **long-stapled wool**. An example of this new cloth was a worsted, named after a village in north Norfolk.

Of greater significance was the arrival from western Europe of textile workers. The outbreak of disturbances in the Netherlands from the mid-1560s and the French Wars of Religion led to large numbers of Protestants seeking refuge in England. They brought with them their skills in textile manufacture. Eventually English manufacturers began to copy these techniques.

12.6 Were there any changes in the pattern and development of agriculture?

A survey of agriculture

Elizabethan England was an overwhelmingly agricultural economy. However, there was a wide variety of agricultural practices across the country. The type of farming depended mainly on geographical and climatic factors. For instance, wool production was dominant in the Fenland area of eastern England. This low-lying, former marshy area was ideal for sheep grazing. In north-west England, in the Cheshire Plain, the climate and terrain allowed the development of the Cheshire cheese industry.

In simple terms, farming could be divided into different categories. Arable farming involved the planting and harvesting of crops such as corn. Arable land was usually divided into three strips with one strip left fallow (with no crop) each year. Pastoral farming involved the grazing of livestock such as cattle and sheep. Mixed farming, as the term suggests, was a mixture of both. An important part of Elizabethan agriculture was woodland farming. This involved the grazing of pigs and cattle. It also involved the cutting of timber, which was the most important building material in Tudor England.

Were enclosures a problem in Elizabethan England?

During the early Tudor period considerable concern was shown by contemporaries towards the adverse effects of enclosure and engrossing. Both processes were associated with the expansion of sheep farming. They were seen as responsible for creating unemployment in the countryside. It took far less workers to tend sheep than to produce arable crops. For instance, Parliament passed laws against enclosure in 1489, 1533 and 1536. However, none of this legislation proved effective in slowing down the rate of enclosure.

By the time Elizabeth I became queen, enclosure was no longer a major issue. However, as Elizabeth's reign came to an end the issue again became important. A succession of bad harvests affected England from 1594. Studies of Leicestershire and Staffordshire had shown an increase in enclosure and rural depopulation in the early 1590s. Parliament passed the Act on Husbandry and Tillage in 1598. This Act, which remained in force until 1624, banned any further conversion of arable land into pasture.

A woodcut from Spenser's *The Shepherd's Calendar*, 1579

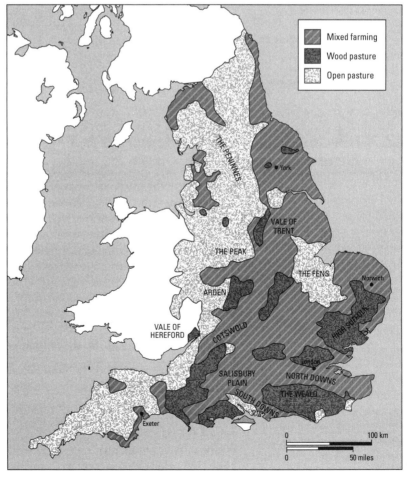

Farming regions in England, 1500–1640

Enclosures in 16th-century
England

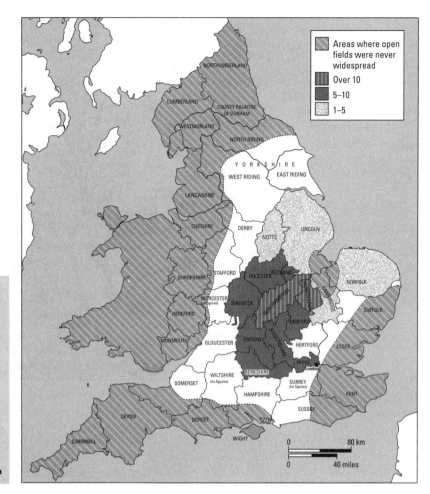

Areas where open
fields were never
widespread

Over 10

5–10

1–5

1. **Describe the pattern
of enclosures in Tudor
England.**

2. **Study the two maps
(right and on page
309). Which types of
farming areas were
most affected by
enclosure? What
reasons can you give to
support this
development?**

12.7 How important were developments in English culture during Elizabeth I's reign?

According to the historian Penry Williams, in *The Later Tudors*, culture can be defined as 'a network of shared values, together with the writings, pictures, performances, festivities, and so on in which they are embodied'. In Elizabethan England it is possible to make a distinction between 'popular culture' and the culture of the educated upper classes, 'high culture'. Popular culture, as the name suggests, was culture enjoyed by most of the population below the educated upper classes. High culture was enjoyed by those who comprised William Harrison's group of 'gentlemen and citizens or burgesses'.

What factors affected the development of high culture?

The development of culture in Elizabethan England was affected directly by social developments earlier in the century. The European Renaissance (see page 23), the 'New Learning', helped increase the level of literacy. Increased interest in learning was aided by the development of printing. Printing helped the development of education and private libraries. Around 5,000 books survive from the late 15th century to 1557. For the period 1580–1603 alone there are approximately 4,300 books still in existence.

In the century before the accession of Elizabeth I many grammar schools were founded. For instance, Stockport Grammar School in Cheshire and Brentwood School in Essex. Edward VI's reign alone saw the creation of a large number of schools which still bear his name. In addition, there was an increase in university places. Cardinal Wolsey founded Cardinal, later Christ Church, College Oxford in the 1520s. To gain a university-level education students could attend Oxford, Cambridge or the Inns of Court in London. The latter provided a legal training. As a result, the level of literacy improved considerably. By 1558 the group William Harrison termed 'gentlemen' were literate. By 1603 so were the majority of yeomen.

High culture was also aided by royal and aristocratic patronage (page 58). Both Henry VIII and Elizabeth I were noted patrons of the arts. Elizabeth's Court became a centre of artistic activity. This was partly due to the 'Gloriana Cult', which was actively encouraged by Elizabeth's supporters. The portrayal of Elizabeth as the centre of national life helped develop popular support for the regime.

How did 'high culture' develop during Elizabeth I's reign?

The two dominant art forms were drama and poetry. To many the 'Age of Elizabeth' is really the 'Age of Shakespeare'. William Shakespeare (1564–1616) began to reach the height of his literary powers during the last years of Elizabeth I's reign. However, Elizabethan drama was not limited to Shakespeare alone. Ben Jonson, who wrote *Volpone the Wolf* and *Every Man out of his Humour*, was also a playwright of repute.

The development of drama was aided not only by patronage but also by the development of theatres, in particular in London. The opening of the Globe Theatre in 1599 and the Fortune Theatre a year later provided the audience for the plays by Shakespeare and other playwrights.

Poetry also went through a period of considerable creativity. Edmund Spenser's *The Faerie Queene* stands out an example of the quality of Elizabethan poetry. It is also an example of literature aiding 'the Gloriana

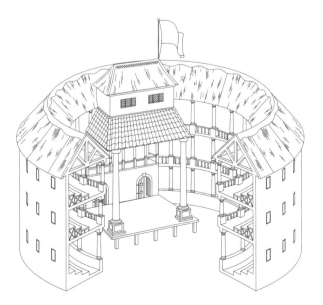

An Elizabethan stage

Cult'. Towards the end of Elizabeth's reign the development of Metaphysical poetry, most closely associated with John Donne, was established.

Unlike drama and poetry, there was little development in either painting or sculpture. In both cases, producing portraits of leading members of society was the main avenue for artists to develop these art forms.

In a broader context there were important developments in English music and architecture. In music, Thomas Tallis, who received royal patronage, wrote in both English and Latin. In architecture, a distinctive English style was developed. Gentry homes such as Little Moreton Hall in Cheshire offer an example of this style.

Little Moreton Hall, Cheshire: an Elizabethan manor house

Study the two Elizabethan houses.

a) What do you regard as the main architectural features of Elizabethan houses?

b) How far are these houses similar in design and construction?

Crooke Hall, near Wigan

How did 'popular culture' develop?

Several medieval pastimes were still popular in Elizabethan England. In rural areas hunting, fishing and archery were followed. Fairs and markets attracted both townspeople and rural dwellers alike. At these events, amateur plays and 'circus-style' acts would take place. There were also spectacles such as bear-baiting and cock-fighting. On a more gory level, public executions attracted large crowds throughout the period. Towards the end of Elizabeth's reign open-air theatres began to attract craftsmen and town dwellers. On a literary level, **ballads** were popular. So were 'chap-books'. These were small, cheap books sold by pedlars.

Ballads: Form of song which told a story.

A feature of 'popular culture' which also survived through to the Elizabethan period was magic and witchcraft. Magic was most closely associated with popular medicine and healing. In a society where a large number of poorer people lacked education, the survival of such ideas is perhaps understandable. In periods of extreme economic hardship, such as the 1590s, the belief that witches were responsible for misfortune was not uncommon.

London from the South Bank in Elizabethan England. London Bridge, with its shops and array of traitors' heads, spans the river, leading to the City (left) and the Tower (right).

1. What factors helped the development of high culture in Elizabeth I's England?

2. How did high culture differ from popular culture? Give reasons to support your answer.

3. To what extent was Elizabeth's reign 'A Golden Age' for English culture?

Further Reading

CHAPTER 2   The reign of Henry VII

Texts designed for GCE AS and Advanced Level students

Henry VII by Roger Lockyer and Andrew Thrush (Longman, Seminar Studies in History series, 3rd edition, 1997)

Henry VII by Caroline Rogers (Hodder and Stoughton, Access to History series, 1991)

The Wars of the Roses: Politics and the Constitution in England 1437–1509 by Christine Carpenter (Cambridge University Press, 1997)

More advanced reading

Government and Community: England 1450–1509 by J. R. Lander (Edward Arnold, 1980)

Henry VII: The importance of his reign in English history by Alexander Grant (Methuen, Lancaster pamphlets, 1985)

Tudor England by John Guy (Oxford University Press, 1988)

Lancastrians, Yorkists and Henry VII by S. B. Chrimes (Macmillan, 1964)

Articles

In *History Review*:
'Henry Tudor and Henry VIII' by C. S. L. Davies (1987 No. 1)
'The reign of Henry VIII and the case of the missing monasteries' by William Makin (Dec. 1993 No. 17)
'Henry VIII: out of the shadows' by Ian Dawson (Sept. 1995 No. 22)

CHAPTER 3   The age of Wolsey

Texts designed for GCE AS and Advanced Level students

Henry VIII by M. D. Palmer (Longman, Seminar Studies in History series, 1978)

The King's Cardinal: The Rise and Fall of Thomas Wolsey by Peter Gwyn (Barrie and Jenkins, 1990)

Henry VIII by J. J. Scarisbrick (Yale University Press, English Monarchs series, 1997)

Wolsey by Alan Pollard (reprinted 1965 with an introduction by Geoffrey Elton)

The Reign of Henry VIII by David Starkey (Collins and Brown, 1991)

England and Europe 1485–1603 by Susan Doran (Longman, Seminar Studies in History series, 2nd edition, 1996)

Advanced reading

Reform and Reformation by Geoffrey Elton (Arnold, 1977)
Tudor England by John Guy (Oxford University Press, 1988)

Articles

In *History Review*:
'Cardinal Wolsey in context' by S. Gunn (March 1991)
'Henry VIII and his ministers' by John Guy (Dec. 1995)

CHAPTER 4   Social and economic change 1485–1547

Texts designed for GCE AS and Advanced Level students

Henry VII by Caroline Rogers, (Hodder and Stoughton, Access to History Series, 1991)

More advanced reading

The Economy of England 1450–1750 by D. C. Coleman (Oxford University Press, 1977)

Inflation in Tudor and Early Stuart England by R. B. Outhwaite (Macmillan, Studies in Economic History, 1969)

Tudor Economic Problems by Peter Ramsey (Gollancz, 1968)

The Age of Plunder: The England of Henry VIII 1500–1547 by W. G. Hoskins (Longman, 1976)

CHAPTER 5   Religious change in Henrician England – the beginnings of the Reformation?

Texts designed for GCE AS and Advanced level students

Henry VIII and the English Reformation by P. G. Newcombe (Routledge, Lancaster Pamphlets 1995)

Henry VIII and the Reformation in England by K. Randall (Hodder and Stoughton, Access to History series, 1995)

Tudor Rebellions by Anthony Fletcher and Diarmaid MacCulloch (Longman, Seminar Studies in History series, 4th edition, 1997)

Advanced reading

Henry VIII and the English Reformation by R. Rex (Macmillan, 1993)

The English Reformation by A. G. Dickens (Fontana, 1967)

The English Reformation by Christopher Haigh (Oxford University Press, 1993)

The Reformation and the English People by J. J. Scarisbrick (Oxford University Press, 1984)

The Stripping of the Altars: Traditional Religion in England, c. 1400–c. 1580 by Eamon Duffy (New Haven, 1992)

The Tudor Parliaments by M. A. R. Graves (Longman, 1985)

The Dissolution of the Monasteries by J. Youings (Allen and Unwin, 1971)

CHAPTER 6   Government, politics and foreign affairs, 1529–1547

Texts designed for GCE AS and Advanced level students

'Foreign Policy in the Reign of Henry VIII' by P. Potter in *The reign of Henry VIII* edited by Diarmaid MacCulloch (Macmillan, Problems in Focus Series, 1995)

'Wolsey, Cromwell and the Reform of Henrician Government' in *The reign of Henry VIII* edited by

Diarmaid MacCulloch (Macmillan, Problems in Focus Series, 1995)

Henry Vlll and the Government of England by K. Randall (Hodder and Stoughton, Access to History series, 1991)

England and Europe, 1485–1603 by Susan Doran (Longman, Seminar Studies in History series, 2nd edition, 1996)

Henry VIII by M. D. Palmer (Longman, Seminar Studies in History series, 1978)

More advanced reading

Tudor England by John Guy (Oxford University Press, 1988)

The Emergence of a Nation State by A. G. R. Smith (Longman, 1984)

Henry VIII by J. J. Scarisbrick (Eyre and Spottiswoode, 1968)

CHAPTER 7   'A Mid-Tudor crisis'?: the reign of Edward VI, 1547–1553

Texts designed for GCE AS and Advanced level students

A Mid-Tudor crisis? by Nigel Heard (Hodder and Stoughton, Access to History series, 1990)

The English Reformation by W. J. Sheils (Longman, Seminar Studies in History series, 1989)

Tudor Rebellions by Anthony Fletcher and Diarmaid MacCulloch (Longman, Seminar Studies in History series, 4th edition, 1997)

More advanced reading

The Emergence of a Nation State: the Commonwealth of England, 1529–1660 by A. G. R. Smith (Longman, 1984)

Tudor England by John Guy (Oxford University Press, 1988)

The Mid-Tudor crisis, 1545–1565 by David Loades (Macmillan, 1992)

The Government Policy of Protector Somerset by M. L. Bush (Arnold, 1975)

The Mid-Tudor Polity edited by Jennifer Loach and Robert Tittler (Macmillan, 1980)

English Reformations: Religion, Politics and Society under the Tudors by Christopher Haigh (Oxford University Press, 1993)

The Later Reformation in England, 1547–1603 by Diarmaid MacCullough (Macmillan, 1990)

CHAPTER 8   'A Mid-Tudor crisis'?: the reign of Mary I, 1553–1558

Texts designed for GCE AS and Advanced level students

A Mid-Tudor Crisis? by Nigel Heard (Hodder and Stoughton, Access to History series, 1990)

The Reign of Mary by Robert Tittler (Longman, Seminar Studies in History series, 1983)

The English Reformation by W. J. Sheils (Longman, Seminar Studies in History series, 1989)

More advanced reading

The Emergence of a Nation State: the Commonwealth of England, 1529–1660 by A. G. R. Smith (Longman, 1984)

Tudor England by John Guy (Oxford University Press, 1988)

The Mid-Tudor Crisis, 1545–1565 by David Loades (Macmillan, 1992)

The Reign of Mary Tudor: Politics, Government and Religion in England, 1553–58 by David Loades (Longman, 1979)

CHAPTER 9   English government under Elizabeth I, 1558–1603

Texts designed for GCE AS and Advanced level students

Elizabethan Parliaments, 1559–1601 by M. A. R. Graves (Longman, Seminar Studies in History series, 2nd edition, 1996)

Elizabeth I by Christopher Haigh (Longman, Profiles in Power series, 1988)

The Government of Elizabethan England by A. G. R. Smith (Arnold, 1967)

William Cecil, Lord Burghley: Minister of Elizabeth I by A. G. R. Smith (Headstart History, 1991)

More advanced reading

The Emergence of a Nation State: the Commonwealth of England, 1529–1660 by A. G. R. Smith (Longman, 1984)

Tudor England by John Guy (Oxford University Press, 1988)

The Later Tudors: England, 1547–1603 by Penry Williams (Oxford University Press, 1995)

The Tudor Regime by Penry Williams (Oxford University Press, 1979)

The Reign of Elizabeth I edited by Christopher Haigh (Macmillan, 1984)

CHAPTER 10   Religion in Elizabethan England

Texts designed for GCE AS and Advanced level students

Elizabeth I: Religion and Foreign Affairs by J. Warren (Hodder and Stoughton, 1993)

The English Reformation 1530–1570 by W. J. Shiels (Longman, Seminar Studies in History series, 1989)

The Elizabethan Parliaments 1559–1603 by Michael Graves (Longman, Seminar Studies in History series, 1987)

English Catholicism 1558–1642 by A. Dures (Longman, Seminar Studies in History series, 1983)

Elizabeth I and Religion 1558–1603 by Susan Doran (Routledge, 1994)

English Puritanism by Patrick Collinson (Historical Association pamphlet, 1983)

More advanced reading

Elizabeth I by Wallace MacCaffrey (Edward Arnold, 1994)

The Reign of Elizabeth I by Christopher Haigh (Addison Wesley Longman, 2nd edition, 1998)

Elizabeth I by Christopher Haigh (Longman, 1988)

The Royal Supremacy in the Elizabethan Church by Claire Cross (Allen and Unwin, 1969)

The Stripping of the Altars by Eamon Duffy (Yale University Press, 1992)

The Elizabethan Puritan Movement by Patrick Collinson (Cape, 1967)

Faith by Statute: Parliament and the Settlement of Religion by Norman Jones (London Swift, 1982)

The Later Reformation in England by Diarmaid MacCulloch (Macmillan, 1990)

The Later Tudors 1547–1603 by Penry Williams (Oxford University Press, 1995)

CHAPTER 11   Elizabethan foreign policy

Texts designed for GCE AS and Advanced level students

England and Europe 1485 to 1603 by Susan Doran (Longman, Seminar Studies in History series, 1986)

Elizabeth I: Religion and Foreign Affairs by J. Warren (Hodder and Stoughton, 1993)

The Tudor Years edited by John Letherington (Hodder and Stoughton, 1994)

More advanced reading

Tudor England by John Guy (Oxford University Press, 1988)

The Emergence of a Nation State by A. G. R. Smith (Longman, 1984)

'The Foreign Policy of Elizabeth I' by G. D. Ramsay in *The Reign of Elizabeth I* edited by Christopher Haigh (Addison Wesley Longman, 2nd edition, 1998)

The Making of Elizabethan Foreign Policy by R. B. Wernham (University of California Press, 1980)

After the Armada: Elizabethan England and the Struggle for Western Europe by R. B. Wernham (Oxford University Press, 1984)

Tudor Foreign Policy by P. S. Crowson (A & C Black, 1973)

The Later Tudors by Penry Williams (Oxford University Press, 1995)

Reformation and Revolution by R. Ashton (Paladin, 1984)

Tudor Ireland by Steven Ellis (Longman, 1985)

CHAPTER 12   Social, economic and cultural history in the reign of Elizabeth I

Texts designed for GCE AS and Advanced level students

Poverty and Vagrancy in Tudor England by John Pound (Longman, Seminar Study in History series, 1971)

The Problem of the Poor in Tudor and Early Stuart England by A. Beier (Methuen, Lancaster Pamphlets, 1983)

More advanced reading

The Age of Elizabeth: England under the Later Tudors 1547–1603 by D. M. Palliser (Longman, 2nd edition, 1992)

The Later Tudors: England 1547–1603 by Penry Williams (Clarendon Press, New Oxford History of England series, 1995)

England's Agricultural Regions and Agrarian History, 1500–1750 by Joan Thirsk (Macmillan, 1987)

The English Woollen Industry, 1500–1750 by G. D. Ramsay (Macmillan, 1982)

English Overseas Trade 1500–1700 by Ralph Davies (Macmillan, Studies in Economic History series, 1973)

Inflation in Tudor and Early Stuart England by R. B. Outhwaite (Macmillan, 1968)

Industry in Tudor and early Stuart England by D. Coleman (Macmillan, 1975)

The Causes of the English Revolution, 1529–1642 by Lawrence Stone (Routledge, 1996) – Chapter 2 'The social origins of the English Revolution'

Index

Glossary terms

Absenteeism 98
Accession Day tilts 220
Acts of attainder 54
Annates 142
Aristocracy 12
Assize Courts 229
Astraea 220
Attaint 76
Avarice 58
Babington Plot 252
Ballads 313
Benefit of clergy 98
Bonds 54
Borough 63
Burgavenny Case 55
Buttery 58
By proxy 45
Capitalism 117
Chamber, The 56
Chantries 131
Chaplaincies 80
Chartered companies 22
Churchwardens' accounts 196
Common land 118
Constable of England 93
Copyholders 297
Cottage industry 293
Council 29
Council's functions 191
Council Learned 29
Coup d'état 183
Courtly romances 74
Court of Augmentations 200
Court of Chancery 19
Court of First Fruits and Tenths 200
Court of Requests 95
Crown 266
Debasement of the coinage 115
Deflationary approach 192
Deputy lieutenants 229
Diocese 81
Domestic service 301
Dowry 47
Duchy of Lancaster 59
Dry Stamp 184
Elevation of the Host 194
Embargo 275
Enclosure 111
Engrossing 119
Escheator 188
Eucharist 193
Evangelicals 193
Excommunication 146
Factional rivalry 184
Fifteenths and tenths 96
Fireship 279
First Fruits and Tenths 241
Foldcourse 188
Freehold 295
Friars 137
Galleys 302
Garrisoning 186
Gentleman usher 80
Gentry 111
Great Councils 43
Habsburg–Valois Wars 84
Hanse 49
Heretics 124
Holy Roman Emperor 38
Homily 185
Household 192
Humanists 133
Hunne Case 136
Husbandry and tillage 300
Iconoclastic Fury of 1556 275
Indulgences 134
Jesuits 252
Justices of the peace (JPs) 13
Kenninghall faction 200
King's Almoner 77
Laity 97
Lay peer 65

Licentious speech 231
Livery 54
Local gentry 30
Lollard 133
Long-stapled wool 308
Lord Chancellor 72
Lord Deputy 36
Lord lieutenant 13
Magnates 11
Maintenance 54
Masques 220
Mercenaries 32
Merchant Adventurers 46
Militia 264
Monopolist 122
Monopoly 115
Musters 201
Nation state 68
'New Learning' 74
New World 116
North West Passage 264
Order of the Garter 53
Over-mighty nobility 43
Oyer and Terminer 76
Palace guard 191
Papal Bull 233
Papal dispensation 33
Papal legate 84
Patronage 58
Patrons 221
Peasants 110
Perfect knight 74
Pluralism 98
Pluralists 136
Poor relief 301
Praemunire 103
Prerogative 61
Primogeniture 285
Principality 65
Privateers 276
Privy Chamber 190
Privy Council 13
Probate 98
Prophesying 257
Proroguing 216
Pulpit 153
Queen's Champion 220
Real wages 117
Recognisances 54
Recusants 229
Regent 78
Regular clergy 98
Relics 136
Relief 59
Religious conservatives 190
Renaissance 23
Requiem Masses 206
Restoration of the coinage 186
Sanctuary 35
Scullery 58
Secular clergy 98
Semi-independent Duchy of Burgundy 43
Sequester 200
Sovereignty 270
Standing army 53
Staple 22
Star Chamber 18
Statute of Uses 155
Statute law 208
Subsistence economy 111
'Te Deum' 206
Tenant farmers 119
Tenants-at-will 295
Tilting 74
Tithes 136
Trade embargo 29
Traditional religious practices 194
Transubstantiation 193
'Tudor despotism' 67
Tudor propaganda 33
Typhus 295
Usurper 29
Vagabondage 119
Vagrancy 12
Wardship 59

Profiles

Alencon, Duke of 264
Allen, Cardinal William 253
Alva, Duke of 269
Anjou, Duke of 264
Aske, Robert 155
Bacon, Francis 217
Boleyn, Anne 139
Brandon, Charles (Duke of Suffolk) 81
Bray, Reginald 30
Cabot, John 49
Cabot, Sebastian 49
Campion, Edmund 253
Cartwright, Thomas 256
Caxton, William 123
Cecil, William (Lord Burghley) 187
Colet, John 133
Coligny, Admiral 269
Cranmer, Thomas 130
Cromwell, Thomas 167
De la Pole, John (Earl of Lincoln) 33
Dudley, Edmund 54
Dudley, John (Earl of Warwick) 183
Dudley, Robert (Earl of Leicester) 220
Empson, Sir Richard 54
Erasmus, Desiderius 124
Farnese, Alexander (Duke of Parma) 278
Field, John 256
Fisher, John 133
Fitzgerald, Gerald (8th Earl of Kildare) 66
Francis I 86
Gardiner, Bishop Stephen 168
Gates, Sir John 183
Grindal, Edmund 257
Hall, Edward 105
Harpsfield, Nicholas 105
Hatton, Christopher 220
Howard, Thomas (13th Earl of Surrey) 35
Howard, Thomas (Duke of Norfolk) 168
James V of Scotland 176
Jerningham, Sir Henry 199
Knollys, Sir Francis 221
Latimer, Bishop Hugh 134
Luther, Martin 129
Margaret of Burgundy 36
Maximilian, Emperor 77
Mildmay, Sir Walter 192
More, Sir Thomas 133
Morton, John 35
O'Neill, Hugh (Earl of Tyrone) 287
Paget, William 167
Parker, Matthew 245
Parr, Catherine 158
Paulet, William 199
Petre, Sir William 200
Pole, Reginald 208
Seymour, Edward 183
Smith, Sir Thomas 186
Stuart, Esme 271
Tyndale, William 134
Walsingham, Francis 217
Whitgift, John 257
Zwingli, Huldrych 194

MAIN INDEX

Abbeys 39, 131, 147–8, 151
Acts of Supremacy 18–19, 24, 156, 193, 214, 233, 239–43, 250, 255, 260
Act of Uniformity (1559) 19, 239–41, 251, 255, 260
Acts of Parliament 60, 64,

70, 96–8, 110, 115–16, 119–21, 128, 140, 143, 146, 151–3, 160, 172, 182, 201, 208, 230, 234, 239–41, 245–7, 251, 260, 292, 299–302, 309
Administration 17–20
Agriculture 12, 22, 110, 117–21, 293, 297, 308–10
Alençon, Duke of 214, 217, 262–3, 269–70, 272
Allen, William 233–4, 253–4
Alva, Duke of 204, 251, 269, 276–7
Amicable Grant 15, 79, 89, 92, 97, 106
Ancrum Moor, battle (1545) 44, 177
Anglicans 245, 248, 252, 255
Anglo–Scottish Treaty (1502) 28
Angoulême, Duke of 51
Angus, Earl of see Archibald Douglas
Anjou 42, 78, 268
  Duke of see Henry of Valois
Annates 142, 145, 150
Anne of Beaujeu 44
Anne of Brittany 44
Anne of Cleves 16, 161–7, 173–5, 178–9, 272
Anne of Denmark 272
Antrim 283–6
Antwerp 22, 46, 50, 113–15, 205, 256, 264, 269, 274–8, 282, 293, 305
Appellants 254
Archpriest Controversy 234, 254
Argyll, Earl of 271
Aristocracy 11–13, 17–19, 22–4, 65, 111, 148, 227, 257, 293–7
Armada see Spanish Armada
Arran, Earl of 272
Arthur, Prince of Wales 16, 28–9, 35, 40, 46–7, 51–3, 60, 64–5, 75, 101, 115, 139, 272–4
Artificers 294–7, 306
Arundel, Duke of 250
Ascham, Roger 234, 238
Aske, Robert 155–7
Attainder 19, 28–9, 33, 40, 53–4, 63, 153, 173, 179
'Auld Alliance' 26, 48, 266, 270
Austria 25, 84–5, 275
Aylmer, John 233
Ayton Treaty (1497) 29, 48

Babington, Anthony 252, 273, 290
Babington Plot 234, 252, 258, 273–5, 279, 290
Bacon, Francis 30, 217
Bancroft, Richard 258
Barnes, Robert 133, 159
Barnet, battle (1470) 32, 52
Barrow, Henry 234, 259
Barton, Elizabeth ('Holy Maid of Kent') 153
'Battle of the Spurs' 71, 77–8
Bayonne 77–8, 268
Beaufort, Margaret 30–2
Beaton, Cardinal 176
Beggars 292, 300–1
Benevolences 35, 107
Berwick 43–4, 177, 304
  Treaty of (1560) 262, 267, 271
Bible 24, 74, 100–1, 123–4,

128–30, 133, 158–60, 174, 236, 242–5, 255–6
Bishop's Book 129, 150, 160
Blackwell, George 254
Blois, Treaty of (1572) 47–8, 262, 269, 277
Blount, Charles (Lord Mountjoy) 263, 280, 288
Boleyn, Anne 16–19, 73, 100–3, 106, 128–30, 139–46, 159, 163–6, 173, 245, 266, 272
Boleyn, Mary 100, 139
Boleyn, Sir Thomas 100
Bonner, Bishop 194, 207
Bonds 29, 53–4, 59–60, 65, 73, 76
Book of Rates 62, 197–8, 201
Books of Common Prayer 24, 182, 185, 193, 227, 238, 245–6, 251, 256–8
Boroughs 63, 201, 224, 227, 231
Boston (Lincs) 113–14, 304, 307
Bosworth Field, battle (1485) 28–30, 33, 38, 43, 52, 59, 63, 81
Bothwell, Earl of see James Hepburn
Boulogne 14, 25, 27, 45, 178, 180, 183–5
  Treaty of (1550) 182, 192
Brandon, Charles (Duke of Suffolk) 16, 21, 71, 81, 107, 272
Bray, Reginald 30, 59, 62, 167
Brehon Law 283, 285
Brest 77–8, 268
Bridgwater 304, 307
Brill 274, 277
Bristol 49, 112–13, 120, 195, 229, 240, 294, 304, 307
  Convention of (1574) 277
Brittany 28, 32, 37–8, 41–5, 78, 268, 280
  Duke of 268
Browne, Robert 259
Bruges, Treaty of (1521) 79, 88
Bryan, Sir Francis 103
Bryant, Alexander 252
Bucer, Martin 162, 193–4, 207, 255
Buckingham, Duke of 25, 32, 35, 52, 71, 81, 93
Burghley, Lord (William Cecil) 167, 187, 191–2, 199, 214–17, 220–7, 231–2, 243–5, 250, 257, 265–7, 273, 277, 289
Burgundy 37, 42–3, 46–9, 58, 74, 78, 268
  Duke of see Charles the Bold
Bury St Edmunds 112–13, 151
Butler of Ormond Rebellion (1570) 262, 283, 286
Byrd, William 222

Cabot, John and Sebastian 49–50, 110, 116, 282
Cadiz 281, 305
Calais 11, 14, 24–7, 40, 43–5, 50, 77–80, 115, 197, 204–5, 234, 262, 266–8, 274, 280
Calvin, John 237, 256
Calvinism 236–7, 246–7, 255–9, 271, 283
Cambrai, League of 77
  Peace of (1517) 86, 102

Cambridge 23–5, 34, 105, 110–13, 124–7, 133, 192–5, 217, 229, 233, 245, 256–60, 299, 304, 311
Camden, William 290–1
Camp, Treaty of (1545) 164, 178
Campeggio, Lorenzo 86, 102, 128, 140
Campion, Edmund 234, 252–3
Canon law 80, 101, 136, 142
Canterbury 23–5, 79–81, 112–13, 126, 131, 150–1, 229, 239–40, 304
   Archbishops of 76, 80, 105, 128–30, 143, 173, 197, 208, 233–4, 239, 245, 255–9
Capitalism 117, 255
Carberry Hill, battle (1567) 262
Carew, Sir Nicholas 103
Carew, Sir Peter 203, 286
Carey, Catherine 221
Carlisle 44, 250, 304
Carthusians 137, 150, 154
Cartwright, Thomas 233–4, 256–8
Carver, Derek 208
Casimir, John 278
Castile 47–8, 77
Cateau-Cambrésis, Treaty of (1559) 84, 242, 262, 266–7, 274
Catherine de Medici 264, 268–9, 272, 277
Catherine of Aragon 16, 23, 27–9, 40, 46–51, 71–8, 89, 99–103, 107, 115, 128–30, 138–44, 165–6, 174, 198, 267, 272–4
Catholic Alliance 269–70
Catholic Counter-Reformation 250, 253–6, 263, 269, 290
Catholic Crusade 273, 278
Catholic League (French) 263, 269, 273, 278
Catholics 23, 105, 122–4, 152–3, 159–61, 204, 226, 232–5, 239, 241–2, 245, 248–54, 260–1, 267–9, 272–6
Catholicism 24, 27, 175, 195–8, 202, 206–12, 216, 234–7, 247–8, 251–4, 259, 263, 272–8, 281
Cavendish, Elizabeth 16, 272
Cavendish, George 80–1, 90, 104, 108
Cecil, Robert (Earl of Salisbury) 17, 21, 214–15, 220–2, 232, 289
Cecil, William *see* Lord Burghley
Chamber 56–62, 91, 170, 219
Chancellor of the Exchequer 163, 168–71, 192, 231
Chancellor, Richard 282
Chantries 131, 143, 160, 182, 186, 194–5
Charles, Duke of Bourbon 88
Charles, Duke of Burgundy 47–8, 77
Charles, Lord Howard of Effingham 218
Charles the Bold (Duke of Burgundy) 43, 77
Charles V (HRE) 49, 71–3, 79, 84–90, 99–102, 134, 139–40, 163–4, 173, 178–80, 193–4, 198, 275

Charles VII of France 32, 38, 43
Charles VIII of France 32, 38, 44–5
Charles IX of France 269
Chaucer, Geoffrey 137
Cheke, John 126
Cheshire 34, 53, 59–60, 228–9, 306–12
Chichester 241–2, 307
Christopherson, Bishop 242
Church in England 13, 19, 23–4, 33, 72, 77, 81, 90–99, 104–6, 110–11, 124–9, 133, 138–47, 150, 155, 158, 169, 193, 204
Church of England 144, 190, 195, 198, 211, 215, 226–8, 232, 239–41, 246, 255, 259–60, 298
Clanrickard, Earl of 284–5
Clarence, Duke of 33, 52
Classical Movement 258
Clement VII, Pope 102, 140–3
Clergy 111, 128, 131, 136–8, 142, 145, 149, 153–5, 185, 210, 240–1, 244–5, 250, 255–60
   benefit of 98, 150
Clifford, Sir Robert (Earl of Cumberland) 16, 21, 38
Cognac, League of 72–3, 89, 100–1
Coinage 23, 64, 110, 115, 122, 178, 182–5, 197, 201, 298–9
Colet, John 123–4, 133
Colet, William 98
Colonisation 282, 286
Commons, House of 19, 54, 63, 96, 111, 121, 133, 141–2, 165, 200, 214, 221, 225–7, 242–3, 248, 256
Communications 12, 64, 228, 289
Compton, William 92, 107
Comptroller of Royal Household 199, 219
Condé, Louis de Bourbon 266–8
Connaught 66, 284, 288
Constable 93, 230–2
Convocation 142, 144, 160, 233, 239–43, 246, 255
Cooke, Sir Anthony 242
Cope, Anthony 227, 234, 258–9
Cope's Bill and Book 214, 234, 258
Cork 37, 283–4
Cornish Rebellion 28, 39–41, 97, 182
Cornwall 15, 186, 229, 280, 306, 310
Council, Royal 29, 80, 142, 183–5, 188, 194, 198–206, 210, 228, 260
Council Learned 18, 30, 54, 59–60, 69, 73, 76
'Council of Blood' 276
Council of the North 19, 25, 34, 60, 163, 170–2, 227–9, 250
Council of Troubles 269
Counting House 58, 219
Court *see* Royal Court
Court of Augmentations 150–1, 170–1, 192, 200
Court of Chancery 19, 72, 90, 94, 168
Court of Requests 95, 119
Court of Wards 170–1, 187, 215, 221
Courtenay, Edward 202–4
Coventry 112–14, 240
Cranmer, Edmund 105
Cranmer, Thomas 105, 128–30, 134–5, 139–43, 152, 158–62, 173,

178–9, 185, 193–7, 207–8
Creighton, Mandell 105
Croftes, Sir James 203
Croker, Sir John 70
Cromwell, Thomas 13, 17–18, 65, 68, 110–12, 121, 126–30, 134–74, 179, 245, 283
Crown 29–30, 37, 49, 52–5, 59–69, 96–8, 113–14, 119–21, 145–7, 156, 167, 182–8, 191–2, 196–7, 200–1, 210, 216, 221–3, 227–32, 246, 266
Culture in Elizabethan England 310–13
Cumberland 25, 34, 44, 65, 177, 214, 229, 304, 310
   Earl of 16, 21, 38
Cusack, Thomas 283
Customs duties 60–3, 114–16, 201

Dacre family 18, 21, 44, 60
Dacre, Lord 44, 65, 93, 250, 296
Darcy, Lord Thomas 157
Darnley, Lord (Henry Stuart) 16, 262, 271–3, 289
Daubeney, Lord 42, 53
Davis, John 282
Davison, William 225, 273
Deane, Henry 80
De la Pole, Edmund (Earl of Suffolk) 40–1
De la Pole, John (Earl of Lincoln) 33, 36
De la Pole, Richard 40
Denmark 50, 235
Denny, Sir Anthony 184, 238
Derby, Earl of *see* Thomas Stanley
Derbyshire 120, 306, 310
Desmond, Earl of 66, 283–7
   Rebellion 262
Devereux, Robert (Earl of Essex) 17–19, 215–23, 263–5, 287
Devon 21, 34, 60, 182, 186, 203, 229, 310
   Earl of 21, 93
Dieppe 268–70, 280
Dissolution of the Monasteries 22–4, 111, 118, 129, 138–9, 147–52, 155–60, 167, 174, 179, 200
Donne, John 293, 312
Dorset, Marquis of 53, 77, 80, 93
Douglas, Archibald (Earl of Angus) 16, 86, 272
Douglas, Lady Margaret 16
Dover 277, 280, 304
Drake, Francis 263, 280–2
Drogheda 66–7
Dublin 24, 36, 65–6, 283–7
Dudley, Ambrose 266
Dudley, Edmund 54, 59, 183
Dudley, Guildford 182–3
Dudley, John (Earl of Warwick; Duke of Northumberland) 12, 21, 33, 37–9, 52, 76, 161, 179, 182–7, 190–200, 203–7, 211–12, 224, 228, 262, 267
Dudley, Robert (Earl of Leicester) 17, 214, 217, 220–1, 224, 227, 231, 234, 250, 256–8, 265–7, 272, 275, 278–9, 289
Durham 25, 34, 44, 65, 98, 151, 177, 195, 222, 229, 240, 249–50, 304, 310
Dutch Revolt 22, 263–4, 269–70, 275, 289

East Anglia 52, 60, 97, 114, 120–1, 182, 186, 198–9, 206–7, 220, 306–7
East India Company 22, 263, 282, 292
East Stoke, battle (1487) 15, 28, 33, 36, 66
Economy 20–3, 293
Edinburgh 44, 177, 267, 271
   Treaty of (1560) 26, 262, 267, 271
Education 12, 23, 111, 123–6, 236, 242, 310–11
Edward III 31–2, 53, 93
Edward IV 17, 30–3, 36–7, 43–5, 49–53, 58, 61–4, 69, 139, 175
Edward V 185
Edward VI 14–16, 19, 24–6, 140, 168, 176, 179, 182–5, 189, 192–200, 207–8, 211–12, 234, 244, 257, 270–2
Egmont, Count of 276
Egremont, Sir John 41
Elizabeth I 11–19, 23–7, 50, 123–5, 128, 140–6, 167–8, 172, 177, 184–7, 190–2, 198–205, 210–27, 233–91, 311–12
Elizabeth of York 16, 28–35, 40, 51, 53, 272
Elizabethan Church Settlement 24, 233–62
Elizabethan government 222–33
Eltham Ordinances 92, 97
Embargoes 275–7, 292, 300, 305
Emden 22, 274–5, 305
Empson, Sir Richard 54, 59, 76
Enclosure 22, 95, 110–11, 118, 122, 182, 186, 308–10
Erasmus, Desiderius 73, 98, 110, 123–6, 133
'Erastian' 236, 239, 247
Essex 174, 195, 206, 215, 229, 253, 258, 275, 307, 311
   Earl of *see* Robert Devereux
Etaples, Treaty of (1492) 28–9, 38, 44–5, 49, 61, 110, 115
Exchequer 18, 57, 60–2, 96, 170, 197, 200
Excommunication 146, 164, 233, 250–1, 260–2
Exeter 112–13, 240, 294, 304, 307–9

Factions 102–3, 156–7, 174–8, 184–5, 222, 289
Farnese, Alexander (Duke of Parma) 263, 278–80
Farsetmore, battle (1567) 286
Ferdinand of Aragon, King of Spain 40, 43, 46–51, 75–8, 85, 99, 275
Ferdinand, Duke of Estrada 51
Feria, Count of 216
Field, John 233, 256–8
Field of the Cloth of Gold (1520) 34, 71, 79, 83, 86–7, 90
First Fruits and Tenths, Court 170–1, 200, 241, 246
Fisher, Bishop John 128, 133, 137, 140, 154
Fisher, Irving 298
Fitzgeralds 66, 283–6
Fitzmaurice Fitzgerald, James 286
Fitzroy, Henry (Duke of Richmond) 16, 100

Flamanck, Thomas 41
Flanders 29, 38, 43, 77, 115, 305
Fleetwood, William 227, 231
'Flight of the Earls' 265, 288
Flodden, battle (1513) 26, 35, 44, 71–2, 78, 177, 267
Florence 42, 50, 85, 101, 115
Flowerdew, John 188
Fotheringay Castle 273, 290
Fox, Bishop Richard 30, 35, 59, 65, 76, 80–1
Foxe, John 162, 207–12, 241–3
France 14–17, 24–9, 32, 38, 42–5, 48–9, 58, 62, 68, 71–3, 76–92, 96, 100–2, 110, 115, 129, 152, 163–4, 174–6, 180, 183–6, 191–2, 197, 200, 204–5, 210–12, 217, 229–34, 238, 242, 248, 256, 262–70, 273–80, 289–91, 305
Franche Comté 46, 85, 264, 275
Francis, Duke of Guise 266
Francis I of France 71, 75, 79, 83–9, 139, 175, 268
Francis II of France 16, 44–5, 266, 271–2
Frederick III 43
Friars 137, 149
Frobisher, Martin 282

Gaelic chieftains 265, 285
Gardiner, Bishop Stephen 137, 154, 163, 167–8, 172, 178–82, 194, 199–204
Garrisons 26, 182, 186, 192, 204, 267
Gates, Sir John 183, 191–2
Genoa 41, 49–50, 305
Genoese Loan 262, 277, 299
Gentry 22, 29, 40, 55, 58–60, 69, 76, 91, 95, 111, 119–21, 147, 155–7, 190, 220, 226, 252–3, 257–8, 293–7
Germany 24, 38, 123, 128, 133, 143, 147, 158, 161, 173, 274, 282, 305
Ghent, Pacification of (1578) 278
Gilpin, George 289
Gloucester, Duke of 52
Gonson, Benjamin 201
Gordon, Katherine 38
Government of England 13, 17–20, 90–9, 116, 167–72
'Grand Enterprise' 79, 88
Granvelle, Cardinal 276
Gravelines 87, 205, 280
Great Seal of England 72, 90, 192
Gregory XIII, Pope 248, 283
Greenwood, John 234, 259
Greenwich, Treaty of (1543) 164, 176
Grey, Henry (Duke of Suffolk) 16, 21
Grey, Lady Catherine 216
Grey, Lady Jane 14–16, 182–4, 191, 197, 203–6, 216, 245
Grey, Lord 267
Grindal, Edmund 233–4, 245, 257
Grocyn, William 123–4
Groom of the Stool 91, 219
Guise, Duke of 269
Guisnes 83, 205
Guistiniani, Sebastian 75, 82

Habsburg, Archduke Charles 272
Habsburg family/lands 38, 43, 73, 84–5, 275
Habsburg–Valois conflict 73, 84–9, 202–4, 266
Hacket Affair 234, 258
Hales, John 96, 186
Hall, Edward 105, 108–9
Hamburg 22, 274–5, 305
Hamilton, James 272
Hampton Court 78, 91, 99, 190
    Treaty of (1562) 262, 266, 276
Harrison, William 294–6, 303, 310–11
Harvests 20–3, 118
Hastings, Henry (Earl of Huntingdon) 21, 221, 228, 256
Hatton, Sir Christopher 214, 220–1, 224, 231, 291
Hawkins, John 262–3, 276–7, 281
Heath, Archbishop 200
Heneage, Thomas 103
Henry of Valois (Henry III of France; Duke of Anjou) 12, 264, 269–72, 277–8
Henry II of France 204, 266
Henry IV of France (Henry of Navarre) 263, 268–70, 280
Henry VII 11–19, 28–70, 94, 106–7, 110–19, 169, 272–4, 282–3
Henry VIII 11–18, 21–9, 34, 38–40, 48–9, 53–4, 62, 71–110, 113–15, 122–86, 192, 198, 204, 208–13, 216, 224, 234, 246, 266–8, 272–4, 283–4, 311
Hepburn, James (Earl of Bothwell) 16, 262, 272
Herbert, Lord (Earl of Pembroke) 21, 32
Heresy 156, 159, 173, 193, 197, 204, 208–9, 276, 279
Heron, Sir John 62
Hertford, Earl of see Lord Protector Somerset
Hicks, Sir Michael 221–2
Holbein, Hans 74, 166–7, 175
Holy Roman Empire 42, 50, 84–7, 102, 175, 234–6, 247, 265
Holy Roman Emperor 38, 43, 71–3, 77, 84–7, 198, 272, 275
Hooper, John 194, 197, 208, 237
Hoorn, Count of 276
Howard, Catherine 16, 158, 161–5, 173–5, 178–9, 272
Howard, John (Duke of Norfolk; Earl of Suffolk) 16, 21–2, 52, 93
Howard family 21, 184, 188, 295
Howard, Sir Edward 77
Howard, Thomas (Earl of Surrey) 33–5, 41, 52–3, 60, 65, 76, 80, 93, 140
Howard, Thomas (Duke of Norfolk) 168, 184
Howard, Lord William 21
Huguenots 266–9, 280
Hull 222, 304–7
Humanists 123–6, 133, 179, 186, 194
Humphrey, Laurence 255
Hunne, Richard 98, 136
Huntingdon, Earl of see Henry Hastings
Husbandry and tillage 22, 292, 300, 309

Inflation 22–3, 111, 117, 121–3, 178, 184–5, 227, 232, 293–300
Influenza epidemic 197–8, 294–5, 300
Injunctions 126, 129, 160, 196, 233, 240–1, 246
Ipswich 25, 79, 93, 98, 112–14, 229, 299, 302–4, 307
Ireland 11, 14–18, 24–8, 33, 36–8, 56, 65–7, 74, 222, 227, 235, 262–5, 274, 279–88, 298
    Church of Ireland 283
Isabella of Castile 40, 43, 46–7, 51
Italy 38, 43–5, 77, 84–6, 89–90, 101, 133, 140, 143, 174, 208, 236, 264, 275, 278, 305

Jackman, Charles 282
James III 48
James IV 16, 29, 38, 48, 64, 71, 74, 77–8, 176, 272
James V 16, 86, 176, 262, 272
James VI/James I 11, 16, 24–6, 31, 41, 215–17, 232, 260, 263–5, 271–2
Jerningham, Sir Henry 199
Jesuits 214, 233–4, 252–4
Jewell, John 245
Joanna of Castile 29, 40
Joanna of Aragon 47–8, 77
John, Don 278
Joinville, Treaty of (1584) 263, 269–70, 273, 278
Jonson, Ben 23, 292, 311
Joseph, Michael 41
Julius II, Pope 47, 71, 75–7, 101, 208
Justices of the peace 13, 18–19, 30, 57, 61, 202, 230–2

Kent 25, 34, 55, 70, 159, 195–8, 203, 206–7, 229, 275, 300, 310
Ket's Rebellion 15, 183–5, 188–90, 198
Kildare (earls) 24, 28, 36, 39, 66, 283–5
    Rebellion 283
King's Book 129, 160
King's Council 165
King's County 284–5
Kinsale, battle (1601) 24, 263, 280, 287–8
Kitchen of Llandaff, Bishop 243
Knollys, Sir Francis 221, 227, 232, 242
Knox, John 256, 271

Lambeth Articles 259
Lancashire 34, 53, 59–60, 155, 195, 229, 232, 248, 252–4, 259, 304, 310
Lancaster, Duke of 59–60
Langside, battle (1568) 262
Latimer, Bishop Hugh 122, 134, 155, 197, 208–9
Law and order 17, 29–30, 56, 60–1, 64–5, 94–5, 116, 121, 164, 185, 224, 230
Lee, Sir Henry 200
Le Havre 252, 257, 268
Leicester 25, 33, 103, 114, 151, 206
    Earl of see Robert Dudley
Leinster 66, 283–4, 288
Leo X, Pope 71, 79, 85–7
Levant Company 22, 282, 304–5
Linacre, Thomas 123–4
Lincoln 81, 137, 149, 240, 307
    Bishop of 60, 65
    Earl of 36
Lincolnshire 159, 229, 310

rising 118, 129, 155
Lisbon 280, 305
Livery 53–5, 70, 93
Lollards 133, 152
London 15, 20, 41–2, 50, 58, 63–7, 79, 84, 90–1, 95–9, 102–4, 110–15, 120–6, 149, 153–4, 157, 169–71, 175, 179, 199, 203, 206–9, 212, 222, 229, 239–40, 245, 250, 253–5, 261, 276, 290, 293–4, 297–8, 300–13
    Bishop of 233
    Bridge 313
    Steelyard 49
    Tower of 33, 37–41, 47, 52, 76, 83, 94, 158, 166–8, 179, 191, 199, 206, 214–17, 258, 273, 290, 313
    Treaty of (1518) 71, 79, 86–9, 182–3
Longland, Bishop 137
Lord Chamberlain 38, 58, 183, 191, 218–19
Lord Chancellor 29, 35, 59, 71–2, 76, 79–81, 94, 103, 107, 128, 133, 140–2, 153, 163, 166–8, 214, 217, 220
Lord Deputy 36, 227, 283–8
Lords lieutenant 13, 18–19, 74, 224, 227–8, 264, 281, 285
Lord Privy Seal 29, 35, 59, 76, 80–1, 163, 168, 171
Lord Protector Somerset see Duke of Somerset
Lord Steward 58, 219
Lord Treasurer 29, 60, 65, 76, 187, 199–201, 214–15, 221
Lords, House of 13, 19, 63–5, 111, 121, 140–2, 166, 200, 226–7, 243, 248, 273, 295
Lords of the Congregation 266, 271, 276
Louis XI of France 43
Louis XII of France 16, 47, 51, 71–2, 78, 81, 84
Lovell, Thomas 35, 59, 61, 167
Loyola, St Ignatius 252
Luther, Martin 71, 128, 133–4, 138, 146, 167, 193–4
Lutherans/Lutheranism 131, 134, 152, 161, 234–8, 246–7

Magnus Intercursus 110, 115
Malus Intercursus 29, 41, 46–7
Man, John 288
Manor houses 312
Marcher lordships 14, 65, 93
Marches, the 19, 44, 53, 60, 177, 228
Margaret of Burgundy 33, 36, 40, 46, 49
Margaret of Parma 276
Margaret of Savoy 47–8
Marignano, battle (1515) 85
Markenfeld, Thomas 250
Marlowe, Christopher 292
Marprelate Tracts 234, 258
Martyr, Peter 194, 207, 255
Mary I/Mary Tudor 11, 15–18, 21, 24–7, 48–50, 71–2, 75, 78, 81, 86–9, 99–100, 130, 145, 167–8, 183–7, 190–2, 195–213, 224, 234, 241, 246, 257, 268, 272–4, 282, 289–91
Mary of Guise 16, 176, 266–7, 270–2
'Mary Rose' 178
Mary, Queen of Scots (Mary

Stuart) 176–7, 186, 214–16, 220, 233–4, 248–52, 258, 262, 267, 271–3, 276–9
Mason, Sir John 266
Master of the Rolls 168–71
Matthew, Sir Toby 222
Maximilian, Archduke/Emperor 37–40, 43–6, 77–8, 85–7
Mayne, Cuthbert 233
Medina del Campo, Treaty (1489) 28–9, 46, 49–50, 115, 274
Medina-Sidonia, Duke of 279
Mercenaries 32, 36, 85, 185
Merchant Adventurers 22, 46, 64, 115, 275, 289, 305
'Mid-Tudor crisis'? 181–212
Milan, Duchy of 42, 51, 85–6, 89, 265
Mildmay, Sir Walter 192, 231
Monasteries see Dissolution of the Monasteries
Monopolies 19, 115, 124, 133, 214, 223, 227
Moray, Earl of 262
More, Thomas 73, 98, 128, 133, 140–2, 153, 157, 163–6, 173
More, Treaty of the (1525) 72, 89
Morton, Archbishop John 30, 35, 59, 94
Morton, Earl of 26, 271
Morton, Nicholas 250
Mountjoy, Lord see Charles Blount
Munster 66, 282–7
    Irish Rebellion 262
Muscovy Company 22, 282, 289, 304–5

Nantes, Edict of (1598) 281
Naples 85–7, 235, 294
National Catholicism 24, 234, 237–8
Naval/militia reforms 201, 210, 264, 279, 281
Naworth, battle (1570) 250
Netherlands (United Provinces) 14, 22, 27, 33, 38, 42–3, 46, 50, 77, 84–8, 110, 115, 152, 204, 225, 233, 256, 259, 263–4, 267–70, 273–82, 289, 292–3, 300, 305–8
Neville, George (Lord Bergavenny) 21, 55
Newcastle 34, 44, 112–13, 177, 229, 249, 294, 304–9
New Draperies 293, 308
Newfoundland 282
New World 116, 276–82, 298
nobility 29, 35, 40, 43–5, 52–6, 59–60, 63, 69, 73, 76–80, 91–2, 95–7, 156–7, 220, 224, 228, 250, 271
Nonsuch, Treaty of (1585) 263, 270, 273, 278
Norfolk 131, 161, 188, 198–200, 206, 229, 307–10
    Duke of 33, 92, 100–3, 106, 148, 152, 156–8, 168, 173–5, 178–9, 184, 214, 233, 250–1
Norris, Henry 92
North America 263–4, 282
Northern Earls see Rebellion of the Northern Earls
Northumberland 25, 34, 44, 229, 310
    Duke of 182–4, 187, 190–200, 203, 206–7, 211–12, 224, 228

Earl of 33, 41, 52, 60, 64, 93, 100, 109, 214, 249–51
North West Passage 264, 282
Norton, Richard 250
Norton, Thomas 226, 231
Norway 42, 50, 235
Norwich 111–14, 120, 151, 198, 240, 259, 294, 299–309
Noyon, Treaty of (1516) 86
Nymegen Convention (1573) 277

Oglethorpe, Bishop 242
O'Neill, Hugh (Earl of Tyrone) 24, 284–8
O'Neill, Matthew 285–7
O'Neill, Shane (Rebellion) 262, 284–6
O'Neill, Turlough 287
Ormond, Earl of 66, 283
Ottoman Empire 86, 235, 265, 282
Over-mighty subjects 43, 58–60, 228
Overseas exploration 49–50, 264, 282
Oxford 23–5, 34–6, 79–80, 95, 110–13, 124–7, 133, 149, 229, 240, 253–5, 310–11
    Earl of 35, 52–5, 60, 76, 98, 206

Pace, Sir Richard 92, 102
Paget, William 167, 180, 183, 187–91, 199–204
Pale, The 18, 24, 65–7, 283–4
Papal bull 233, 250–1, 260–2, 276
Papal legate 71–2, 79, 84–6, 98, 108–9, 136, 140, 197, 208
Papal States 77, 85, 204, 235, 265
Paris 88, 124, 216, 262
Parker, Matthew 233, 245, 255–7
Parkyn, Robert 206
Parliament 19, 30–3, 37, 40–1, 45, 55, 59–64, 72, 76–9, 94–8, 105, 123, 127–30, 138–46, 151–3, 161–71, 180, 187, 212–17, 225–7, 231–4, 239–43, 247–52, 256–9, 272–3, 283, 293, 301, 308–10
Parma, Duke of see Alexander, Farnese
Parr, Catherine 16, 127, 158, 161, 164–5, 179, 238, 272
Parry, Dr Thomas 252
Parsons, Robert 234, 253
Pate, Richard 208
Patronage 58, 91, 98, 220–3, 227, 231, 311–12
Paul IV, Pope 204–5, 208, 242, 248
Pavia, battle (1525) 72–3, 79, 85–6, 89–90, 100–1
Peasants 20, 113–14, 118
Pembroke, Earl of see Lord Herbert
Penry, John 234, 259
Percy family (Earl of Northumberland) 18, 21–2, 41, 52, 295
Percy, Henry 100, 109
Pett, Arthur 282
Philip of Burgundy 40–1, 46–8, 77
Philip II of Spain 12–17, 27–9, 43, 168, 197–204, 209–13, 248, 262–3, 266–9, 273–80, 289
Pilgrimage of Grace 15–17, 97, 119–21, 129, 152–7, 163, 170, 176, 212, 250

Pinkie, battle of (1547) 44, 177, 182, 186
Pius V, Pope 248, 260
Plague 232, 267, 276, 292, 300
Plessis du Tours, Treaty of (1578) 270
Pluralism 98, 136–7, 141, 150
Plymouth 25, 34, 70, 262, 277, 307
Pole, Reginald 197, 204, 207
Pontefract Articles (1536) 156
Poor law 214–15, 227, 230, 292, 299–303
Popes 11, 23, 33–5, 73, 77, 81, 84, 98–102, 129–47, 150, 154, 158, 175, 180, 200, 208, 236, 248–52, 260, 276, 289
Population 12, 22, 25, 110–13, 117–18, 122, 229, 259, 293–300
Portugal 42, 49, 68, 235, 263, 279, 300, 305
Poverty 12, 23, 119, 202, 293, 299–303
Poynings, Sir Edward 28, 66, 283
Praemunire 103, 108–9, 128, 136, 142–4, 150
Prayer Book 194–5, 206
Predestination 246, 255, 259
Presbyterianism 234–7, 254–60, 283
Principal Secretary 167–71, 289
Privy Chamber 34, 58, 76, 91, 102–3, 107, 190, 218–19
Privy Council 13, 17–18, 22, 91, 95, 125, 142, 161–3, 167–73, 179, 183, 187–91, 198–200, 204, 214–16, 224–7, 230–2, 242–3, 257–9, 267, 273–5, 278, 289, 302
Protestantism 23–4, 129–30, 135, 142–9, 158–62, 171, 175, 194–6, 206–8, 234–50, 254, 259, 267–9, 271, 276, 279, 283
Protestant Church in England 143, 244–5
Protestants 11, 131–6, 139, 152, 156–61, 166, 180, 184, 192–210, 216, 221–4, 232–5, 241–8, 256, 260–2, 266–7, 271, 275–6, 283, 308
Puritanism 24, 192, 254–60

Queen's County 284–5

Radcliffe, Thomas *see* Earl of Sussex
Ralegh, Walter 259, 282
Rebellion of the Northern Earls 15–17, 35, 118, 214, 233, 248–51, 272, 276, 279, 301
Recoinage 201, 210, 214, 292
Recusancy 214, 228, 252–4, 261
Redon, Treaty of (1489) 28, 45
Reformation 128, 134–6, 142–3, 159, 252, 266
Parliament 19, 23, 72, 127–8, 140, 144–5,150
Regency Council 129, 158, 184
Regional government 228–31
Religion 12–13, 23–4, 128–62, 271–3

Renaissance 23, 74, 123–4, 310
Renard, Simon 202–4, 209
Requesens, Louis de 269
Retaining 55, 60, 70
Richard II 31, 52
Richard III 17, 28–38, 43, 52, 59, 61, 185
Richard, Duke of York 36
Richmond, Duke of *see* Henry Fitzroy
Treaty of *see* Treaty of Hampton Court
Ridley, Bishop 197, 208–9
Ridolfi Plot 214, 233, 251, 269, 272, 276, 279, 290
Rivers and roads in England 304
Robsart, Amy 272
Rochester 133, 137, 149, 154, 240
Roman Catholic Church 129–36, 142–9, 154, 158, 174, 179, 192–3, 244
Rome 72–3, 79, 84, 99–102, 106–8, 128–34, 138–53, 174, 179, 197, 200, 204, 208, 233, 254, 287
Roper, William 105
Royal Council 33–5, 54–6, 92, 95–7, 100–3, 107, 170
Royal Court 17–22, 56, 74, 80, 91–8, 107, 140, 158–61, 166, 176, 192, 204, 218–23, 226–7, 275, 311
Royal Courts of Justice 90
Royal Divorce (Henry VIII and Catherine of Aragon) 139–46, 164, 169
Royal Household 61–2, 168–70, 184, 191, 218–21
Royal Injunctions 245–6, 254
Royal palaces 34, 58, 63, 90, 96, 218, 233, 293
Royal Proclamations 252
Royal Supremacy 158, 168, 185–6, 190, 212–14, 243–7
Royal Treasury 78, 97, 114
Russell, Lord (Baron Russell; Earl of Bedford) 21, 190, 256
Russia 22, 235, 305
Ruthven Raid 271

Sable, Treaty of (1488) 45
Sadler, Sir Ralph 176
Salisbury 112–13, 149, 240, 245, 304, 309
Earl of *see* Robert Cecil
Sampson, Thomas 255
Schwarz, Martin 36–7
Scotland 11–18, 24–9, 34, 38, 42–4, 48, 63, 78, 86, 93, 163–4, 176–7, 180–92, 214, 225–9, 233–8, 248–52, 256, 262–72, 276, 280, 289, 291
Church of 271
Sea Beggars 277
Secretary of State 187, 200, 214–17, 225, 231, 267, 273
Seminary priests 214, 233, 251–4
Separatists 234, 259
Seymour, Edward 161, 168, 182 (*see also* Duke of Somerset)
Seymour, Jane 159, 165, 183, 272
Seymour, Thomas 183
Seymour of Sudeley, Lord 143
Shakespeare, William 23, 111, 292–3, 311

Sheffield, Sir Roger 94
Sheriffs 62–4, 209, 224, 230, 249, 255
Sherwin, Ralph 252
Shipbuilding 115, 306
Shrewsbury 25, 32, 304
Countess of 208
Earl of 52, 93, 220
Sidney, Sir Henry 285–6
Silver 23, 298–9
Simnel, Lambert 15, 28, 33–6, 66
Conspiracy 29, 42, 54
Six Articles Act (1539) 158–62, 168, 175, 182, 193
Skeffington, William 283
Skelton, John 74, 82, 91, 104
Smith, Sir Thomas 194, 217, 286, 294, 298
Sodor and Man, Bishop of 243
Solway Moss, battle (1542) 44, 163, 176–7
Somerset, Duke of (Lord Protector) 15–17, 26, 164, 176–9, 183–93, 211, 221, 245, 298
Southampton 114, 120, 262, 277, 304, 307
Earl of *see* Thomas Wriothesley
Spain 17–22, 27–9, 38–50, 68, 72–7, 83–9, 115, 163, 174, 197, 228, 232–4, 248, 252, 263–82, 288–91, 298, 305
Spanish Armada 211–15, 234, 252, 258, 263, 278–81, 288, 298
Spenser, Edmund 23, 292–3, 309–11
Spes, Don Guerau de 277, 289
St Albans 98, 149
St Bartholomew's Day Massacre (1572) 256, 262, 269
St Germaine-en-Laye 71, 82
Stafford, Edward *see* Duke of Buckingham
Stafford Conspiracy 197
Stafford, Humphrey 204
Standard of living 297–300
Stanhope family 220
Stanley family 60, 295
Stanley, Sir William (Earl of Derby) 21–2, 28, 33, 38
Stanley, Thomas (Lord Stanley; Earl of Derby) 35, 53
Stanney, Thomas 253
Star Chamber 18, 57–9, 70–2, 90–4, 106, 119, 191, 214, 258–9
Statute law 208
Statute of Artificers 292, 296–300, 306
Stuart, Henry *see* Lord Darnley
St John, Elizabeth 67
St Leger, Sir Warham 283
Strickland, William 227, 256, 259
Stuart, Lady Arabella 16
Stuart, Charles (Earl of Lennox) 16, 272
Stuart, Lord James 271
Stuart, Mathew (Earl of Lennox) 272
Suffolk 79, 196–8, 212, 229, 232, 307–10
Duke of 16, 21, 71, 92–3, 103, 152, 155, 203
'Supplication against the Ordinaries' 142
'Surrender and regrant' 24, 283
Surrey, Earl of *see* Thomas Howard, Duke of Norfolk

Sussex 207, 229, 248, 252–3, 300, 310
Earl of 21, 218, 278, 285
Sweden 42, 235
Switzerland 24, 38, 143, 147, 235–7, 265
Symonds, Richard 36

Tallis, Thomas 222, 312
Taxes 41, 45, 57, 61–3, 88, 96, 113, 136, 155, 164–7, 170, 186–8, 200, 215, 231, 241, 246, 301–2
Ten Articles 155, 160
Tewkesbury 148, 151
battle (1471) 32, 35
Textiles 306, 309
Theatres 292, 311–13
Thérouanne 77–8, 268
Thirty Nine Articles 233, 241, 246, 251–7
Throckmorton (Guise) Plot 214, 234, 252, 272
Tilting 74, 81, 87
Tournai 14, 27, 37, 77–8, 81, 86, 268
Trade and industry 49–50, 64, 110–16, 167, 282, 304–9
Treason 54, 73–9, 94, 103, 133, 145–6, 153, 159, 163, 167–8, 182, 200, 204, 214, 223, 233, 251–4, 263, 291
Troughton, Richard 206
Troyes, Treaty of (1564) 27, 262, 267–9
Tudor, Edmund (Earl of Richmond) 31–2, 40
Tudor, Jasper (Duke of Bedford) 31–2, 35, 52, 65
Tudor, Margaret 16, 29, 39, 48, 64, 75, 78, 86, 176, 216, 272
Tudor, Owen 31–2
Tunstall, Cuthbert 140
Tyndale, William 128–30, 134–5
Tyrone 284
Earl of *see* Hugh O'Neill
Rebellion 24, 263, 274, 283, 287–8

Ulloa, San Juan de 262, 277
Ulster 26, 66–7, 284–7
Unemployment 95, 300–2, 308
Union of Crowns (1603) 11

Vagabondage 119–21, 292, 301–3
Vagrancy 11, 23, 60, 185, 224, 231, 293–303
'Valor Ecclesiasticus' 128, 150–1
Venice 41, 49, 77, 85, 101, 114–15, 265, 289, 305
Vere, John de *see* Earl of Oxford
Vergil, Ploydore 69–70, 82, 104, 108
Vestiarian Controversy 245, 255
Visitation of the Clergy 128, 149, 245

Wales 11, 17–19, 24–5, 32–4, 42, 56, 60, 65, 93, 163, 167–71, 228, 239, 255, 280, 285
Act of Union with (1536) 18, 24
New Council 163, 170–2
Walsingham, Francis 167, 214–17, 221–4, 231, 251–2, 256–8, 273–5, 278, 289–90
Warbeck, Perkin 15, 28–9, 35, 38–42, 45–6, 49, 63, 66, 115
Conspiracy 28, 38–42

Warham, William 76, 81, 90, 94, 99, 142
Wars of the Roses 11–17, 30, 33, 37, 52, 55, 69, 99, 153, 155
Warwick, Earl of 33, 37–9, 52, 182, 186–90, 262, 267 (*see also* John Dudley)
Waterford 38, 66, 284
Watson, Thomas 208
Wentworth, Peter 214
West Country 114, 306
Western Rebellion 15, 185, 188
West Indies 263, 273, 276–7
Westminster, Treaty of (1527) 89
Westmorland 25, 34, 44, 65, 177, 229, 304, 310
Countess of 221
Earl of 65, 214
Weymouth 35, 41, 47, 304
Whitgift, Archbishop John 224, 234, 256
Wilcox, Thomas 256
William the Silent 225, 263, 278, 289–90
Willoughby, Sir Hugh 282
Wilson, Thomas 294–5
Wilton, Abbess of 103
Winchester 81, 98, 108, 149, 168, 199, 240
Windsor, Treaty of (1506) 47, 71–2
Wine 49–50, 114, 131
Wolsey, Cardinal Thomas 35, 71–110, 119, 124, 128, 136–49, 163, 166–8, 173, 179, 311
Woodville, Elizabeth 37
Wool/woollen cloth trade 22, 27, 46–50, 90, 110–15, 264, 275, 282, 292–3, 304–7
Worcester 112–13, 126, 134, 151, 229, 257
Worsted 307–8
Wriothesley, Thomas (Earl of Southampton) 21, 190
Wyatt, Sir Thomas 203, 207, 212
Wyatt's Rebellion 15–17, 197, 200–4
Wynter, Sir William 267

Yarmouth 112–13, 199, 304–5
Yellow Ford, battle (1598) 263, 288
Yeomen 295, 311
York 34–5, 41, 103, 108, 112–14, 120, 131, 136, 150–1, 195–6, 206, 229, 239–40, 261, 294, 304, 309
York, Archbishop of 60, 65, 79, 98, 239, 249–50, 257
Yorkist pretenders 15, 43, 46–7, 66, 115
Yorkshire 34, 41, 64, 114, 148, 154–5, 177, 187, 195–6, 202, 206, 228–9, 250, 254, 304–6, 309
Rebellion 41, 156–7

Zwingli, Huldrych 193–4, 236
Zwinglianism 236–8, 245–7